Introduction to
Behavioral Science in Medicine

Frederick R. Hine
Robert C. Carson
George L. Maddox
Robert J. Thompson Jr.
Redford B. Williams Jr.

Introduction to Behavioral Science in Medicine

Springer-Verlag
New York Heidelberg Berlin

Frederick R. Hine, M.D.
Professor of Psychiatry
Director of Medical Student Education in Psychiatry
Duke University Medical Center
Durham, North Carolina 27710, U.S.A.

George L. Maddox, Ph.D
Professor of Sociology and Medical Sociology (Psychiatry)
Director
Center for the Study of Aging and Human Development
Duke University Medical Center
Durham, North Carolina 27710, U.S.A.

Redford B. Williams, Jr., M.D.
Professor of Psychiatry
Associate Professor of Medicine
Lecturer in Psychology
Duke University Medical Center
Durham, North Carolina 27710, U.S.A.

Robert C. Carson, Ph.D
Professor and Chairman
Department of Psychology
Duke University Medical Center
Durham, North Carolina 27710, U.S.A.

Robert J. Thompson, Jr., Ph.D.
Associate Professor and Head
Division of Medical Psychology
Department of Psychiatry
Assistant Professor
Department of Pediatrics
Duke University Medical Center
Durham, North Carolina 27710, U.S.A.

With 25 Figures
Sponsoring Editor: Chester Van Wert

Library of Congress Cataloging in Publication Data
Introduction to behavioral science in medicine.
Includes index.
1. Medicine and psychology. I. Hine, Frederick R., 1925- . [DNLM: 1. Behavior. 2. Mental disorders. WM 100 I675]
R726.5.I63 1982 616.89 82-19439

Typeset by Information Sciences Corporation, Washington, D.C.

9 8 7 6 5 4 3 2 1

ISBN-13: 978-0-387-90736-9 e-ISBN-13: 978-1-4612-5452-2
DOI: 10.1007/978-1-4612-5452-2

Contents

Preface

This book is the product of many years' experience teaching behavioral science in a way that demonstrates its relevance to clinical medicine. We have been guided by the reactions and evaluations of many first-year medical students. The result is a conceptual framework different from those that we and others had tried before.

Because the clinical relevance of knowledge about human behavior is less apparent to many first-year students than that of the other traditional preclinical courses, books and courses organized as brief introductions to psychology, sociology, and behavioral neurology have often been poorly received. Various medical schools and texts have explored ways to overcome this difficulty. One text organizes the presentation around very practical problems which are of unmistakable interest to the future physician: the therapeutic relationship, death and dying, sexuality, and pain, to give a few examples. Another emphasizes stages of development, periods of the human life cycle, as its organizing principle. Both of these approaches have merit and have been used successfully in various schools. They seem to us, however, to have a potentially serious shortcoming. They focus student attention too much on the more immediately intriguing issues of specific clinical problems or on the more easily recognized age-specific behavioral issues. In the limited time available, the teaching of general principles of human behavioral functioning may then be neglected. Our experience, which includes work with students later in their training, suggests that understanding basic principles of human behavior is the soundest foundation for future physicians, who need to be able to think broadly and creatively about the human condition and about the problems of thinking, feeling, and acting experienced by their patients.

The approach we take in this book emphasizes clinical relevance while retaining a behavioral science orientation. That body of knowledge from the basic behavioral sciences considered most important for medicine is divided into five *behavior function areas,* each of which, when impaired, is directly related to a corresponding area of behavior disorder or psychopathology. We begin with an introductory chapter in which this concept and its relation to behavior pathology are discussed and illustrated with case examples. This general introduction is followed by five units, each of which examines a behavior function from psychological, sociological, developmental, and neurobiological perspectives, and includes information about typical disorders associated with impaired functioning in that area. Throughout, we recognize and stress that the presentations in each unit are simplifications for purposes of conceptualization and teaching. Any one aspect of a person's behavior is intimately bound up with all of the others.

The final unit extends the discussion of behavioral science beyond its relation to behavioral disorders to consider its relevance for disorders of bodily functioning. Cardiovascular disease is used as the principal example. The relevance of this basic knowledge not only for psychiatric medicine but for all areas of medical practice thus becomes clear. This unit draws extensively upon the developing field of behavioral medicine.

Among the many colleagues, students, and associates who have assisted us with this project, we wish particularly to express our appreciation to Mr. Chet Van Wert of Springer-Verlag New York for his encouragement and support, and to Ms. Betty Ray and Ms. Deborah Coley of the Duke University Medical Center for their devoted processing and reprocessing of our words.

1

Introduction: Behavior Function Areas and Dimensions of Psychopathology

Human and animal behavior may be classified for study and teaching in many different ways. All classification systems are to some degree arbitrary, reflecting both the preconceptions and the interests of their creators. There are no truly "natural" systems of classification and no theoretical systems which are finally or absolutely correct. Such systems are judged not for their ultimate truth but for their usefulness in ordering the observed data in ways which provide satisfying explanations, permit some prediction and influence of future events, and foster new observations by raising additional questions. The usefulness of a classification or other theoretical system is itself a relative matter, depending in large part upon the particular purposes for which it is intended.

The purpose of this book is to provide the student of medicine with a background of knowledge in the areas of behavioral science important to understanding individual human misery and its alleviation. Its aim is to present information of current clinical importance as well as to provide a basic grasp of topics and approaches in behavioral science which will enable the student to keep abreast of future developments in the understanding and treatment of the psychosocial contributions to bodily illness (behavioral medicine) as well as the specifically behavioral disorders that have been the traditional province of psychiatry.

The physician is most centrally concerned with the distress of individual patients. Our presentation of behavioral science knowledge will therefore be organized around Units which correspond as closely as possible to the major areas of disordered behavior as it has been understood by psychiatrists and clinical psychologists studying and treating individual patients. Defining *behavior* as the aggregate of an individual's thoughts, feelings, and actions, we conceive five major areas of disordered behavior or psychopathology: (1) organic brain disease, (2) schizophrenia, (3) affective disorder, (4) neurosis (including personality disorder), and (5) impulse disorder (i.e., "impulse control" disorder). Related to each is a corresponding *behavior function area:* (1) basic biobehavioral functions, (2) biobehavioral dispositions (so-called "constitutional" predispositions), (3) affect and mood, (4) personality and interpersonal functioning, and (5) social integration. These five behavior function areas constitute the framework for the organization of this book. An additional Unit 6 draws on all five of these areas to demonstrate the relevance of behavioral science for physical as well as for psychological disorders. Each requires for its understanding the combined inputs of several behavioral science disciplines: behavioral neurobiology, psychology, and sociology. Psychopathology itself is also a basic behavioral science; many of the most important insights concerning normal function in the various areas have come from the study of the abnormal.

Classification of Behavioral Disorders

Because the individuals and events actually observed in any particular situation have features unique to that one time and place, there is inevitably an element of oversimplification in any effort to classify. Needless oversimplification may sometimes be avoided, however, by choosing the appropriate type of classification system. Psychopathology is most frequently classified in terms of a list of disease *categories* which carries the presumption that clear evidence of one disease precludes the possible coexistence of the others—as if nature were under some constraint to limit diseases one-to-a-customer. The practice of approaching a patient with this "either-or" question may have been useful when medicine was mainly concerned with identifying the particular infection from which he suffered. (The likelihood of diphtheria and whooping cough both striking at the same moment is probably rather small.) However, in the disorders of behavior it is often the case that more than one psychopathological process is important, two or more interacting to produce the total impairment. We therefore urge our clinical students to avoid categorical thinking about psychiatric diagnosis and to adopt a *multidimensional* approach in which the question is not which disease the patient has but how much of each process is involved in his disability and discomfort (Hine and Williams, 1975).

Thus when we turn to consider the basic behavior functions associated with each dimension of psychopathology, similar precautions against categorical oversimplification are necessary. No single behavior function area is exclusively associated with one particular dimension of abnormal behavior. The information we shall present about affect and mood, while centrally relevant for the affective disorders, is also essential to an understanding of the neurotic process, schizophrenia, impulse disorders, and organic brain syndrome. A similar statement can be made for each of the other behavior function areas. The behavior function areas themselves do not represent isolated processes. Emotions are clearly dependent upon both memories and current interpersonal processes, and interpersonal behavior is inextricably bound to the person's internal integrative function as well as to his social integration.

Some case examples may serve to illustrate the general points made so far. Discussions following each case include initial definitions of several dimensions of disordered behavior.

> P.B. was 23 years old at the time of his first psychiatric admission. He was working at that time as a junior executive in the small manufacturing plant owned by his family and managed by his father. After completing college, P. had returned to live with his father who had separated from the patient's mother during the time he was away. College had been difficult for him, not because of inadequate talent for the work but because he demanded of himself continuous excellent performance. Although always a friendly, even gregarious person, P.B. had avoided most social activities because of his preoccupation with grades and the need to study. During college and after he entered the business, P.B.'s relationships with both men and women were casual and even superficial; he had no close friends and had never gone steady. It was assumed in the family and in the business that P.B. would succeed his father in the management role. Father expected the patient to begin participation in the civic, religious, country club, and golfing circles which he, himself, found valuable to his own success. It was also expected that P.B. would display the keen business judgment characteristic of several generations of B.s. The patient himself accepted these expectations without conscious question. He continued to work very hard during the day and to spend his evenings and weekends studying trade publications, business magazines, and the stock market reports. He joined the clubs and accepted the invitations as he sensed father wished. He was not successful in these efforts, however. His co-workers did not turn to him for leadership, apparently finding that he was unable to think through problems to useful solutions despite his eagerness to be in the executive role. Friends did not repeat social invitations beyond those "required" by their ties to his family, reporting later that the patient was limited, repetitious, and superficial in his conversations and interests. Father expressed to P.B. his growing concern and P.B. tried harder. He became so eager to win the approval of his fellow employees that he assumed, at times, the role of spokesman for the underdog in their complaints against top management. His judgment regarding timing and presentation was not adequate to produce success in these activities, however, with the result being that he anta-

gonized both his colleagues and his father. Gradually he began to show more distinctly abnormal behavior: increasing social withdrawal and brief outbursts of intense rage with very minor provocation.

The several days immediately before his admission had been particularly difficult for P.B. A long-time supervisory employee at the plant had died suddenly. The patient attempted to assume the role of benefactor and guardian of this man's family, personally offering them large sums of money from his own savings and assuming responsibility for funeral and other arrangements for a family he scarcely knew. They were both bewildered and offended, and called the patient's father who immediately "jumped all over him." P.B. himself became confused and began to speak unintelligibly to his father. Father responded by sending P.B. home, where the patient made an ineffectual attempt to set the house on fire. Later that night he returned to the plant and demolished most of the equipment in the area in which his own office was located. The family doctor sedated the patient and he was brought to the hospital.

Physical examination upon admission was unremarkable, but the patient was severely agitated and hyperactive, anxious, and at times angry and assaultive. Verbal expressions of anger were fragmented and included both father and others from his family and friends outside the hospital, as well as being directed unpredictably and without provocation toward ward staff and other patients. His thinking in general was disorganized and without apparent purpose, any single idea being held for only a brief time and seldom developed to make any point or accomplish any goal. He shifted frequently from one topic to another or simply "ran down" on a subject without completing it. At times his thoughts would alternate between two incompatible ideas (for example, "I must go visit my mother . . . I can't visit my mother, she makes me feel bad . . . I must go visit my mother"), these alternations occurring within a few seconds and without any successful "resolution" by the patient or any apparent recognition on his part of a need for resolution.

P.B. was provided the support of an accepting hospital staff and removal from the demands of his outside life, together with drug therapy involving chiefly moderate to high doses of a phenothiazine antipsychotic agent (chlorpromazine). His agitated, assaultive behavior subsided in a few days. The difficulty in thinking coherently and purposively gradually improved over some three months, although some traces of the problem continued to be apparent to experienced observers. P.B.'s personality settled back into a pattern of superficial friendliness, eagerness to please, concern about being away from work, and worry about father's anticipated displeasure at his lack of reliability and competence.

As P.B. became more capable of grasping and retaining communications, cautious efforts were begun to help him reduce his exaggerated tendency to fear any deviations from parental expectations or from his own self-imposed demands. This psychotherapy, together with direct support and support enlisted from his family, was continued following discharge from the hospital.

The case of P.B. illustrates the possibility of impairment in two major dimensions of psychopathology: (1) the schizophrenic or ego-disintegrative and (2) the neurotic, which we view as including the so-called personality disorders. These terms will be more fully defined and their implications will be discussed in much greater detail in later chapters. At this time it may simply be noted that the schizophrenic element in P.B.'s illness was reflected in the disorganization of his thinking and of his goal-directed behavior, extending over many weeks and relatively uninfluenced by changing circumstances. At the same time, the neurotic element was apparent in that this patient had learned to fear the consequences of independently and assertively determining his own life in defiance of father's expectations—learning these fears in excess of the real dangers. He was driven by these fears to pattern his behavior in self-defeating (maladaptive) ways which involved inhibiting natural independence and assertion while exaggerating compliance and submission. P.B. also illustrates the frequently observed interaction between the dimensions of psychopathology. The activation of his neurosis precipitated by return to the family business and daily contact with father, in addition to the neurotic consequences of maladaptive interpersonal behavior, seems also to have activated his predisposition (possibly genetically determined) toward disruption of certain more basic capacities for unity and coherence in his behavioral life. These capacities, impaired in schizophrenia and often termed the integrative or synthetic ego functions, are among the "dimensions of biobehavioral disposition." Beyond the two most central areas of impairment, however, it is clear that the patient's emotional life as well as his social integration were severely affected in his illness, although most likely their involvement was secondary to that of the ego functions and the personality-interpersonal life.

Only the basic mental functions—consciousness, memory, and general intelligence (those characteristically impaired in organic brain disease)—were not impaired to a clinically significant degree in this patient. This fact illustrates a further point intended in the order of arrangement of the psychopathology dimensions and behavior function areas. They are arranged hierarchically from the most basic to the most complex. An important clinical implication of that arrangement is that all functions above those primarily involved will, in that patient, themselves be to some degree impaired. Thus in the next chapter we shall see that organic brain syndrome, while specifically involving the basic functions of consciousness-sensorium, memory, and intelligence, also typically involves all of the higher functions as well.

> R.L.[1] was a married woman in her late 20s, the wife of a tenant tobacco farmer. She was referred for psychiatric care after numerous visits to medical and gynecological clinics failed to provide relief from episodes of severe abdominal pain accompanied by nausea and vomiting. These episodes

occurred mostly at night and often required that her husband and children get out of bed to take the patient to the emergency room of the local hospital where her family doctor would give her medication for pain and sleep. This illness increased in severity over a period of several months. Physical symptoms were more frequent, and the patient became increasingly depressed and less able to function in her household and maternal activities. She said she felt desperate and helpless to bring about any changes—quite at the "end of my rope."

During a series of meetings with R.L. it became apparent that, in addition to her preoccupation with her physical health, she was quite dissatisfied with the relationship with her husband. Particularly during the winter, when the patient was not needed to help with the farm work, her husband paid little attention to her, rarely staying home during the waking hours. As her illness and complaints increased, he became even less attentive. Mrs. L. presented herself as a loving but deeply hurt wife. To the sensitive observer it was clear that she also felt intense resentment and anger which she was quite unable at first to accept or recognize in herself. Trapped in this conflict (again of the aggression-fear variety, with many independence-fear feelings as well), the patient came to feel more and more helpless and without hope—cardinal signs of depressive illness.

After some initial support (consisting chiefly of acceptance by the therapist and a commitment on his part to work with her—thus implying hope), it was possible to begin a gradual program of reeducative psychotherapy in which she was encouraged to confront her fears in words and, later, to attempt the previously feared behaviors so that they were gradually increased. Maladaptive substitute behaviors, including her bodily symptoms, gradually diminished. She became much more free to insist that her needs be considered in any relationship and when they were not, to express her feelings in a manner which convinced others that she was a person to be reckoned with. Her depression disappeared and anxiety was no longer a dominating experience in her life.

Mrs. L. illustrates the interaction of neurotic (including psychosomatic) and affective disorder elements in a single patient. Prolonged states of depressed "spirits" and/or elevated mood, together with corresponding changes in activity levels, are the principal symptoms of the mood disorders. In this patient the depressive element was moderately severe but probably largely secondary to the neurotic, although it is not possible to rule out some biological predisposition to extremes of mood. As we shall see in later chapters, there are patients in whom such predispositions may play a part equal to or greater than the coexisting neurosis. There is even an occasional case in which neurotic elements may play no part in the development of a severe affective disorder, but interaction is the most usual case, pointing up

[1]The case of Mrs. L. is presented in more detail in an earlier publication (Hine et al., 1972, pp. 90–94, 107–108, 111–112, 136, 143–144, 150n, 174) to illustrate various aspects of the psychodynamics of neurosis.

the importance of avoiding an oversimplified, categorical approach to behavior and behavior disorders. This same point is demonstrated in the remaining case examples which will also serve to make more concrete those dimensions and behavior function areas which we have not as yet illustrated.

C.D. was a 28-year-old man referred by the criminal court for psychiatric hospitalization in lieu of a prison sentence. He was charged with illegal possession and discharge of firearms, having been arrested during the night while shooting out store windows on the main street in his home town. His explanation was that he was angry and disillusioned with people and found relief from his tensions in this activity. C.D. had no previous record of arrests, but his adult life had been a very stormy one in other respects. He had been married three times, each marriage lasting only a brief time, apparently largely because of his abusive behavior toward his wives. He had, in fact, just broken with his third wife at the time of his arrest. After each separation he was sad and remorseful, but also resentful and bitter. C.D.'s work history was as erratic as his marital life. He had been fired from innumerable jobs, often after an auspicious beginning during which his intellect and verbal abilities had earned him early promotion and the confidence of his employers. Invariably, however, as he became more highly esteemed and those around him began to express confidence and regard for him, C.D. would provoke some violent verbal or physical fight which resulted in his dismissal. The patient lived with his mother when he was not married or off in another town at some new job. His returns to her home usually occurred when he was depressed and included promises to do better in return for her support. Within a few weeks, however, he would swing to a position of arrogance and domination of the household, flagrantly exploiting his mother (who adopted a posture of long-suffering but helpless devotion to C.D.) and at times stealing from her or involving her in serious social and financial difficulties, such as liability claims for his frequent auto accidents.

In the hospital C.D. was at first uncooperative and menacing in this attitude. After several weeks he developed friendships with a few patients and staff members and seemed to be establishing a useful relationship with his therapist, a relationship of sufficient warmth that the therapist was induced to relax and himself become somewhat more open and warm toward the patient. Within a day or two C.D. began to find flaws in the therapist: he was really duplicitous and did not feel real warmth toward the patient—witness his callous treatment of another patient on ward rounds; he was really not very intelligent—having completely misunderstood the point of some information provided by the patient in the previous session. After three or four days the patient reported that he had "completely lost respect" for the doctor, could never work with him, and should be transferred to another therapist or another hospital. It was then necessary to start again from the beginning and rebuild the relationship. While rebuilding was possible, the same pattern of patient-instigated disruptions was repeated over and over during the six months of hospital stay. Similar "approach" followed by "avoidance" patterns were seen with a series of women patients with whom the patient became close and then turned upon in bitter denunciation and abuse. C.D. was also frequently disruptive to the administration of the ward, "escaping" only to return on his own, but with concealed alcohol or drugs which he then distributed to other patients. He used his expertise as a locksmith to break into the nurses' station, where he was discovered, and into his therapist's office, where he left his calling card in the form of a totally dismantled telephone.

Despite repeated approaches to involvement in therapy, C.D. was not significantly improved at the end of the six-month period set by the court. He was declared by the hospital administration unsuitable for further treatment in that particular facility and returned to the court for disposition.

The case of C.D. again illustrates the interaction of two major psychopathological processes. His illness was administratively diagnosed "sociopathic personality disorder," a diagnosis corresponding to our term "impulse disorder." When used as a single diagnosis—in categorical oversimplification—such a diagnosis implies that the individual is inadequately socialized and has not acquired the fears and inhibitions of his natural impulses necessary to function in his society. One does occasionally see cases of "true sociopathy" in which this lack-of-inhibition element alone accounts for the disordered behavior. Certainly C.D. lacked some self-restraints which would have been useful to him, but there is certainly more to his illness. Even with those restraints he would have been an unhappy, miserable person, although the behavioral reflections of his misery would undoubtedly have been quite different: withdrawal perhaps, a suspicious, misanthropic personality, but one less abrasive to those around him. We suggest that in addition to a pathological lack of social inhibition, C.D. also suffers from fears and an *excess* inhibition of his natural impulses toward tenderness, intimacy, and dependence upon others (as described, for example, by Vaillant, 1975). We suggest that these processes of excessive inhibition of trust, intimacy, and related needs fall within the range of fear-generated neurotic conflicts.[2]

L.O. was a 46-year-old married woman who had been in treatment with another psychiatrist irregularly for about six years before he referred her for inpatient evaluation. Throughout her life L.O. had been a striving, perfectionistic person who made extreme demands upon herself and members of her family. Her ambitions for a professional career (type unspecified) had been thwarted by financial problems. After college she married a young lawyer and devoted herself to furthering his career through participation in social and community activities. Their two daughters also became the focus of her intense drives for accomplishment and success. There were minor disappointments and short periods of family dissension during the first 20

[2]The reader who has become aware of the prominence given to neurotic processes in these case examples may wish to know that we do consider neurosis to be, in varying degree, ubiquitous in human affairs and an important element in most psychopathology. Having admitted this bias, we encourage the reader to evaluate its validity in his own growing clinical experience.

years of her marriage, but L.O. and those important to her were "successful," and she experienced no persisting distress until she entered her 40s. Then she found herself less able to maintain the life schedule she had set for herself. Periods of depression became more frequent and her demands upon others increased and threatened more severe disruption of relationships, especially with her daughters who were now young adults. It was for these problems that she had consulted a psychotherapist six years earlier. He had provided support, including antidepressant medication, during periods of lowered mood and, at other times, worked with her to relieve some of her perfectionistic, "compulsive" personality traits by efforts to help her free herself from neurotic conflicts which included both aggression-fear and submission-fear elements.

The doctor's reasons for hospital referral centered principally around events of the preceding two months. After an absence from therapy of nearly a year, the patient had asked to resume her visits. Expecting again to find her "uptight" about some disruption of family relationships, her therapist was surprised to find Mrs. O. complaining mainly of inability to control her emotions. Always a very controlled person, she now found herself exhibiting outbursts of anger, tearfulness, and even extreme joy which she found quite out of character. Her main complaint was the embarrassment she felt at having "made a fool of myself," although her affective displays were not beyond the bounds of social custom and had elicited no more than mild surprise from family and friends. The psychiatrist also noted, during several visits, that Mrs. O. was not as meticulous about her dress and grooming as she had previously been, nor was she as precise about choosing her words nor as careful about being "fair" to everyone she described. The patient herself seemed unaware of these changes. With her permission, the therapist made inquiries of her family and learned that they were relying on her less because she was now often late or less careful in performing the domestic tasks which had previously given her so much satisfaction. One or twice she had forgotten some family matter entirely, a most unusual thing for her. Of even greater significance was her lack of concern over the inconvenience her lapses had caused others. In the past she would have been greatly distressed.

Mrs. O. was admitted to the hospital where the initial behavioral picture was essentially as described by the referring physician. However, while laboratory, x-ray, radioisotope, and psychological examinations were in progress, she began to deteriorate rapidly in her mental status. The earlier affective lability was largely replaced by an emptiness of emotional response, and her thinking became increasingly difficult to follow. Over a period of about six weeks L.O. became less and less concerned about her appearance and about the effect her behavior had upon others. At times one could see remnants of her old "compulsivity" as she briefly chided other patients for their tardiness for meals or ward meetings, but the patient herself was becoming increasingly forgetful and disorganized in her habits. She could no longer discuss the events reported on the TV news programs nor could she perform the simple calculations required for participation in card games with patients and staff.

Meanwhile, brain scans and contrast radiographs had revealed evidence of multiple, bilateral cerebral tumors. Surgery was not deemed possible. The patient experienced two grand mal seizures, the first of her life. She became unsteady and then totally unable to walk, disoriented with respect to the month and year as well as to the place where she was located. She no longer recognized family members and required assistance to eat and to care for her other needs. At 13 weeks after admission L.O. became increasingly impaired in her attention and consciousness, and four days later became comatose. She died shortly thereafter. Post-mortem examination revealed multiple cerebral metastases of a tumor primary in the mediastinum.

The case of Mrs. O. illustrates the interactive involvement, primarily or secondarily, of all five dimensions of psychopathology and all five behavior function areas. The hierarchical nature of their arrangement is also apparent in that once the basic organic area became impaired, there were secondary effects in functions previously normal for all practical purposes, namely the dimensions of biobehavioral disposition (decreasing ability to organize her activities, to work for a purpose) and social integrative areas (diminished sensitivity to the needs and feelings of others).

The four cases presented so far have all been "psychiatric patients" in that the principal signs and symptoms involve the individual's behavior—his thoughts, feelings, and actions—rather than malfunctions or lesions of specific tissues or organ systems. Mrs. R.L., to be sure, manifested psychosomatic (or psychophysiological) dysfunction of the gastrointestinal system in the form of nausea and vomiting. Mrs. L.O. had multiple, intracranial, space-occupying, and tissue-destroying lesions, as well as her asymptomatic mediastinal tumor, but her symptoms were essentially behavioral until the final phases of her illness. These cases were selected for the clarity with which they illustrate and define (in a preliminary way, at least) the essential features of the several areas of disordered behavior around which we have chosen to consider behavioral functions. The final case to be discussed, a medical-surgical patient, illustrates the importance of behavioral elements and a knowledge of biopsychosocial principles in the management of, and treatment outcome of, an illness clearly "organic" in its major aspects.

F.S.[3] was a 42-year-old married businessman at the time of his admission to the cardiology service. He had been referred by his internist for cardiac catheterization and evaluation for possible valve replacement surgery. The patient had a history of rheumatic fever and rheumatic heart disease at age 12. Over the three years before admission he had three bouts of minor congestive heart failure. The patient agreed to the in-hospital studies, but once admitted became anxious and refused to sign permission for the catheterization. The cardiologist knew that the patient a was successful businessman, that he had married late in life, and that he had no children.

[3]This case example was modified for the purpose of illustrating the role of the nonpsychiatric physician in the management of combined psychosocial and medical disorders (Houpt et al., 1977).

The charge nurse on the patient's unit reported that the patient had initially appeared relaxed but on the second afternoon was found to be quite anxious, especially about anyone "probing around my heart," and was terrified at the thought of surgery.

The patient himself told the cardiologist that he had hesitated for some months before accepting his local doctor's recommendation that he be evaluated for surgery. He had read extensively on valve replacement and investigated different centers. He had to "force" himself to sign in because of anxiety but had previously rejected the idea of psychiatric help because "I don't like to talk about it . . . It makes me feel worse . . . I have to work too hard to avoid thinking about it." Having made the decision, however, he initially felt more comfortable, but on the morning of his second day the house staff examined him and discussed their findings in his presence so that he overheard discussion of two murmurs. Assuming this meant multiple valve involvement which would require replacement of two valves and having read that mortality increased to 50% for such surgery, he became acutely anxious and requested discharge.

The patient reported that his parents were immigrants, his father a laborer who preached the virtues of hard work and education as the route to improving one's station in life. Father died while the patient was in college. For six months thereafter the patient was sleepless, aimless, and unusually introspective. His mother shared the father's values but was more warm and caring. The patient remembered her care when he was ill at age 12 and also the family doctor's statement that the patient would be "lucky" to live beyond the age of 18. He ignored the doctor's advice to take it easy, completed high school, played competitive sports, and worked very hard in college despite finding his studies very demanding. He was determined to succeed but, through it all, there was a vague sense of doom, a sense that all his efforts would be useless and that perhaps he would "drop dead." For this reason he avoided marriage until age 35 and insisted on not having children. He worked long hours and had been promoted to a position of independent responsibility shortly before his admission to the hospital. His wife, when interviewed, confirmed the patient's story and added that he did not allow her to take care of him in relation to his health problems.

Reasoning that the patient's present severe anxiety was the result of (1) misconception about the number of valves involved, (2) lack of confidence in physicians' prognostic ability, (3) long-standing anxious preoccupation with illness and death, and (4) a pattern of chronic anxiety about performance and failure, the cardiologist carefully clarified his diagnostic impressions and plans and advised the patient that all future information would come only directly from him. He also met daily with the ward staff to make certain that they understood these plans and the patient's needs. For example, it was decided that nurses would acknowledge the patient's frequent calls on the intercom but respond a short time later, rather than immediately rushing to his room, thereby reducing his sense of being in immediate danger.

Brief daily private visits (in addition to rounds with house staff) were used by the cardiologist to reinforce clarification of information provided and to help Mr. S. see how his increased anxiety was triggered by the incident during house staff rounds. Although aware of the etiological importance of earlier life experiences and relationships and of the patient's striving, hyperindependent, emotionally constricted personality patterns, and in view of the need to reduce anxiety during the period of surgical stress, he avoided exploration of these areas with the patient, concentrating instead upon here-and-now matters and the patient's positive accomplishments in life.

Mr. S. agreed to cardiac catheterization and then underwent valve replacement surgery. The postoperative course was uneventful. Brief daily visits limited to supportive material were continued as before. Psychiatric referral was offered at the time of discharge but the patient declined. It was learned six months later that the patient had returned to work, had consulted his local doctor with feelings of depression, and had been referred to a psychiatrist in his own community.

The disordered behavior elements in this patient's illness were essentially neurotic in nature, i.e., learned patterns of exaggerated, unrealistic fears and resulting self-defeating actions. He feared death or some "doom" as a consequence of defying parental requirements that he strive and achieve success, but he had also been threatened with death if he did not "take it easy." His early experience had also left him with a fear of painful outcome as a consequence of putting himself in the hands of another person. These fears are understandable in the light of the patient's earlier life experiences, but they led to self-defeating behavior when triggered into activity in adult life by the threats and demands of his heart disease. As a result, the real dangers of Mr. S.'s illness are compounded by the possible consequences of his unrealistic fears.

Conclusion

The main purpose of this introductory chapter has been to present and illustrate the concept of the five behavior function areas in their relation to the dimensions of disordered behavior. This concept forms the organizing principle for the entire book. In addition, it has been suggested that a useful understanding of any of these areas or dimensions requires input from the neurobiological and social sciences as well as psychology itself. The basic science investigator may perhaps argue the legitimacy of limiting his interest to a single level in order to isolate one aspect of behavior for study. The physician, on the other hand, has practical responsibilities which require his knowledgeable intervention, when intervention is feasible, at whatever levels can be useful to his patient. This consideration, in addition to the important intellectual satisfactions inherent in viewing nature from several perspectives, makes a multidisciplinary approach essential to this presentation.

Another important perspective in understanding behavior, one not thus far mentioned, involves the sequence of developmental periods through which the individual passes from conception to death. No single schema of development is adequate for all purposes. Our charts of the developmental stages will be somewhat different for each of the behavior function areas. But it seems clear that sequences of maturational events in interaction with influences from the environment constitute an essential facet of our knowledge about any aspect of behavior. The developmental stage at which loss of a parent occurs has much significance for the effect of that event upon later emotional, interpersonal, and other functions, just as the stage of a central nervous system infection may be critically important for later intellectual and other ego functions. It is not a mere formality that medical and psychiatric workups begin with a statement of the patient's age, although this does not, of course, always tell us everything we wish to know about the current developmental stage of the patient. (Development is innately variable across individuals, and that innate variability is increased still further by the variations in outside influences at each stage.) The physician's desire for a personal history reflects his recognition that knowledge of earlier stages in the patient's life often contains clues to the understanding of present functions, assuming we know enough developmental principles to interpret the information and assuming that reliable information can be obtained.

Finally, we wish to alert the reader to an evolutionary-adaptational perspective which we shall use on occasion in considering the possible contribution of innate, species-typical response patterns to normal and pathological behavior. This perspective can best be explained by an example. It has been suggested that grief, including its extreme, depression, has evolved in some mammalian lines as an adaptation to certain conditions of environmental stress. If this is true (and our later discussion will suggest that it probably is), that knowledge may enable us to more fully understand depressive illness in terms of the range of stressful situations likely to precipitate it, the ways in which we may best intervene to relieve the most significant stresses, the neural and neurochemical pathways likely to be involved, and perhaps even the enzyme systems through which genetic variations in predisposition to depressive illness are determined. Our conviction that such a biological capacity does in fact constitute a part of human nature will certainly be strengthened by observing similar patterns in nonhuman species, particularly those which stand in some evolutionary relationship to man. In our presentations, therefore, we will be alert for studies of animal behavior, both naturalistic and experimental, which may throw light upon innate human behavioral capacities and their adaptational significance.

References

Hine, F.R., and R.B. Williams. Dimensional diagnosis and the medical student's grasp of psychiatry. Arch. Gen. Psychiat. 32:525–528, April 1, 1975.

Hine, F.R., E. Pfeiffer, G.L. Maddox, P.L. Hein, and R.O. Friedel. Behavioral Science: A Selective View. Boston, Massachusetts: Little, Brown, 1972.

Houpt, J.L., H.M. Weinstein, and M.L. Russell. The application of competency-based education to consultation-liaison psychiatry. I-Data gathering and case formulation. II-Intervention knowledge and skills. Internat. J. Psychiat. Med. 7:295–307, 309–320, 1977.

Vaillant, G.E. Sociopathy as a human process: A viewpoint. Arch. Gen. Psychiat. 32:178–183, February 1975.

Unit I

Basic Biobehavioral Functions

In this Unit we shall describe those three psychological functions noted in Chapter 1 to be fundamental for behavioral life. From the most basic to the most complex, these are: (1) consciousness and perceptual function (consciousness-sensorium), (2) memory, and (3) general intelligence. The three chapters making up this Unit will describe each of these function areas in the order noted above, considering first normal and, where relevant, developmental issues. Each chapter includes a consideration of those situations encountered in medical practice wherein each of these basic biobehavioral functions is impaired, for it is such impairment which the physician must be alert to detect. Together these functions define the first, or *basic biobehavioral function area.* They are directly impaired only in organic dysfunction of the central nervous system. Moreover, in slowly progressive organic brain disease they are typically the last mental functions to be affected. This observation suggests their close relationship to those even more resistant vegetative functions essential to life itself, and therefore their fundamental place in the hierarchy of psychological processes.

2

Consciousness-Sensorium

Consciousness and the related functions of sensing, alertness, and attention are basic behavioral functions in the sense that they form the foundation without which the other, more complex mental functions would not be possible. The mental life of the individual rests upon this bedrock, which we shall call *consciousness-sensorium*. Without this function the organism is not in *behavioral* contact with its environment. The complete abolition of consciousness-sensorium, while not incompatible with life, results in a state of interaction with the world less like that which we associate with behaving animals and more like that of the plants. Recognition of this fact is reflected in the use of the term "vegetative" to refer to the neurobiologic functions which remain when consciousness and sensorial processes are seriously impaired, and to the clinical conditions resulting from disruption of consciousness-sensorium and the higher functions which it makes possible.

The memory and intelligence functions are only slightly less basic to a behavioral existence than consciousness-sensorium. The capacity for memory and learning, by making possible the retention and reactivation of information based upon previous experiences, frees the individual from the need to approach each moment as if it were his first. Without this capacity one would be utterly bound in the immediate present or forced to depend entirely upon adaptational patterns acquired through evolutionary processes. Such phylogenetic stores of wisdom are, of course, not without great value, but alone they cannot provide sufficient flexibility or specificity for the behavioral life of a complex, wide-ranging organism. It is frequently suggested that mankind represents the highest level of an evolutionary trend toward greater capacity for storage of information acquired through individual experience. This does not mean that inherited, species-typical patterns are without importance for man. It does mean, however, that memory and related functions are of enormous importance in all human behavior.

Before experiences can be retained or recalled, they must be experienced and registered. Thus memory and learning are based upon an intact consciousness-sensorium. In this relationship between these two most basic behavioral functions is the pattern for a hierarchy of functions in which each higher level depends upon the integrity of those more basic. The next level in the behavior function hierarchy is the more complex area of general intelligence, the capacity for organization and reorganization of current stimuli and stored information in ways which serve the needs of the organism.

As noted above, consciousness-sensorium, memory, and intelligence are the most stable of the mental functions, and the least vulnerable to disruption by the day-to-day variations in the organism's environment, directly impaired only in organic conditions affecting the brain. When impaired, they are considered indicators of central nervous system (CNS) pathology, the organic brain syndrome (OBS) which will be described later in this chapter. They may be secondarily affected by impairments of one or more of the higher functions. For example, intellectual activities, such as judgment or reasoning, may be changed in states of intense emotional arousal; states of consciousness or memory may be altered as part of a pattern of efforts (defenses) employed by the individual in attempts to solve problems of relating to others and his concept of himself. (These latter alterations of consciousness or memory have been called neurotic or "hysterical" dissociations and amnesias. For further discussion, see Chapter 16. Such secondary disturbances of the basic functions, however, fluctuate with changes in the higher level dysfunctions and can usually be understood as purposive within the context of the life problems of the individual. Direct impairment of the basic functions themselves, by contrast, has the quality of impersonal deficit, i.e., it occurs and persists independent of personal interpretation of the meaning of events and their variations in the individual's circumstances. Such impairment is thus unaffected by social events and unresponsive to treatments using conversation and the techniques of human interaction.

Description

"Consciousness" refers essentially to the organism's adaptive sensory contact with the surrounding world, i.e., to those processes which give significance to stimuli from the environment. While sensory processes are obviously an essential first step in adaptive interaction with the world, sensation alone does not produce a state of intact consciousness. Electrical evidence of a sensory organ and afferent nerve firing would not constitute an index of the conscious state. In the clinical as well as the research setting, consciousness is evaluated by observing the presence or absence and the quality of motor response to stimulation. Does the patient reply or turn his head or shift his gaze when we call his name? If he has failed to show evidence of awareness of our presence, does he withdraw when we inflict pain with a needle or a forceful squeeze of an extremity, or does he at least emit the primitive grimace and grunt? At times autonomic motor responses may be used, as in observing respiratory changes or flushing in response to stimuli, and in special situations the polygraph has been employed to make subtle assessments of state of consciousness. The electroencephalogram is also used on occasion—an exception to the statement that motor responses provide the criterion of consciousness. But by and large we depend upon somatic motor behavior viewed in the setting of the stimulus situation. There are some problems with this indicator of consciousness. It has been reported, for example, that patients completely paralyzed by curarization (a treatment sometimes used to control contractions in severe tetanus), although they are completely unresponsive and therefore, from a motor standpoint, quite indistinguishable from patients in coma, may be acutely aware of events taking place around them and able to report these memories upon recovery. Despite inherent problems of definition and assessment, the clinical evaluation of level of consciousness does focus upon the patient's appreciation of the significance of sensory stimuli, as reflected in his motor responses. This focus upon perceptual interaction with the world has meant that, in clinical usage, the terms "consciousness" and "sensorium" are often employed interchangeably.

In the state of full consciousness, the individual is capable of responding to a wide range of types and intensities of stimulation. He does, of course, attend to some more than others. This capacity for selective attention-inattention is, in fact, an important indicator of the conscious state. Selection obviously involves appreciation of the relative importance and significance of various stimuli, a perceptual process one or more steps removed from peripheral sensation. Distractibility, the inability to maintain attention in the face of multiple stimuli, is often an important clinical sign of impaired consciousness. A balance between attention and a capacity to shift focus is clearly the most adaptive state. The fully conscious cook will ignore the gently simmering pot but shift attention to it immediately when it begins to boil over.

It will increase our understanding of the definitions of consciousness if we consider its absence as impairment. One obvious choice for the condition at the other extreme from full consciousness is deep sleep. Although the sleep-wakefulness axis is important in the total behavioral life and for understanding certain areas of psychopathology, it does not represent impairment of consciousness. Although consciousness is unquestionably reduced during sleep, significant changes in stimulus conditions will usually produce prompt awakening. Note also that what is "significant" will vary from person to person: a mother will often wake at the first sound of her baby's crying. Clearly the sleeping person is still in some adaptive contact with the environment. There are, moreover, converging lines of neurophysiological evidence suggesting that the CNS mechanisms mediating sleep are not those affected in the disturbances of consciousness characteristic of organic brain disease.

In certain pathological states (in contrast to normal sleep), even the most intense stimulation—even stimuli which signal grave danger to the organism—elicits no reactions to suggest arousal or a return to consciousness. As we have seen, the production of intense pain is a classic test to determine the presence and depth of the comatose condition. Between coma and full wakefulness there is a continuum of levels of consciousness which may often be observed in the same patient over a period of time. The stages of this wakefulness-coma axis are, for clinical purposes, usually given as: consciousness, confusion, clouding, stupor, and coma. Organic *confusion* represents the mildest level of impairment. Responses to stimuli, including verbal stimuli, are slower than usual, and questions of any complexity may provoke signs of perplexity and irritation. Spontaneous speech may be rambling and pointless. Attention is no longer flexible, with the patient showing either distractibility or fixation on a single subject from which he cannot be distracted. Sensorimotor coordination is somewhat impaired so that gait is unsteady and speech is slightly slurred. Orientation, particularly for time, may be impaired, with the patient unable to correctly state the time of day or month. It should be noted that orientation, while usually described as a sensorial function, also involves memory operations. Memory and intellectual performance are also usually impaired in the organically confused patient and serve as confirmatory evidence of the nature of the problem. The deficit of consciousness-sensorium itself, however, is most often the key to identifying the organic element in mild states of erratic behavior, because testing memory and intelligence depends more upon the frequently unavailable cooperation of the patient.

In states of *clouded* consciousness, the patient appears dazed and "out of it," and there is severe misperception of the nature and significance of his situation. It is often necessary to shout at him repeatedly or to shake him in order to obtain and keep his attention. Little effort is made by the patient to follow directions and, if he is ambulatory, he may blunder into dangerous circumstances. All motor functions are grossly impaired. Orientation for time and place are disturbed, and there is marked impairment of memory and intelligence.

Patients may shift back and forth between the various levels of consciousness within brief time periods. This is particularly true of brain impairments produced by acute illnesses.

In *stupor*, the patient is no longer ambulatory and, although he may be restless, discrete, and meaningful reactions to environmental stimuli are lacking. The individual appears unaware of the elements in his surroundings and typically reacts with diffuse global patterns. Total motor movement, which in milder stages may have been increased, is now more often diminished. Purposive movements of the eyes may be present, but attention span is minimal. The basic protective reflexes, especially those to pain, remain intact.

In *coma*, the most severely disturbed state of consciousness, the patient is motionless and unresponsive. Even intensely painful stimuli and those arising from interference with the respiratory passages are without effect. Essentially only the autonomic (vegetative) functions remain, and these too may be gradually depressed with death the result unless the underlying pathology can be arrested or reversed or mechanical life supports are applied. Coma is, of course, the final stage of many illnesses, systemic as well as neurological. This fact, however, should not cause the physician to lose sight of the reversibility of many comatose states if the underlying cause is clarified and early treatment vigorously pursued.

Clinical Issues: Organic Brain Syndrome

As we shall see below, organic brain diseases, pathological processes which interfere directly with brain tissue function as reflected in demonstrable changes in chemistry, physiology, or anatomy, may affect all aspects and levels of behavior. However, the basic biobehavioral functions of consciousness-sensorium, memory, and general intelligence are impaired only when there is impairment of brain tissue function (see Fig. 2-1). Thus, demonstration of impairment of any of the three basic function areas should always alert the clinician to the existence of tissue pathology.

In the hierarchy of behavior function areas which form the organizing concept of this book, we have arranged these areas in a sequence intended to reflect varying contributions to each area of biological, psychological, and social determinants. Thus the basic mental functions and their abnormalities are relatively more determined by biological (organic) factors than by the types of events studied by the psychological and social sciences. Social integration, the last in our hierarchical list, clearly depends to a very large degree upon social determinants. However, *it would be a serious error to assume that any behavior is not, in some complex pattern of interaction, determined by all three.* Our immediate point is that brain pathology, if sufficiently diffuse, typically affects all behavior functions. Organic brain syndrome (OBS) is the term used for the symptomatic, behavioral reflection of diffuse organic brain disease.

In early OBS, the most immediately vulnerable functions are not the basic behavior functions, the impairment of which, as we have seen, is characteristic of organicity. The most vulnerable—those usually "first to go"—are those highest in the hierarchy, that is, the most complex, most recently evolved, most exclusively human: those involved in socialization and social

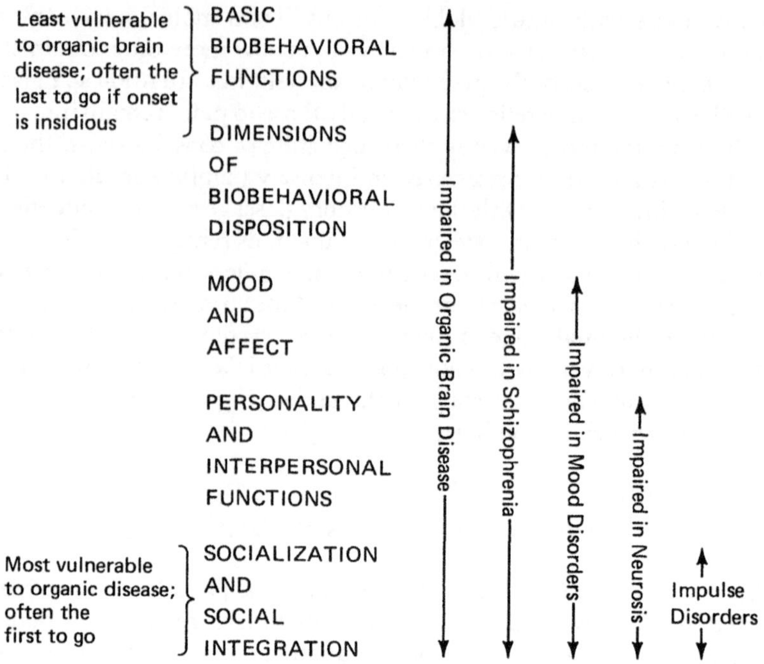

Fig. 2-1. The hierarchy of behavior function areas and their relationships to areas of disordered behavior. (Note that patients most often have disturbances in more than one behavior function area which produce the total disordered behavior picture. They may be said to suffer from more than one illness.)

integration. However, if carefully searched for, signs of impairment in basic biobehavioral functions can often be found, even in early stages of organic brain disease.

In chronic OBS, which often develops slowly enough to permit observation of a sequence of symptoms, the first indicator of illness is frequently loss of social inhibitions and sensibilities. A man or woman previously sensitive to societal expectations and keenly aware of the feelings of others and the finer nuances of personal relationships may become noticeably insensitive to the communications of other people, awkward in social interactions, less responsive, unpredictable, and thus less pleasant and comfortable to be with. In more advanced stages of the syndrome, these signs may progress to flagrant disregard for the feelings of others, tactlessness, and coarseness of speech, quite in contrast to earlier habits. The picture may include bizarre demands and expectations toward others, including sexual advances which are inappropriate both with regard to place and person approached. Appropriation of the belongings of others is also frequent. Impairment of the social integrative functions is, of course, often the result of factors other than organic brain disease. However, when such changes occur and particularly when other explanations are insufficient, the possibility of early OBS must certainly be entertained.

Very closely related to social integration is the area of personality and interpersonal functions. Many writers consider "personality change" to be the most frequently reported initial sign of OBS. The possible variety of such changes is, of course, nearly unlimited. A previously shy and reserved person becomes extremely gregarious and outgoing. A sociable, friendly individual rather suddenly changes to become sullen and withdrawn, without known situational precipitant and without signs of emotional conflict sufficient to explain the transformation. Easygoing persons become easily provoked; previously hard-driving individuals lose their former interest in occupations and in civic or church affairs. Again it must be emphasized that causes other than organic produce such changes, probably more frequently than brain disease, and their presence must also be investigated. However, the possibility of OBS must not be overlooked simply because the classic, basic signs of organic pathology have not appeared, especially when the initial signs of personality change occur after age 40. Personality changes may become very profound. When OBS is advanced, the personality itself may be almost totally destroyed, leaving only fleeting remnants of an earlier human being to remind and sadden relatives and friends. These individuals often tell the physician, "He is now only a shell of his former self."

Emotional lability is so frequently a part of the behavioral pattern in diffuse brain disease that many texts list it as an integral element of OBS. It is not, however, distinctively characteristic of this type of pathology, as are the basic mental functions. Also, unlike impairment of consciousness-sensorium, memory, and intelligence, emotional abnormalities are not as likely to be late symptoms in the development of the illness but may occur at relatively early stages. The problem is largely one of loss of the finer aspects of emotional control and modulation. Events or circumstances which previously would have elicited mild concern now evoke intense fear or defection. Minor irritations become rages. Pleasure may assume the quality of euphoria. Emotional reactions are quickly triggered and as quickly evaporate. Extremes of one reaction often seem to rebound, without external cause, to produce extremes of the polar opposite emotion. Relatives and others who provide the physician with historical information are often troubled by the unpredictability of the patient's feelings. "We just never know what to expect anymore." Irritability and hostility are, of course, the emotions which cause the greatest concern to those around the patient and are most frequently reported when present. The doctor should inquire about unusual emotions in other directions as well. In advanced stages of OBS, emotional abnormality may become an almost constant behavioral feature, usually manifesting as intense irritability and "fussiness" or as intense depression.

In our hierarchy of behavior function areas there is a group of mental activities nearly as basic as those which form the subject of this chapter. For this cluster of behaviors we have adopted the term "dimensions of biobehavioral disposition" (to be discussed in detail in Unit II). These are dimensions thought to be determined in some significant degree by innate factors. Among those dimensions of biobehavioral disposition of particular significance for medicine are those concerned with the general function of integration (often spoken of as an "ego" function). For present purposes we may say that the ego-integrative functions include: (1) reality testing and a sense of the boundaries between oneself and the outside world; (2) coherence and purposiveness of the thought processes or "associations" and (3) integration (synthesis) of the various aspects of the mental life—thoughts, emotions, behavior—into a coherent whole. Their impairment, *in the absence of organic brain disease*, is characteristic of the schizophrenic group of disorders. They are also affected with some regularity in the moderate and severe stages of OBS. Problems of differentiating organic and schizophrenic behavior are not infrequent in clinical practice. However, it is usually the case that by the time the illness is sufficiently advanced to produce impairment of the ego-integrative functions, there are also distinct basic organic signs as well, i.e., consciousness, memory, and intelligence. Exceptions to this rule are certain organic brain syndromes due to focal lesions of the brain, particularly tumors, which may develop organic indicators very late in the course, but suffer schizophrenia-like symptoms for periods up to several years. In conditions of more acute onset, the difficult differential diagnosis is most frequently between intoxication with various drugs which do not depress the level of consciousness-sensorium and therefore produce a state almost indistinguishable from acute schizophrenia. The patient is typically hyperalert and hyperactive. Speech is incoherent, and the emotions may be unrelated to the content. Visual hallucinations (which are more characteristics of organic brain disease than auditory) may occur, but they may be absent and persecutory delusions may form the most prominent element of the mental content. Amphetamines and hallucinogens such as LSD, are the most frequent compounds producing this schizophrenia-like acute organic psychosis.

When chronic OBS has advanced to the severe stage reflected in extremes of social, personality, emotional, ego function, and basic function impairments which we have now described, the condition is known as *dementia*. Use of this term in the clinic implies that all of the "higher" functions are affected to a significant degree and that intelligence and memory are significantly impaired. Consciousness, on the other hand, is often unaffected until the very latest stages of the illness. Thus the patient may appear at first glance to be alert and well, but attempts to engage him in conversation reveal the severe loss of the other mental functions. If the underlying disease is progressive, changes of consciousness often signal the terminal period, which is characterized by successive stages of clouding, stupor, and coma, during which the patient loses somatic and visceral motor control, is bedridden, incontinent, and requires total nursing care. In the past it has been the custom to use the terms "chronic OBS" and "dementia" to connote irreversibility. Many types of chronic OBS do indeed prove to be irreversible, since central neuronal tissues, once destroyed, do not regenerate. On the other hand, it is now the practice to emphasize that some conditions showing all the symptoms of chronic OBS and the severity of dementia may, if the underlying cause is treated, permit arrest and even some restoration of function. Within this emphasis, which directs attention toward active clarification of the nature of the cause and vigorous treatment whenever possible, it is becoming commonplace to speak of "reversible dementia," a phrase which, until recently, would have been viewed as a contradiction of terms.

It is beyond the scope of this book to present detailed descriptions of the symptomatology, course, and treatment of the many different sources of organic brain pathology which may produce the behavioral picture of OBS. This information will be found in textbooks of clinical psychiatry and internal medicine. We will, however, provide a listing of the types of pathological processes which may be involved:

1. Drug or poison intoxication (including alcohol)
2. Intracranial infection
3. Cerebral arteriosclerosis and other cerebrovascular disturbances
4. Epilepsy
5. Intracranial neoplasm
6. Degenerative and atrophic disease of the CNS
7. Brain trauma
8. Endocrine disorder
9. Metabolic or nutritional disorder
10. Systemic infection

Most of these pathological processes may produce chronic or acute OBS depending upon the severity and rate of progression of the process itself. Acute states may, of course, develop into more chronic conditions, and it is not uncommon for chronic conditions to erupt into acute episodes.

Acute OBS has often been described as a reversible state, but this conceptualization, like the designation of chronic OBS as irreversible, is in practice misleading. While it is unusual for severe acute OBS, the state called *delirium*, to last more than a week or two, a fatal outcome for this state or progression to chronicity is quite common. It would be unwise to take a casual view of acute OBS on the assumption that it is a benign condition.

Because the onset is more rapidly progressive in acute OBS than in the chronic form, the progression of symptoms from higher order to basic may be obscured; organic signs are present from the beginning, and impairment of consciousness-sensorium is the hallmark of the delirious state. [Intoxication with amphetamines and hallucinogens have already been mentioned as exceptions to this rule. Some acute conditions resulting from alcohol and sedative *withdrawal* and from states of severe sensory deprivation, such as may occur in hospital intensive care units, are additional exceptions.] In delirium, the affective functions are usually markedly disturbed, most often in the direction of anxiety and agitation which may reach levels of terror and panic. Restlessness is common and hallucinations, particularly visual, are also frequent. Intellectual functions, especially judgment, are disturbed so that the patient is prone to behavior of the most irrational nature.

It is customary to think of OBS, chronic and acute, as the symptomatic reflection of *diffuse* brain pathology, whereas focal lesions are described symptomatically in terms of their sensorimotor ("primary neurological") and more localized behavioral signs. Review of the list of possible causes of OBS, however, makes it evident that many processes which produce focal brain lesions (benign tumors, for example) are quite capable of producing the general behavioral picture of OBS—in addition to, or particularly in early stages instead of, the classical localizing signs. This fact is of importance for proper diagnosis and early treatment. Unless it is possible to clearly establish the etiology of an OBS in one of the diffuse CNS pathologies or in a systemic illness, more detailed studies such as electroencephalography and isotope brain scans should be considered in order to further investigate the possibility of a focal lesion.

Epidemiological Considerations

Documenting and explaining the distribution of pathology in populations are major objectives of epidemiology as a field of medical inquiry. Distribution is expressed in several ways. The frequency of events is commonly expressed as *incidence* (how many new cases per 1000 population in a year) and as *prevalence* (how many new *and* continuing cases per 1000 populations in a year). In addition to population incidence and prevalence of cases for a total population, rates may be calculated for subpopulations by age, gender, socioeconomic status, or ethnicity. The incidence and prevalence of common pathologies such as cardiovascular disease or cancer in the general population and in subpopulations have been studied in detail for many years. Consequently, the distribution of rates in our society and in other societies currently and over time are well known.

The incidence and prevalence of pathologies of intellectual functioning have not been documented definitively, but some facts are known. Consider, for example, mental retardation. Debate continues on the definitive diagnosis of mental retardation and hence the identification of cases. With this caution in mind, the estimated prevalence of mental retardation in the U.S. population is 30 per 1000, or 3%. The incidence of mental retardation is not documented, but the rate is suggested by an estimated 10 per 1000 (1%) children diagnosed as retarded in the preschool years; the highest incidence of this diagnosis was for children aged 10–14.

Three signs of impaired intellectual functioning of diagnostic significance for physicians are orientation (location of oneself in terms of time and place), loss of memory, and inability to reason. These signs are commonly summarized with the diagnostic label of dementia or under a label that suggests the general etiology of the signs, OBS. As noted earlier in this chapter, OBS includes both acute and chronic malfunction of the central nervous system. Dementia and OBS are known to have multiple etiologies, including both irreversible and reversible CNS change. Dementia appears secondary to a variety of disease processes or their pharmacologic management.

Systematic population studies of dementia and OBS have not been made. Consequently, their general incidence and prevalence are not known. However, their age-specific prevalence has been of considerable interest in studies of older persons. The association of age and CNS malfunction is suggested by the frequency with which both physicians and the lay public refer to *senile* dementia and associate OBS with the later years of life. In common terminology, senility connotes impairment of orientation, memory, and judgment. We know from evidence that the great majority of older people, even at advanced chronological age, are not senile; but we also know that the incidence and prevalence of impaired intellectual functioning increases with age in the later years. Consider the following evidence.

The Duke University Center for the Study of Aging and Human Development has conducted sample surveys of noninstitutionalized persons 65 years of age and over. The survey instrument used employs a series of questions designed to establish whether the respondent is sufficiently intellectually intact to be interviewed. Significantly impaired intellectual functioning has been observed in about 6% of older individuals contacted in these surveys. Studies of institutionalized older persons provide additional information. About 5% of persons over age 65 are institutionalized, primarily in nursing homes. Among these individuals, about 50% are significantly impaired in intellectual functioning, and the rate increases with age. For those aged 65–74, the estimate of intellectual impairment is 45%; 75–84, 61%; and for those 85 and older, 71%. In such institutions, the classification of chronic conditions includes OBS, senility, and mental retardation; the rates for these three classifications are 25%, 32%, and 6% respectively. These figures are crude estimates of the prevalence of these conditions, and estimates of incidence are not available. It is worth noting that about 10% of persons in nursing homes are younger than 65. Among those younger than 65 the rate of intellectual impairment is 15%, and among those younger than 45, 6%.

Estimates of the incidence of OBS in outpatient psychiatric clinics range from 25% to 33% among older patients. First admissions to mental hospitals for older persons, a rough indicator of incidence in this particular subpopulation, is 75% for those aged 65–74 and 90% for those 75 and older. There are no comparable estimates for younger patients, although one would expect the incidence to vary by the medical specialty with which one makes contact.

Psychiatrists, for example, would be more likely to encounter intellectually impaired patients than would internists.

Population studies of dementia and OBS in the U.S., the United Kingdom, Sweden, Denmark, and Japan produce estimates for severe intellectual impairment among older persons of around 5%; there is consensus that prevalence increases with age from below 5% at age 65 to 15%–20% at age 80.

Estimates of the incidence-prevalence of intellectual impairment are very important for the general physician whose practice, on average, involves older persons who are seen as ambulatory patients or in institutions. Older persons now constitute almost 11% of the U.S. population, and early in the next century this proportion is projected to increase considerably.

The facts and figures cited above do not give the complete picture, however. Behavior in public places which suggests that a person is physically but not functionally present (i.e., is not oriented in terms of time, place, and persons, and is unable to meet conventionally expected standards of performance) is disordered and requires an explanation. Is the individual demented, retarded, subnormal, or a social deviant? Is the condition explained by organic damage, by sickness, by drugs? Is the condition reversible?

Occasions for such questions are common in medical and psychiatric practice, particularly because older patients constitute a large proportion of both inpatients and outpatients. The answers tend to be complex precisely because altered states of consciousness demonstrably have multiple potential explanations and, in any case, are frequently difficult to diagnose with precision. As noted above, the relationship between pathological states of consciousness and late life is well known and provides a good illustration both of problems of diagnosis and of the consequences of routine application of convenient diagnostic labels.

Over 1 million long term care beds in the United States are occupied by persons over the age of 65, and surveys of the U.S. National Center for Health Statistics indicate that over half of these persons are significantly disoriented in terms of person, place, and time. More generally, the observed association of old age with organic brain pathology, with memory loss and intellectual decline as prominent features, is commonplace; this association invites the application of a commonplace label at the disposal of lay persons and health professionals alike: senile dementia.

Dementia is a label that is applied with caution by experienced clinicians. As a description of behavior, the basic meaning of dementia is straightforward: the term denotes a state of confusion—a disorientation of place, time, and person—which is sustained and associated with failing memory and loss of intellectual functions. The observed caution is occasioned by a number of connotations of dementia, such as "dementia is expected to be a concomitant of later life." Dementia is, in fact, most often discussed in connection with OBS, which the American Psychiatric Association defines as a "mental condition characteristically resulting from diffuse impairment of brain tissue function *from whatever* cause" (emphasis supplied). The commonly identified causes are numerous, including circulatory disturbances, metabolic disturbances, brain trauma, drugs, toxicity, infections, intracranial neoplasms, and epilepsy. This list is not exhaustive, but it is sufficient to indicate why the presence of sustained confusion should occasion a search for its sources and a determination of whether the identified etiological factors are reversible or, if not reversible, modifiable.

From the list of causes just noted, modifiability would be presumed until demonstrated otherwise. Moreover, even if irreversible brain damage is demonstrated, health professionals are familiar with the concepts of compensation and decompensation. *Compensation* refers to the reestablishment or maintenance of function in a defective organ or organ system; *decompensation* refers to loss of function which appears to be unexplained by the demonstrated anatomical defect. Processes of compensation and decompensation would, therefore, be expected to attenuate the relationship between brain and behavior and provide a substantial reason for caution in simple extrapolations from behavior to organic status of the brain and vice versa. This caveat is particularly consequential for the diagnosis and management of older patients.

The association between age and disability, which is well-grounded in epidemiologic evidence, tends to be exaggerated by both health professionals and lay persons. The probability of all kinds of impairments does tend to increase with age and, concomitantly, these impairments are translated into disabilities which increase utilization of health resources. These epidemiologic facts, however, do not justify the conclusion that old age per se explains observed disability. Clinicians who are experienced in working with older patients are very much aware that the psychological or psychiatric assessment of a confused or depressed older person is particularly affected by the general state of health, intelligence, education, vocational experience, and demands of the environment in which the person operates from day to day. Clinicians are also aware that the ready availability of a diagnostic label may mask the complexity of a condition and subvert adequate diagnostic study and vigorous corrective intervention. Senile dementia is a label to be used with caution.

An association between age and the probability of dementia is certainly indicated by the available evidence, but it is equally clear that significant dementia and the presumptively underlying chronic brain impairment are not inevitable in late life and not even a highly probable outcome until very late life. Moreover, the evidence available provides no adequate basis for estimating the degree of organic impairment underlying the observed behavior, whether this impairment is reversible, or the degree to which compensation is possible. In the absence of such information, sustained states of confusion exhibited by persons of any age are an inadequate basis for conclusions about the etiology of the behavior and about reversibility. There is a realistic basis for optimism that dementia which is secondary to treatable physical illness (drug addiction, or malnutrition, for example) is reversible. Moreover, even in the presence of diagnosed organic brain damage, some compensation can be achieved through behavioral training in reality orientation. Such training, which concentrates on orientation of the confused person to time, place, and person, has a beneficial effect in increasing the independence of the patient, but also has a beneficial effect on health care personnel on whom the burden of the dependent patient falls most heavily. The families of the OBS patients who often attempt to care for them at home also can be assisted in understanding the behavioral problems involved and in techniques of effective management. A national organization with local chapters, the Alzheimer's and Related Disease Association (ARDA) has recently experienced rapid growth in response to a broadly felt public need for assistance against one of the most common forms of OBS among older persons.

As our understanding of consciousness, memory, and intelligence has improved and as diagnostic procedures have become increasingly precise, undifferentiated labels like retardation and senile dementia will be used less often. Correspondingly, as diagnosis of the etiology of sustained confused states becomes more precise, more precise interventions will become possible. In the final analysis, a number of individuals with irreversible chronic brain damage and related severe behavioral disability will be identified. But the number of such persons will be much smaller than those usually labeled as senile. Even for those very impaired individuals who are correctly classified, it is possible to construct supportive environments that will enhance their capacity for independence and increase the satisfaction of the health personnel who care for them.

3
Memory

As was discussed in Chapter 2, *memory*, the capacity to retain a record of past experience, is a mental function only slightly less basic to adaptive behavior than consciousness itself. Conditions producing functional impairment of neural processes in the brain almost always result in discernible loss of certain memory processes, and indeed the diagnosis of organic brain syndrome (OBS) is frequently ultimately dependent upon the demonstration of such losses. The present chapter undertakes a review of basic memory processes insofar as these have become known through appropriate laboratory research, conducted chiefly by experimental psychologists.

Three concepts have dominated the history of research on memory and, in somewhat modified form, they are still with us today. These are the concepts of consolidation, decay, and interference of/with the memory trace. *Consolidation* refers to the well-established fact that the successful retention of an experience requires time for it to be "processed" following its occurrence. Distraction or disruption of CNS functioning (as with electroconvulsive shock) occurring shortly following the experience produces decrements in recall. *Decay* is a term referring to the inverse proportionality between the probability of retrieval of an experience and the time elapsed since its occurrence; conceptually it is associated with the notion of gradual "erasure" of the memory trace by ongoing metabolic processes. It is by no means certain (although it has not been disproved) that such erasing occurs, and *interference* mechanisms have long been postulated as an alternative explanation of the commonly observed decrease in the retrievability of memorial contents over time. The essential idea is that more recently acquired material interferes with and "inhibits" recall of earlier-formed memories. The parameters of this process, termed *retroactive inhibition*, have been well-explored: for example, maximum inhibition tends to occur where the interpolated (newer) material bears a moderate degree of similarity, but not approximating identity, to that of the original learning. A related process is that of *proactive inhibition*, where certain types of prior learning experiences interfere with the retrievability of subsequently occurring experiences. Proactive inhibition may be an important element in loss of memory function with age (the more the prior experience, the greater the amount of potentially proactive inhibiting material in memory), quite independent of age-related organic changes. Of course, organic changes, involving deterioration of the supporting neurophysiology, may also contribute to memory deficits in old age.

Until fairly recently, memory had been conceived in holistic, unitary terms; little attention was paid to the idea that there might be different sorts of memory having differing operating characteristics. Beginning some 25 years ago, investigators increasingly noted that the well-established principles of remembering and forgetting, which by and large were not substantially different from the observations of Aristotle, sometimes did not hold true. Eventually it became necessary to postulate separate systems of memory in order to account for its seemingly different properties under varying conditions of retention. Specifically, memory is conventionally conceived at present as three partially independent systems: (1) sensory information storage (SIS), (2) short-term memory (STM), and (3) long-term memory (LTM). The distinction between the last two of these, in particular, should be regarded as chiefly heuristic in that the implied dichotomy is becoming difficult to sustain in the face of mounting evidence of process continuity (Postman, 1975). In any event, it *is* the case that some memories are much more evanescent than others, and a great deal has come to be known about the processes implicated in at least the end-points of the retention-interval continuum. It seems wise, therefore, to briefly describe each of these memory systems in conventional terms in order to provide a convenient framework for discussion (Table 3-1).

In identifying the several memory systems, we follow the conventions of the psychological and neurobiological research literature. Unfortunately, the terms do not correspond fully with those of the clinical literature. The following table is provided for guidance in translating from one convention to the other.

It is noteworthy that despite the clinical tradition of distinguishing recent from remote memory because remote is thought to be more resistant to organic brain pathology, the modern clinical literature emphasizes that *both* are usually impaired in most cases of organic mental syndrome. This recognition tends to support the research classification in which both recent and remote memory are viewed as mediated by the same LTM process.

Table 3-1. Memory Systems.

Approximate Time Span	Research Term	Clinical Term	Method of Clinical Assessment
500 ms	Sensory information storage (SIS)	(No clinical equilavent)	
20–30 s	Short-term memory (STM)	Immediate memory	Immediate repetition of a series of numbers (digit-span test)
Variable	Long-term memory (LTM)	Recent memory or short-term memory	Recall of digit series or name after several minutes of unrelated activity; recall of events of recent hours, days, weeks
Unlimited	Long-term memory (LTM)	Remote memory or long-term memory	Recall of events from more-distant past

Sensory Information Storage

A variety of evidence indicates that the reception of a stimulus in the sensory apparatus, whatever the modality, is not an instantaneous event, as common sense would perhaps suggest. Rather, the sensory "image" lingers with decreasing experiential clarity for approximately 500 ms after termination of stimulation. Virtually any stimulus contains more information than the organism can effectively utilize. Discrimination of the essential from the inessential apparently occurs during the brief period of sensory information storage. The SIS system is therefore chiefly a mechanism that permits feature extraction and pattern recognition, a limited but perhaps quite crucial aspect of memorial retention. Little is known about the neural basis of SIS, although it is extremely likely to be related to processes involved in the "orienting reflex" or "what is it?" alerting response to any new stimulus originally described by the Russian physiologist Pavlov. It is quite conceivable that the SIS system would be subject to disruption by damage or dysfunction in localized brain tissue, in which case the organism would suffer deficits in the appropriate encoding of its experience, with resultant memory impairment. Clinical phenomena suggesting impairment at this level of sensory registration are by no means rare (e.g., certain aphasic and other disorders of the communicational faculties), but as yet no such specific causation has been isolated in patients with neurological disorders.

Short-Term Memory

With pattern recognition, the contents of an experience enter short-term memory where, in humans, they remain for perhaps 20–30 s in the absence of (overt or covert) rehearsal or of interpolated mental activity of a demanding sort. Continuous rehearsal can maintain items in STM for an indefinite period, but there are practical limits on the *amount* of material that can be continuously rehearsed in consciousness without loss. In the past, these items were considered to be numerically specific (maximum of about seven items, with the allowance that an "item" might be quite complex and contain several subitems, a hierarchical process known as "chunking") in consequence of an unfortunate analogy with address capacity in the memory units of computers. More recently, the concept of a limited STM capacity has been seen as ambiguously relating to both numerical units and to the rate at which successive units of a given type can be accommodated (Craik and Lockhart, 1972). In any event, estimates of the size of STM capacity vary widely in differing experimental contexts. About the only conclusion that can be justified at present is that there *are* magnitude limits of a fairly stringent order for the retention by maintenance rehearsal of unprocessed experiential data. Performance on the digit-span test, used clinically to test mental status, is an example of the application of this principle in medical practice. It is not clear whether forgetting in STM is a product of decay, displacement (interference), or both.

Maintenance rehearsal involves recycling of the items-to-be-remembered in consciousness. Anything that interferes with this recycling, such as a compelling distraction, produces losses in retention that are quite obliterative in extent. Mere maintenance rehearsal without further processing of STM contents, which in the pure case may be quite rare, apparently accomplishes little or nothing toward the formation of relatively permanent memories (i.e., transfer to LTM). The message format of information in STM is prevailingly acoustic or phonemic (articulatory), even where stimulation has been by other than the auditory modality. That is, the material is actually verbalized over and over. It is clear, however, that recoding of nonauditory stimulation into an acoustic format is not mandatory for STM storage (Postman, 1975).

The neural bases of memory, whether of brief or long-term duration, have not been precisely worked out. However, as we shall see later in this chapter, it seems very likely that retention in SIS and STM—the two systems are obviously in contact with each other—is somehow mediated through electrical activity of the reverberating circuit variety. The precise nature of this reverberation remains obscure. As will be seen, LTM seems dependent on the synthesis of new proteins. Sokolov (1977), in reviewing work on the neuronal mechanisms of memory, proposes a distinction between DNA-dependent (involving permanent alteration of the neural net) and DNA-independent memories, where the latter are conceived as nonpermanent modifications of the responsiveness of synaptic receptor sites. While DNA-independent memories can apparently be of considerably greater duration (at least in animals) than the presumed limits of human STM, continued exploration at the biochemical level has obvious promise of deepening our understanding of different types of memory processes.

The chief importance of the STM system consists in its being essential to the formation of long-term memories, i.e., those that persist for perhaps a few hours to virtually a lifetime. The formation of these persistent memories is dependent upon time for processing of informational input and very probably also for the manufacture and transport of proteins to pertinent synaptic sites. The required temporal buffer is provided by the retention within STM of material-to-be-processed. Apparently, there are no other routes of input to long-term storage. It follows that damage or dysfunction in neural tissues that support the operations of STM (which in all likelihood include at least certain hippocampal structures) will produce severe impairment of the ability to learn new information. Fascinating descriptions of two patients seeming to exhibit such a syndrome have been provided in a series of papers published several years ago (Millner et al., 1968) and are briefly summarized in a later section of this chapter. These patients have intact LTMs that are, however, impervious to the input of *new* information, a circumstance that produces quite bizarre behavioral phenomena. For example, the process of introduction of a person entering the patient's life space *after* the injury may have to be repeated on every occasion in which an interaction occurs.

Long-Term Memory

"Integrative" or "constructive," as opposed to mere maintenance, rehearsal appears to be the necessary and sufficient condition for the storage of information in LTM. Such rehearsal organizes new information and keys it into content structures that already exist within the LTM, thereby making available multiple cues for retrieval. Mnemonic systems of various kinds essentially capitalize on this principle. There is reason to believe that information once stored in LTM is never entirely "erased," and that the storage capacity of LTM is without practical limits. Recall, then, is principally (and perhaps exclusively) a matter of retrieval. The probability of retrieval of an item of information from LTM is a function of the extent and quality of the embeddedness of that item within the network of information that is the LTM system, assuming functional intactness of the neural base. The "strength" of a memory trace is therefore critically dependent upon the depth of processing to which its constituent information has been subjected. Very often, of course, and perhaps always in the case of nonredundant experience, processing depth is determined at or shortly following the occurrence of the experience. The context surrounding the acquisition of information is a major determinant of its subsequent retrievability. Some hold that it is the *only* such determinant, a position identified as the "principle of encoding specificity." Thompson and Tulving (1970), major figures in the psychology of memory, make the following strong assertion: "No cue, however strongly associated with the (to-be-remembered) item or otherwise related to it, can be effective unless the (to-be-remembered) item is specifically encoded with respect to that cue at the time of storage" (p. 255). The controversy provoked by this assertion has to date not been resolved.

The above quotation in essence relates to a fundamental distinction concerning the contents of the memory store; that is, these contents are organized in terms of both concepts and events, referred to respectively as the semantic and the episodic memory systems. In making their assertion, Thompson and Tulving are essentially relying upon evidence that retrieval operates upon the episodic memory store, the memory system that is involved in the recording of *events*. The semantic store, as the term implies, is concerned with the denotative and connotative meanings of words and their associative and classificatory bonds. If retrieval does indeed operate exclusively on the episodic system, then it would seem to follow that no cue could be effective in retrieval unless it were somehow associated with the pertinent event. Quite obviously, in any case, the semantic and episodic stores are only partially independent and must make contact at many points. Nevertheless, it is important to note that certain types of brain damage produce highly selective memory deficits such that only one of the two systems seems affected. Some patients (e.g., with Korsakoff's syndrome) forget events but do not suffer discernible loss of language or semantic functioning; others (e.g., aphasics) undergo severe disruption of semantic memory without impairment of memory for past events.

While the semantic and episodic systems together constitute the most significant aspects of LTM storage, it is clear that other systems are also capable of retaining information over long periods of time, i.e., those systems concerned with the "imaging" of past events in what is essentially a sensory format. Thus, visual images of past experiences can be called up at will, frequently with striking vividness and apparent veridicality. The scanning of such images may reveal new information that was heretofore encoded in some other form. Probably all of the senses have at least some limited capacity to store their contents in this manner, and deliberate imaginal encoding may be a substantial aid in memory in general. However, little is known in detail about such processes; they have not been studied with anywhere near the intensity of other forms of long-term storage.

The facility and efficiency with which the LTM performs its essential functions depend upon the adequacy with which it is *organized.* To some extent organization depends upon the acquisition of associative links common to most people, or at least most people in a given culture and language community. Much of this organization, however, is highly idiosyncratic. The human mind is such that it seems irresistibly drawn to discriminating, categorizing, coding, and organizing anything it stores away for future reference, and in so doing it relies perforce on its own previously established rules (and metarules) or principles of organization, much as do the administrators of library card catalogues. It goes without saying that some organizational systems are better, richer, more elaborated, and more flexibly adaptive than others in terms of their functional utility, and here we touch on the issue of general intelligence, to be discussed in Chapter 4.

As has been suggested, retrieval of material from LTM is basically a matter of discovering a route into the pertinent subsystem, a route that will permit us to recreate the sought-after content. Ease of discovery is dependent upon the richness of available connections, some of which may be quite remote. This bears on the question of recall versus recognition—we frequently "know" more than we can report, as demonstrated by our ability to recognize a correct response on a multiple-choice examination even though we may not have been able to reproduce (recall) it spontaneously. It also relates to the commonly experienced "tip-of-the-tongue" phenomenon (Brown and McNeill, 1966), where it can be demonstrated that the associations we do produce in searching for the elusive word or name are by no means random with respect to the characteristics of the target. Certain types of brain injury (e.g., to the medial temporal lobe) apparently interfere with the effective (i.e., duly processed) transfer of memories from STM to LTM. The interference seems to be of a limited type, however, inasmuch as such patients can often *recognize* the items to be remembered while being wholly unable to *recall* them. This phenomenon (in addition to the often striking loss of recent memory) is common in the amnestic-confabulatory (Korsakoff's) syndrome referred to earlier in this chapter, and it highlights the central role of the retrieval mechanism in disorders of this type. Needless to say, such observations raise fascinating questions about how the mind and brain work. At present, unfortunately, we have many more questions in this area than we have answers.

Neurobiological and Clinical Considerations

The physiology, biochemistry, and anatomy of memory are largely matters of speculation, as has been indicated. However, given what we know about the functioning of neurons, the possibilities of trace retention at the biological level can be reduced to a finite array of general models. This is especially true of the SIS and STM systems which, as has been indicated, probably are mediated by ongoing electrical activity. Basically, there are three possibilities to account for the retention of single units or items of information within these systems. All of them relate to the manner in which individual neurons may conceivably be recruited as highly discriminative carriers of information, broadly speaking. The possibilities are:

1. An unique cell, which is somehow programmed to fire only with a specific pattern of input stimulation
2. An unique pattern of cells whose mutual, simultaneous firing is information-specific
3. An unique *code*, such that the temporal order of firing of predesignated cells is information-specific

As can readily be appreciated, these possibilities (or conceivably combinations of them), while quite likely exhaustive, provide little in the way of satisfaction of one's curiosity about the mechanisms of short-term retention. The concept of DNA-independent memory, mentioned earlier, does provide a reasonable explanation of how time-limited alterations in synaptic efficiency, a process implicitly assumed in each of the above models, might occur. Briefly, Sokolov's (1977) conception is that the action of the transmitter substance on the receptor neuron produces conformational changes of neuronal protein whose activation/inactivation causes a modification of the responsiveness of the receptor site. While thoroughly consistent with current knowledge of neuronal functioning, it is not clear how such a view could be proven (or disconfirmed) as the neuronal mechanisms of short-term memory storage.

There is a growing consensus that relatively permanent memories involve the manufacture of new proteins. Perhaps the strongest evidence bearing on this question is the negative effect upon long-term memory formation of drugs that inhibit protein synthesis (e.g., anisomycin). On the other hand, the inhibition of protein synthesis has no discernible effect on short-term memory.

As we have seen, it appears that short-term memory function is dependent upon electrophysiological events for its integrity. In one study carried out to demonstrate this phenomenon, chickens learned to avoid, after one trial exposure, an object which was coated with a substance having a noxious taste. They were immediately re-presented with an object identical to that which had been coated with the noxious substance but now uncoated, and all chickens immediately responded by pecking at the new object even though it was not covered with the noxious substance. Thus they "remembered" the association between the object and the unpleasant taste.

Pretreatment with a protein synthesis inhibitor, cycloheximide, had no effect on this *immediate* recall of the object by the chickens. On the other hand, pretreatment with the drug ouabain caused a rapid loss of retention (indexed by loss of pecking behavior) of the object which had been coated with the noxious substance. That is, chickens pretreated with ouabain, upon representation of a similar object to that which had been coated with a noxious substance, no longer pecked at it or showed any other signs of recognition. Ouabain is known to have several effects which would impair electrophysiological responses. It inhibits the adenosine triphosphatase in nerve membranes on which the sodium pump is dependent. Furthermore, it is known to abolish the after-potential sequence which is generated in some neurons by sodium pump activity after repeated discharges. Therefore, this study would suggest that short-term memory is dependent upon electrophysiological events within the brain. The locus of these electrophysiological events is not known. However, short-term memory is clearly impaired by gross alterations of central nervous system metabolic activity.

Learning may be conceived as the process whereby information is transferred from short-term to long-term memory and is later retrieved either spontaneously or in response to some new environmental demands. The anatomical location in which transfer to storage or retrieval from long-term memory occurs appears to involve the so-called Papez circuit, which extends from the mamillary bodies, to the anterior nuclear group of the dorsal thalamus, to the cingulate gyrus, to the hippocampal gyrus (hippocampus and amygdala), to the septum, and back to the mamillary bodies. Bilateral lesions of any part of this circuit appear capable of causing so-called amnestic syndromes. These syndromes appear to be examples of "pure short-term memory," i.e., the individual has intact short-term memory as tested by such tasks as the digit-span test but has no ability to either store or perhaps retrieve information in long-term memory. Korsakoff's syndrome, described earlier, provides one example of this problem in which the mamillary bodies undergo damage secondary to vitamin deficits.

Another classic example of the amnestic syndrome is provided by the case of H.M., which is described in greater detail by Millner et al. (1968) in the following case study:

> H.M. had suffered from seizures since the age of 7, resulting in his being unable to work upon graduation from high school, despite an IQ level of 112. Because he appeared to have bilateral temporal lobe seizure foci, a bilateral extirpation of temporal lobe tissue was undertaken at age 32. Postoperatively, his seizure problem was markedly diminished. However, he appeared to have an unusual memory deficit in which his early memories were clear and vivid and his short-term memory (e.g., digital span), speech, and other behaviors were both normal and appropriate. The main problem appeared to be an inability to recall any events occurring post-op once they departed his immediate attention. That is, as long as events were being maintained in short-term memory, he could recall them, but once he was distracted there appeared to have been no transfer from short-term to long-term memory. For example, he could mow the lawn, but he never could remember where he left the mower after he quit mowing the lawn. He would read and reread the same newspapers and books over and over again. He failed to recognize friends and neighbors unless he had known them for years preoperatively. Each time he learned of the death of his

> uncle, which had occurred three years preoperatively, he became moved and tearful, treating it as though it were a new event. In short, as long as his attention was maintained toward a given stimulus event or series of stimulus events, H.M. was able to recall those events, but as soon as his attention was distracted it was as though those events had never happened.
>
> Fifteen years postoperatively, H.M.'s seizures continued to be under good control, but the memory deficit was essentially as it had been immediately postoperatively. His IQ was still at the level of 118, but he was still unable to recall or learn any new verbal or visual material when tested extensively on follow-up examinations.
>
> The most poignant description of his dilemma comes from H.M. himself: Every day is alone in itself. Whatever enjoyment I've had and whatever sorrow I've had . . . right now I'm wondering, "Have I done or said anything amiss?" You see, at this moment everything looks clear to me but what happened just before? That's what worries me. It's like waking from a dream. I just don't remember.

Another similar case in which bilateral destruction of hippocampal tissue occurred was that of a high school math teacher who suffered bilateral destruction of the hippocampus in association with encephalitis at age 42. Even though he had an IQ of 125, his memory deficit was quite similar to that of H.M. described above. An even more poignant example of the tragedy involved in this kind of memory deficit is that this patient was unaware of the birth of his last two children which occurred 2–5 years before his illness. Thus the loss of the ability to store or retrieve information in long-term memory essentially robbed this patient of knowledge of his children.

We do not yet know the precise nature of the deficit involved in these amnestic syndromes involving bilateral damage of the Papez circuit. Three possible explanations exist, and evidence has been presented which supports each. First of all, there may be a consolidation problem or failure to transfer information from short-term to long-term memory. The second possibility suggests that there is an encoding problem, that is, a problem in translating information into a form appropriate for transfer or recall. A lack of ability to verbally rehearse information would be an example of this problem. Finally, there may be no problem with transfer from short-term to long-term memory or in encoding, but the problem could be in retrieval of information from long-term memory. Probably the true state of affairs is some combination of all three. If the information can no longer be retrieved from long-term memory, then it remains inaccessible to the individual. Hopefully, further research will help unravel this mystery.

In addition to its dependency upon the structural integrity of the Papez circuit components, the transfer of information to long-term memory appears to involve the RNA-dependent synthesis of new proteins. In one study of the biochemistry of transfer of information into long-term memory, rats were trained to jump to a ledge in their cage to avoid footshocks administered through the wire grid floor of the cage. The rats learned in 10–12 trials to jump to the ledge to avoid the footshocks. In this study, control animals were in two groups. One group was yoked to the animals being trained to avoid footshocks—that is, they received the same shocks as the experimental animals but had no ledge to which they could escape. When the experimental rats had learned to escape the shocks, then the yoked animals were no longer shocked. Thus the yoked group received the same physical stresses as did the trained animals but had no opportunity to engage in learning. A second control group just sat in the cage for a comparable amount of time. The relationship between learning and transfer of information into long-term memory and RNA-dependent protein synthesis was studied by injecting the animals with radioactively labeled uridine intracranially 30 min before a 15-min training or yoked period. A 28% increase in incorporation of labeled uridine into nuclear RNA and a 40% increase of incorporation into polysomal RNA was found in trained versus yoked animals. This increase in uridine incorporation was mainly confined to the diencephalon. The increase in uridine incorporation also appeared to be limited to the acquisition phase—that period when information is being actively transferred from short-term to long-term memory, since animals trained prior to retesting did not show increased uridine incorporation relative to yoke controls if they were injected with radioactively labeled uridine prior to retesting. In contrast, animals that had been yoked controls in prior testing did show increased uridine uptake during actual training administered later to avoid the footshocks. Subsequent studies have shown an increased rate of incorporation of radioactively labeled amino acids into protein in association with training, but not with the general stress experienced by yoked controls.

In other studies, inhibition of protein synthesis with such drugs as puromycin or cycloheximide was similarly found to inhibit or to retard the consolidation of sensory information (i.e., the transfer from short-term to long-term memory and/or the retrieval from long-term memory). Thus there are two lines of evidence supporting the conclusion that RNA-dependent synthesis of new proteins is involved in the storage or transfer of sensory information from short-term to long-term memory. First, coincident with this process there is an increase in the rate of incorporation of uridine into RNA; second, pretreatment with drugs which either inhibit RNA synthesis or protein synthesis are found to disrupt such transfer.

Other influences undoubtedly play a role in the consolidation of sensory information into long-term memory. For example, it has been proposed that the ACTH response to the stress of novel stimuli occurring in a learning situation may be an important contributor to learning, in that ACTH in the brain has an effect on increasing the rate of protein synthesis. Moreover, hypophysectomized animals have been found to learn poorly in the standard learning paradigms, and this deficit is reversed by pretreatment with ACTH. The neuropeptide vasopressin also appears to facilitate learning.

Developmental studies have been carried out to determine the ontogeny of learning. In one study, rat pups at 6–10 days of age were found to be able to gradually learn (i.e., to remember) to discriminate a stimulus for the reward of being returned to their home cages. At 15 days of age, rat pups learn to remember or discriminate the stimulus much more quickly in comparison to the 6- to 10-day-old rats. This superiority of the 15-day-old rats is destroyed by x-ray treatment which reduces the granular cell population of the hippocampal dentate gyrus.

The neuroscientist, Seymour Kety, has proposed that, in addition to the learning situation with its various parameters and other factors such as the age and species of the organism which is doing the learning, the affective state of the organism also plays a role in memory processes. It has long been known that memories associated with strong emotional states are more firmly established. For example, almost everyone can recall in great detail exactly where they were and what they were doing at the exact moment they learned of President Kennedy's assassination. That is, the transfer of information from short-term to long-term memory appears facilitated by the presence of a strong emotional state. In addition, it appears that information stored under such conditions is more easily retrieved. Kety proposes that the central nervous system noradrenergic systems may be involved in mediating this effect of affective states upon memory consolidation. He cites evidence that central nervous system norepinephrine may be involved in modulating protein synthesis at synapses. Indirect evidence for a role of noradrenergic neurons in facilitating transfer of information from short-term to long-term memory is provided by the observation that amphetamine or electric footshock, both of which are known to increase functional norepinephrine levels at the synapse, are found to counteract the suppression of memory consolidation (i.e., transfer from short-term to long-term memory) which is caused by inhibition of protein synthesis with agents such as cycloheximide. Further studies have shown that agents which deplete central nervous system catecholamines, such as reserpine, impair transfer from short-term to long-term memory if given immediately after training. This impairment by catecholamine depletors of memory consolidation is prevented by administering, simultaneously with the reserpine, precursors of the catecholamines such as L-DOPA. Finally, bilateral lesions of the locus ceruleus (that collection of cell bodies in the brain stem which supply most of the noradrenergic terminals to the cerebral cortex, cerebellar cortex, and parts of the hypothalamus) have been shown to impair the acquisition of ability of rats to learn to run an L-shaped maze runway for a food reward.

While final answers are obviously wanting at the present time, the evidence which is available clearly implicates the central nervous system catecholaminergic systems in the processes of memory at all levels, from the sensory information storage through the short-term memory through the long-term memory systems.

Inasmuch as transfer of information from short-term to long-term memory appears to involve the synthesis of new protein, the nutritional status of a child both intrautero and postnatally has a possible strong influence upon the ability of the child to acquire and learn new information. Thus, aspects of the social system which may determine the amount of amino acids available from the child's diet have potentially important implications for the ability of that child, no matter what the genetic endowment, to learn new information. Therefore, research such as that carried out in rats and chickens, showing the role of various anatomical and neurochemical systems in the central nervous system in the transfer of sensory information from short-term to long-term memory, may have important implications for such socially relevant questions as what kind of diet should we be sure to make available to our children. It would appear on the basis of such research that it is important to provide a balanced diet for children, not just because it will help them not to be hungry, but so that they may also have the capacity to develop to their fullest potential the ability to transfer information from short-term to long-term memory.

Certain other conditions relating to clinical conditions flesh out somewhat our understanding of memory mechanisms. Among these are the effects of trauma to the head, purposely induced or accidental, upon memory consolidation. Electroconvulsive shock delivered up to 1 h following a learning experience produces a marked anticonsolidation effect in animals. This phenomenon seems related to the well-known retrograde amnesia experienced by humans undergoing electroconvulsive therapy (ECT). It is not clear whether the effect is due to disruption of the STM system, preventing transfer to LTM (in which case it must be assumed that animals have a longer retention span in STM than humans), or whether the LTM consolidation process is itself directly affected. Many accidental head injuries produce similar effects, with loss being directly proportional to the recency of pretraumatic events. As the patient recovers, older memories return first, followed progressively by those relating to events closer in time to the trauma. Full return is the rule, except for events occurring in the last few minutes prior to injury—i.e., those events that had not yet made it into LTM. These observations establish the important point that head trauma does not produce, in the typical case, an erasure of memory, but rather that it somehow interferes (temporarily) with the retrieval process. Notice, too, that in these instances we are dealing with losses from episodic memory; semantic functioning typically remains intact.

We normally think of the passage of time as weakening memories, and that our strongest memories are those of recent events. Yet a multitude of evidence seems to show that our most robust memories are our older ones, the record of recent events being by comparison rather fragile and more vulnerable to assault. The paradox is partially resolved by reference to the distinction between the existence or strength of a memory trace and its retrievability. Newer memories, by and large, should clearly be more retrievable than older ones because of the salience of their associated cues, leading to the perhaps illusory sense that they are "stronger." The retrievability-dependent advantage of newer memories would, of course, evaporate in the face of conditions which disrupt the retrieval process. It remains unclear, however, why older memories return first during recovery from injury, and why they seem in some sense to be "protected" from a variety of influences that impair the retrieval of more recent acquisitions. Could it be that the relative irretrievability (under normal circumstances) of older memories somehow renders them less vulnerable to assault? We simply do not know.

The question of the localization of memory traces within the brain has a long and quite distinguished history. The psychologist Karl Lashley spent the better part of a professional lifetime in search of the engram (the anatomical locus) of specific memories, concluding finally that the idea was essentially chimerical, and proposing as a substitute his well-known law of "mass action" of brain tissue. According to this principle, the probability of memory obliteration is proportional to the *amount* of tissue rendered inoperative, not to its location. However, if it is magnitude of tissue damage that determines loss, then we should expect to observe at least some memory impairment with massive lesions. By and large we do, but there are notable exceptions; on occasion, huge areas of brain destruction produce no discernible memory deficit, although there might be other quite notable effects. This remains another of the puzzling phenomena for which we lack an entirely adequate explanation. It should be noted that these observations relate chiefly to episodic memory whose neural basis does indeed appear to be distributed broadly throughout the brain, and that such losses as occur seem to be predominantly losses of the retrieval function. A variety of evidence suggests quite strongly that the semantic memory is much more specifically localized to the left cerebral hemisphere although, within the implicated areas, little is known about the neural organization of the system.

Previously "lost" memories can be reactivated by the application of a minute electrical current to the surface of the brain. The retrieval process is somewhat random, however, in that repeated stimulation of the same point frequently gives rise to very different experiences. Wilder Penfield, the distinguished neurosurgeon, attributes such effects to activation by the stimulus of gray matter distant from the site of application, a spread of effect that is, of course, not readily controlled. Penfield (1975), in contrast to most contemporary investigators, offers certain anatomical localization hypotheses concerning the memory system. He locates the data base or storehouse of information of (episodic) memory in the higher brain stem or diencephalon, not in the cortex as intuition would have it. Probably correctly, he notes that the memory system requires an interpretive mechanism capable of scanning the data base, an inference that can be arrived at on exclusively psychological grounds; *something*, probably something that operates in conjunction with the

STM, must be capable of establishing connections (via "processing") between the contents of STM on the one hand and LTM on the other. Penfield suggests that the site of this function is a strip of tissue along the temporal lobe, an area he refers to as the "interpretive cortex." Damage to this area would presumably break a vital connection between these two data systems, and certain clinical phenomena, alluded to above, are generally consistent with this notion.

Having now considered the psychological and neurological processes whereby environmental events are retained in the memory banks of the organism, we shall move on in Chapter 4 to a consideration of individual differences in the ability to encode and retrieve past events, or general intelligence.

References

Brown, R., and D. McNeill. The "tip of the tongue" phenomena. J. Verb. Learn. Behav. 5:325–337, 1966.

Craik, F.I.M. and R.S. Lockhart. Levels of processing: A framework for memory research. J. Verb. Learn. Behav. 11:671–684, 1972.

Penfield, W. The Mystery of the Mind. Princeton, New Jersey: Princeton University Press, 1975.

Postman, L. Verbal learning and memory. In M.R. Rosenzweig and L.W. Porter (Eds.) Annual Review of Psychology, vol. 26. Palo Alto, California: Annual Reviews, Inc., 1975, pp. 291–335.

Scoville, W.B. and Milner, B. Loss of memory after bilateral hippocampal lesions. J. Neurol. Neurosurg. Psychiat. 20:11–21, 1957.

Sokolov, E.N. Brain functions: Neuronal mechanisms of learning and memory. In M.R. Rosenzweig and L.W. Porter (Eds.) Annual Review of Psychology, vol. 28. Palo Alto, California: Annual Reviews, Inc., 1977, pp. 85–112.

Thompson, D.M., and E. Tulving. Associative encoding and retrieval: Weak and cues. J. Exp. Psychol. vol. 86:255–262, 1970.

4
Intelligence

Intelligence, though a commonly used word, is a concept which has no simple definition. Our understanding of the processes and capacities that underlie the construct of intelligence continues to evolve and so do our definitions. A brief consideration of this evolution will serve to emphasize the dynamic character of this construct.

Evolution of the Concept of Intelligence

Individual differences in abilities have long been an area of interest. The consideration of individual differences was significantly influenced by Darwin and his theory of evolution. Darwin's raising of the question regarding continuity between animal and man with respect to mind as well as body stimulated interest in problems of mental inheritance. Galton's work on a tendency for genius to run in families followed and contributed to the eugenics movement, that is, substituting intelligent selection for natural selection in the interest of racial improvement. To foster this selection, various means of measuring man's abilities were developed. Originally these surveys were of sensory discrimination capabilities, but by the turn of this century they also included higher mental functions such as memory, imagination, and comprehension. Subsequently, instruments and tests were constructed to measure these abilities. Thus the field of mental testing emerged with the goal of assessing human faculties. Binet contributed to the emerging concept of intelligence by replacing the idea of separate functions or mental abilities with the idea of general ability-intelligence. In addition, Binet, along with Simon in 1905, devised the first "test of intelligence." The Binet-Simon scale was built around three main conceptions about the nature of intelligence. The mental processes that constituted intelligence were considered: (1) to be goal-directed, (2) to involve the ability to show adaptive solutions, and (3) to involve the capacity to show selectivity or self-judgment and self-criticism of choices (Chaplin and Krawiec, 1968). In addition to Binet's conceptualization about the nature of intelligence, the basic assumption underlying the original scale was that "a person is thought of as normal if he can do the things persons of his age normally do, retarded if his test performance corresponds to the performance of persons younger than himself, and accelerated if his performance levels exceed those of persons his own age" (Terman and Merrill, 1960, p. 5). Thus a person's performance on the test was measured in terms of mental age (MA) which was compared to his chronological age (CA) and expressed as a quotient of intelligence (MA ÷ CA × 100).

Subsequently, others expressed ideas about what constituted intelligence. For example, Spearman's two factor theory assumed that all mental tests required a general ability (G) and a specific ability (S), while Thurstone's theory assumed that seven primary mental abilities (verbal, number, spatial, perceptual, reasoning, memory, and word fluency) constituted intelligence. A more recent model, that of Gilford's structure of the intellect, views intelligence as a dynamic information processing system with 120 factors. Undoubtedly, our understanding of the processes underlying the construct of intelligence will continue to evolve.

Developmental Changes in Intelligence

In addition to the evolution of the concept of what constitutes intelligence, there has also been a focus on the development of intelligence within the individual which has been concerned not with the "what" of intelligence but with "how" or the process of thinking. The primary contribution in this area has been the work of Jean Piaget, leading to his theory of human cognitive development. It is not the content of performance which has been of primary interest to Piaget but the emergence and change of the thought processes underlying the functioning. Piaget viewed intelligence as developing hierarchically in a series of stages, with functions developed early being incorporated in later stages. Intellectual growth is seen as moving from the various stages of the sensorimotor period, which characterizes infancy, through the preoperational period, through the phases of the period of concrete operations, to the period of formal operations.

The *sensorimotor* period is thought of as extending from birth to age 2. During this stage the child becomes able to coordinate and integrate information from the various sensory modalities and exhibits goal directed behavior. While the behavior of the child during this period is genuinely adaptive and intelligent, it is still very concrete because of the lack of corresponding conceptual schemata.

The *preoperational* period follows the sensorimotor period and occupies the time from about age 2 to age 7. During this stage the child's internal cognitive picture of the external world is gradually evolving. It is a transitional period marked by inconsistencies in the logical aspects of thinking. Laws and relationships are gradually appreciated as the child develops his/her cognitive schemata.

The period of *concrete operations* occurs from about age 7 to age 11. During this stage the child acquires concepts of space, number, and time, and his/her thought processes become more stable, logical, and reasonable. The child demonstrates an understanding of the concrete operations of events and objects and the order or relationship among them.

The period of *formal operations* is seen as emerging around age 11. During this period the adolescent understands the basic principles of causal thinking, and his/her thought processes are characteristic of adult abstract thinking.

In Piaget's theory, the driving force behind the process of ever-more-complex cognitive organization is equilibration. That is, we strive to do what we can but also to increase the adaptiveness and complexity of our behavior. Intellectual growth is related to the continuous interaction of the organism and environment which Piaget terms *adaptation*. Two complementary concepts are postulated to provide for adaptation. One is *assimilation* which refers to restructuring environmental data so that they are congruent with existing schemata (behavioral patterns) and can be incorporated. This is a conservative process which tends to maintain the status quo. The other process is *accommodation*, which refers to the modification and elaboration of existing schemata so that they will be consistent with aspects of the environment. To adapt to the environment, the organism's schema must accommodate to the demands of the environment so that assimilation can occur and equilibrium can be obtained. The principles of Piaget's theory apply to all of his stages of development. The stages are not considered to be variable in the sequence order in which they appear, but the ages at which they are achieved can vary from individual to individual.

Intelligence: A Dynamic Definition

This brief consideration of some of the thinking about the "what" and "how" of intelligence can provide some appreciation of the continual evolution of this concept. It is important to emphasize that intelligence is a logical construct abstracted from things we observe people doing and from observed individual differences in such doing. It is operationally defined as "the aggregate or global capacity of the individual to act purposely, to think rationally, and to deal effectively with his environment" (Wechsler, 1958, p. 7). Intelligence is more than the sum of the various abilities which contribute to it, such as memory or reasoning. It is not a quality in the mind per se nor is it a singular or unique trait. It is a many-faceted entity that is not merely cognition, reasoning, memory, or any particular combination thereof, and excesses in any given ability may add relatively little to the effectiveness of the individual's behavior as a whole. Thus it is the configuration of capabilities along with other factors such as drive and incentives which constitutes intelligence. It is a general integrative function which is not localized in any particular cortical area. In essence, intelligence is an aspect of behavior reflecting a capacity to understand the world and to cope with its challenges.

Just as it is important to differentiate intelligence from some of its component parts, it is also necessary to differentiate it from the methods of measuring it. As there has been a continuing evolution in the construct, there has also been a corresponding evolution in measures or tests of intelligence. Typically, a particular measuring instrument is based upon a theory of what constitutes intelligence, and an individual's performance on such a measure is contrasted with that of a particular reference group. The comparison made, for either a child or an adult, is with the empirically determined expectancy for the reference group at a specific development period. The Stanford-Binet Intelligence Scale and the Wechsler Intelligence Scale are examples of instruments of this type. Some tests are constructed to delineate particular stages of development of intellectual functioning within the individual with less emphasis upon comparing one individual with a reference group—e.g., the instruments designed to determine characteristics of an individual's thinking in relation to Piaget's theory of intellectual development. Thus, in evaluating the usefulness of any measure of intelligence, the essential questions relate to what was being measured, with whom the individual was being compared, and for what purposes. In clinical situations, the intention is not to derive a label or a category which will enable classification, but to elicit behavior in response to specific questions and tasks that can be evaluated in terms of the individual's strengths and weaknesses in functioning, interacting, and adapting to his or her environment.

Clinical Issues

A consideration of those instances in which the intelligence function is impaired can serve to illustrate this complex construct. The recognition that some individuals have been impaired in their ability to cope with their environment has always been with us. Just as there have been changes in our thinking regarding the nature of general mental ability or intelligence, there also have been changes in our thinking about what constitutes subnormal mental ability.

Mental subnormality can be defined as "subnormal general intellectual functioning which originates during the development period and is associated with impairment of either learning and social adjustment or maturation, or both" (Knobloch and Pasamanick, 1974, p. 149). There are several important components to this concept of subnormality. First, the impairment is of *general* intellectual functioning, and it can affect maturation, learning, and social adjustment (which differentiates the impairment from a specific deficit such as a language disorder). Second, it can have numerous organic and environmental etiologies. Third, it occurs during the developmental period (which differentiates the impairment from other later-life phenomena such as senility—e.g., organic brain syndrome, as discussed in Chapter 2).

Mental subnormality can be further delineated in terms of the degree of functional impairment. Mental subnormality can be subdivided into mental deficiency and mental retardation. *Mental deficiency* refers to subnormal intellectual ability which is due to a pathological condition of the brain which could result from a variety of specific, known disease processes. As previously noted, the intellectual manifestations may also be accompanied by other manifestations of chronic organic brain disease—such as sensation, perception, and neuromotor difficulties—or may be the only expression. *Mental retardation* refers to intellectual and educational deficits that appear to an undetermined but important extent to be related to a constellation of social, familial, and cultural factors. Recently the term mental retardation has been utilized synonymously with mental subnormality. This has occurred because it is frequently difficult to ascertain that a specific pathologic condition of the brain exists and to avoid the implication of limited gains in skills that have been historically associated with the idea of brain impairment. In addition, the recent focus has been upon functional rather than categorical approaches to disorders of development. The point is made that the needs of the particular individual are many times more directly related to the degree of functional impairment than to the presumed etiological factor. However, we believe that both an etiological and functional perspective are necessary, not only to enhance the understanding about the nature of mental subnormality but also to enhance appropriate treatment and remedial services.

Functional Perspectives

It is important to appreciate that a continuum of functioning underlies normal and subnormal intelligence. Intelligence scores are distributed according to the normal curve, with the mean IQ scores assigned the standard score value of 100. The standard deviation of IQ scores is usually 15 to 16 points depending upon the particular assessment instrument used. The normal curve distribution can be used then to indicate percentage of the population included within successive standard deviations from the mean. It can be seen from Figure 4-1 that 68% of the population will fall within ±1 standard devi-

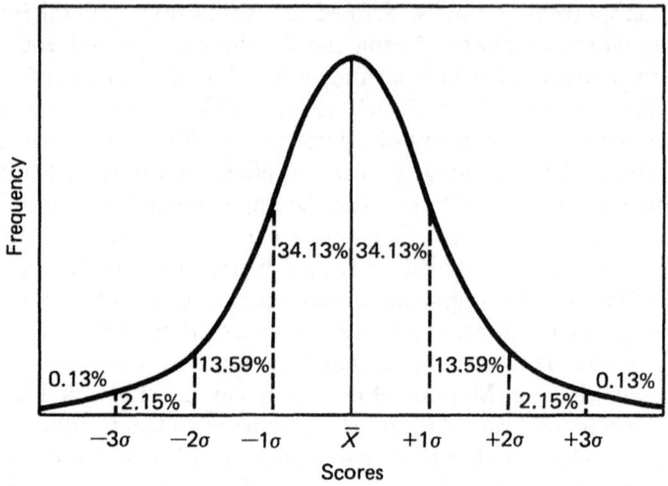

Fig. 4-1. Normal curve distribution of IQ scores with percentage of scores falling within successive standard deviations from the mean. (From Thompson and O'Quinn, 1979.)

ation from the mean, that is, between IQ scores of 85 and 115. Ninety-five percent of the population will fall between ±2 standard deviations from the mean, that is, IQ scores between 70 and 130.

In addition to depicting the number of people falling within various standard deviations from the mean IQ score of 100, the normal curve distribution has also been utilized in various classification systems to describe various levels of intellectual functioning. For example, the classification system utilized by the American Association of Mental Deficiency (AAMD) identifies mental subnormality as functioning more than 2 standard deviations below the mean. Thus, approximately 2.5% of the population would be categorized as demonstrating mental subnormality. Functioning within the general area of mental subnormality can be further delineated with respect to degree of functional impairment. Table 4-1 depicts the various AAMD categories of subnormal intellectual functioning and the corresponding IQ score ranges on the Stanford-Binet and Wechsler Scales of Intelligence. Recognition of the continuum of functioning underlying these descriptive categories is necessary for a full appreciation of the degree of impairment in self-help, communication, and social skills necessary to adapt to various age and cultural expectations. Some of those functioning within the mildly retarded range of intelligence can achieve independent adult functioning. Those with moderate, severe, or profound retardation need varying degrees of assistance and care to function adequately even in situations of reduced expectations.

Table 4-1. Ranges of Intellectual Functioning Impairment.

AAMD Category	σ	Stanford-Binet (σ=16)	Wechsler (σ=15)
Mild	−2 to −3	67–52	69–55
Moderate	−3 to −4	51–36	54–40
Severe	−4 to −5	35–20	
Profound	−5 and less	19 and below	

Etiological Perspectives

Only rarely are the precise reasons for mental subnormality known. We know that various genetic and environmental influences are associated with mental subnormality. However, what actually transpired on a cellular or subcellular level in the central nervous system to result in mental subnormality is typically not known. While various theories have been proposed, it can

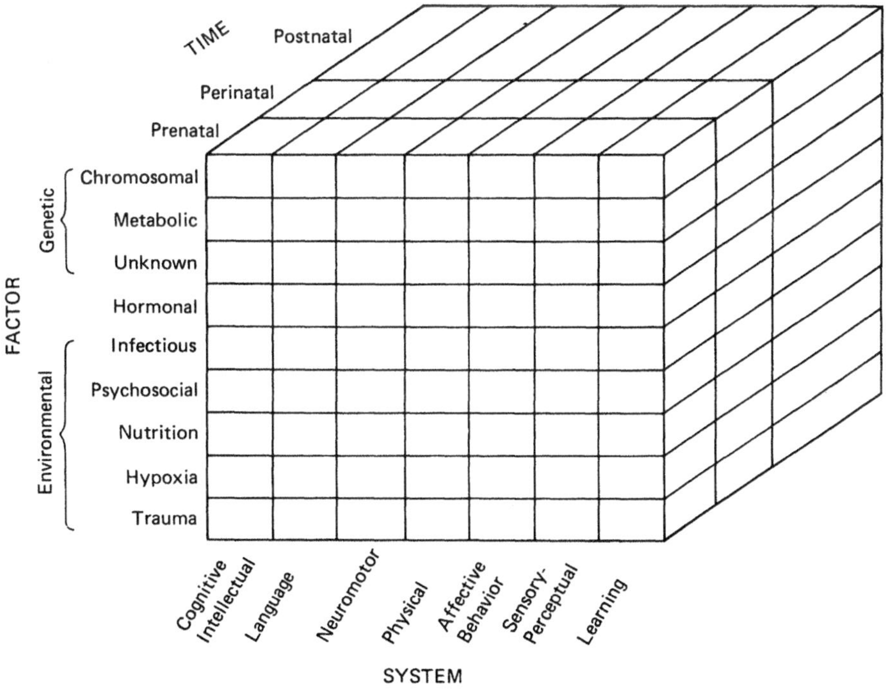

Fig. 4-2. Developmental disabilities cube depicting the interaction of etiologic factors occurring during a time period of development resulting in manifestations in various systems. (From Thompson and O'Quinn, 1979.)

be said that the processing of information from the environment, storage, and retrieval for decision making or action is impaired. In addition to uncertainty about the precise etiological factor, it must be recognized that etiology and resulting manifestations are related to interaction of both genetic and environmental factors and the specific developmental period in which these factors are operative.

One useful way to conceptualize this multidimensional approach and to provide a schema for considering disorders of functioning is by way of the cube shown in Figure 4-2. In this schema, behavior is perceived as a consequence of the multiple interaction of specific etiological factors occurring during particular periods, affecting various dimensions of functioning.

Table 4-2. Factors Associated with Mental Subnormalities

	Incidence per 1000 Live Births	Average Age of Diagnosis	Average Life Expectancy
PRENATAL PERIOD			
A. Genetic Factors			
1. Inborn Errors of Metabolism			
Cerebral lipidoses		prenatal-infancy	2–6 yrs
Infantile Gaucher's			
Nieman-Pick			
Tay-Sachs	0.28 among Ashkenazi Jews		
Mucopolysaccharidoses	0.04		
Hurler's syndrome		prenatal possible	variable
Hunter's syndrome		prenatal achieved	
Sanfilippo syndrome		prenatal achieved	
Disorders of protein metabolism			
Aminoacidopathies			
Phenylketonuria	0.05–0.1	newborn	adult
Homocystinuria	0.01	prenatal possible	variable
Lesch-Nyhan syndrome		prenatal possible childhood	variable

Table 4-2. Factors Associated with Mental Subnormalities (*con't*)

	Incidence per 1000 Live Births	Average Age of Diagnosis	Average Life Expectancy
Disorders of carbohydrate metabolism			
Galactosemia	.013	prenatal-infancy	adult
Glycogen storage disease		childhood	variable
2. Chromosomal Disorders	5	prenatal	variable
Disorders of the autosomes			
Down's syndrome (trisomy 21)	1.5	prenatal-newborn	variable
Edward's syndrome (E) (trisomy 18)	0.15	prenatal-newborn	<1 yr
Patau's syndrome (D) (trisomy 13)	0.13	prenatal-newborn	<1 yr
Cri-du-chat syndrome	0.02	prenatal-newborn	adult
Disorders of the sex chromosomes			
Klinefelter's syndrome	0.7	puberty	adult
Turner's syndrome	0.25	puberty	adult
3. Multiple Malformations			
Neural tube defects			
Anencephaly	0.1–6.7	prenatal or birth	perinatal
Meningomyelocele	1–2	prenatal or birth	variable
Syndromes of multiple malformation			
Neurofibromatosis (Von Recklinghausen's)		midchildhood	adult
Tuberous sclerosis		variable	adult
4. Other Inherited Syndromes			
Muscular dystrophy		2–5 yrs	early adult
Kernieterus as a result of blood group incompatibility		perinatal	
B. Environmental Factors			
Congenital infections			
Toxoplasmosis	1.3	perinatal	variable

Table 4-2. Factors Associated with Mental Subnormalities (*con't*)

	Incidence per 1000 Live Births	Average Age of Diagnosis	Average Life Expectancy
Rubella	rare	preventable due to vaccine	variable
Cytomegalovirus (CMV)	10	perinatal	variable
Herpes simplex virus (HSV)	0.01	perinatal variable	variable
Other maternal factors			
Psychosocial disadvantage			
Malfunction of the materno-placento-fetal unit			
PERINATAL PERIOD			
A. Metabolic Factors			
Hypoglycemia		perinatal	adult
Hypocalcemia		perinatal	adult
B. Environmental Factors			
Hypoxia-asphyxia-inchemia	variable	perinatal	variable
Trauma	variable	perinatal	variable
Malnutrition	variable	perinatal	variable
Infection (meningitis)	0.4	perinatal	variable
POSTNATAL PERIOD			
A. Metabolic-Hormonal Factors			
Congenital hypothyroidism	0.12	infancy	adult
Hypoglycemia		variable	variable
B. Environmental Factors			
Trauma			
Hypoxia			
Infection			
Meningitis (bacterial)			
Meningoencephalitis (viral)			
Poisoning			
Psychosocial disadvantage	frequent	infancy-childhood	adult

From Thompson and O'Quinn, 1979.

Etiological factors can be viewed as genetic (innate) and environmental. The consequences of the etiological factors depend not only upon the type of factor but also upon the particular developmental period in which it occurs. Thus there can be distinctly different patterns of consequences across the various dimensions of functioning depending upon, for example, the type of viral agent and the developmental period in which infection occurs. Furthermore, an etiological factor might be operative during one developmental period, but the functional consequences might not be manifested until a later period. This is particularly true of the chromosomal disorders and inborn errors of metabolism, which are prenatal in etiology but which might not be recognized until the perinatal or postnatal period. Etiological factors operating in a developmental period may have manifestation across a number of dimensions or systems of functioning such as the cognitive-intellectual, language, or neuromotor, or may primarily affect only one dimension. This multidimensional cube can be a useful schema for conceptualizing the complexity of behavior as a whole, which is important to keep in mind as we consider disorders in the intellectual dimension of functioning.

Table 4-2 presents some of the known genetic and environmental etiological factors associated with mental subnormality that occur during the prenatal, perinatal, and postnatal periods, along with representative examples and incidence estimates. It can be seen that the genetic factors of importance during the prenatal period include inborn errors of metabolism, chromosomal disorders, and multiple malformations. The environmental factors of importance during this period include congenital infections as well as other factors that may cause damage to the developing fetus. During both the perinatal and postnatal periods, it can be seen that metabolic factors and hormonal factors which may have had their origin during the prenatal period result in manifestations during these later periods. In addition, the environmental factors of importance have to do with situations such as trauma or infection which may impair functioning of the developing central nervous system.

Representative Examples. Consideration of several conditions involving known etiological factors occurring in the prenatal period will serve to illustrate several of the points that have been emphasized with regard to subnormal intelligence.

The *environmental* factors that are of importance in the etiology of mental deficiency in the prenatal period include intrauterine infection and maternal health factors. Congenital infections frequently involve the TORCH virus group, which is an acronym for Toxoplasmosis, Rubella, Cytomegalovirus, and Herpes Simplex virus. The manifestations vary depending upon localization of the infection in the fetus. Many affected infants do not survive the newborn period. In those that do, severe central nervous system involvement with mental deficiency and/or cerebral palsy is frequent.

Overuse of drugs and alcohol by the mother during pregnancy is also an environmental factor that has been associated with mental deficiency. Recently, there has been considerable interest in the effects of maternal alcohol consumption on offspring, and the existence of a fetal alcohol syndrome has been postulated (Jones and Smith, 1973). It has been reported that infants exposed prenatally to chronic alcoholism are subject to craniofacial, limb, and cardiovascular defects as well as growth deficiency and mental subnormality. While there is some cause for caution about the evidence for a fetal alcohol syndrome and the degree of alcohol consumption likely to result in maternal subnormality (Thompson, 1979), chronic consumption of large amounts of alcohol during pregnancy increases the risk of mental subnormality. The identification of this etiological factor is of most importance because of the possibilities for prevention.

The *genetic* factors of importance during the prenatal period include chromosomal disorders and inborn errors of metabolism. Chromosomal disorders are one of the major prenatal causes of mental deficiency, and Down's syndrome (trisomy 21) is probably the most common of the autosomal disorders, with an incidence in the U.S. of 1 out of 600 live births. About 50% succumb during the first five years with respiratory infections and congenital heart disease. However, recently there has been a drop in the mortality rate, and now a life expectancy of 30 years is a conservative estimate. Little was known about the cause of this congenital syndrome until 1959 when the first abnormality of human chromosomes was described: the association of 47 chromosomes with Down's syndrome. The extra chromosome material was attached to the 21-22 group, and it came to be known as trisomy 21.

Trisomy 21 accounts for 95% of all cases of Down's syndrome and is thought to occur as a result of nondisjunction in the first or second meiotic division of gametogenesis. This produces an abnormal ovum with a functional extra chromosome. There is no clear explanation why this happens, but there is a higher incidence of Down's syndrome in children of older mothers. One hypothesis is that the older an ovum gets, the more likely it is to exhibit nondisjunction. Solomons (1969) reports that 65% of all children with Down's syndrome are born to mothers over 30 years of age, and a mother over 40 years of age runs a risk 30 times greater of having a Down's child than does the mother below 20 years of age. Recent reports have suggested an increased frequency of Down's syndrome associated with older fathers as well. The recurrence risk of having another child with trisomy 21 for any given family is 1 or 2 out of 100. One or two percent of all children with trisomy 21 are mosaic—one cell line being normal and the other being trisomy 21. In general, the mosaic form of Down's syndrome is more mildly affected.

Translocation accounts for 3.3% of all cases of Down's syndrome and occurs when chromosome material from chromosome 21 attaches itself to another chromosome, usually in the D group (13–15) or less frequently in the G group (21–22). Thus a mother who is a balanced carrier for D–G translocation would have 45 chromosomes rather than 46 and would look perfectly normal. Because of the translocation, she would have an expected incidence of a Down's child of 1 in 3. If the father is the carrier, the incidence is slightly less, probably due to a competitive disadvantage with normal sperm. If either parent has a G–G (21–22) translocation, the child with Down's syndrome will actually have a chromosome count of 46 but will have extra genetic material in the long arm of chromosomes in the G or D group. Solomons (1969) reports that there is no correlation between maternal or paternal age in this disorder.

In terms of the cube in Figure 4-2, Down's syndrome results from a chromosomal, genetic, etiological factor occurring during the prenatal period with manifestations along several dimensions of functioning. In the cognitive-intellectual area, Down's syndrome is typically characterized by moderate to severe retardation (IQ of 30–50), although estimates vary. Historically, there has been an unwarranted pessimistic prognosis about intellectual development, probably because of studies using only institutionalized children. Speech and language delays are particularly marked, but most do learn to speak in sentences. They frequently have nasal speech and articulation problems. In the neuromotor area, the Down's syndrome infant follows a relatively normal motor pattern during the first six months; thereafter, there is gradual discrepancy in subsequent progress. Walking often does not occur until age 2 or 3. Hyperextensible joints and generalized hypotonia are characteristic.

In the behavioral-affective area of development, the Down's syndrome child has been noted to have a generally amicable disposition. Although studies are somewhat unclear, there appears to be no greater risk of emotional disturbance in the Down's syndrome child than in other children. Social maturity is likely to exceed intellectual maturity. Hyperactivity is not uncommon.

Another type of genetic disorder occurring during the prenatal period are the inborn errors of metabolism which can have severe effects upon the intellectual dimension of functioning during the perinatal and postnatal periods. Phenylketonuria (PKU) is a disorder of protein metabolism which follows the laws of autosomal-recessive inheritance and is associated with mental deficiency. The metabolic defect in classic PKU is a deficiency of phenylalanine hydroxylase, with the resultant elevation of blood phenylalanine levels, which is thought to interfere with the myelination of the brain. The incidence of PKU is 1 out of 10,000 to 20,000 births.

PKU represents a metabolic genetic factor occurring during the prenatal period with classic manifestations along several dimensions of functioning. In the cognitive-intellectual area, moderate to severe mental retardation is typical. Language is affected in relation to the mental retardation, as is learning. In neuromotor functioning, individuals with PKU are clumsy but are not definitely athetoid or spastic. Irritability is a noted behavioral characteristic in infancy, but later in childhood individuals are described as "good-tempered." Physically, babies with PKU often have a "mousy odor" and eczema, and are typically blond, blue-eyed, and fair. Other characteristics of severe cases include kyphosis or humpbacked curvature of the spine, hyperkinesis (digital mannerisms), and seizures in infancy and childhood. Seizures and autistic behaviors occur in 25%–85% of all PKU patients.

What makes PKU so important is that even though etiology is related to a metabolic defect occurring during the prenatal period, the influences and subsequent manifestations are primarily postnatal. Furthermore, if the elevated phenylalanine level in the blood can be reduced, CNS pathology and consequent manifestations can be reduced and even prevented. Thus PKU represents an example of a genetic condition which has potential for mental deficiency, but in which the mental deficiency can be prevented by improving environmental factors—in this case, improving the environment means treatment consisting of a low phenylalanine diet. Research has shown that each week treatment is delayed results in some loss of intellectual functioning, because brain development is taking place postnatally. The possibility of prevention has led to intensive screening efforts to identify affected individuals at birth and prior to manifestations, so that dietary treatment could be initiated as soon as possible. In 45 states, legislation exists for mandatory newborn screening and treatment.

Remedial Issues

The previous failure to distinguish between mental deficiency and mental retardation, along with the statistical necessity for reliable IQ scores, interacted with the conceptual view of intelligence that emphasized hereditary genetic aspects and resulted in a belief that intelligence was immutable. The view that intelligence was immutable influenced treatment programs. If intelligence level could not be changed, the most humane reasonable treatment for mental subnormality was custodial care. To change this view that intelligence is immutable, it was necessary to also change the view that mental abilities reflect primarily hereditary factors. Gradually it became apparent that correlates of poverty, in terms of poor health care, nutrition, prematurity, and impoverished environment, were at least as deleterious as genetic factors. Furthermore, the Armed Forces induction efforts brought about by World War II revealed a larger number of people to be functioning subnormally than hitherto appreciated, and the markedly nonrandom geographic distribution of these individuals forced a consideration of the relationship of intellectual functioning to educational and social conditions.

Gradually a new view emerged: in a majority of cases of mental subnormality, environmental factors were prominent and could be altered to improve functioning and prevent deterioration or deficiency. This led to a more hopeful outlook and to efforts to improve environments and to develop special educational techniques to foster development of intellectual ability to the fullest extent possible. In addition, efforts were directed at identifying etiological factors associated with mental subnormality so that appropriate preventive measures could be developed.

It need not be assumed that mental deficiency is reversible to posit that changes in functioning over time are possible. The assumption is that, although ultimate functioning is related to the integrity of the central nervous system even with a condition of mental deficiency reflecting CNS pathology, some learning can take place and some improvement of intellectual functioning can be achieved through proper programs and experiences. Thus in each clinical situation a functional analysis should be undertaken and, where possible, a determination of etiology made. This leads to the question of what can be done to improve functioning and, ultimately, what is the potential for such improvement and at what cost. In most cases meaningful prediction is impossible, and attention is better directed toward generating an empirical answer. That is, each individual needs to be provided with an opportunity over time to demonstrate change in response to special approaches. The empirical observation of how much change occurs in relation to particular remedial efforts is the appropriate base on which expectancies can be set and decisions about subsequent programs made.

References

Chaplin, J.P., and T.S. Krawiec. Systems and Theories of Psychology. New York, New York: Holt, Rinehart, and Winston, 1968.

Jones, K.L., and D.W. Smith. Recognition of the fetal alcohol syndrome in early infancy. Lancet 2:999–1001, 1973.

Knobloch, H., and B. Pasamanick. (Eds.) Gesell and Amatruda's Developmental Diagnosis, 3rd ed., Hagerstown, Maryland: Harper and Row, 1974.

Solomons, G. Mongolism. Hospital Medicine 58–69, 1969.

Terman, L.M., and M.A. Merrill. Stanford-Binet Intelligence Scale. Boston, Massachusetts: Houghton Mifflin, 1960.

Thompson, R.J., Jr. Effects of maternal alcohol consumption on offspring: Review, critical assessment, and future direction. J. Pediatr. Psychol. 4:265–276, 1979.

Thompson, R.J., Jr., and O'Quinn, A.N. Developmental Disabilities: Etiologies, Manifestations, Diagnoses, and Treatments. New York, New York: Oxford University Press, 1979.

Wechsler, D. The Measurement and Appraisal of Adult Intelligence. Baltimore, Maryland: Williams and Wilkins, 1958.

Unit II

Biobehavorial Dispositions: "Constitutional" Factors in Behavior

In Unit I we considered the first behavior function area—basic biobehavioral functions of consciousness-sensorium, memory, and intelligence—and its relationship to disordered behavior in the form of organic brain syndrome. In Unit II we are going to consider the second behavior function area—dimensions of biobehavioral dispositions—and its relationship to disordered behavior, primarily in the form of schizophrenia.

5

Introduction to the Concept of Biobehavioral Dispositions

Definition

The biobehavioral dispositions generally equal or exceed in complexity the more complex of the "basic" functions considered in Unit I. Thus, although the behavior function hierarchy is extended in the direction of "higher" mental activity, there is no implication of sharp discontinuity between these first two areas (or, for that matter, between any areas in the total schema). The constitutional core of general intelligence could certainly have been included in this part, and the points made here about biobehavioral dispositions should certainly be understood to apply to that function. The decision to discuss intelligence in Unit I was based largely on its traditional association with the clinical definition of organic brain syndrome. Like intelligence, most of the functions to be considered next include central, integrative, as well as sensory and motor aspects and therefore fall to some degree under the laws of mass action and equipotentiality. These are not sharply localized in a particular brain area or system.

Variations between individuals with respect to the dimensions discussed in this part are thought to be determined to a significant degree, though by no means entirely, by innate factors which exist prior to experience and subsequently interact with environmental events of the person's life to produce behavioral effects. For this reason the term "constitutional" is often applied to these behavior areas, an obvious oversimplification unless its meaning is restricted to the implication that, whatever the relative contribution of innate determinants, they may not be totally ignored in general considerations of the behavior without risk of losing important understanding.

Thus, in addition to considering dimensions of biobehavioral dispositions and their relationship to behavior disorder, we shall also have to consider the role of constitutional factors in behavior.

Description

Among the dimensions of biobehavioral disposition are those concerned with the general ego function of integration or synthesis. The ego functions include (1) reality testing (accurate perception of the environment, and reality sense) perception of the boundaries between oneself and the outside world; (2) coherence and purposiveness of the thought process which involves cognitive focusing (the capacity to scan information selectively, attending to essentials and ignoring irrelevant stimuli), reasoning (drawing logical inferences about relationships between objects and events), and concept formation (interpreting experience at appropriate levels of abstraction); and (3) integration (the ability to synthesize and organize various aspects of the mental life—thoughts, emotions, behaviors—into a coherent whole).

The impairment of these functions occurs with some regularity in the moderate and severe stages of organic brain syndrome. The impairment of these functions in the absence of organic brain disease and with retention of the autonomous or basic biobehavioral functions is characteristic of the schizophrenic group of disorders. Schizophrenia, as we shall see, is thought to reflect an innately determined predisposition toward disruptions of the person's basic capacities for unity and coherence in behavioral life. To understand dimensions of biobehavioral dispositions more fully, it is necessary to consider the role of constitutional factors in human behavior from both conceptual and methodological perspectives. This consideration will be focused upon issues such as nature vs. nurture and continuity, and areas of individual differences reflecting constitutional factors.

Nature vs. Nurture

The questions of nature or nurture, innate or acquired, genes or environment are historic, frequently but inconclusively discussed, and persistently important. The enormous difficulties in separating the innate and the experimental once the organism has lived for a single instant in interaction with its environment (including the intrauterine) are now more fully recognized. The prevailing conclusion is that neither biological reductionism and determinism nor sociological reductionism and cultural determinism in explaining behavior is warranted by the evidence. Attention is no longer directed toward determining whether a given behavioral attribute is either hereditary or environmental in its origin, nor to efforts to determine the rates of their contribution to a particular trait. Attention is now directed to the question of how these factors interact, in what sequences and at what points in the life span to produce the observed behavior. The dominant theoretical perspective emphasizes the interaction of biological substrates and environmental factors over time and in very complex ways. The dominant perspective has profound consequences for the kind of research which is required to explain observed similarities and differences between groups of individuals and of individuals within groups. For example, research which employs an interactional perspective requires the simultaneous measurement of biological, psychological, and contextual factors. This is obviously difficult to do since any single investigator or group of investigators is unlikely to have the skills or the instruments for measurement necessary for such a task, particularly outside the controlled conditions of a laboratory. Moreover, an interactional perspective is necessarily probabilistic, and at best produces conclusions which at most identify main effects, that is, variables or clusters of variables which account for modest proportions of the total variance in the behavior to be explained. At best, the investigator identifies variables which account for enough variance to be considered a necessary condition of some observed behavior but not necessarily a sufficient condition. An illustration is provided in discussions of schizophrenic process in which genetic factors are important, perhaps necessary, but not sufficient to account for the process. Von Bertalannfy (1952) has concentrated on this general problem of scientific explanation in his discussion of the equipotential of different organic and organizational structures for producing the same outcome, and of the same structures for producing different outcomes when moderating contextual or environmental variables are introduced. Similarly, Walter Mischel (1969, 1973, 1976) has argued that the observed continuity of behavioral responses which individuals and scientific observers perceive and conceptualize as self or personality can be explained as easily by stable environmental stimuli as by stable intrinsic traits. In summary, single-factor reductionistic explanations of human behavior are *out*; explanations which emphasize the interaction of multiple factors are *in*.

The necessity of an interactional perspective in understanding behavior does not ensure its acceptance. The scientific community, which tends to be organized by discrete disciplines whose tutors and trainees believe, for practical reasons among others, in theoretically parsimonious explanations, slips with ease into univariate, reductionistic analysis of the problems it chooses. While such behavior on the part of the scientific community is understandable and may facilitate the understanding of one or more subcomponents of human behavior, the necessity for interdisciplinary endeavors and interactional perspectives must continually be reiterated.

Continuity

The process of development requires a consideration of the degree of continuity of a particular system or function. Frequently, the implicit assumption is that development is roughly continuous in a somewhat linear fashion. This assumption typically underlies the effort to use observation or measure of functioning at one time to predict future functioning. It has also served as a basis for evaluating the continuing impact or influence of the factor, characteristic, or component of behavior such as size, intelligence, and neuromotor coordination in the individual's life. The belief that there are aspects of the individual which are relatively stable and persist over time is widely held. Consequently, both constitutional and environmental components of behavior have been evaluated in terms of the evidence for continuity in assessing the importance or utility of the particular factor in subsequent development.

The emphasis on continuity in assessing the importance of constitutional, environmental, and transactional factors may be an inappropriate criterion, because biological and psychological development is increasingly being recognized as noncontinuous, as we discussed in relation to Piaget's conceptualization of mental development in Chapter 4. Furthermore, with the increasing complexity of behavior as development proceeds, the relationship of current behavior to previous behavior may be obscured. The environmental demands are also constantly changing in response to the increasing development of the individual. Development is likely to be characterized by periods of integration and reorganization. For example, the crying of an infant might be reflective of "irritability" or response to frustration, but we would not expect the same behavioral manifestations when the individual is an adolescent. Rather, we would look for other expressions of irritability or poor response to frustration, such as interpersonal relationships characterized by curtness and lack of tolerance or perhaps outburst of angry behavior when goal attainment is interfered with or frustrated.

Sameroff (1975) has discussed the evidence for the hypotheses of a continuum of reproductive (i.e., biological) casualty and continuum of caretaking casuality. It is clear that neither constitution nor environment are necessarily constant over time and, furthermore, the differences are interdependent. The view is offered that it is not because of inability to locate critical links in the causal chain from antecedents to consequences that long range predictions based on the initial characteristics of the infant on his/her environment have been unsuccessful. Rather, linear sequences are seen as nonexistent, with development proceeding "through a sequence of regular restructuring of relations within and between the organism and his environment" (p. 285). It is the character of the specific transactions between child and environment that influences developmental outcome. Thus the focus of search for constants in development is not on some set of inborn characteristics and traits, but on the processes by which these characteristics are maintained in transactions between child and environment.

Genes and Biobehavioral Dispositions

A behavior pattern, normal or abnormal, to which heredity appears to have contributed significantly is a guidepost to those more basic behavioral dimensions which stand at the interface between the levels of molecule, cell, and tissue and the levels of the behaving organism—an interface represented in the term biobehavioral. Gottesman (1968, pp. 60–61) is quite eloquent in reminding us that, "There are no genes *for* behavior or any other phenotypic trait. Genes exert their influence on behavior through their effects at the molecular level of organization. Enzymes, hormones, and neurons may be considered as the sequence of path markers between gene and a behavior characteristic." One might add that the path continues through numerous levels once it has crossed into the realm of the behavioral or psychosocial before reaching the level of patterned, integrated behavior. Each step on this path is an interactive one. It is thus a truism that all behavior is both hereditary and environmental. This interaction between the innate and the experiential begins at the moment of fertilization and continues throughout the life of the individual in an incredibly complex process of *building upon* what has preceded. In a later context we shall refer to such a process as *epigenetic.*

Despite the complexity of gene-environment interactions when viewed developmentally, it is sometimes possible to isolate and clarify some portion of the sequence. Witness the interaction between the phenylalanine–hydroxylase–deficient, PKU-predisposed neonate (described in Chapter 4) and the phenylalanine-laden world to which he or she must adapt. In that situation, clarification has led directly to a therapeutic "breakthrough," illustrating the wisdom of Anastasi's (1958) advice to avoid asking whether a trait or illness is hereditary or environmental, to avoid even the question of how much heredity or environment contributes to a given trait, and to ask instead *how* the two interact to produce the observed effects.

Questions about the relative contributions of heredity and environment to a given trait leads us directly to the concept of *heritability.* The definition in Rosenthal's (1970, p. 280) glossary reads: "The proportion of the total variation regarding a given characteristic that is accounted for by genetic factors." That seems straightforward enough so that, if it can be determined, it might be a very nice thing to know about a number of behavioral and other characteristics. Indeed, one can consult large tables in various sources (e.g., Thompson and Wilde, 1973, p. 219) and read out numerical heritability estimates for a variety of mental diseases and behavior traits. One may also select from the table cited almost any heritability for schizophrenia (as an example) that pleases the fancy. The numbers range from .10 to .83! Something is clearly wrong here. Perhaps another, somewhat more complete definition will begin to explain why heritability, as a statistic, should not be applied to human behavior traits or disorders: "Heritability may be defined as the proportion of the total variance of a trait, in a *specified population* under *specified environmental conditions* [emphasis added], that can be attributed to genetic differences" (Shields, 1973, pp. 557–558). When we speak of the trait of human "aggression" or the disorder "schizophrenia," we are not limiting the meaning to a particular isolated tribe living under environmental conditions constant for all relevant variables. (We don't know all the relevant variables to begin with.) It would obviously be a mistake to view any number as a fixed constant applying to a given trait for all populations and under all circumstances. This being the case, it is also obviously a mistake to take any such number and apply it, as a given that goes with the trait name or diagnosis, to the particular case of an individual who displays the trait or is thought to suffer from the disorder.

David and Snyder (1962, pp. 16–17) suggest that genetic contributions to "human behavior in general," that is, to individual differences in such continuously distributed variables as intellectual capacity, personality leanings, and psychosocial response tendencies, are typically of a polygenic type in which phenotype is many interactive steps removed from genotype. They propose a rather sharp contrast between such genetic processes and those involved in the rare, sharply delimited diseases such as PKU and Huntington's chorea. These latter, they suggest, result more directly from abnormal genes at a single major locus which produce extreme developmental-behavioral disturbances. As noted earlier, we are in agreement with their emphasis on the complex, interactive passage from genes to behavior. Their sharp dichotomy between the two varieties of behavioral inheritance, however, seems open to question.

Gottesman and Shields (1976b), in discussing the question, "What is to be regarded as a genetic disease?" make some illuminating suggestions bearing on the issues raised by David and Snyder:

> It is necessary to clarify what is meant by saying that a disorder or a disease is regarded as a "genetic" one, or that it results from the interaction of genetic predispositions (diatheses) and environmental factors (stressors). To the extent that we ... all subscribe to the value of a diathesis-stressor framework for explaining the appearance (and remission) of schizophrenia, compromise without appeasement should be feasible. *Our* emphasis, however, is on a large and rather specific genetic "something" interacting with nonspecific, rather universal, environmental factors....
>
> There is no reluctance to calling galactosemia a genetic disease; all babies homozygous for this recessive disorder become affected when exposed to the universal agent in their diets, milk. *When the genetic predisposition is relatively rare and the relevant environmental factor is common, it is clear that the disease is an inherited one* [emphasis added]. At the other end of this contin-

uum of cause-specificity and weighting come the typical environmental diseases such as plague; everyone adequately exposed to the environmental vector becomes affected. *When the genetic predisposition is relatively common and the relevant environmental factor is infrequent or rare, the disorder is called an environmental one* [emphasis added]. Favism, a hemolytic anemia that follows the eating of fava or broadbeans, provides a textbook example of genotype X environment interaction. Only those persons with the particular X-linked G6PD enzyme variant develop favism, and then, only after eating the bean. Both the gene and the bean are necessary for the disease to appear, neither alone is sufficient, and the disease is *both* a genetic and an environmental one. Schizophrenia falls between the two extremes of galactosemia and plague and has aspects analogous to the interaction in favism. It is the relative prevalence of the genetic predisposition to developing schizophrenia compared with the relative prevalence of alleged environmental causes that leads us to prefer calling it a genetic disorder. (p. 447)

While there may be some question about calling conditions anywhere near the midpoint of their continuum genetic diseases (it seems to subtly bias in favor of ignoring the environmental factors), the continuum itself, as conceived by Gottesman and Shields, may provide a useful framework in which to order our knowledge about both environmental and genetic contributions to various disease states.

Methods of Study in Behavior Genetics

Knowledge about the presence and transmission pattern of the genetic factors in a particular behavior trait may derive from several types of study. The three principal methods used in human behavior genetics research are: (1) the family-risk or consanguinity method (a refinement of the classical pedigree method); (2) the twin method; and (3) the adoption method, and its variant, cross-fostering. Brief descriptions and examples of the use of these methods are presented below. Details of the related statistical techniques are beyond the scope of this presentation, as are discussions of the biochemistry and cytology of genetics. Readers interested in those topics should consult more specialized presentations (Rosenthal, 1970; Rainer, 1974).

Traditional studies of human heredity utilized a pedigree chart showing several generations of the lineal (parents, grandparents, and offspring) and collateral relatives of the affected individual (index case). Presence or absence of the trait in question was, of course, indicated for each relative. Inspection of the charts of several generations of a number of families in which the trait appeared provided evidence regarding its probably genetic nature and indication of the presence or absence of a typical Mendelian transmission pattern.

The *family-risk* or *consanguinity method* is a refinement of pedigree studies in that incidence of the trait in the (consanguinous) family is carefully calculated for comparison with its frequency in the general population. In addi-

Table 5-1. Risk of Schizophrenia for Relatives of Schizophrenics

Monozygotic co-twin	86% (40–50% in more recent studies)[a]
Dizygotic co-twin	15%
Full sibs	14%
Parents	9%
Half-sibs	7%
Grandchildren	4%
Nephews and nieces	4%
First cousins	3%
General population	0.85%

[a]Data, from Gottesman and Shields, 1976, p.373. See discussion in text.
Adapted from Thompson and Wilde, 1973, p. 220.

tion, relative incidence within the family is compared with degree of genetic relatedness to the index case, on the assumption that such incidence should be higher for close relatives (given a sufficiently large sample) since they share more genes with the affected person. *Incidence* (how many relatives will be affected during their lifetimes) is the essential datum here, not mere *prevalence* (number affected at any given time) or even how many are affected thus far. Mathematical corrections for those family members not yet past the age of possible onset, as well as those dying before passing that age, must therefore be made. (For this purpose, the age of risk for schizophrenia is usually given as 15–45 years.) Careful attention to the inclusion of all relatives, some of whom may be difficult to locate, is also an important methodological issue. Table 5-1 shows a family-risk or expectancy table for schizophrenia.

The essence of the *twin bond-method* lies in the fact that monozygotic (MZ) twins have identical genotypes while dizygotic (DZ) twins simply have the genotypic similarities of any pair of siblings. Genetic factors contributing to a trait should therefore result in a higher coincidence or *concordance* in MZ than in DZ twins. With a single exception, all studies comparing MZ/DZ concordance ratios for schizophrenic psychosis have shown significant differences in the direction predicted by the hypothesis of a genetic element in the etiology. For many years, MZ concordance for schizophrenia was listed at .86 (as in Table 5-1). More recent studies, with more attention to sampling and careful determination of zygosity, have consistently reduced MZ concordance to the range of .40 to .50, but when the same methods are used to determine DZ concordance a MZ/DZ ratio of about 3:1 is consistently found (Gottesman and Shields, 1976a, p. 373). While this ratio is far below that of the classical studies (.86/.15 = 5.7:1), it is nonetheless highly significant and sufficient, together with the family-risk studies, to warrant a strong presumption of genetic contributors to this condition. The fact that the MZ concordance ratio is not 1.00, of course, is equally strong evidence that factors in addition to the genetic are also important in determining the actual occurrence of the clinical illness.

The twin method, in itself, does not provide information bearing on the mode of transmission of genetic determinants, and neither the twin nor family-risk methods can truly separate the effects of environment and heredity. Twins are usually raised in the same home and, while it may be argued that DZ twins serve as controls for the MZ twins since they too are usually raised by the same family, the objection has been raised that identical (MZ) twins are very likely to be treated more identically than fraternal (DZ) twins. Until 1966, only family-risk and twin studies of the genetics of schizophrenia were available. Because most subjects were reared by their biological parents, no clear separation of the effects of heredity and environment in this condition was possible. Beginning with the study of Heston (1966) and those of Rosenthal et al. (1968) and Kety et al. (1968), the *adoption method* of investigation has been applied in this area. This method examines the prevalence of schizophrenic psychoses (and conditions assumed to be milder degrees or variants of the typical psychosis—often termed "schizophrenic spectrum" conditions) in: (1) the children of parents with schizophrenia who have been adopted away from those parents in early life or (2) in the biological parents of early-life adoptees who later develop schizophrenia. These prevalences are, of course, compared with appropriate controls: (1) the adopted-away children of normal parents; and (2) the biological parents of normal adoptees and the adoptive parents of adoptees with schizophrenia. In an extension of the adoption methods, known as *cross-fostering*, Wender et al. (1974) were able to locate a small number of cases in which the adopted-away offspring of normal parents were reared by parents with schizophrenia, and to compare the prevalence of schizophrenia in such adoptee subjects with that in adopted-away offspring of normal parents reared by normal parents and the adopted-away offspring of parents with schizophrenia reared by normal adopting parents. The essential findings are: significantly more schizophrenia and schizophrenia-related disorders in the adopted-away children, at least one of whose biological parents had schizophrenia, and in the biological relatives of adopted children with schizophrenia.

In his textbook on the genetics of abnormal behavior, Rosenthal (1970, pp. 131–132) summarized the importance of the adoption studies: "In all the studies done so far that have used this research strategy, the evidence has turned up so consistently and so strongly in favor of the genetic hypothesis that this issue must now be considered closed. Genetic factors do contribute appreciably and beyond any reasonable doubt to the development of schizophrenic illness. Any theory of schizophrenia must take this fact into account." He did, to be sure, deal at length (pp. 138–162) with the possibility of the *biological heterogeneity* of schizophrenia, the possibility that what we call schizophrenia may not be one homogeneous entity to all cases of which genetic and related biological processes contribute the same or about the same amount of etiological input. More recently, Rosenthal has co-authored a paper with the other members of the group conducting the adoption research (Kety et al., 1976). [This paper, it is interesting to note, was written in response to criticisms of the adoption studies based on issues of sampling, data analysis, diagnostic ambiguity, and neglect of alternate interpretations of the findings (Gottesman and Shields, 1976; Lidz, 1976).] In this later paper, the adoption researchers present their conclusions somewhat more cautiously:

> We feel that our findings permit the conclusion that genetic factors play an important etiological role in the *majority* [emphasis added] of patients suffering from schizophrenia. Our studies do not indicate that schizophrenia is a homogeneous syndrome, nor have they yet contributed to the mode or modes of genetic transmission. Neither have they cast doubt on the importance of environmental factors, although they indicate that one type of environmental influence—schizophrenia or severe psychopathology in the rearing family—is not necessary for the development of schizophrenia. (Kety et al., 1976, p. 422)

References

Anastasi, A. Heredity, environment and the question "how?" Psychol. Bull. 65:197–207, July 1958.

David, P.R., and L.H. Snyder. Some interrelations between psychology and genetics. In S. Koch (Ed.) Psychology: A Study of A Science: Biologically Oriented Fields, Vol. 4. New York, New York: McGraw-Hill, 1962, pp. 1–50.

Gottesman, I.I. Beyond the fringe—personality and psychopathology. In D.C. Glass (Ed.) Genetics. New York, New York: Rockefeller University Press, 1968, pp. 59–68.

Gottesman, I.I., and J. Shields. A critical review of recent adoption, twin and family studies of schizophrenia: Behavioral genetics perspective. Schizophrenia Bull. 2:360–401, 1976a.

Gottesman, I.I., and J. Shields. Toward optimal arousal and away from original din. Schizophrenia Bull. 2:447–453, 1976b.

Heston, L.L. Psychiatric disorders in foster home reared children of schizophrenic mothers. Brit. J. Psychiat. 112:819–825, 1966.

Kety, S.S., D. Rosenthal, P.H. Wender, and F. Schulsinger. The types and prevalence of mental illness in the biological and adoptive families of adopted schizophrenics. In D. Rosenthal and S.S. Kety (Eds.), The Transmission of Schizophrenia. Oxford, Great Britain, Pergamon Press, 1968, pp. 185–199.

Kety, S.S., D. Rosenthal, P.H. Wender, and F. Schulsinger. Studies based on a total sample of adopted individuals and their relatives: Why they were necessary, what they demonstrated and failed to demonstrate. Schizophrenia Bull. 2:413–428, 1976.

Lidz, T. Commentary on "A Critical Review of Recent Adoption, Twin and Family Studies: Behavioral Genetic Perspective." Schizophrenia Bull. 2:402–412, 1976.
Mischel, W. Continuity and change in personality. Amer. Psychol. 24:1012–1018, 1969.
Mischel, W. Toward a cognitive social learning reconceptualization of personality. Psychol. Rev., 80–252–283, 1973.
Mischel, W. Introduction to Personality, 2nd ed. New York, New York: Holt, Rinehart and Winston, 1976.
Rainer, J.D. The genetics of man in health and mental illness. In S. Arieti (Ed.), American Handbook of Psychiatry: The Foundations of Psychiatry, Second Edition, vol. 1. New York, New York: Basic Books, 1974, pp. 131–155.
Rosenthal, D. Genetic Theory and Abnormal Behavior. New York, New York: McGraw-Hill, 1970.
Rosenthal, D., P.H. Wender, S.S. Kety, F. Schulsinger, J. Weiner, and L. Ostergaard. Schizophrenics' offspring reared in adoptive homes. In D. Rosenthal and S.S. Kety (Eds.), The Transmission of Schizophrenia. Oxford, Great Britain: Pergamon Press, 1968, pp. 377–391.
Sameroff, A. J. Early influences on development, fact or fancy? Merrill-Palmer Quarterly. 21:267–294, 1975.
Shields, J. Heredity and psychological abnormality. In H. Eysenck (Ed.), Handbook of Abnormal Psychology, Second Edition. San Diego, California: Knapp, 1973, pp. 540–603.
Thompson, W.R., and G.J.S. Wilde. Behavior genetics. In B.B. Wolman (Ed.), Handbook of General Psychology. Englewood Cliffs, New Jersey: Prentice-Hall, 1973, pp. 206–229.
VonBertalannfy, L. Problems of Life, London, Great Britain: Watts, 1952.
Wender, P.H., D. Rosenthal, S.S. Kety, F. Schulsinger, and J. Weiner. Crossfostering: A research strategy for clarifying the role of genetic and experiental factors in the etiology of schizophrenia. Arch. Gen. Psychiat. 30:121–128, January, 1974.

6

Dimensions of Individual Differences in the Neonate

There has been an increasing recognition of the capacities and competencies of the newborn infant, and an appreciation of the infant's active role in eliciting, shaping, and determining aspects of his/her environment. This recognition and appreciation has fostered a change of view about the infant's development from that of a relatively passive recipient of environmental socialization factors to an active participant in the determination of outcome. As a result, there has been a focus upon some of the characteristics which an infant manifests from the time of birth, in terms of the effect these have on the infant's interaction with the environment and ultimately on the infant's growth and affective, cognitive, and personality development. These characteristics are variously referred to as inborn, congenital, or constitutional.

Along with this new recognition of the competencies of the infant and his/her ability to influence the environment, the environmental context with which the infant interacts has not been ignored. The context of major importance is the parent-child relationship, especially the mother-child relationship. Why especially the mother-child relationship? Because infants typically have a relatively greater amount of contact and time with their mothers than with anyone else. The mother-infant bond or attachment has been considered the formative relationship in the course of which the child develops a sense of self and which is the wellspring for future attachments.

Because the mother-infant relationship reflects the confluence of constitutional and environmental factors, it is useful to assess the association between this relationship and future development along many dimensions. As a transaction, it is necessary to consider what each person—in this pair, the infant and the mother—bring to the developing relationship. One of the main points to be emphasized is that the synchrony of the mother-infant relationship is a primary factor that influences the infant's development. By synchrony we mean the extent of dovetailing of behaviors of the infant and mother. Synchrony is expected to facilitate development because it enables the infant's needs to be appropriately met, and feedback from the caretaker enhances the infant's communication skills. Each of the participants has a role to play in establishing synchrony. The infant must emit accurate cues as to needs or status, the mother must be sensitive and responsive to these cues, and in turn the infant must be responsive to the mother's interventions and ministrations.

There is much mutual learning that must occur for both infant and mother about the nuances of behavior patterns of each other and the rules of interaction which change constantly as a consequence of maturation and previous interactions. Mothers develop a sensitivity to their infant's capacity for attention and nonattention, and utilize periods of interaction to model more increasingly complex behaviors. In turn, complexity is altered in relation to the stage of infant development.

Individual differences in constitutional factors reflect the unique pattern of characteristics that each neonate presents to the environment and to the developing parent-child relationship. This unique pattern of characteristics has been referred to as the "stimulus value" of the child in recognition of the role of these characteristics in the infant's ability to evoke responses from his/her environment. Some of the behavioral dimensions in the neonate along which infants differ include physical characteristics, sex, birth order, state, and temperament. We will consider each of these constitutional factors in terms of their influence on subsequent development both directly as well as indirectly through their impact on the parent-child relationship and the effect of that relationship on subsequent development.

Physical Characteristics

Neonates vary considerably in their physical characteristics, the most prominent of which are birth weight, birth length, shape and body composition, and physical maturity (Tanner, 1974). Even with equal time in utero, the degree of maturity can vary overall and among different body systems. Variations of three to four weeks in maturity have been found with babies all born at 40 weeks gestation. These physical characteristics are affected by other factors such as length of gestation, parity, sex, maternal uterine and systemic characteristics, and socioeconomic circumstances and habits of the mother.

One of these characteristics, birth weight, has been the focus of substantial research efforts, not only because of its influence on the response of the caretaker, but also because of the biological vulnerability associated with low birth weight (<2.5 kg) and subsequent increased frequencies of intellectual impairment and other development delays. Firstborn children average about 0.10 kg less than later-born infants, but grow a little faster and make up the deficit by the end of the first year. There is a negative correlation between birth weight and weight increment during the first six months and between birth length and length increment. However, with babies of poorly nourished mothers, catch up may continue for at least a year.

In terms of sex differences, males are larger than females from the time of 35 weeks gestation, and by 40 weeks gestation average about 0.15 kg heavier and 1.1 cm longer. Males tend to be particularly larger in the head and face regions, considerably more muscular, slightly less fat as newborns and considerably less at nine months of age, and tend to grow faster in length and weight from birth to about seven months but then more slowly and decelerate in growth faster than girls. On the other hand, girls are more advanced in skeletal maturity from about 30 weeks gestation and are ahead of boys at birth by about two weeks in bone age and one to two weeks in neurological maturation.

Maternal habits or behaviors can also influence the physical characteristics of the neonate. For example, maternal smoking during the last two months of pregnancy has been found to lower birth weight on the average of 0.17 kg. Excessive maternal alcohol consumption during pregnancy has been associated with lower birth weight and birth length, other congenital abnormalities, and impaired intellectual development.

Sex

We can consider the constitutional factors of sex from several perspectives. We can think of the sex-role attitudes and values of the mother and environment which are elicited by the stimulus value of the infant by virtue of being male or female. We can also consider individual differences in characteristics and behavior as a function of sex of the infant and the interaction of sex with other constitutional factors. We will consider some evidence related to the constitutional factors of infant's sex in this section but will also consider this factor when relevant to other factors such as birth order, state, and temperament.

Mothers do respond differently to males and females, and some of this difference is due to difference in infant characteristics as well as to attitudinal and sex role differences. There is evidence of sex differences in many infant characteristics (Korner, 1974). Females emerge as possibly having greater tactile sensitivity, more responsiveness to sweet taste, and tend to engage in more frequent reflex smiling. While not significantly different in visual tracking of moving objects, the frequency and duration of the state of alert inactivity, or in visual responsiveness to maternal types of ministration, the female's response to photic stimulation appears to be significantly faster than that of the male. Sex differences are not reported in auditory receptivity and spontaneous active and expressive behaviors, frequency or rate of ordinary spontaneous sucking, or in reduction of crying response to maternal soothing. There is suggestive evidence of greater physical strength and muscular vigor in males.

Babbling to human face or voice is reportedly more stable for girls during the first year of life than for boys (Kagen, 1969). An environmental interpretation of this finding would argue that mothers are motivated to accelerate their daughters' mental development, and spend a lot of time in face-to-face vocal interactions and not so much time with their sons. Support comes from the associated findings that well-educated mothers engage in more distinctive face to face vocalizations with females than do less-educated mothers, but this difference does not occur with mothers of males. Furthermore, middle-class mothers are more likely to imitate the vocalizations of 3-month-old females than males. A biological interpretation of the data would contend that vocalization is more prepotent for females, and that vocalizations and fixation times are more stable for females from 8 to 13 months of age. This view is paralleled by other data indicating greater long term stability for girls in a variety of cognitive dimensions, including intelligence and decision time in problem situations, and a variety of physical growth variables including onset of ossification centers.

Mothers of males have been found to touch and give more attention to their infants than do mothers of female infants. These mothers of male infants were also found to express more dyadization (the desire to spend time with their infants) and were higher in self-evaluation of competence than were mothers of female infants (Leiderman and Seashore, 1975).

Thus it can be seen that infants do vary in the characteristics they present to the environment on the basis of their sex, and mothers, in turn, express different attitudes and respond differently to male and female infants. Additional sex differences will be considered as they interact with other variables such as state and birth order.

Birth Order

Birth order has been shown to account for some of the variance in individual differences, and experiential differences as a function of ordinal position in the family are usually thought of as the primary reason. Review of the literature in terms of the influence of birth order on various aspects of social behavior (Warren, 1966) has shown substantial support for the contentions that: (1) firstborns of both sexes attend college in relatively greater numbers, are more susceptible to social pressures, and are more dependent than laterborns; and (2) firstborn women, when apprehensive, desire the company of others more strongly than do later born women. The evidence in support of the relationship between birth order and volunteering, identification, delinquency, and alcoholism is tenuous and spotty in relation to schizophrenia.

Recently (Schooler, 1972), the relationship between birth order and various normal and abnormal psychological characteristics have been surveyed in three ways: (1) by looking at the prevalence of different birth ranks in various relevant populations, (2) by comparing the characteristics of individuals of known birth ranks, and (3) by examining parents' reports of their treatment of children of different birth ranks. It has been pointed out that biases can occur in studies purporting to show an increased frequency of birth ranks in certain populations because of the influences of long-range trends in number of families started, and in size of families on the prevalence of different birth ranks in any sample. In terms of psychiatric abnormalities, with the exception of an indication of a slight surplus of last-born individuals from small families among hospitalized American female schizophrenics, there does not seem to be any reliable evidence of a relationship between birth order and the occurrence of any psychiatric disorder, if the effects of long-term trends in the number and size of families started are taken into account. Comparison of the characteristics of psychiatrically impaired people in terms of birth rank does provide some evidence that last born females who were hospitalized with schizophrenia demonstrate more flagrant symptomatology and a lower level of social competence than do firstborns both before and during hospitalization.

Studies of the prevalence of different birth ranks among different normal populations and the performance of individuals of different birth ranks in various psychological tests and experiments "fail to reveal any consistent and replicable pattern of relations between birth order and normal aspects of personality" (Schooler, 1972, p. 172). The frequently reported association between firstborns and intellectual and occupational achievement can be more easily explained in terms of differences among social-class trends and family size. That is, family size is related to socioeconomic status. Families of higher socioeconomic status tend to be smaller in size than those of lower socioeconomic status. One exception appears to be that early-borns are more often present than later-borns in high-scoring groups on verbal achievement tests. Evidence is lacking concerning meaningful and replicable patterns of differences in parents' reports of children of different birth ranks.

Thus it can be seen that consideration of the effect on development of the single factor of birth order is not likely to be very productive. Well-designed studies that control for age, social class, and family size and that identify relevant interactions with sex, socioeconomic factors and environmental characteristics will be necessary to gain an appreciation of the influence on development of the constitutional factor of birth order.

Carefully controlled studies have demonstrated that birth order does have an effect on mother-infant relationship, and that infants are responded to differently on the basis of birth order. Mothers have been found to spend significantly less time in social, affectionate, and caretaking activities (with the exception of feeding) with their second-born than they had with their firstborn (Jacobs and Moss, 1976). This decrement was less if the second-born was a male, greatest for females with older sisters, next greatest for females with older brothers, and virtually no decrease for males with firstborn sisters.

Mothers of firstborn infants have also been found to demonstrate significantly more distal attachment (talking, laughing, looking) and attention during noncaretaking periods to firstborns than to laterborn infants (Leiderman and Seashore, 1975). These differences in distal attachment were significant by the first week of age. Attitudinal differences were also present. Mother's feelings of wanting to be alone with, and in fact spending time with, her infant (dyadization) was significantly greater for mothers of firstborns than later-born infants. In terms of her feelings of her own competence in dealing with noncaretaking activities, multiparous mothers scored higher than primiparous mothers. In terms of self-confidence, primiparous mothers of premature infants have somewhat lower self-confidence than multiparous mothers shortly after birth, but not significantly different at one month after discharge (Seashore et al., 1973).

Perhaps the influence of the factor of birth order itself and in its interaction with sex is best summarized as follows:

> If the mother's handling of the infant has any particular effect on the subsequent cognitive and social growth of the infant, then from our observations we might conclude that first born males are a particularly favored group and later born females a less favored group. (Leiderman and Seashore, 1975, p. 227)

State Characteristics

The variability of neonates and infants in behaviors and states reflecting neurophysiological developmental status is substantial. Reliable and significant differences have been reported in capacity for visual pursuit; frequency and duration of periods of spontaneous alertness; alerting behaviors in response to maternal types of ministrations; readiness to respond to auditory stimuli; high or low thresholds across sensory modalities; frequency and type of motions; frequency of spontaneous mouthing and sucking; frequency, skill, and persistence of hand-mouth coordination; irritability and soothability; and autonomic reactivity as reflected in heart and respiration rates (Korner, 1973, 1974).

For several reasons, individual differences in the state of the infant have become the focus of current investigations. In this context, state refers to behavior reflective of neurophysiological status such as sleeping, wakefulness, and alertness. State is a ubiquitous characteristic, and relationships between state organization and central nervous system functioning have been documented, as have associations between neurological defects and patterns of state behaviors. Furthermore, state is a composite characteristic presented by the infant to the environment, especially to the mother, and changes in state occur by virtue of the activities of the mother. Thus state is a good vehicle for assessing transactions (Thoman, 1975).

Data on the duration and pattern of state transitions between and within the sleep and wake stages reflect degree of organization of infant states against which marked differences can be viewed as aberrations of state organization. There are some indications that state behaviors are consistent over the first few weeks of life. For the developing mother-infant relationship to go well and be synchronous, the mother must be sensitive and responsive to the particular characteristics and needs of her infant. As in other dimensions, there is also a consideration of association of particular state characteristics with subsequent developmental difficulties. The poorly organized infant interacting with a relatively insensitive mother is seen as constituting a relationship that is at risk (Thoman, 1975).

One condition which is known to be associated with an aberrant state is prematurity. The states of sleeping and wakefulnesss in prematures, even when attaining full-term chronological age (CA), differ markedly from that of full-term infants. Sleep is not as well-organized, and periods of wakefulness, active sleep, and quiet sleep are of shorter duration than in full-term infants. Also, a lower percentage of regular respiration and of low-voltage EEG patterns, a more rapid cardiac rate, and a more irregular respiratory rhythm have been noted in prematures (Dreyfus-Brisac, 1974).

As can be anticipated, state characteristics can interact with other constitutional factors such as gender in influencing the mother-infant relationship. An interesting study (Moss, 1967) has shown that male infants slept more and cried more than females, and that mothers held male infants longer than female infants. However, the sex-related differences were more pronounced at three weeks of age than at three months. Maternal contact and infant irritability positively co-varied for female infants both at three weeks and three months, but there was no relationship between maternal contact and irritability of males at three weeks; there was a negative relationship at three months, with mothers spending less time with irritable male infants. These results are interesting, but when the state of the infant was controlled, most of the sex differences no longer were significant. The only exception was that mothers still stimulated and aroused male infants more, and imitated vocalizations of female infants more.

Thoman (1975) provides an interesting example of the effect of an infant's state behavior on the mother-infant relationship. One infant demonstrated a great deal of open-eyed sleep. This confused the mother, and she responded to the infant as though he were awake. She would pick him up and try to feed, change, or bathe him. The infant would either awaken and cry or sleep through the procedures. Mother expressed frustration at her infant's unresponsiveness or fussy response to her ministrations.

The development of the Brazelton Neonatal Assessment Scale provides a reliable, standardized instrument and method of assessing the subtle state and behavior capabilities of the neonate. Furthermore, the various state and behavioral items form four clusters or dimensions of functioning: (1) interactive processes, (2) motoric processes, (3) organizational processes—state control, and (4) organizational processes—physiological response to stress. Profiles are obtained for each infant based on typology determination of worrisome to very good on each dimension. The scale has been found to be a good predictor of later functioning without a high false-positive rate and to be sensitive to: mild dysfunctions of the central nervous system during the neonatal period, cultural-racial group differences, maternal and neonatal abnormalities such as low birth weight and mild drug effects, and differences between infants with adolescent and nonadolescent mothers.

The Brazelton Scale has also been utilized to evaluate the relationship between neonatal style and the early mother-infant relationship (Osofsky and Danzger, 1974). Strong relationships were found between the dimensions of the Brazelton Scale and independent rating of infant characteristics during the mother-infant interaction. Furthermore, there was a strong interrelationship between the mother's stimulation in a particular domain (visual, auditory, tactile) and the infant's responsivity in that domain. What was demonstrated was the consistency of measures of infant characteristics across situations during the early days of life, the utility of the Brazelton Scale assessing these characteristics, and the interrelationship of infant and maternal behaviors. Attentive and sensitive mothers had responsive babies or vice versa.

Temperament

The study of temperament has received considerable impetus from the work of Thomas et al. (1968). Thomas and Chess (1977) view temperament as a general term which refers to the "how" of behavior, as opposed to ability, the what and how well of behaving, and to motivation, the why of behavior. Temperament is the way in which an individual behaves. It is a phenomenologic term which has no implication as to either immutability or etiology, and is influenced by environmental factors. Using parent interview data from the New York Longitudinal Study, nine categories of temperament, each scored on a three-point scale, were established by inductive content analysis. These are:

1. Activity level: (high, medium, low) the motor component present in a given child's functioning and the diurnal proportion of active and inactive periods
2. Rhythmicity (regularity): (regular, variable, irregular) the predictability and/or unpredictability in time of any function

3. Approach or withdrawal: (approach, variable, withdrawal) the initial response to a new stimulus
4. Adaptability: (adaptive, variable, nonadaptive) response to new or altered situations in terms of ease of modifiability in desired directions
5. Threshold of responsiveness: (high, medium, low) the intensity level of stimulation necessary to evoke a discernible response
6. Intensity of reaction: (positive, variable, negative) the energy level of response
7. Quality of mood: (positive, variable, negative) amount of pleasant, joyful, and friendly behavior, as contrasted with unpleasant, crying, and unfriendly behavior
8. Distractibility: (yes, variable, no) effectiveness of extraneous environmental stimuli in interfering with or altering the direction of the ongoing behavior
9. Attention span and persistence: (yes, variable, no) continuation of an activity in the face of obstacles

Using these nine categories, three temperamental constellations have been defined. The "easy child" is characterized by regularity, positive approach, high adaptability, and mild or moderately intense mood which is preponderantly positive. The "difficult child" is characterized by irregularity, withdrawal, non- or slow adaptability, and intense mood expressions which are frequently negative. The "slow-to-warm-up child" is characterized by a combination of negative responses of mild intensity to new stimuli, with slow adaptability after repeated contact. Not all children fit into one of these groups, and within each there is a wide range in degree of manifestation. Only an appreciable genetic role is postulated in the determination of temperamental individuality in the young infant, which is seen as well-established by the second or third month but is not viewed as immutable. There are only modest sex differences reported, but sociocultural factors seem to have some influence. In terms of continuity of temperament, qualitative analyses have shown significant correlations, with the exception of approach/withdrawal, distractibility, and persistence, for the categories of temperament from one year to the next. The number of significant correlations decrease over longer time periods. Continuity and predictability are not assumed for a specific attribute of the child. Consistency is seen as resulting from continuity of the organism and the environment, and discontinuity from change in one or the other.

Temperament is not always a significant factor in the ontogenesis and course of behavior disorders, but it is a factor that can contribute. Studies of the relationship of temperament to behavioral problems have been reported by Thomas and Chess (1977). A significant correlation has been reported between the temperament signs of the difficult child and the occurrence of behavioral disturbance. Children with developmental deviations are also seen as more vulnerable to developing behavior disorders and, thus, as requiring a particularly good fit or consonance between their temperamental characteristics and environment demands and expectancies to foster optimal development and prevent behavior problems. Temperamental scores at age 5 have been correlated with academic achievement scores at various points in schooling, and a substantial relationship between lower academic achievement scores and characteristics of the slow-to-warm-up child has also been reported.

Several important points with regard to temperament and behavioral disorders need to be made, and these are illustrated nicely in an extensive case report by Thomas et al. (1968, pp. 154–156; 166–168). The child's temperament characteristics change as the child increases in age and as environmental demands change. The goodness of fit, or lack thereof, between the child's characteristics and environmental demands, structure, and flexibility can lead to dissonant stress. In turn, the dissonant stress can result in behavioral disturbance, the form of which is seen as reflecting the child's temperament characteristics. Modification of the environment to lessen dissonant stress and therapy to foster recognition of capacity for self-control are utilized to resolve the behavioral disturbance.

More recently, an interaction temperament model has been advocated by Buss and Plomin (1975). Their view of temperament is similar to that of Thomas and Chess in that temperament is seen as concerned more with style than with content; more with broad personality disposition than with highly specific acts or traits. However, there is more focus on heredity, with temperaments seen as inherited tendencies. The main criterion utilized in deciding which personality disposition should be called temperament is inheritance, which leads to the other criteria of: developmental expectations of stability during childhood, retention into maturity, adaptive value, and presence in our animal forebearers. This view reflects a strong biological and etiological emphasis but is also an interactional model. The concern is with inborn dispositions, the subsequent course of which is determined by a complex interaction with the environment, which in turn is also affected by dispositions. Thus temperaments are not immutable. They "predispose an individual to a limited range of a phenotype, but the interaction between the temperament and environment, especially during the critical developmental years, determines where the phenotype falls within this range" (Buss and Plomin, 1975, p. 209). Temperament may determine which environments are selected, and they shape the social environment initially or through feedback. Temperament-environment mismatches can occur and lead to "strain," which is similar to the Thomas and Chess (1977) notion of goodness of fit.

Four specific dispositional dimensions or temperaments have been postulated by Buss and Plomin (1975): (1) activity—total energy output; (2) emotionality—intensity of reaction evidenced by arousal, reactivity, and excitability; (3) sociability—affiliativenesss; and (4) impulsivity—tendency to respond quickly rather than inhibiting the response.

Gender differences in these temperament dimensions have been reported, with American boys being more active and lower on emotionality and sociability than girls. However, these differences are thought to be due to socialization, and more evidence is required to substantiate inborn gender differences in temperament.

In this model, temperaments have also been combined in an effort to identify constellations which would be found to be related to subsequent disorders or explain in part some commonly seen patterns of behavior. For example, hyperkinesis could be considered as a combination of high activity and high impulsivity; hysteria could be viewed as reflecting high emotionality and high impulsivity; and psychopathy could be viewed as reflecting high impulsivity, low sociability, and low emotionality. Potential adjustment difficulties are seen when emotionality or impulsivity is combined with the extreme of another temperament. What is now needed are some actual prospective experimental studies to evaluate these contentions, which must be currently viewed as only hypotheses.

Summary

Various major constitutional factors, such as sex and birth order, and other dimensions in which there are significant individual differences, such as physical characteristics, temperament, and state, have been presented. These constitutional factors reflect the unique pattern of characteristics which each individual neonate presents to the environment. These characteristics are considered in terms of the potential they provide for differential responses from the environment and the consequences they are likely to have on the mother-infant relationship. This relationship, in turn, is seen as affecting the development of the infant and child. In addition to an appreciation of the range of individual differences, the very demanding and challenging task of the mother to be sensitive and responsive to the particular needs and characteristics of her infant is recognized. Within these various dimensions of differences, various combinations or clusters of factors are postulated as being associated with subsequent disorders of development or as placing the mother-infant relationship at risk. A strong foundation has been laid for the subsequent consideration of these hypotheses through prospective experimental studies. Through these efforts not only will our knowledge of the impact and significance of various dimensions and clusters be advanced, but it will also result in a better understanding of when and how to utilize environmental factors to foster affective, cognitive, and personality development.

References

Buss, A., and R. Plomin. A Temperament Theory of Personality Development. New York, New York: Wiley, 1975.

Dreyfus-Brisac, C. Organization of sleep in prematures: Implications for caretaking. In M. Lewis and L. Rosenblum (Eds.) The Effect of the Infant on its Caregiver. New York, New York: Wiley, 1974.

Jacobs, B., and H. Moss. Birth order and sex as determinants of mother-infant interaction. Child Development 47:315–322, 1976.

Kagan, J. Continuity in cognitive development during the first year. Merrill-Palmer Quarterly, 15:101–119, 1969.

Korner, A. Early stimulation and maternal care as related to infant capabilities and individual differences. Early Child Development and Care 2:307–327, 1973.

Korner, A. The effect of the infant's state, level of arousal, sex, and ontogenetic stage on the caregiver. In M. Lewis and L. Rosenblum (Eds.) The Effect of the Infant on its Caregiver. New York, New York: Wiley, 1974.

Liederman, P.D., and M.J. Seashore. Mother-infant separation: Some delayed consequences. In Ciba Foundation Symposium 33, Parent-Infant Interaction. Amsterdam: Associated Scientific Publishers, 1975.

Moss, H.A. Sex, age and state as determinants of mother-infant interaction. Merrill-Palmer Quarterly 13:19–36, 1967.

Osofsky, J., and B. Danzger. Relationships between neonatal characteristics and mother-infant interaction. Developmental Psychology 10:124–130, 1974.

Schooler, C. Birth order effects: Not here, not now. Psychological Bulletin 78:161–175, 1972.

Seashore, M.J., A.D. Leifer, C.R. Barnett, and Leiderman, P.D. The effects of denial of early mother-infant interaction on maternal self-confidence. J. Personality and Social Psychology 26:369–378, 1973.

Tanner, J. Variability of growth and maturity in newborn infants. In M. Lewis and L. Rosenblum (Eds.) The Effect of the Infant on its Caregiver. New York, New York: Wiley, 1974.

Thoman, E. Sleep and wake behaviors in neonates: Consistencies and consequences. Merrill-Palmer Quarterly 21:295–314, 1975.

Thomas, A., and S. Chess. Temperament and Development. New York, New York: Brunner/Mazel, 1977.

Thomas, A., S. Chess, and H. Birch. Temperament and behavior disorders in children. New York, New York: New York University Press, 1968.

Warren, J. Birth order and social behavior. Psychological Bulletin, 65:38–49, 1966.

7
Socialization

Culture as Construction of Reality

The potential range of behavior responses by *Homo sapiens* is enormous. Language is a case in point. Based on biological and neurological substrates which are distinctively human, language as we recognize it is potential behavior which is learned through social interaction. The particular patterns of sounds and the structured presentation of symbols appear in impressive variety. Well over 200 identifiably different language systems have been documented. Particular language systems are shared by groups of individuals and are transmitted both formally and informally by adult members of a group to their offspring. Theoretically, a child is capable of learning any known language; practically, a child learns the dominant language of his parents.

Language is the prototype of the learned patterns of behavior and the products of that behavior (values, ideologies, roles, statuses, artifacts) which are shared by a group and transmitted from generation to generation. The anthropologist designates these shared, transmitted ways of behaving as culture. Cultures are literally social constructions of reality which are meant to, and which in fact do, constrain the behavioral repertory of dependent young. Socialization is the process by which an individual develops, through transactions with others, the specific patterns of socially relevant behavior and experiences (Ziegler and Child, 1969). The dependent young do not construct social reality *de novo*, but encounter shared definitions of preferred behavior and the roles and rules which differentiate acceptable and unacceptable behavior. Through the process of socialization, then, the potentially large behavioral repertory of the young is narrowed into a socially expected range. Social groups construct the situations to which persons respond and within which they interact.

The typical outcome of the socialization process is behavior which falls within a culturally recognizable, socially expectable and predictable range. Ordered behavior is the rule, and disordered behavior is literally a rare event in a statistical sense. Intersocietal variations and intrasocietal consistency of behavior testify to the effectiveness of the socialization process. Most persons, most of the time, perceive what Erik Erikson called "a satisfying sense of sameness and continuity" in their behavior, and attribute consistency to the behavior of others.

Cultural Universals, Cultural Differences, and Intracultural Variation

The imputed effectiveness of the socialization process in producing orderly behavior within a predictable range, while correct in general, requires qualification. All societies take account of some basic biological facts and some universal aspects of human experience. For example, all societies differentiate male and female roles. This differentiation includes a recognition of a distinctive female role in childbearing and a very elaborate set of assumptions about physical prowess, temperament, and ability. The extent to which societies structure sex roles to accommodate sexual differences and/or superimpose social preferences through socialization on males and females is difficult to disentangle precisely, as the review of evidence in Chapter 8 will illustrate. However, it is very clear that differential social power associated with sex roles is largely a culturally determined phenomenon; the patriarchal, patrilineal kinship (that is, male-dominated) groups which have been historically predominant in Northern Europe and the United States are not universally observed.

Similarly, all societies grade individuals by age, differentiating infants, children, adults, and old persons. These gradations acknowledge in broad terms a life span which has a beginning, end, and gradations in between. Of particular interest is the near-universal marking of puberty by rites of social passage. However, the social significance of age grading varies considerably across societies. Aries (1962) has documented that, historically, children in most societies have been considered adults-in-training; childhood as a socially valued and distinctly important and somewhat romanticized period has not been universally recognized. Similarly, adolescence is a distinctly modern phenomenon associated exclusively with technologically developed societies (Eisenstadt, 1956). Margaret Mead began her distinguished career in anthropology in the late 1920s with a demonstration that the troublesome adolescent period between childhood and adulthood in the United States was not the inevitable experience and was therefore better explained by sociological rather than biological or psychodynamic variables. Old age is also a universally recognized life stage with very different social meaning across cultures (Simmons, 1945). The relatively low status of older persons frequently observed in technologically advanced societies reflects a preference for conspicuous productivity, activity, and independence favoring youthfulness which is peculiar to such societies. Sex and age, therefore, are a universal basis for differentiation and for the development of distinctive expectations about behavior. The context of such expectations is largely specific to particular societies. In addition to differentiating roles by sex and age, all societies stratify individuals by status. Access to goods and services, honor, and power are differentially distributed. In the United States, the shorthand designation for stratification by status is social class. The significance of social stratification is well-documented in a variety of areas. Lower status is associated with elevated birth rates, death rates, and morbidity rates; lower status individuals are less likely than others to do well on standard intelligence tests or to finish high school. Individuals of the same social class tend to marry, and there is a substantial body of literature documenting the ways in which adults within a socioeconomic stratum transmit distinctive patterns of behavior to their offspring (Ziegler and Child, 1969).

Sociological and anthropological research thus documents consistency of behavior within groups, and different patterns of consistent behavior between groups. Socialization as a process of social learning is advanced as the principal explanation of the observed consistencies and the patterned variations. Although culture and the related social structuring of the context of behavior have a large effect on the behavior of individuals, individual differences also should be recognized as a variable in behavior.

Persons and Situations

Behavioral continuities do appear to characterize the behavior of individuals, and these continuities in cognitive style and in preferred ways of interacting with others may well reflect innate biological differences and a complex interaction of biological differences and social learning. Accounting for continuities in this behavior of individuals and for distinctly personal differences in response to social situations has been a major task of psychologists who study personality (Mischel, 1976, Chapter 21).

Personality theorists have accumulated a great deal of evidence that relatively stable cognitive and interpersonal styles (traits) characterize individuals, that the pattern of these traits constitute personality, and that personality is therefore an important predictor of behavior in and across various social situations. The field of personality studies has for at least a decade been unsettled by challenging evidence that the observed behavior of a person may be largely situation-specific (a state) rather than person-specific (a trait) across situations. Current evidence rather clearly supports the conclusion that persons are capable of extraordinary adaptiveness and discrimination as they cope with the demands of different social contexts. The evidence which emphasizes the responsiveness of persons to situational stimuli does not require the abandonment of the concept of stable traits, but does require that such traits be considered as behavioral preferences or tendencies subject to situational modification. Moreover, the documentation of discriminative response to situations as typical implies that behavioral styles or tendencies which are not responsive to situational demands may be maladaptive and characteristic of disturbed individuals. Some individuals are consistent in some behavior in some situations.

Research on stabilities in behavioral response at any time and over time clearly requires measurement and interaction of personal characteristics *and* situations. A new field of inquiry, psychological ecology, has emerged which focuses attention on person-situation interaction. Personality psychology is not, however, willing to concede that person variables are irrelevant to understanding behavior. Within a conceptual framework that acknowledges the centrality of person-situation interaction, theorists like Mischel concentrate on types of variables which provide relatively stable anchor points as persons negotiate the demands of various situations in which they find themselves. These types of person variables are summarized in Table 7-1. Whether these relatively stable tendencies are expressions of innate factors or are learned is an unanswerable question, and is the wrong question anyway. The question of primary interest is the interaction of person and situation. In pursuing this question, social scientists are primarily interested in the structuring of behavioral situations and the process of socialization in which definitions of situationally appropriate behavior are transmitted from generation to generation.

Table 7-1. Summary of Cognitive Social Learning Person Variables

1. Compentencies: ability to construct (generate) particular cognitions and behaviors. Related to measures of IQ, social and cognitive (mental) maturity and competence, ego development, and social-intellectual achievements and skills. Refers to what the person knows and can do.
2. Encoding Strategies and Personal Constructs: units for categorizing events and for self-descriptions.
3. Expectancies: behavior-outcome and stimulus-outcome relations in particular situations.
4. Subjective Values: motivating and arousing stimuli, incentives and aversions.
5. Self-Regulatory Systems and Plans: rules and self-reactions for performance and for the organization of complex behavior sequences.

From Mischel. 1976.

Patterns of Childrearing

Socialization is frequently discussed as though it is synonymous with childrearing. The equation is incorrect but understandable. Some psychological theory (particularly theory derived from Freud, for example) has argued that biological mechanisms largely determine basic behavioral responses and that these responses are set in the early years of life and continue over the life course. More generally, studies of animal behavior have suggested plausible and intuitively appealing analogs in the behavior of the human animal. Terms like orality, anality, territoriality, imprinting, and instinct became associated with the socialization of children. One practical consequence was disinterest in socialization beyond childhood. References to *adult* socialization have appeared in the sociological literature relatively recently (Brim and Wheeler, 1966), and discussion of socialization over the entire life span is quite rare (Erikson, 1959; Cummings and Henry, 1961).

The literature on *childhood* socialization is enormous, indicating the importance attached by social and behavioral scientists to understanding the transmission of cultures from generation to generation (Ziegler and Child, 1969). This literature illustrates the encounters of biological organisms with constraining environments and the behavior products of these complex encounters. Ziegler and Child organize their review of this literature around six specific "systems of behavior" to which societies devote attention and explicit training: oral, excretory, sexual, aggression, dependence, and achievement. In turn, behavior of apparent social significance has received attention from investigators interested in how the training takes place and the consequences of that training. The first four items of interest have an obvious practical importance to social groups. These items are also of special interest to students of the interaction of social and biological variables; patterns of eating, excreting, and aggressive behavior are observed early in the development of infants and children, have physiological substrates, and, based on analogies from animal studies, may reflect innate components which drive the observed developmental sequences. The other two items—dependence and achievement—have equally important practical implications for social groups, but a less obvious relationship to physiological substrates. One may conjecture that dependence and achievement are of special interest in cultural contexts, like our own, which place extraordinary value on independence and high achievement. More than scientific curiosity is involved in the attention given by social and behavioral scientists to the socialization of these specific behavior systems. How social groups or, more specifically, the parents, who are typically the agents of society with primary responsibility for socialization, train offspring is important, because the procedures used presumptively have fateful consequences for the development of personality and the capacity of the socialized organism to adapt successfully over the lifespan.

Those who are interested in an exhaustive review of research on the process and consequences of childrearing will find a convenient and perceptive summary in the work of Ziegler and Child (1969). A few illustrations of the kinds of issues will suffice here, and primary attention will be given to generalizations about socialization which are warranted by current evidence. Studies of oral and excretory behavior have concentrated extensively on weaning and toilet training. Does the procedure and timing of social constraints placed on these elemental types of behavior affect subsequent development and behavior in a predictable way? The available evidence suggests not, in spite of the fact that this conclusion may appear counterintuitive. It should be noted, however, that methodologically adequate studies which could trace the effects of specific childhood behavior to adult behavior do not exist; the practical problems in developing adequate longitudinal research over long periods of time, say from childhood through adolescence into adulthood, are substantial.

Interest in socialization regarding sexuality and sexual preference reflects the impact of Freud's observations about male and female children to their parents, the high emotional loading which has surrounded sexual behavior, and the documentation of anthropologists regarding the elaborate attention given in most societies to social controls of the relationship between the male child and his mother. A common theme of puberty rites is the obligation of the pubescent male to identify with adult males. Anthropological findings have provided evidence that the Oedipus myth mirrors real problems in the authority relationships between sons and fathers, but also that these interpersonal problems are, as a rule, successfully negotiated within a tolerable range. Of particular interest are societies in which a child's father is his mother's sexual partner but not the person responsible for disciplining the child. In such instances, the conflict between son and father predicted by Freudian theory is not observed, although conflict is observed between the male child and the adult male authority figure. In recent decades, scientific interest in identity formation has shifted from *sexual* identity to a more general *ego* identity, a part of which is, of course, sex-role identification (Erikson, 1959).

Animal studies of aggression, which initially stressed instinctual mechanisms, have demonstrated that aggressive behavior observed in young animals may be altered, reduced, or eliminated by subsequent experience. Human research on aggression has progressively emphasized social learning. Even the frustration-aggression hypothesis, which has influenced much of the published research, has emphasized learned rather than innate components. An interesting finding of recent research is that parental permissiveness rather than restrictiveness increases aggressive behavior in children, and that "parental warmth" (accepting, supportive behavior) coupled with restrictiveness (nonacceptance of overt, hostile activity) is least likely to produce overt aggression, particularly in the absence of adult figures who provide models of successful aggressive behavior.

Dependence and achievement, the behavior systems which most obviously have an interpersonal component and which have least often been considered to be explained by innate processes, can conveniently be discussed together. This is so because research on independence typically concentrates on two criteria: the extent to which nurturance is sought, and the extent of personal initiative and achievement-striving. The evidence suggests that early social deprivation (frustration of early nurturance needs) does have lasting effects on children, such as increased motivation for nurturance and social reinforcement and conformist behavior in the interest of securing social approval. The previous discussion of person-situation interaction and the emergence of cognitive and interpersonal styles (Table 7-1) suggest how such behavior could become stable over time and affect patterns of personal responsiveness. Also interesting is research which indicates that striving for independence and achievement-striving are only modestly correlated. The extensive literature on internal-external locus of control (fate control, field independence/field dependence) has been generated from a social learning theory perspective. This perspective emphasizes expectancy sets, learned and reinforced in social interaction, which appear to constitute relatively stable perceptual styles that emerge in childhood and continue at least into young adulthood (Rotter, 1966; Witkin, 1962; Mischel, 1976). An especially interesting variant of research on locus of control has focused on fate control and the particular variant of learned helplessness (Lefcourt, 1973), which is of special interest to health professionals who have so many occasions to observe extensive dependency behavior among ill individuals. Lefcourt used as a point of departure the work of B.F. Skinner and the inference invited by that work that freedom (personal control) is an illusion. If personal control is an illusion, Lefcourt argues, it is an illusion with interesting behavioral consequences. He reviews animal research to indicate that experimental inducement of total helplessness in the face of punishing stimuli in laboratory animals leads to rapid disappearance of appropriate striving and, with interesting frequency, to death from causes that have no apparent physiological explanation. Animals that have experience with aversive action that reduces punishment continue to strive, as though their behavior will be efficacious even when they are physically restrained from doing so. However, animals that sustain such striving behavior over long periods of time in the absence of relief from noxious stimuli do tend to develop physical pathology. If an expectancy set of positive fate control is an illusion, it may be an useful illusion, at least in the short run. Extrapolating the implications of such findings to human behavior, Lefcourt approvingly cites an observation of Mower made over a quarter century ago:

> One is ill and suffering from pain and inconvenience. The physician arrives, diagnoses the difficulty, prescribes treatment, and intimates that in a day or two one will be quite hale again. It is unlikely that the examination or the ensuing exchange of words has altered the physical condition of the patient in

> the least; yet he is likely to "feel a lot better" as a result of the doctor's call. What obviously happens in such instances is that initially the patient's physical suffering is complicated by concern lest his suffering continue indefinitely or perhaps grow worse. After a reassuring diagnosis, this concern abates; and if, subsequently, the same ailment recurs, one can predict that it will arouse less apprehension than it did originally. (Lefcourt, 1973, p. 420–421.)

Conclusions

What general conclusions are warranted from research on the forms and consequences of early socialization? *First,* all societies give some attention to each of the specific behavior systems discussed above, but the amount of attention and the kind of attention given varies between societies and, to some extent, within societies. For example, some societies are rigid; others are permissive regarding weaning procedures, toilet training, overt aggression, and training for independence and achievement striving. *Second,* all of the variants observed appear to have behavioral outcomes which fall within a socially specific tolerable range for most persons most of the time. Nature appears to tolerate various forms of nurturing. *Third,* societies train their dependent young, usually successfully, to want to and to be able to behave in ways that are socially accepted and rewarded. *Fourth,* the behavior of the society's official socializing agents, initially parents, is a key variable in understanding why different styles and content have an equipotential for successful outcome. This variable has been conceptualized by Sears, et al. (1957) as "the responsiveness of the (socialization) environment." By this they mean the positive acceptance by the adult socializers of each other, the child, and of the responsibility for and to the child. Future research on childrearing should appropriately give as much attention to the socializers of children as to the child being socialized.

These conclusions cannot possibly be satisfying to anyone who would like to have a simple formula or a regression equation specifying the ingredients of foolproof socialization procedures. There is some consolation in knowing, however, that success does not depend on the implementation of any single formula, and that outcomes depend a great deal on the general context of socialization provided by adults.

References

Aries, P. Centuries of Childhood. New York, New York: Knopf, 1962.

Brim, O.G., Jr., and S. Wheeler. Socialization after Childhood. New York, New York: Wiley, 1966.

Cummings, E., and W. Henry. Growing Old: The Process of Disengagement. New York, New York: Basic Books, 1961.

Eisenstadt, S.N. From Generation to Generation, 2nd ed. New York, New York, The Free Press, 1956.
Erikson, Erik H. Identity and the life cycle. Psychological Issues, 1:1, 1959.
Lefcourt, H.M. The function of the illusions of control and freedom. American Psychologist 28:417–425, 1973.
Mischel, W. Introduction to Personality, 2nd ed. New York, New York: Holt, Rinehart and Winston, 1976.
Rotter, J.B. Generalized expectancies for internal versus external control of reinforcement. Psychological Monographs 80:1, 1966.
Sears, R.R., E.E. Maccoby, and H. Levin. Patterns of Child Rearing. Evanston, Illinois: Row, Peterson, 1957.
Simmons, L.W. The Role of the Aged in Primitive Societies. New Haven, Connecticut: Yale University Press, 1945.
Witkin, H.A. Social influences in the development of cognitive style. In D.A. Goslin (Ed.) Handbook of Socialization Theory and Research. New York, New York: Wiley, 1962.
Ziegler, E., and I.L. Child. Socialization. In G. Lindzey and E. Aronson (Eds.) The Handbook of Social Psychology/III, 2nd ed. Reading, Massachusetts: Addison-Wesley, 1969.

8

Gender Differences in Behavior: Confluence of Nature and Nurture

It has, in recent times, become fashionable in some circles to deny that there are gender-related behaviors to be addressed; to assert that there are no differences between men and women apart from trivial anatomical ones and perhaps certain superficial behavioral traits that are exclusively the product of differential socialization experience, often a socialization experience that is said to favor males. The political goal of equality of opportunity of the sexes does not require for its validity the assumption of biobehavioral sexual homogeneity, needless to say; in any event, that assumption is in fact empirically untenable. Psychological differences between males and females, in terms of central tendency, are manifold across a broad range of traits, and they are often "basic" in the sense of making their appearance prior to any substantial contact with the social environment. Julia Sherman (1971) provides a thorough review of these findings. On the other hand, as will be seen in what follows, the sex-typing proclivities of the social environment *are* normally exceedingly intense in their deployment and extremely powerful in their effects. However, to reiterate again, the central issue is not that of determining how much of the outcome variance is attributable to nature and how much to nurture (even if that were possible) but of understanding the manner in which innate predispositions affect and are affected by the vicissitudes of life experience.

The notion of "central tendency" is invariably of crucial import when seeking to compare the behavior of groups of people—*any* groups:

males/females, schizophrenics/normals, blacks/whites, medical students/law students, etc. With respect to virtually any behavioral characteristic there is always a substantial overlap, some individuals being more similar to at least some members of the "other" group than they are to a large proportion of their own. Such is clearly the case with respect to gender-related behaviors. This observation alone justifies a certain caution in speaking of "typical" male or "typical" female behaviors. Beyond that, it seems increasingly likely that psychological masculinity and femininity, as personality or behavioral traits, are not most profitably conceived as opposite poles of a single dimension, but rather as separate and somewhat independent dimensions in their own right. Thus some individuals, described as androgynous (Bem, 1975), have strong dispositions to engage in some behaviors conventionally regarded as "feminine" and some that are, by convention, "masculine." There is even some evidence that such androgynous persons are better adjusted and more psychologically "healthy" than those oriented strongly and exclusively to their particular gender-"appropriate" roles. Note that we are not speaking here of gender-identity confusion, which is often correlated with various forms of behavior disorder, but rather of a type of individual who securely incorporates into his/her behavioral repertoire aspects of both the male and female roles, as conventionally conceived. There is a vast difference between the individual who is both strongly "masculine" and strongly "feminine" and the individual who is neither. Notwithstanding the force of these general caveats, the psychological differences between men and women, *in general*, are sufficiently compelling to provide an instructive case of nature-nurture interaction in the development of characteristic styles of behavior.

What are these sexually dimorphic differences in behavior? The matter is by no means entirely settled at this time. However, at some risk of oversimplification, it is possible to list those findings in the areas that have shown a reasonable degree of empirical stability. Relative to men/boys, women/girls tend to exhibit, in terms of greater strength and/or frequency, the following characteristics:

1. More rapid physical development, accelerating up to puberty
2. Precocity of language development and verbal skills, retaining superiority into adulthood
3. Less physical strength and more sedentary activity level
4. Less analytical ability, possibly limited to the area of spatial relations
5. More global, as opposed to analytical, approach to cognitive tasks
6. Less physical aggressiveness, assertiveness, and striving for dominance
7. Less sexual drive, although greater capacity for orgastic response
8. Greater readiness to express fear, weakness
9. More conformity, guilt, resistance to temptation
10. More envy of the opposite gender role
11. Greater stability of dependency behavior beyond childhood

12. Cyclical emotionality, associated with the menstrual cycle
13. Greater attention to self-adornment in matters of grooming and dress
14. More focus on personal relationships than functional aspects of career enhancement, etc.
15. Less objectified response to erotic stimulus materials, i.e., greater tendency to project self and preferred partner into the situation, in fantasy
16. Less irritable, fussy, and problematic as children
17. Fewer speech and reading problems
18. Less skilled in mathematical problem-solving and tasks requiring mechanical aptitude
19. Superiority in tasks requiring fine hand coordination
20. Slower reaction time
21. Less willingness to take risks
22. Less ambitiousness and achievement-striving, and less achievement in career

Undoubtedly, many of these differences are strongly determined at least in part by differential social reinforcement and expectations, and to that extent they cannot be considered immutable in the face of changing cultural traditions that may mute, accentuate, or rechannel any innate tendencies in the male or female constitution. In any event, these physical and behavioral differences are only part of the story; to these differences must be added the very important differences in cognitive organization deriving from a sense of oneself as male or female, which in the normal case provides a crucial anchoring point of personal identity. The latter is almost certainly of causal significance in itself in the production of many sex-typed behaviors. Accordingly, we shall be very concerned in what follows with gender identity and its development.

Experimentation (in the sense of the active manipulation of variables) at the human level in this area is subject to very stringent constraints. There is therefore an unavoidable inferential quality to some (actually very little) of what follows. A good example is the notion of gender-specific neural pathways in the brain, believed to be the product of dimorphic fetal hormones. No such pathways have as yet been anatomically identified in the human brain. They have not been specifically and unequivocally demonstrated in animal brains either, but many studies of the modification of normal adult gender behavior (e.g., reversed copulating position) by the experimental alteration of fetal or neonatal hormone uptake suggests very strongly indeed that they are there (Money and Ehrhardt, 1972, Chapter 5).

Psychological maleness or femaleness in the adult human being is the product of a richly interconnected sequence of causes, both biological and social. The accompanying chart (Figure 8-1) summarizes these influences. We shall discuss each of them in turn.

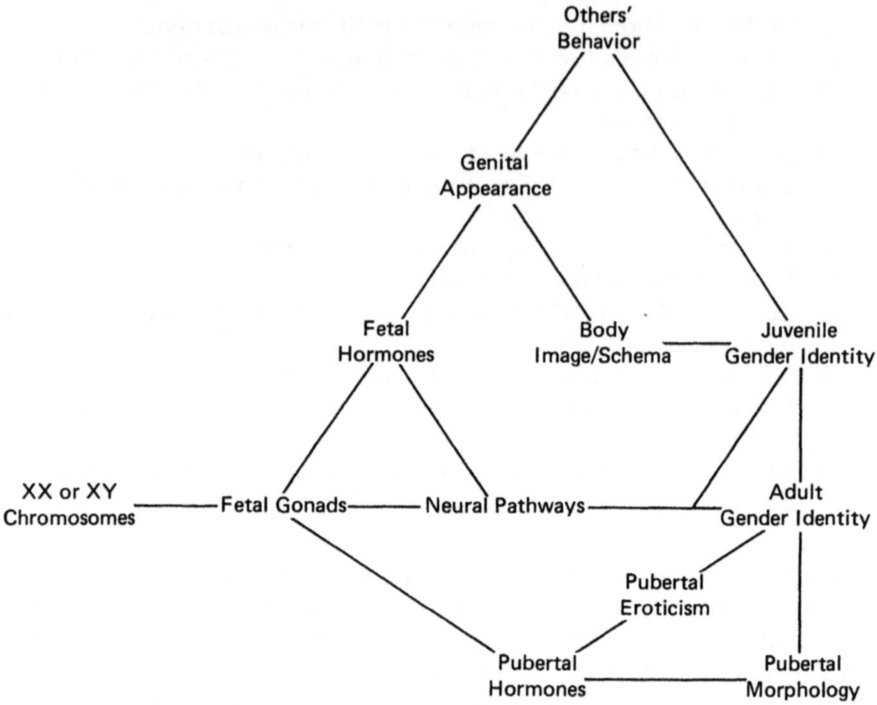

Fig. 8-1. Sequential and cumulative components of gender identity differentiation. (From Money, 1974).

Beginnings

The development of a genetically and morphologically normal female or male neonate begins when the sperm, bearing an X or a Y chromosome, penetrates the X-bearing ovum of the mother, thus initiating the "little moment of glory" (Money, 1974) played by these genetic materials in controlling future sexual differentiation. The glory is brief because, so far as is known, the sex chromosomes play no role in such differentiation following their determination of the character of the fetal gonads. These gonads will differentiate as male in the presence of Y genetic material (provided there is also some X, required for viability); otherwise, the gonads will develop as female. The primordial gonad remains undifferentiated until after the sixth week of gestation, whereupon, under the influence of a Y chromosome, it begins to develop typical testicular tissue. Specific ovarian tissue does not develop, if that is to be the organism's fate, until some six weeks later. In the absence of substances produced by testicular tissue, the fetus will develop female morphological characteristics, regardless of chromosomal endowment. The prototype human fetus is thus in some basic sense female. Two testicular substances are believed critical in producing the typical male morphology: (1) a müllerian-inhibiting substance, known only by inference, which in effect renders impossible the development of a uterus, fallopian tubes, and the inner portions of the vaginal canal; and (2) testosterone, whose influence causes the development of the internal and external male sexual organs. The overwhelming majority of human neonates are clearly and accurately recognized as either males or females at birth. Some few are born with ambiguous sexual morphology, and fewer still with frankly deceptive anatomical characteristics. Tragic and problematic as these anomalous cases often are to the affected individuals and their loved ones, they constitute the basis of an "experiment of nature" that has been very productively exploited by researchers seeking to understand the origins of psychological gender.

There are a number of ways in which deviations from the norm may occur, including chromosomal and hormonal aberrations affecting the fetus and, in rare instances, accidental alteration of the neonate's genital morphology, as in surgical destruction of the penis. The known, nonlethal anomalies of the sex chromosomes involve either the loss of a chromosome or the addition of one or more chromosomes to the normal 46,XX or XY complement. There are four basic patterns, with variants, each associated with a recognized clinical syndrome. They are: (1) 45,X (Turner's syndrome), involving female body type, ovarian deficiency, and absence of puberty; (2) 47,XXX, with female body type, diminished fertility, and occasionally mental retardation; (3) 47,XYY, the so-called supermale syndrome, with diminished spermatogenesis, varied congenital and developmental anomalies, and, arguably, increased body dimensions and psychological impulsiveness; and (4) 47,XXY (Klinefelter's syndrome), with male body type, underdeveloped male organs and resultant infertility, low testicular androgen output, and increased risk of varied psychopathology, including those involving gender-identity anomalies. Quite obviously, any of these syndromes might produce difficulties in gender identity formation by virtue of both their manifest effects on body structure and function and, quite conceivably, latent effects on neural organization, although such difficulties are by no means an invariant outcome of chromosomal defects and may often be counterbalanced by appropriate hormone replacement therapy. Much depends here on the nature of the child's upbringing, and especially on the extent to which it is uniform and unambiguous with respect to sex-typing (Stoller, 1974; Money and Ehrhardt, 1972). On the other hand, as will be discussed in greater detail below, certain of these individuals prove intractable to all such efforts at sex-typing, as though the assigned sex were in some basic sense "wrong." It is observations of this sort, which obviously relate in some measure to the problem of transsexualism, that lend substantial credence to the notion that brain pathways are implicated in the earliest beginnings of psychological gender formation.

Chromosomal abnormalities apparently produce their anomalous effects on the developing sex organs (and probably neural pathways) of the fetus by way of fetal hormones. Hormonal anomalies, however, are not limited to those produced by gross defects in the sex chromosomes. In the more interesting of these other syndromes, the sex chromosomes are normally male (XY) or female (XX), but the genital morphology is either ambiguous or distinctly appears to be that of the opposite sex. Two such syndromes have received special attention, especially in the notable and long-standing program of the Johns Hopkins group (Money and Ehrhardt, 1972; Money, 1974). These are (1) the adrenogenital syndrome, in which a genetic female is masculinized by the improper synthesis in the adrenals of an androgen in place of cortisol, and (2) the androgen-insensitivity (testicular-feminizing) syndrome, wherein a genetic male is feminized by a genetic defect involving inability to utilize androgen. As has been indicated, the fetus differentiates as a female in the absence of a positive masculinizing influence. Either syndrome may range from mild to extreme in severity, producing varying levels of morphologic hermaphroditism and genetic-morphologic discrepancy. Indistinct or frankly discrepant genital morphology at birth presents a serious dilemma for which a leisurely solution is rarely acceptable. At birth, an announcement of gender must be made; one that equivocates on sex is not likely to be greeted with rampant enthusiasm. The "decision" is frequently an improvised one, and it is frequently wrong from the standpoint of genetic constitution and/or, perhaps even more importantly, from the standpoint of ease of subsequent correction of discrepancies between assigned sex and bodily structure and function. For example, a sexually satisfactory and serviceable vaginal opening may be surgically constructed, but there is no known means of constructing a penis with these characteristics. Therefore, other things being equal, the preferred sex assignment for the hermaphroditic neonate would usually be female. The fact that some of these children are assigned as males, however, provides the basis of an informative research strategy concerning gender-identity formation which has been much-utilized by Money and his associates—namely, the study of pairs of hermaphroditic youngsters matched for approximate age and genetic sex, but reared with opposite sex assignments (Money, 1974). The main conclusion of these studies is dramatically clear: When, from an early age (generally not later than 18 months), one of these children is consistently raised as a male, he becomes, psychologically, a boy; when raised consistently as a female, she becomes, psychologically, a girl, although she may have a certain tomboyishness believed due to her prenatal androgenization. The obverse of tomboyishness (although we have no term for this) in androgen-insensitive genetic males is rarely seen, because such children will usually have been raised as girls, thereby masking the effects of presumed prenatal neural feminization.

Sex-Typing and Juvenile Gender Identity

To return to the normal course of things, it is clear from observations like those reported above that the social environment is an enormously powerful influence in the shaping of gender identity and gender-related behaviors, whatever the effects of biologically determined behavioral predispositions. It is easy to overlook, but impossible to overemphasize, the massive if often subtle forces brought to bear differentially upon the child in consequence of his/her having been declared a boy or a girl. These forces are unleashed virtually at the first sight of the child's genitals (provided they are unambiguous), and they continue in a mutuality of organism-environment stimulation throughout the person's life. The occasional parental assertion that their sons and daughters are treated exactly alike is at best a benign delusion; it can be proven false with no greater instrumentation than a video recorder. Much of this differential response seems related to the adult's own achievement of gender identity, which involves not only the acquisition of behaviors appropriate to his/her gender role, but also vast experience with the complement of that role, i.e., the typical vis-à-vis behaviors of members of the opposite sex, suitably corrected for age. It would be a mistake to conclude, however, that these differential adult behaviors directed toward children considered as either boys or girls are wholly preprogrammed and independent of the characteristics (other than an accepted sexual designation) of the infant or child. Children—even children of the same sex—differ enormously in their characteristic behavior; these varying behaviors evoke varying responses in parents and other significant adults, these responses in turn being affected by idiosyncratic tendencies in the responding adult. Granting such individual differences in both children and adults, whatever their sex, there are nevertheless certain regularities of behavior in both groups that are sex-related. Thus, as detailed further in Chapter 6, boys and girls present, on average, a somewhat different stimulus configuration to their parents, quite aside from their designations as boys or girls. These differential sex-linked behaviors in turn control to some extent the experience the individual will have with his/her parents or other significant adults, contributing thereby to the further differentiation of the child's sense of identity, including gender identity. The process is, to be sure, a rather complicated one; its study—indeed even its description in broad terms—is arduous and taxing. But that seems to be the way it is.

In any event, if all goes well, boys develop a gender identity as boys and girls as girls, typically many years before the advent of puberty. They are considerably aided in this by their singular awareness of their own body structure, particularly its genital aspects, and by their considerable appreciation of the manner in which it differs from that of the other sex (the doctor's game, or any of its many variants, having an extremely widespread popularity among moppets). Modeling of and identification with the parent of the same sex, or even certain characteristics of the parent of the opposite sex, are clearly involved in the majority of instances, although evidence is sparse supporting the specifically Freudian theory of the oedipal origins of sex-typing in the juvenile period. In other words, there is little good evidence that the boy's fear of castration, or the girl's alleged promissory compensation for her lack of a penis through childbirth, have much if anything to do with the promotion of appropriate gender identities.

Gender identity develops surprisingly rapidly in the early childhood years, and in the majority of instances appears to become at least partially irreversible by the age of 3 or 4; changes of sex assignment attempted after this period are fraught with psychological hazards to the reassignee, a common result being identity confusion and gross personal disorganization. There are, however, exceptions to this general rule, where sex reassignment even in a mature adult may be accompanied by an increase in personal happiness and apparent effectiveness in living. These are the unfortunate individuals whose early socialization as boys or girls—usually occurring on sound anatomical grounds—was in conflict with some form of core gender identity, presumably one embedded in the neural substrate. They are the true transsexuals, not to be confused with the many individuals who seek sex reassignment for essentially psychopathological reasons. The "differential diagnosis," incidentally, should obviously be left to experts in the field.

These observations raise the question of the origins of homosexuality, especially as many homosexuals date the onset of their awareness of being "different" to the prepubertal years. It should be underscored, however, that transsexuality and homosexuality are not the same thing; while most transsexuals are homosexually inclined in terms of choice of partner, as indeed might be expected, very few homosexually oriented individuals desire a change of sex. Transvestism, the desire to dress in the manner of the opposite sex, is yet another differing pattern. While most transsexuals report a history of cross-dressing, most transvestites do not desire a change of sex, nor are they, by and large, homosexually inclined. The evidence suggests that all three of these variants are associated with some form of confusion or reversal in prepubertal gender-identity formation, but little other commonality can definitely be said to exist. The antecedents of a homosexual orientation, in particular, seem to be many and varied, and it may well be the case that the male and female forms of it are of a very different psychological character (Bell, 1974); that is, lesbianism is probably not the mere psychological obverse of male gayness. In any event, insofar as all three (or four, if we separate male and female homosexuality) variant forms will normally have developed counter to very strong social pressures in the opposite direction, there is a basis for believing them to have some type of "constitutional" element in their origins. This does not necessarily imply irreversibility of the condition, particularly where the individual harbors conflict and ambivalence concerning it. For example, successful therapeutic reversal of a conflictful homosexual orientation is not uncommon, but neither should it be lightly undertaken by an overzealous clinician.

Lest the reader be unduly influenced by the foregoing in favor of an excessively "nativist" view of gender identity, we close this section on juvenile happenings with an unique case history, supplied by Money (1974). It involves monozygotic (and therefore genetically identical) twin boys, one of whom lost his penis shortly after birth by virtue of an accident with the electric cautery employed in an attempt at circumcision. Professional opinion was that this child should be raised as a girl, a decision that was not finally effectuated in a formal way until the child had reached 17 months of age. Four months later the necessary surgical reconstruction was begun, not to be completed until adolescence. In the meantime, the parents of the children made special efforts, under professional guidance, to sexually differentiate and clearly sex-type the two youngsters according to plan: the intact one was to be a boy, and his identical twin (brother) was to be a girl. At last report (the twins being 9 years old), that is exactly the way it has turned out. The girl is very much a little girl and very different from her brother in taste, in posture, in appearance, in behavioral style, and even in height and growth rate, the latter presumably the effect of differential endogenous hormonal influence resulting from her orchidectomy. She shows every sign of becoming a very attractive young women when, under the influence of exogenously supplied estrogen, she blossoms into adolescence. Of considerable interest, however, is the fact that she is a bit of a tomboy!

Puberty and Adolescence

Some time after the first decade of life, but in any event occurring some two years earlier in girls than in boys, the pituitary signals the already sexually differentiated gonads to begin producing the pubertal hormones that will complete the physical differentiation of the sexes. These phenomena are too familiar to require recapitulation here. Suffice to say that they are very striking—to the individual and to others. Gender identity is thus consolidated for the normal pubescent via achievement of the external paraphernalia signifying manhood or womanhood, and by virtue of his/her awareness of an internal procreative capacity that is gender-specific. There is a great deal of variation in the timing of the onset of these events for different youngsters, and indeed even the mean timing is not stable across time; for unknown reasons, and on a very widespread geographical scale, puberty has been occurring at younger ages in successive recent generations. Extreme precocity or delay in onset is not uncommonly associated with hormonal derangements of one sort or another, often initially discovered at this time as, for example, in the failure of development of the secondary sex characteristics in the Turner's syndrome girl. More modest precocities or delays are normal and quite standard, but because they carry a heavy freight of psychosexual meaning, they have behavioral effects that are disproportionate to their biological significance.

While much remains to be discovered concerning the relationships between pubertal morphology and the attainment of adult gender identity (it is a much-neglected area of research), certain findings seem reasonably well-established. For girls, early maturation is not so problematic as was once thought to be the case. While they may have some problems of embarrassment early on, they seem to be better adjusted to being female in later adolescence than are the late maturers. There is, however, a problem of interpretation with this finding, because it is conceivable that good adjustment promotes, on a psychophysiologic basis, early maturation, rather than the other way around. They may also appear better adjusted because early maturation produces high status among peers. Or, it may be that both early maturation and good adjustment are causally independent and initiated by one or more extraneous factors, such as prepubertal body build. We do not have the data to resolve this uncertainty.

In general, boys start out with a disadvantage relative to their female age-peers: their growth spurt and adolescent maturation is delayed by some two years. They catch up, of course, and in terms of body dimensions surpass the girls in short order. Promissory notes on the future, however, are small compensation at this juncture, and many a youth has suffered grievously in observing his younger sister attain the physique and body mass that, in most respects, he enviously desires for himself. The problem is compounded should the boy be late in developing, for now he has not only the girls but also his male friends to utilize in social comparisons that can only be negative in their effects on self-esteem and sense of manliness. Early maturation, not surprisingly, seems advantageous right from the start with boys. Late maturing boys have a hard time, and the effects not uncommonly persist beyond the duration of the cause. These young men tend to be anxious and to display inordinate needs for attention and recognition. Persistent feelings of inadequacy and the anticipation of social rejection commonly accompany significant maturational delay among young men. These effects, needless to say, can be a substantial impediment to the on-schedule attainment of an integrated adult gender identity.

Quite aside from these physical changes and their attendant implications for the self-image, the advent of puberty abruptly enhances the complement of motives with which the youngster must in some manner cope. While younger children are certainly capable of sexual excitation, and at least in some girls even a rudimentary form of orgasm, the sexual drive per se typically does not develop its more insistent qualities until the establishment of puberty (Freud notwithstanding). It is difficult to discern what effects these new tensions might produce in their pure or natural state, because they are invariably subject to very strong cultural prescriptions. Nevertheless, it is possible to sketch out in broad outline certain important differences in male and female eroticism that have their beginnings in puberty and that are incorporated into adult gender identity. Our discussion will largely be limited to conditions obtaining in our own and closely related "advanced" societies.

Gender differences in eroticism are determined in part, of course, by structural and physiological differences between sexes. The focal point of the male's erotic feeling (and associated behavioral dispositions) is his penis (particularly its glans), an organ that serves the dual purpose of excretion. Erotic feeling in the female appears more physically disseminated beyond the genitals per se, and specifically includes for most women the breasts and nipples. Contrary to much folklore, vaginal tissue itself is relatively bereft of erotic stimulability, although lubrication—the female counterpart of the male's erection—originates in the vagina. The clitoris, the embryological homologue of the male penis, is by far the most erotically sensitive female organ, and its stimulation is a precondition for orgasm in the vast majority of women (Masters and Johnson, 1966). Its location ensures that for most women it will in fact be stimulated during penile thrusting into the vagina, but perhaps not sufficiently to bring about orgastic relief, which is a principal reason (there may be others) why many women require supplemental stimulation.

The earliest manifestations of pubertal eroticism are largely limited by cultural constraints to the realm of fantasy, the raw materials for which are the usual sources also employed by inactive or otherwise frustrated adults. The grosser forms of these media materials are much more likely to be found in boys' bedrooms than in girls', possibly because boys are more wont to take risks, but more likely because they are just more explicit in their tastes and more insistent in pushing things to the limits of their curiosity. They are apparently much more likely to discover, and to practice regularly, the pleasures of masturbation, although one must be careful here owing to the enormously greater reticence of girls to admit to such things even to their closest chums. Information derived from peers (and, in many cases, even from parents) also feeds these preparatory fantasies, although much of it is apt to have a distorted if not downright mendacious character. The pajama party is perhaps not quite so asexual an institution as the parents of teenage daughters would like to believe. Girls seem to objectify less than boys the characters in their erotic fantasies, as noted above, and these fantasies of girls tend to be more symbolic, and less explicitly sexual. Apparently, boys rarely fantasize about being "forced" into erotic activity, whereas this is a favorite among girls (and, for that matter, women), perhaps because of the diminished responsibility implied. In one sense at least, boys get more out of their pubertal eroticism than girls; nearly all will have had extensive experience with orgasm, if not via masturbation (which is practically universal) then by so-called wet dreams, well in advance of their first opportunity for direct sexual experience with a girl or young woman. By contrast, only some 50% of young women have achieved orgasm by any means by the age of 20.

This last-noted difference may be even more important than it seems at first glance, because there is reason to believe that the experience of orgasm reinforces (stamps in, as it were) as erotically attractive the content of the fantasies accompanying it. Thus, if the boy masturbates to fantasies of female breasts, as many do, then female breasts will get to be very attractive indeed; we need not belabor the point that they often do.

By and large, we know next to nothing about the primary origins of pubertal erotic fantasies, including those that involve homosexual and other variant forms. There is much evidence to suggest that a later "fix" on unusual object choices or activities in respect to adult sexual gratification is often preceded by pubertal erotic-masturbatory fantasies of a contentually similar variety. It is not known whether such pubertal proclivities are innate or acquired. Modern forms of redirection of sexual interest among adults, notably in so-called "behavior therapy" approaches, often employ directed masturbatory fantasy as a means of redirecting erotic interest into more conventional channels. Not infrequently, such an approach is successful, which suggests that the system remains plastic and subject to alteration, whatever its origins. Females are markedly less subject to unusual sexual tastes and behaviors than are males. Their eroticism also seems more diffuse and nonspecific, although limited to a more narrow range of potentially gratifying activities. We have also seen that they are apparently less likely to masturbate or to regularly experience orgasm in the early adolescent years. Is there a connection among these varied behavioral phenomena? The possibility exists, but we do not know.

Sooner or later, most adolescent boys and girls venture out into "trial runs," behavioral samplings of the sorts of activities which have heretofore occupied a large proportion of their private mental preoccupations. Lurking here are many opportunities for interpersonal disaster, particularly where expectations do not mesh—a common occurrence in life where expectations are largely based on fantasy, as they are here. Apparently, certain normative expectations intervene to regulate such budding relationships, and even those that are beyond the budding phase. The regulation is so complete as to be almost (but not quite) boring. A variety of independently generated data on male heterosexual experience indicates that it proceeds in a most standard fashion from kissing and "deep kissing," through various manual fumblings and breast-sucking to ventral-ventral intercourse, thence to reciprocated oral-genital contact, and finally to intercourse in the dorsal-ventral position. There seems to be no inherent rationale to the system; that's just the way it is for the large majority of young men. And if it's that way for the men, one may compellingly surmise that it's also that way for the women, all the more so since by cultural prescription it is the women who control, in most instances, what is and what is not going to happen at a given point in any relationship.

Eventually, despite their divergent histories, developmental trends, and behavioral predispositions, most young men and women discover a particular set of merits in some member of the opposite sex, a process romantically known as falling in love. The differences and divergences do not disappear at this juncture, as most couples ruefully discover sooner or later. However, they can often be worked through in a spirit of compromise and understanding, following which, if they survive the pitfalls, the two can truly get to know each other—even love each other in a sense that transcends, but does not obliterate, the wonder and excitement of the romantic. Obviously, the cards are not particularly stacked, at the outset, in the couples' favor. On the other hand, in acquiring their own gender identities, the partners will have learned a great deal about what to expect from the other.

The establishment of coupling behavior is by no means the end of the story of developmental gender differences in behavior. For most there are still the milestones of parenting, career solidification, the postparenting relationship, the climacterium, retirement, and the approach of death. The main guidelines will have been laid down by this point, however, and it seems as convenient a place as any to stop, especially as solid knowledge from research becomes increasingly sparse after the adolescent years.

References

Bell, A.O. Homosexualities: Their range and character. In J.K. Cole and R. Dienstbier (Eds.) Nebraska Symposium on Motivation, 1973. Lincoln, Nebraska: University of Nebraska Press, 1974, pp. 1–26.

Bem, S.L. Sex role adaptability: One consequence of psychological androgyny. J. Personality and Social Psychology 31:634–643, 1975.

Masters, W.H., and V.E. Johnson. Human Sexual Response. Boston, Massachusetts: Little, Brown, 1966.

Money, J. Prenatal hormones and postnatal socialization in gender identity differentiation. In J.K. Cole and R. Dienstbier (Eds.) Nebraska Symposium on Motivation, 1973. Lincoln, Nebraska: University of Nebraska Press, 1974, pp. 221–295.

Money, J., and A.A. Ehrhardt. Man and Woman, Boy and Girl. Baltimore, Maryland: Johns Hopkins University Press, 1972.

Sherman, Julia. On the Psychology of Women. Springfield, Illinois: C.C. Thomas, 1971.

Stoller, R.J. Sex and Gender. New York, New York: Jason Aronson, 1974.

9

Disorders of the Area

Mechanisms for Expression of Genetic and Environmental Influences

It has been emphasized that biobehavioral dispositions—e.g., toward a more schizophrenic way of interacting with the world—cannot be logically considered as the result of *either* genetic influences *or* environmental factors. Rather, the point was made that innate and environmental factors act in concert to produce observable patterns of behavior. Furthermore, it was noted that even with the evidence presently available to support the role of heredity in expression of schizophrenic illness, the mechanisms whereby such genetic influences are expressed remain to be elucidated. Also, there are a variety of characteristic psychological functions which have been proposed as basic aspects of the schizophrenic process. At the extreme, these functions are expressed in the full-blown syndrome of a patient with a schizophrenic breakdown. However, it was also noted that these functions may be expressed within the "normal" ranges of human behavior. That is, it is possible to identify, to a less pronounced degree, basic behavioral "tendencies" which, in the individual with schizophrenic disease, are expressed to a more extreme degree.

One means of representing the interaction of genetic and environmental factors in facilitating the behavioral expression of psychological functions characteristic of the schizophrenic process—from the normal range to the acutely psychotic state—is illustrated in Figure 9-1. Let us assume that the "dopamine theory" of schizophrenia (to be described below) is correct, and that the genetic contribution to the schizophrenic process(es) may be ade-

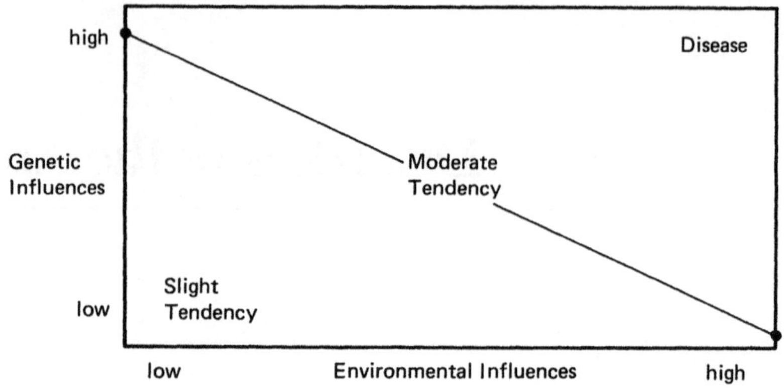

Fig. 9-1. Hypothetical distribution of the varying degrees of expression of schizophrenic process(es) in the population, as a function of both genetic and environmental influences.

quately described as a functional excess of the neurotransmitter dopamine at certain receptor sites within the brain. Thus genetic influences to increase functional dopamine levels would enhance the likelihood that schizophrenic behavioral tendencies would be expressed, even in those individuals not actively psychotic.

A number of mechanisms can be advanced whereby such genetic influences might be expressed. First, the synthesis of dopamine might be accelerated by increased levels of enzymes involved in neurotransmitter synthesis [e.g., tyrosine hydroxylase (TH), the rate-limiting enzyme in catecholamine biosynthesis]. Second, the reduction of levels of enzymes catalyzing the breakdown [monoamine oxidase (MAO)] or conversion of dopamine to other neurotransmitters [dopamine beta-hydroxylase (DBH)] would result in a buildup of dopamine in nerve terminals. Thus genetic influences to increase the levels of TH and/or to decrease the levels of MAO and/or DBH would result in an individual being placed higher on the ordinate of Figure 9-1. For any given "dose" of genetic factors (i.e., the above-described enzyme changes), a certain level of environmental influences (here the reader might wish to insert "stress") would be required to result in a schizophrenic breakdown. As is shown in the illustration, it is likely that with extremely high levels of genetic influences, the amount of environmental stress required to precipitate a schizophrenic psychotic breakdown becomes less—until a point is reached where even the most common of stresses (e.g., going away to college) is sufficient to result in active disease. As illustrated in Figure 9-1, it is proposed that a certain "threshold" dose of genetic factors is required before an active schizophrenic illness would be expressed, even in the face of the highest levels of environmental stress.

The reader should be aware that the schema in Figure 9-1 is not intended as a representation of scientifically established facts (for example, alternative placements of the intercepts of the curves are entirely possible on the basis of the available data and would greatly alter the conclusions to be drawn; e.g., if the solid line separating disease from tendency intersected the ordinate, this would mean that with sufficiently high levels of genetic factors anyone would develop disease, no matter how low the stress levels), but rather as a means of illustrating the point that genetic and environmental factors can intersect in *varying ways* to cause an individual to arrive at the same position—in the case of Figure 9-1, the solid ("disease") portion of the box.

Insofar as the tendency to develop an illness such as schizophrenia is transmitted via hereditary factors, the mode of transmission must involve effects of genes upon protein molecules that in some way are involved in regulating those behaviors which are disturbed in association with a schizophrenic breakdown. In the remainder of this chapter, we shall first consider the manifestations or clinical characteristics of schizophrenia and some of the basic psychological defects postulated to underlie schizophrenic processes. Next, we shall consider the evidence that the biochemical abnormality underlying expression of schizophrenic processes involves an excess of the neurotransmitter dopamine at certain brain sites. Thereafter, we shall review experimental studies demonstrating the influence of both genetic and environmental factors upon enzymes involved in dopamine metabolism. The behavioral effects of such alterations will be discussed, as they may relate to the role of genetic and environmental factors in the schizophrenic process via the mechanism of raising brain dopamine levels.

Manifestations of Schizophrenia

Schizophrenia is a puzzling, elusive, ambiguous, and controversial concept. It would be difficult to find another illness about which it is said that it is both responsible for more hospital days and incapacitation than any other known, and that it does not exist and should therefore be removed from the official classification of diseases. And yet schizophrenia will not go away. Whether it is a single disease, in any meaningful sense of that phrase, is still moot. It may be that what today we call schizophrenia will turn out to be the result of a number of different causes or combination of causes. The term "schizophrenia" may not survive the early twenty-first century, as the term "nephritis," as the name of a definitive disease, did not survive the early twentieth century once the multiple sources of renal dysfunction began to be understood. But there is confronting the clinician of today a cluster of symptoms—a syndrome—sufficiently distinctive in its description or "phenomenology" and in its implications for care and treatment to compel continuing interest and attention. We turn now to the behavioral indicators by which the presence of that syndrome is recognized.

First systematically described by Kraepelin in the 1890s under the term *dementia praecox*, the concept was restricted to patients with unremitting, nonorganic mental illness of major, socially incapacitating (i.e., psychotic) degree.

The condition, he thought, was usually characterized by progression toward total loss of higher mental functions (hence "dementia"), and most typically began in late adolescence or early adulthood (thus "praecox," precocious or early dementia). Eugen Bleuler (1911), a Swiss psychiatrist, recognized the importance of Kraepelin's description of symptoms. It did not seem to him, however, that these indicators occurred only in patients with psychotic degrees of impairment, or that early onset was a defining characteristic of the condition. He therefore proposed to substitute the term *schizophrenia* (meaning split mind) for dementia praecox to emphasize the fragmentation of the mental processes, which he believed to be the essential feature of the condition.

This area of psychopathology is of major interest in our discussion of a hierarchy of behavior function areas because its phenomenology—the experience of its signs and symptoms by the observer—suggests to many the necessary presence of an innate, constitutional deficit which predisposes certain persons to impairment and breakdown of the distinctively schizophrenic type. Most of this section will be an attempt to provide the reader with a sense of what it is for behavior to be distinctively schizophrenic.

Bleuler (1911), who coined the term, viewed schizophrenia as a deficiency of certain mental functions occurring in varying degrees in different individuals, and constituting a predisposition to the incapacitating mental disorder termed "dementia praecox" by earlier workers. In Bleuler's opinion, however, not all persons with detectable degrees of the predisposition develop the full-blown psychotic illness. The current diagnostic trend in clinical psychiatry (American Psychiatric Association, 1980) is to limit the use of the term schizophrenia to those cases having at least a period of the fully developed psychosis. Our purpose, however, is to provide an example of a dimension of biobehavioral disposition which may at times interact with other influences in the life of an individual to produce clinical illness. Bleuler's description of the fundamental symptoms of one such predisposition provides an understanding of the predisposition to schizophrenia as the pathological range of such a biobehavioral disposition and will therefore be presented in some detail here. (The nonpathological range of this same dimension is often termed "integrative capacity" or "ego strength.")

In presenting the essentials of Bleuler's description of fundamental symptoms in schizophrenia, it is customary to speak of the "four A's:" associations, affect, ambivalence, and autism. *Associational deficit* is the first "A." Bleuler believed that normal thought flows largely because of "associative threads" established in one word (idea) for a number of others. If these threads are lacking, the thought processes, as reflected in the speech and writings, will be fragmented and incoherent in varying degrees depending upon the severity of the *associational deficit.* The most severe degree of such *incoherence* is often called "word salad." The speech suggests that the patient's words were being picked at random from a salad bowl vocabulary in which they had been randomly mixed. Although placed end-to-end in the manner of sentences, and punctuated or inflected like sentences, they are lacking in syntax and meaning: "Dairy Jones is see so always milk doesn't." Such total incoherence, while rare, is unmistakably schizophrenic in its implications except in the presence of organic brain disease or during periods of intense, disruptive emotional arousal (e.g., panic). The same basic symptom may occur, however, in all ranges of severity, from dissociation at the word level (as illustrated) to loosening or weakening of the associations in which the breaks occur at the level of sentences or paragraphs. The effect of fragmented associations at any level, as Bleuler points out, is that *the sense of purpose or goal-directedness is lost* from the patient's thoughts and speech. This may be nearly complete or more subtle, as when a first paragraph appears intended to develop a theme but the second and third bear little relationship to the first or to each other.

Irrelevance in response to questions is the counterpart of irrelevance in the spontaneous speech. Thought sequences, once the normal associative threads are lacking, may become pointlessly fixed on one topic (stereotype, perseveration). Ideas may become "condensed" so that two or more are contracted into the same sentence or even into single words (e.g., Judaism and judicial), often producing the so-called "clang associations" in which the sounds enter into the word selection and newly created words (neologisms, such as "sadsome"). Thought processes deprived of associational connections may simply run down, often in mid-sentence, a symptom probably best termed "thought deprivation" or "emptiness of thought," although often called "blocking."

Inappropriateness of affect is the central concept in the second "A." Again, the theme is fragmentation or disorganization. Feelings may be inconsistent with what the patient is talking about or with what is going on around him. Such extreme, qualitatively inappropriate affect (laughter, say, while speaking of the tragic death of a dear friend, or inexplicable giggling in the absence of any apparent stimulus), if sustained over time and in the absence of organicity, is unmistakably schizophrenic. So too are sudden, unprovoked emotional outbursts, typically quite unmixed or "unbalanced" by other feelings than the primary rage or terror, and incomprehensible to the observer. More difficult diagnostic problems arise around questions of subtle, quantitative variations in the appropriateness of the emotions. Feelings may be of higher amplitude than appropriate and labile, but these symptoms are also found in most other types of disordered behavior. More distinctively schizophrenic is inappropriately diminished affect. The patient may appear in varying degrees indifferent to events in his surroundings. The condition has a quality of shallowness or emptiness, often called "flatness" or "blunting," which is in some contrast to the constriction of emotions one senses in the inhibitory processes typical of neurosis. There is an absence of that fullness of emotional expression which elicits an emotional response of similar authenticity in those around him.

The third "A," schizophrenic *ambivalence*, is somewhat difficult to describe because of its intricate relationship with neurotic conflict. In fact, the term "ambivalence" is used alternately with "conflict" in the psychoanalytic literature. In that usage it does not imply the presence of schizophrenic process. Of even greater importance, however, is the fact that the content of schizophrenic ambivalences usually reflects the patient's coexisting neurotic conflicts. What makes the expression schizophrenic is the absence to some degree of that particular mental function which, in the absence of schizophrenic disorder, causes the person to experience conflicting or incompatible thoughts, feelings, or impulses. This sense of something requiring resolution and the activities (often called ego-integrative or synthetic functions) mobilized to produce that resolution is precisely what appears to be deficient in schizophrenia.

Bleuler designated impairments of the associations and affects, together with schizophrenic ambivalence, *simple* fundamental symptoms, whereas the fourth "A," *autism*, was considered by Bleuler as a *compound* fundamental symptom, "disturbed to the extent that the simple functions on which it depends are altered" (Bleuler, 1911, p. 63). In the same passage he also speaks of autism as a "detachment from reality, together with the relative and absolute predominance of the inner life." We interpret "schizophrenic autism" to mean: to the degree that a person is unable to think and speak to others coherently and purposively, to the degree that he or she is unable to respond with emotions appropriate to thoughts and circumstances, and to the degree that, given a reasonable time following initial recognition, he or she is unable to synthesize a coherent reaction pattern to conflicting pressures, to that combined degree will such an individual be de facto cut off from the world of other people and external affairs. In speaking thus of de facto autism as the uniquely schizophrenic phenomenon, we believe we are in some agreement with Oppenheimer (1971, pp. 248–271) and Pincus and Tucker (1978, p. 89), who emphasize distinctions between schizophrenic autism and alterations of reality resulting simply from those "affective-dynamic" processes within the normal or neurotic range. An important implication of this view of autism as deficit rather than defense is that it clarifies the essentially nonschizophrenic, neurotic nature of the behavior patterns called "paranoid" or "schizoid," the two major clinical forms taken by defensive withdrawal.

To conclude our discussion of Bleuler's fundamental symptoms it is necessary to note, without extensive description, that he also described *accessory symptoms*. Unlike the fundamental four "A's," which are characteristic of schizophrenia, the accessory symptoms are found in other types of mental illness. They include hallucinations (most often auditory), delusions or false ideas (often persecutory but also grandiose or bizarre somatic, as of some weird bodily transformation), and *catatonic* symptoms (chiefly states of motor excitement or immobility often including unusual movements or postures).

That the predisposition to schizophrenia may reflect a constitutional disposition rather than an acquired pattern of defenses is suggested by: (1) the phenomenologically deficit-like quality of the fundamental symptoms, as described above, even in their milder forms; and (2) the genetic findings reviewed, in part, in an earlier section. Other phrasings of this distinction are found in the literature on this condition. Schizophrenia, it is said, reflects a disturbance in the form, rather than the content, of the mental life; disturbance of the ways in which the person thinks, feels, and attempts to reach decisions rather than what he thinks about, a distinction analogous to a breakdown of the computer itself rather than a poorly done program. Schizophrenic symptoms are said to be impersonal. It is said that in these various respects they resemble more closely the deficits of organic brain syndrome than they do the highly individual neurotic group of disorders. We shall suggest that the term schizophrenia be reserved for behavioral phenomena showing the fixed, pervasive, formal, and impersonal qualities just described, and showing at the same time the disorganization or disintegration of the unity of mental life which Bleuler found sufficiently characteristic to designate the illness a "splitting of the mind."

Basic Psychological Defect(s)

Having considered the clinical characteristics of schizophrenia, we will now review some of the specific psychological defects postulated to underlie the schizophrenic process. The list of proposals included here is by no means exhaustive of the literature. Our chief purpose is to provide a picture of the types of psychological function/malfunction which might be considered for this process, and thus of the possibilities inherent in the concept of biobehavioral dispositions. Additional information about the deficits presented here, and others, may be found extensively reviewed in the excellent monograph of Chapman and Chapman (1973). Because this source is available, we will not cite individual references for studies of each of the proposed deficits unless there is some special reason to do so.

It is again important to bear in mind that there is no reason to assume a single basic defect for all schizophrenia, a point made repeatedly by Chapman and Chapman, who devote an entire chapter to the heterogeneity of schizophrenia.

Broken Associative Threads (Bleuler). Bleuler, as we have seen, proposed absent or weakened associative threads as the basic defect. He believed that other symptoms were derived from loss of normal associative processes. Any word or idea normally has many associative ties from which, at a given moment, one chooses those which further his overall purpose. If some are lacking, choices are narrowed and will likely become tangential (off target), incoherent, or bizarre. Bleuler described a patient who was asked if something "weighed heavily on his mind." He responded by saying, "Yes, iron is heavy." It is assumed that the normal associative threads involving the figurative meaning of "heavy" were unavailable to him, the one involving "iron" among those remaining. Impoverishment of thought is explained by a profound absence of associative threads, so that there are not enough to keep the thoughts moving. Failure to recognize the incompatibility of opposites, because of broken threads for the two ideas, is thought to lead to the symptom of ambivalence. Similar explanations are offered for the other fundamental symptoms and for the accessory symptoms, in so far as they have particular schizophrenic coloring. Bleuler usually considered the loss of associative connections to be essentially random or "haphazard." This proposal for the basic defect has been studied chiefly by the word association test, in which the subject is asked to give his first immediate association to words provided by the examiner. Chapman and Chapman (1973, p. 117) review the evidence and conclude that the demonstrated differences between performance of patients with schizophrenia and normal subjects on such tests is insufficient to confirm Bleuler's choice of random loss of associative meanings as the basic psychological defect of that illness. They point out, however, that Bleuler's closely related concept of impairment of goal-directedness (purpose) is not contradicted by these findings and may represent a still-viable candidate for the position of basic defect.

Loss of Abstract Thinking (Vigotsky, Goldstein). While no longer considered a very likely prospect for basic defect, loss of abstract thinking (concretization) remains prominent in the clinical examination of schizophrenic processes. The usual examination procedure involves the patient providing general meanings of some common proverbs. In addition there are a number of formal tests in which the subject is asked to sort (classify) objects such as toys, tools, and other common objects or specially constructed blocks of different sizes, shapes, and colors in ways more complex than mere size, shape, etc. In other words, the subject must conceive categories or classifications new to him (but known to the examiner) in order to perform successfully on the test. When such tests are applied to groups of subjects with and without schizophrenic elements in their illnesses, the evidence does not support concreteness as a general accompaniment of schizophrenia. At least the "concreteness" found in such patients is not the same as that of organically impaired persons, but rather a tendency to use more private, idiosyncratic, unusual, and bizarre concepts for the sorting and proverb interpretation tasks. Interestingly, in several studies, patients who showed both true organic concreteness and the idiosyncratic responses of schizophrenic "concreteness" were subsequently given phenothiazine antipsychotic medication, which treatment relieved the latter symptom but not the former.

Errors in Logic (Von Domarus, Arieti). In Aristotelian logic, it is correct to reason: All men are mortal. Socrates is a man. Therefore, Socrates is mortal. The following, however, is incorrect: Certain Indians are swift. Stags are swift. Therefore, certain Indians are stags. The error lies in accepting identity of the subjects on the basis of identical predicates (i.e., on the basis of identical adjectives, identical attributes). Von Domarus called this type of thinking "paralogical," and thought it might be at the core of schizophrenic disruptions of thinking. Arieti, using the term "paleologic" to indicate a possible relation to the thinking of primitive peoples, postulates that patients may purposively adopt this form of reasoning in order to reduce the anxiety which results when they think normally. (Again we see a combined deficit-defense formulation of schizophrenic symptomatology.) Attractive as this theory is, research has demonstrated that reasoning by Von Domarus' principle is very common in subjects without schizophrenia and not significantly more frequent in those who have the condition. Moreover, it is not only a common form of reasoning but quite normal in the sense of reality oriented and adaptive. Aristotelian logic contains the principles of proper deductive reasoning, from accepted premises to necessary conclusions. But much of ordinary reasoning properly involves making tentative, probabilistic inferences from incomplete observational data. Chapman and Chapman (1973, p. 183) very cogently point out that the chemist who reasons: Sulfur is yellow powdery material; some of these test tubes contain yellow powdery material; therefore, some of these test tubes (probably) contain sulfur, is not displaying some mental abnormality, although he would certainly need to check his conclusion further if the nature of the substance were of real importance to him.

Excessive Yielding to Normal Biases (L.J. Chapman). The proposal of Chapman, like that of Bleuler, implicates broken associations as the central element in schizophrenic thought disorder. Unlike Bleuler's concept of randomly disrupted threads, however, Chapman suggests that the associational deficit follows a predictable patterns: The patient "yields" to the most common meaning of the word and is, therefore, unable to make the associations appropriate to the context (goal, purpose) in which the word or idea is actually occurring. Bleuler's example involving problems "weighing on the mind" and "heavy" iron may be reinterpreted by noting that, without other contextual cues, the word "weighing" is most often associated by normal people with heaviness in the sense that iron is heavy, rather than with troublesome, preoccupying thoughts. The patient described, however, was unable to utilize the contextual cues supplied by the phrase "on your mind" and remained stuck, as it were, on the common, normal bias meaning of "weighing." Chapman suggests *failure to attend to contextual cues* as an alternative wording of his phrase, excessive yielding to normal bias. Chapman and his associates, in a series of studies, have shown that subjects with and without schizophrenic disorder have the same preferred meaning responses (i.e., share normal biases) in the absence of contextual cues. They demonstrated, however, that subjects with the illness, who were asked to select meanings for the sentence, "Robert said he likes rare meat" chose "Robert likes the kind of meat that is extremely uncommon" much more frequently than normal subjects, who most often selected, "Robert likes partially cooked meat." Chapman acknowledges that, although his name for the defect suggests some central process of sorting or screening associations for appropriateness, the findings may also be explained in terms of one of the theories which place emphasis on disruption of the process of attention, disruptions which might reduce the cues available for the screening process. We shall turn now to some proposals specifically implicating defects of attention.

Overinclusion (N. Cameron). Although Cameron later modified his definition of overinclusion to mean any response to inappropriate stimuli, his original meaning was the inability to limit attention, including a tendency to overgeneralize. The frequency with which patients suffering from schizophrenia are observed to be *distractible*, to respond to irrelevant stimuli (the examiner's ring or the color of his desk blotter, rather than the test card), is very great. Not only is this observed by others, but patients frequently report that they cannot prevent attending to the variety of stimuli found in almost any setting. This striking feature of the illness is, of course, not unrelated to the loss of goal directedness. Chapman and Chapman consider Cameron's original definition the more testable, and report studies involving sorting tasks; in one, for example, patient subjects, more frequently than normals, included vegetables when asked to sort a large group of objects as fruits. The various findings suggesting that overinclusion (in this sense of overgeneralization or excessive broadening of abstract concepts) is a part of the schizophrenic process should be kept in mind in view of the common tendency in clinical practice to put major emphasis on the contrasting tendency, concreteness, or inability to generalize.

Loss of Major Set (Shakow). After more than 50 years of working with the experimental psychopatholgy of schizophrenia, David Shakow's position is that the basic psychological defect is best characterized as disturbances of the normal "set." This term is used in psychology to mean a state of readiness to respond to stimuli. In schizophrenia, Shakow suggests, the individual is unable to normally use the stimuli of preceding moments to develop a "major set," the term "major" here having the meaning of appropriate or adaptive to the current stimulus situation. The classical study compared subjects with and without schizophrenic illness with respect to ability to utilize varying preparatory intervals (PIs) between warning stimulus and reaction stimulus to shorten their reaction times, i.e., to develop an appropriate readiness to respond. Normal subjects were faster in their reaction times (more accurate in their prediction of PI) when the preceding series of PIs were held constant. Patients whose illness included schizophrenia were slower under the condition of constant PI than when those intervals were varied! From this and many succeeding studies, Shakow and co-workers conclude that inability to maintain a major set results in a state in which "minor" or "segmental" sets are constantly intruding. There is some evidence that any most recent stimulus has a strong capacity to induce a new segmental set. The result, clearly, is a state of poor attention and high distractibility.

Numerous other workers have attempted refinement and further clarification of the attentional deficit. This work is reviewed by Garmezy (1977) who writes, "Clearly we are at flood tide in the study of attention in schizophrenics," and by others (Chapman and Chapman, 1973, pp. 253–285; Neale and Cromwell, 1970; Corbett, 1975; Zubin, 1975; Nuechterlein, 1977; Wynne et al., 1978, pp. 159–396). Some emphasize failure to filter out irrelevant stimuli, others, inappropriate constriction of the range of stimuli to which the individual responds. Other theories have attempted to include variables of emotions, especially anxiety, and drive state as steps in the process leading to disruptions of perception and eventually of thought (Chapman and Chapman, 1973, pp. 224–242, 286–309).

This section will conclude with reference to an interesting suggestion for a major modification of perspective in the search for basic defects in the investigation of the etiology and pathogenesis of schizophrenia. Cromwell (1975) suggests, and provides arguments to support, a shift from behavioral variables at the level of attention, abstract thinking, logic, or associations, to those at the lowest possible level still within the behavioral range, to the absolute limits of psychology—the point at which it becomes physiology or biochemistry. The studies reported by Cromwell, which he believes to be encouraging, focus on behavioral variables such as visual size estimation and reaction time ("the simplest level of response at which schizophrenic patholgy occurs"). To these he juxtaposes physiological measures of arousal such as galvanic skin response and heart rate. His major integrating theoretical concept, stimulus redundancy, derives from neurophysiological studies of rate of stimulus processing. All of these variables involve study of responses in the few seconds or fractions of a second following presentation of an ambiguous, difficult, "briefly presented stimulus." This final phrase, Cromwell notes, is taken from a statement about an essential feature of patients with dementia praecox having particular problems with such stimuli. The statement was made by Emil Kraepelin!

Cromwell (1975) concludes his argument:

> Perhaps the great tragedy in the study of schizophrenia in the past eight decades has been that the interview to study clinically manifest symptoms has been the major tool. In the [review] we have seen how these manifest symptoms are obscured by the cognitive style, social competence, and preexisting personality of the individual. We have seen that premorbid history rather than clinically manifest symptom is more relevant for predicting outcome of hospitalization and drug treatment. Advances in understanding etiology may also require that we turn away from our preoccupation with these clinically manifest symptoms, from our preoccupation with the necessity of interview and projective techniques. The observation and concern with coughing is clinically relevant in deciding that a person needs relief from respiratory misery; however, the classification and factor analysis of

> coughs does not permit an understanding of the etiology of a respiratory infection, its definitive treatment, or its prognosis. While schizophrenia is unlikely to be explained by this model, the disorder has indeed been susceptible to such a misguided orientation of study. The laboratory measures of reaction time and other factors on a more molecular level of behavior have often been dismissed as not clinically relevant. The time has come to accept the fact that what is clinically relevant may not be etiologically relevant. (p. 615)

Whether or not one subscribes to Cromwell's call for abandonment of research at the more molar and clinical levels of behavior, the need to include research models of the type he describes is clearly of the greatest importance.

The "Dopamine Theory" of Schizophrenia

Since heredity does appear to play a role in the expression of schizophrenic behavior, and since the mechanism of transmission of such genetic influences upon behavior most likely involves the brain's biochemistry, a vast amount of work has been done in trying to identify the biochemical "defect" in schizophrenia. The first work in this area attempted to isolate abnormal substances in the blood or urine of schizophrenic patients. A group at Tulane University reported the discovery in the serum of schizophrenic patients of a protein they called taraxein that was not present in normal individuals and that could cause hallucinations when injected into normals. Subsequent investigation showed, however, that the serum proteins of schizophrenic patients are different from those of normal individuals only in ways that can be accounted for by factors related to chronic illness and institutionalization. Even the hallucinatory effects in normals appeared to be due more to effects of placebo and suggestion than to any specific effects of the substance(s) identified. Another initially promising lead was the discovery of the so-called "pink spot" in the chromatographic examination of urine from schizophrenic patients. This compound was tentatively identified as 3,4-dimethoxyphenylamine, a substance structurely related to both the neurotransmitter dopamine and the hallucinogen mescaline. Further work, however, showed that the pink spot was in fact composed of many compounds, the major component being a metabolite of the drugs the patients were taking.

A more promising approach involves investigation of the biochemical effects of drugs which appear to exert selective effects on schizophrenic behavior. The term *neuroleptic* has been coined to describe such drugs. These drugs fall mainly into two chemical families: the phenothiazines and the butyrophenones. The first such drug to be introduced into clinical practice, chlorpromazine, was initially employed with the hope that it would sedate hyperactive patients. It was subsequently found, however, that this agent would activate withdrawn schizophrenic patients. This was in contrast to sedatives, which only served to make withdrawn patients even more withdrawn. Antianxiety agents such as diazepam (Valium) were effective in reducing anxiety, but exerted no clearly beneficial effect upon the disordered thinking which characterizes the schizophrenic patient.

The neuroleptic drugs have widespread biochemical effects, and the task of identifying which effect is responsible for their therapeutic effect in schizophrenia has been an arduous one. The most effective approach has involved evaluation and comparison of drugs with similar structure and biochemical effects to the clinically effective neuroleptics. For example, promethazine is closely related in structure to chlorpormazine but is lacking in antischizophrenic activity. Its major biochemical property is to antagonize the actions of histamine. By this process of elimination, extensive research over the years has revealed only one biochemical action that is consistently present in those neuroleptics which are effective in reducing schizophrenic behavior: the ability to block receptor sites in the brain that are activated by the neurotransmitter dopamine.

Dopamine, along with epinephrine and norepinephrine, is one of the body's three principal catecholamines [catechol referring to a benzene ring with two attached hydroxyl groups, and amine referring to the presence of an amino (bond-NH_2) group in the molecule]. The ultimate source of dopamine in the body is dietary intake of its precursor, the amino acid tyrosine, which is converted by tyrosine hydroxylase (the rate-limiting step in catecholamine synthesis) to dihydroxyphenylalanine (dopa). Dopa is decarboxylated to form dopamine, which in turn is hydroxylated at the beta-carbon position by dopamine beta-hydroxylase (DBH) to form norepinephrine. In some areas of the brain, DBH is not present, and in these areas dopamine rather than norepinephrine must serve as the neurotransmitter. The best known of these areas is the corpus striatum (which includes the caudate nucleus and the putamen), where dopaminergic receptors serve to mediate the coordination of fine motor movements. These dopaminergic neurons are selectively destroyed in patients with Parkinson's disease. Parkinsonian symptoms can be reduced by administration of the dopamine precursor, L-Dopa, indicating that dopamine depletion is causally related to the disease. Significantly, the neuroleptic drugs themselves can produce extrapyramidal, parkinsonian-like symptoms, but presumably by blocking the dopamine receptors in the corpus striatum rather than by depleting dopamine stores.

The dopaminergic neurons which terminate in the corpus striatum originate in cell bodies in the substantia nigra. It is likely that dopaminergic neurons originating in the area of the substantia nigra but terminating in other brain areas are more important in the expression of schizophrenic processes. Projection sites of such dopamine pathways from the substantia nigra include the olfactory tubercle, the nucleus accumbens, and parts of the frontal, cingulate, and entorhinal cortex—all of which are part of or have been functionally linked to the limbic system. It is reasonable to suspect, therefore, that abnormalities in these dopaminergic pathways would induce emotional abnormalities that neuroleptic drugs, by further changing the pathways' functioning, would alleviate or abolish.

Several lines of evidence support the concept that nuroleptics do in fact act on the dopaminergic system. From a number of animal experiments, the Swedish pharmacologist Arvid Carlsson concluded that the behavioral changes observed with neuroleptics seemed most consistent with a *depletion* of brain dopamine. However, when he measured brain levels of dopamine and its breakdown products, he found them to be increased, suggesting an increased firing rate in dopaminergic pathways. He hypothesized that the neuroleptics must be having their effect by blocking dopamine receptors, with the secondary effort of an increased firing rate due to biochemical feedback. That is, the blocked dopamine receptors in turn stimulate the dopamine-releasing cells to fire more frequently, thereby producing the observed excess of the neurotransmitter. Other studies, involving direct recording from brain areas rich in dopaminergic neurons have conclusively demonstrated that neuroleptics do indeed accelerate the firing of such neurons.

Another line of evidence supporting the notion that neuroleptics reduce schizophrenic symptoms by blocking dopamine receptors involves studies of the effects of drugs which result in increased dopamine levels at receptor sites. The amphetamines exert their clinical actions by increasing the amount of both norepinephrine and dopamine in the synaptic cleft. Interestingly, it has been found that even in very low doses amphetamines can dramatically exacerbate the symptoms of schizophrenic patients. Experiments using different amphetamine analogs, with differential effects on the dopamine and norepinephrine systems, indicate that the exacerbation is more likely mediated through effects on the dopamine, rather than the norepinephrine neurons. L-dopa administration, which would also be expected to increase functional dopamine levels, has also been reported in several clinical studies to exacerbate schizophrenic symptoms.

If amphetamines can exacerbate schizophrenic symptoms by engendering an excess of dopamine, it might also be expected that in sufficiently large doses these agents could induce psychotic symptoms even in individuals without schizophrenic predispositions. Such appears to be the case. Amphetamine addicts—especially the "speed freaks" who often administer to themselves intravenous doses of up to 500 mg, or 50 times the normal therapeutic dose—will almost invariably, at one time or another, develop acute paranoid psychosis that can be clinically indistinguishable from acute paranoid schizophrenia. The use of amphetamine psychosis as a model for schizophrenia has been attacked on the grounds that such illness does not present all the abnormalities of thought and action typical of schizophrenia. In addition, while amphetamine psychosis is invariably paranoid in form, paranoid schizophrenia is only one form of the disease. While not entirely destroying the argument, such objections do indicate the need for more direct evidence concerning the mechanisms underlying the antischizophrenic effects of the neuroleptics.

The most promising of this evidence comes from studies of the binding of neuroleptic drugs to dopamine-binding sites in brain tissue which have been carried out by Creese and colleagues (1976). By isotopically labeling dopamine and its antagonists, and incubating brain tissues with these labeled compounds in the presence and absence of various other compounds, it has been possible to relate the clinical efficacy of antischizophrenic drugs to their ability to inhibit binding to brain dopamine receptors of dopamine itself or of a typical antagonist, the butyrophenone antischizophrenic drug haloperidol (Haldol). These studies have shown that isotopically labeled dopamine and haloperidol both are bound to different brain areas in the same proportion. That is, for both dopamine and haloperidol, the greatest amount of binding is in the caudate nucleus, followed in turn by the globus pallidus, the anterior putamen, and the olfactory tubercle. By destroying presynaptic terminals with 6-hydroxydopamine and finding no reduction in dopamine or haloperidol binding, Creese and co-workers were able to show that the binding in question does not involve presynaptic dopamine receptors.

These studies have further demonstrated that the receptor site appears to exist in two states—one with greater affinity for the agonist dopamine and another with greater affinity for antagonist compounds. Thus dopamine inhibits dopamine binding 30 times more effectively than it does haloperidol binding, while haloperidol inhibits haloperidol binding 300 times more effectively than it does dopamine binding. Creese and his colleagues have ranked a whole series of antischizophrenic drugs on the basis of their ability to inhibit the binding to brain dopamine receptors of dopamine and the representative antagonist haloperidol (see Figure 9-2). They find that the clinical potency of these agents correlates far better (.84) with ability to inhibit haloperidol binding than with their ability to inhibit dopamine binding (.58). These studies provide good evidence that the brain's dopamine pathways are involved in the therapeutic effects of neuroleptics in schizophrenic patients. The findings are also consistent with the dopamine theory of schizophrenia—that the disordered behavior of the schizophrenic patient results from excess functional activation of brain dopamine receptors—but they are by no means conclusive proof of the theory. Creese et al. explain this through the analogy of the electric circuit breaker: the fact that a dangerous short circuit in the kitchen can be abolished by the appropriate circuit breaker in the basement does not mean that the short is in the basement. Similarly, the fact that schizophrenic symptoms can be reduced by "breaking" the dopaminergic circuits in the brain (by administering dopamine antagonists) does not necessarily imply that the symptoms' primary cause is some defect in release or reception of dopamine. The primary neurochemical deficit in schizophrenia could involve systems (e.g., noradrenergic or cholinergic) several steps removed from the dopamine system, but which can be modulated by changes in dopamine transmission.

With the caveat that the dopamine theory of schizophrenia remains subject to the qualifications just outlined, we shall now proceed, for purposes of

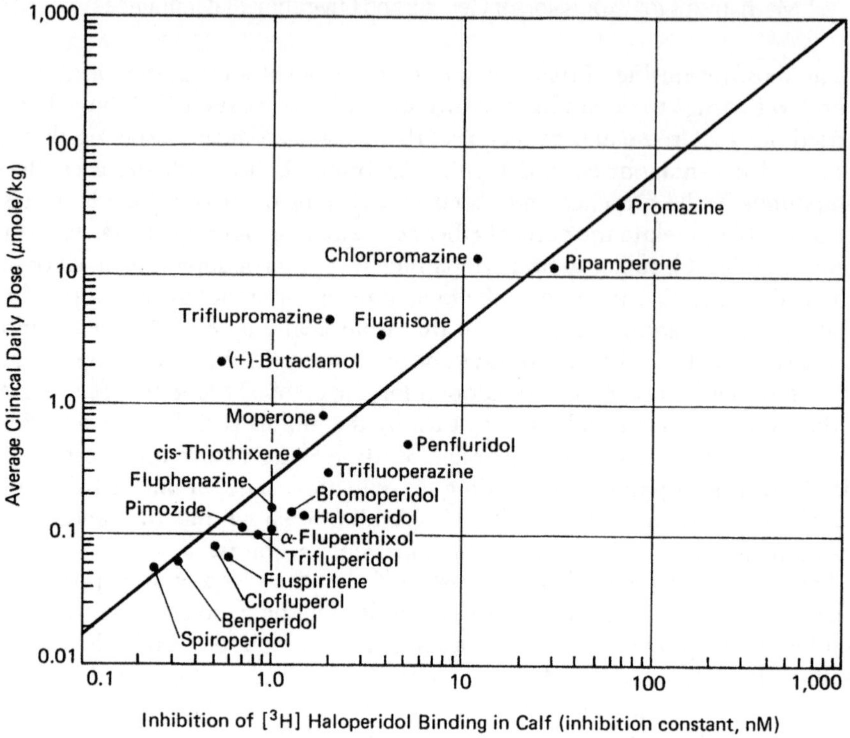

Average Clinical Daily Dose (μmole/kg)
Inhibition of [3H] Haloperidol Binding in Calf (inhibition constant, nM)
Promazine
Chlorpromazine
Pipamperone
Triflupromazine
Fluanisone
(+)-Butaclamol
Moperone
Penfluridol
cis-Thiothixene
Trifluoperazine
Fluphenazine
Bromoperidol
Pimozide
Haloperidol
α-Flupenthixol
Trifluperidol
Fluspirilene
Clofluperol
Benperidol
Spiroperidol

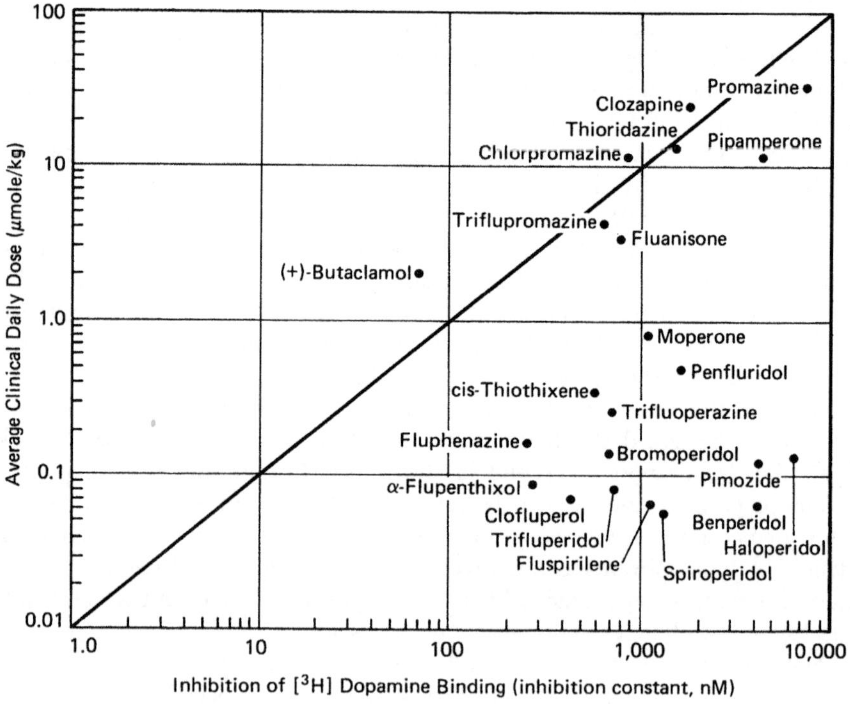

Average Clinical Daily Dose (μmole/kg)
Inhibition of [3H] Dopamine Binding (inhibition constant, nM)
Promazine
Clozapine
Thioridazine
Pipamperone
Chlorpromazine
Triflupromazine
Fluanisone
(+)-Butaclamol
Moperone
Penfluridol
cis-Thiothixene
Trifluoperazine
Fluphenazine
Bromoperidol
Pimozide
α-Flupenthixol
Clofluperol
Trifluperidol
Fluspirilene
Benperidol
Haloperidol
Spiroperidol

continuing the argument, as if it were proved that excess dopamine reaching brain receptors is indeed the primary biochemical abnormality in schizophrenia. Given this assumption, we might now pose the question, "How might genetic and environmental influences act to increase functional levels of dopamine at brain synapses?" To illustrate possible answers to this question, we shall first consider experimental evidence derived from the "biochemical high risk" approach, which recently been developed by Buchsbaum and colleagues, (1978), as an example of how genetically determined biochemical characteristics might influence brain dopamine levels in ways that would predispose to the expression of schizophrenic processes. The potential role of environmental factors to increase brain dopamine levels will be illustrated in terms of the effects of stress upon brain catecholamine metabolism using an animal model.

"Biochemical High Risk" Approach

The traditional "high risk" approach to the study of psychiatric disorders involves initial selection of a pool of apparently healthy individuals who are considered to be at risk of developing a specific disorder—e.g., schizophrenia—on the basis of having a parent or close relative with that disorder. Thus, the basis for selecting the vulnerable individuals is genetic. The vulnerable sample so identified can then be followed with regard to subsequent development of active schizophrenic disease, or with regard to certain biochemical parameters which theory suggests would be altered in persons predisposed to expression of schizophrenic illness. An example of this latter approach has been the demonstration of low levels of monoamine oxidase (MAO) in platelets of patients with chronic schizophrenia and in twins of schizophrenic patients (Wyatt, et al., 1973).

Rather than selecting the at-risk sample on the basis of genetic material in common with a patient with schizophrenia, the biochemical high-risk approach selects individuals as being at risk on the basis of possession of biochemical characteristics which theory suggests will predispose toward psychiatric disorder. Buchsbaum et al.(1978) adopted this approach in a study of 375 normal young adults. First, the sample was assayed for platelet MAO levels, and the top 10% and the bottom 10% were selected for more detailed study. In addition, plasma samples were obtained for assay for

---

Fig. 9-2. Inhibition of haloperidol and dopamine binding to calf brain tissue by various antischizophrenic drugs. It will be noted that clinical potency is much more strongly related to inhibition of binding of the dopamine antagonist haloperidol than it is to inhibition of binding of dopamine itself. (From Creese, Burt, and Synder, 1976)

DBH. Based on the dopamine theory of schizophrenia, it was postulated that subjects with low levels of both MAO and DBH would be a higher risk, since both degradation of dopamine by MAO and conversion to norepinephrine by DBH would be expected to be proceeding at a slower rate, thus resulting in accumulation of excess dopamine in synaptic clefts. An additional assumption, supported by some evidence but by no means conclusively proven, was that peripheral levels of these enzymes are reflective of brain levels. Although platelet MAO and plasma DBH levels are not highly correlated, both are under genetic control and, hence, reflective of hereditary biochemical characteristics which would predispose to high levels of dopamine.

The first finding of interest emerged from interviews of the low and high MAO groups. Compared to high MAO subjects, low MAO subjects reported: (1) a history of more frequent psychiatric or psychological counseling, (2) a higher family history of suicide or suicide attempts, and (3) higher scores on a scale measuring stimulus-seeking. In addition, these subjects were studied in terms of performance on the continuous performance test (CPT), a test requiring subjects to employ selective attention to detect critical signals in a set of ongoing stimuli which are presented at the rate of one per second. That is, subjects were instructed to pay attention to a TV screen on which numbers flashed at the rate of one per second, and to press a button every time a "4" appeared if, and only if, it were preceded by a "6." Subjects with low MAO but with high DBH levels made significantly fewer errors of commission (pressing the button in the absence of a "4" preceded by a "6") than subjects with low MAO and low DBH—the type of error which is also increased in the performance of remitted patients with schizophrenia on the CPT.

Another measure of selective attention employed to evaluate the high and low MAO and DBH groups was the average evoked response (AER). Visual AERs were determined by light stimuli of four increasing intensities under conditions of attention to the lights (to perform a discrimination task) and under conditions of inattention to the lights (to count auditory tones randomly presented with the light flashes). Since attention to the stimuli from which the AER is derived is a major determinant of AER waveform amplitude, those subjects with a large increase in AER amplitude when attending to the lights as compared to when listening to tones would be considered as showing neurophysiologic evidence of better selective attention. In both high and low MAO groups, it was found that subjects with low DBH levels showed a smaller AER amplitude increase with attention to the lights compared to high DBH subjects. This effect was particularly evident for the low intensity light flashes, where attentional effects upon evoked response amplitude are known to be most important.

Thus, poorer attentional performance was found among a group of nonhospitalized, nonpatient young adults with low levels of MAO and DBH. This would indicate that the poorer performance associated with these biologic indicators is not merely an artifact of hospitalization or of illness but is related to influences of these biochemical factors upon psychological variables of possible relevance to schizophrenic processes. One means of conceptualizing the psychological expression involved in these effects was discussed previously in terms of Shakow's "loss of major set" theory of the psychological deficit in schizophrenia. This theory states that individuals with schizophrenia are unable to maintain a major set—i.e., maintain a focus of attention—but rather are continually distracted by minor sets. That is, they tend to "segmentalize" sets, and they are distracted by irrelevant stimuli to the extent that the irrelevant stimuli become the major set or focus of attention. Thus, it would not be surprising that patients with schizophrenia show poor performance on the CPT, which requires prolonged maintenance of a constant focus of attention. It is extremely interesting, therefore, that nonpatients with biochemical indicators predictive of high dopamine levels also show poorer performance on the CPT. The smaller increases in AER amplitude among low DBH as compared to high DBH subjects is also indicative of impaired ability to focus selective attention on one aspect (set) of the stimulus field—a "deficit" which has also been observed in schizophrenic patients. The reader may question the clinical relevance for schizophrenia of commission errors on the CPT or of smaller AER attentional effects, among healthy young adults. If such is the case, the reader is advised to refer back to Cromwell's statement, which was quoted at the conclusion of the section Basic Psychological Defects, to the effect that "what is clinically relevant may not be etiologically relevant."

Environmental Stress and Brain Catecholamine Metabolism

In the preceding section, it was shown that genetically determined variations in levels of enzymes involved in catabolism and anabolism of dopamine are associated in nonpatients with alterations in psychologic functioning which resemble those observed among schizophrenic patients. In this section, we shall consider the role of environmental factors, acting independently of genetic influences, in the control of brain catecholamine metabolism and, hence, of behavior.

To illustrate such a role, a specific experiment (Lamprecht et al. 1972) using a standard "stress paradigm," immobilization stress in the laboratory rat, will be described. In the first part of this experiment, one group of male Sprague-Dawley rats was subjected to immobilization stress for 2 h daily over a four-week period. A second group was not stressed and served as controls. At the end of the four week period of daily immobilization stress, the stressed rats were found in comparison to controls to have increased blood pressure, increased plasma DBH, and increased aggressive behavior as indexed by percentage of attacks in the shock-induced fighting paradigm. Both groups were sacrificed at this point, and the stressed group was found to have increased levels of tyrosine hydroxylase (TH) in the hypothalamus but not in the remainder of the brain stem or the cerebral cortex. Since hypothalamic norepinephrine levels were not decreased in stressed as compared to control rats, the increased TH levels among stressed rats appear to be indicative of increased catecholamine synthesis and release as a result of the stress.

In the second part of this study, two more groups of rats were subjected to four weeks of daily stress periods or served as nonstressed controls, just as in the first part described above. Instead of being tested as above directly at the end of the four-week stress period, both groups in this second part were allowed to remain in their cages receiving normal care without testing or stress of any sort for an additional four weeks. At the end of this four-week "recovery period," the animals were tested and sacrificed. First of all, the peripheral manifestations of increased sympathetic nerve activity—the increased DBH and blood pressure—were no longer evident in comparing those rats which had been stressed four weeks previously to the nonstressed controls. The behavior of the formerly stressed rats remained altered in that they still showed significantly more attacks in the shock-induced fighting paradigm in comparison to nonstressed controls. Of greatest interest for the present discussion, the formerly stressed animals also continued to show significantly higher hypothalamic TH levels than did the controls.

Although hypothalamic dopamine levels were not measured in this study, it is likely that with the increased levels of TH, which catalyzes the rate-limiting step in catecholamine biosynthesis, there was increased synthesis and release of dopamine as well as norepinephrine. Furthermore, the hypothalamus forms a major component of the brain system concerned with regulation and expression of emotion, the limbic system. The persistence, long after cessation of stress, of stress-induced alterations in hypothalamic catecholamine synthesis and release, along with the possibly related persistent behavioral alterations, suggests a mechanism whereby environmental influences could act to increase brain dopamine levels and, hence, predispose to expression of schizophrenic processes. Presumably, such influences would be more pronounced among individuals who also have genetically determined low levels of those enzymes which would enhance the removal or conversion of the increased dopamine resulting from such stress-induced increases in TH activity.

Summary

In the preceding sections, we have reviewed evidence that a basic mechanism underlying the behavioral expression of schizophrenic processes involves a functional excess of the neurotransmitter dopamine at certain sites in the brain. In addition, we have cited evidence that both genetic and environmental factors which can act to engender such dopamine excess are associated with behavioral characteristics which are at least relevant to schizophrenic behavioral characteristics. It is impossible to say at present whether what remains to be known for the full understanding of the neurobiological basis of such "biobehavioral dispositions" as that involved in schizophrenia will constitute a radical departure from the evidence and conclusions presented in this chapter. The evidence presented does, however, serve to make the point which is illustrated in Figure 9-1; it is highly likely that the final answer to the puzzle of schizophrenia will not be found in genetic *or* environmental influences, but in their *interaction* to influence some crucial aspect of brain functioning.

Disordered Behavior as a Social Construction

Medicine, which might theoretically have given equal attention to health and illness, has, for a variety of reasons, tended to concentrate on illness. So far our consideration of the socialization process has focused on the high probability of order rather than disorder in behavior—not out of lack of recognition or appreciation of behavioral disorder, but in order to make several important points. Pathology in general and specific forms of pathology in particular are, in a statistical sense, relatively rare events. Moreover, the social context in which behavior is learned has a main effect, that is, accounts for a significant part of the variance in most of the behavior which we have any interest in explaining. Finally, the awareness that behavior is best explained by multiple variables which potentially have causal significance leads naturally to including biological variables as potential contributors to behavior, even when we do not know exactly which biological parameters to measure or how to measure them. Current behavioral research is quite open to the inclusion of both biological and social factors.

Research on disordered behavior, insofar as such behavior is traceable to socialization processes, does not require consideration of a distinctly different set of variables. The variables that account for ordered behavior presumably, in different combinations and magnitude, account for disordered behavior. It follows from the previous discussion of socialization process that no single, simple formula exists for predicting disordered behavior. One can imagine the exposure of children to extreme conditions of socialization in any specific behavior system which would have a high probability of deleterious behavioral outcome—for example, conditions which approximate Lefcourt's description of helpless animals in the face of sustained punishment. If one were going to advance a single social variable most likely to produce behavioral disorder it would be "the response quality of the (parental) environment" in which rejecting, punishing behavior directed by adults to children is sustained. Such theorizing has been common in accounting for

Table 9-1. Frequency of Symptoms in a Pooled Sample of Schizophrenic Patients Examined in Nine International Centers[a]

Common: Frequency > 30%	Uncommon: Frequency > 4% < 10%	Rare: Frequency < 4%
Loss of interest	Hostile, negativistic	Absence of voluntary movement
Less energy	Outburst of anger in interview	Waxy flexibility
Difficulty in concentration	Fails to respond verbally	Imitation of examiner's movements
Continuous worrying	Ecstatic mood	Automatic obedience
Trouble sleeping	Ambivalence	Lips moving soundlessly
Wants to stay away from people	Suggestibility	Talks to self incoherently
Depressed	Visual hallucinations	Echolalia
Cries	Nihilistic delusions	Neologisms
Variable mood	Confused in interview	Verbigeration
Anxiety	Difficult life situation	
Flattened affect		
Auditory hallucinations		
Delusional		
Behavior abnormalities		

[a]Adapted form World Health Organization. Report of the Internation Pilot Study of Schizophrenia. Table 8.1 Geneva: Word Health Organization, 1973.

schizophrenic processes, but as the discussion has indicated, we are quite a distance from establishing with evidence the relative importance of biological and social factors in the development of schizophrenic processes.

For the scientific observer interested in schizophrenic processes there is at least one insight from comparative study of schizophrenia in various societies worth noting. While there do appear to be some core characteristics of schizophrenic processes which are found across societies, a number of characteristics tend to be relatively culture-specific. A summary of the evidence is found in Tables 9-1 and 9-2. This evidence is a specific reminder of an important general principle. Complex processes of illness typically have specific behavioral manifestations which complicate the identification of the central pathological process of interest. Reality is a social construction and, to some degree, individuals learn and share ways of disordered behavior just as they learn ways of ordered behavior.

References

Bleuler, E. Dementia Praecox oder die Gruppe der Schizophrenien. Leipzig: Deuticke, 1911. [Transl. J. Zinkin. Dementia Praecox or the Group of Schizophrenias. New York, New York: International Universities Press, 1950.]

Table 9-2. Reliability Units of Schizophrenic Symptoms Analysis Across Nine International Centers[a]

Units of Analysis		
>0.93 (high)	0.62–0.60 (medium)	0.59–0.47 (low)
Sucidal	Change of interest	Stereotyped behavior
Elated thoughts	Dissociation of speech	Increased libido
Ideas of reference	Perplexity	Negativism
Delusions of grandeur	Lability	Perseveration
Thought-hearing		Body hallucinations
Derealization		Morose mood
Lack of concentration		
Hopelessness		
Delusions of persecution		
Delusions of reference		

[a]Adapted from World Health Organization. Report of the International Pilot Study of Schizophrenia. Table 8.3. Geneva: World Health Organization, 1973.

Buchsbaum, M.S., D.L. Murphy, R.D. Coursey, et al. Platelet monoamine oxidase, plasma dopamine-beta-hydroxylase and attention in a "biochemical high risk" sample. J. Psychiatric Research 14:215–224, 1978.

Chapman, L.J., and J.P. Chapman. Disordered Thought in Schizophrenia. Englewood Cliffs, New Jersey: Prentice-Hall, 1973.

Creese, I., D.R. Burt, and S.H. Snyder. Dopamine receptor binding predicts clinical and pharmacological potencies of antischizophrenic drugs. Science 192:481, 1976.

Corbett, L. Perceptual dyscontrol: A possible organizing principle for schizophrenia research. Schizophrenia Bull. 2:249–265, 1976.

Cromwell, R.L. Assessment of schizophrenia. Ann. Rev. Psychol. 26:593–619, 1975.

Diagnostic and Statistical Manual of Mental Disorders, 3rd ed. Washington, D.C.: The American Psychiatric Association, 1980.

Lamprecht, R.B., Eichelman, and N.B. Thoa, et al. Rat fighting behavior: Serum dopamine-beta-hydroxylase and hypothalmic tyrosine hydroxylase. Science 1977:1214, 1972.

Matthysse, S.W., and K.K. Kidd. Estimating the genetic contributions to schizophrenia. Am. L. Psychiat. 133:185–191, 1976.

Neale, J.M., and R.L. Cromwell. Attention and Schizophrenia. In B.A. Maher (Ed.) Progress in Experimental Personality Research, vol. 5, New York, New York: Academic Press, 1970, pp. 37–66.

Nuechterlein, K.H. Reaction time and attention in schizophrenia: A critical evaluation of the data and theories. Schizophrenia Bull. 3:373–428, 1977.

Oppenheimer, H. Clinical Psychiatry: Issues and Challenges. New York, New York: Harper and Row, 1971.

Pincus, J.H., and G.J. Tucker. Behavioral Neurology, 2nd ed. New York, New York: Oxford University Press, 1978.

Wyatt, R.J., D.L. Murphy, R. Belmaker, et al. Reduced monoamine oxidase activity in platelets: A possible genetic marker for vulnerability to schizophrenia. Science 173:916, 1973.

Wynn, L.C., R.L. Cromwell, and S. Matthysse (Eds.), The Nature of Schizophrenia: New Approaches to Research and Treatment. New York, New York: Wiley, 1978.

Zubin, J. Problem of attention in schizophrenia. In M.L. Kietzman, A. Sutton, and J. Zubin (Eds.) Experimental Approaches to Psychopathology. New York, New York: Academic Press, 1975, pp. 139–166.

Unit III
Affect and Mood

As we consider each additional area in our hierarchical schema of behavior functions, the artificiality of an approach which divides behavior into separate functions becomes increasingly apparent. At the same time, we have no choice but to break down the whole into manageable components. A radical holism simply boggles the mind, preventing not only controlled experimentation but ordinary observation and conceptualization as well. One cannot simultaneously observe or theorize about all aspects of so complex a phenomenon as the behaving human organism. We propose to discuss, in this Unit, the affects. However, we shall try to remember that emotion cannot be understood except in association with thought and memory processes, sensorial contact with the environment, learning, innate capacities and limitations, and patterns of interpersonal living and social integration. We have titled Unit III Affect and Mood. Affect, or emotion, is the more general term; mood, as we shall see, is perhaps best viewed as a special case or extension of the affective response state.

10

Definitions and Conceptual Orientations

This chapter attempts to develop a functional definition of the emotional aspects of behavior, of emotion as subjective and bodily response to those features of the environment (external and internal) experienced by the organism as significant, and of emotion as motivation or pressure to act upon the environment to change or maintain it. Learning in certain of its basic forms (association, learning, conditioning) is intimately connected with emotional (motivational) processes. As we shall see, those types of learning deriving from Pavlov's original experiments (classical conditioning) are involved in the process whereby circumstances and events come to have emotional significance (the learning of motives). Similarly, the learning of effective ways of meeting needs (satisfying motivations or drives) is an essential feature of the other major type of basic learning (operant or instrumental conditioning, reward learning). For this reason, we will deal with these more "simple" varieties of learning here rather than in a separate presentation.

As an aid to describing the place of emotion in the functioning organism, we shall consider in this chapter three major aspects: (1) the *perceptual-cognitive* or *appraisal* aspect in which stimuli are received and evaluated for their significance to the well-being of the organism. This appraisal becomes in turn, the major stimulus for (2) the *motivational-effector* or *drive-discharge* aspect involving a pressure for certain activities at both metabolic-visceral and somatomotor levels (the former providing the energy supplies and other enabling background for the latter) and the actual performance or "discharge" of those behaviors, as a result of which (3) an *interpersonal-*

communicational or *transactional* aspect may be described involving the impact of those behaviors on the organism's interactions with the outside world, particularly other organisms which inhabit it.

Although we speak of the emotions as reactions, it is clear that we are really speaking of a continuously changing affective response state in which new stimuli are constantly received and interpreted, and the emotions adjusted in both intensity and quality. Some of these stimuli are fortuitous but others are the result, in large measure, of recent behaviors of the subject, so-called feedback effects. Stimuli are never simple, single events such as one might attempt to structure in the psychological laboratory, and responses never occur in isolation either. We attempt to point out the patterned nature of stimuli and responses by always using the plural form. Finally, it may be noted that the list does not include important aspects of affect for the conscious, subjective experience of the emotions. This is not an attempt to deny this phenomenon as an aspect of the affective life. The experience and report of feelings is well known to all, and in some theories is considered to be emotion.

In clinical work, the patient's report of emotional responses and mood states is of great importance. But it is also true that the entire sequence of emotional life may take place without conscious awareness, on the subject's part, of the emotions involved. This may be the result of those feelings being very mild and/or very transient, but it may also be the result of a defensive effort to avoid awareness. In Freudian terms this constitutes an important use of the defense mechanism of repression, a maneuver of self-deception which the person himself typically does not recognize. We shall have much more to say about defenses in Unit IV, when neurosis is the focus of our attention. Repression of the emotions is introduced here to make the point that subjective awareness is not an essential element in the sequence of emotionally involved behavior, and to alert the reader to the need for observing autonomic and somatomotor behavior when assessing affective state, as well as noting the subject's verbal report of how he or she feels.

Perceptual-Cognitive or Appraisal Aspects

There are some stimulus patterns that innately possess emotional significance. To list a few of the more obvious: pain, hunger, and other related discomforts give rise to states of fear and anger; ingestion of certain foods and fluids evoke pleasure or satisfaction, as do certain warm, gentle tactile sensations, certain soothing sounds and, perhaps, certain visual cues such as the human face. These innately significant stimuli may originate from events external to the organism or from bodily processes. To say that stimuli have emotional meaning is to say that they possess some power to move us into some motion of our own, some power to affect us so that we feel in turn impelled to do.[1] Thus circumstances to which we respond with emotion are those experienced (not necessarily consciously) as of some significance to our well-being. Stimuli of primary (innate) emotional significance presumably have acquired that position through evolutionary mechanisms in which their presence conferred some survival advantage upon individuals and species (Hamburg, 1963). For example, in most situations the organism phylogenetically "wired" to respond with internal activities pressing for and enabling active escape from or aggressive removal of a pain-producing circumstance will have some survival advantage over one that remains "unmoved" while bodily tissues are being painfully destroyed or distorted. The argument can be extended to the other innately significant stimuli, those such as food, physical discomfort, pleasant companions, and sexual partners that evoke affects leading to positive (approach, maintain) behaviors as well as to negative (avoidance) patterns.

The innately significant stimuli that have been mentioned above do not, certainly, represent a complete list of circumstances to which the human organism has been phylogenetically programmed to respond with emotion. We probably do not have a complete list. Some stimuli which were until recently considered biologically neutral, acquiring significance only through association with those more primary (see Classical Conditioning, below), are now recognized as themselves biologically primary. An example is the infant's positive attraction to the human face, formerly thought to become significant only by virtue of association with the feeding activity of the mothering person. Even if additional stimuli of innate affective significance are revealed, (as part of the current return to an interactive balance in the nativism-environmentalism controversy, see Unit IV), it is inconceivable that evolutionary programming alone could provide response habits of sufficient complexity *and* specificity to provide for the motivational needs of members of a species adapting to widely varying, changing environments. Clearly the individual organism needs to add some tendencies of its own to those provided by membership in a species, and to develop a sense of meaning appropriate to the particular world in which it is to survive (or not survive). A major task of early development, for all but the simplest organisms living in the most uniform environment, is to become able to appraise a wide variety of situations in terms of their potential benefit or danger. This fact will perhaps be better appreciated if we note that the facet of emotional behavior we have called perceptual-cognitive has also been termed the "signal scanning" aspects of emotion (Engel, 1962, 1963), calling our attention to the living organism's constant searching of the environment for evidence (signals) of opportunity and danger.

[1] For the etymology buff: "emotion" derives from the Latin *emovere*, to move out or, in the passive voice, to be moved out; "affect" is derived from *afficere* (*ad* + *facere*), to do to or be done to, to impress, to affect.

The simplest model of a process by which initially neutral stimuli acquire emotional meaning for the individual is found in the process known as classical or Pavlovian conditioning. The basic laboratory paradigm does not constitute the entire story of how the individual human being develops a sense of which aspects of his world are significant and what that significance is, but classical or associational conditioning does provide a picture of what the core of that acquisition process is (and the essence of what is required to modify appraisal patterns when they are producing needless distress to the individual). A clear understanding of this learning process is absolutely essential to the clinical student.

Classical Conditioning

In Pavlov's original experiment, a dog which naturally salivated (unconditioned response, UCR) when food powder was placed in the mouth (unconditioned stimulus, UCS) was trained to salivate (conditioned response, CR) to the sound of a clicker (conditioned stimulus, CS), a previously neutral stimulus that before the training elicited no more than a mild alerting and exploratory turning of the head. The necessary condition for such training was the repeated pairing of the CS with the UCS, that is, the click was sounded just before the presentation of the food (see Figure 10-1). In simple physiological terms, an autonomic reflex has been expanded to include new stimuli. However, from the standpoint of psychological importance, one must recognize that salivation is one preparatory or enabling element in a larger motivational pattern involving other glandular, visceral, CNS-activating, and somatomotor activities such as approaching, chewing, etc. necessary to the consummatory behavior of feeding—a pattern closely related to, if not identical with, the "emotion" of hunger. Traditional descriptions of classical conditioning emphasize a single visceral response or, at most, the autonomic pattern. Somatomotor outflow is largely ignored—the dog is typically immobilized in a harness. The present point is that response in classical conditioning, while regularly including a prominent ANS-mediated visceral or metabolic component, also typically involves an expectancy of significant events to follow—in consequence, a pressure to

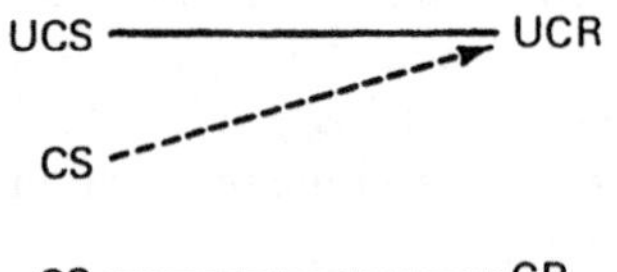

Fig. 10-1. Classical conditioning. Pairing of the conditioned stimulus with the unconditioned stimulus results, after some trials, in the evocation by the conditioned stimulus alone of essentially the same response, now called the conditioned response (see text).

move, a motivation to approach or avoid the active stimuli. This fact suggests that the acquisition of emotional significance may be the important function of this type of learning.

Another example of the importance of classical conditioning in affect—an example of major importance in psychopathology—is the pairing of pain such as an electric shock to the paws (UCS) with a tone or a visually distinctive chamber (CS), so that the tone or experimental chamber comes in itself to elicit tachycardia, pupillary dilatation, hyperventilation, lowered skin resistance, and other autonomic signs associated with avoidance. Following our same line of reasoning, we shall assume that the previously neutral stimulus now also elicits the powerful emotion of fear. In this circumstance, fear is said to be "reinforced" by the occurrence of the shock.

Reinforcement, in the classical conditioning model, consists of the pairing in time of the already effective UCS and the to-be-learned CS. The term *reinforcement by contiguity*, referring to close temporal juxtaposition, is often used to describe the required conditions for this type of learning.

Presentations of the CS in the absence of the reinforcer (UCS) will result in the gradual diminution of the probability of occurrence of the learned response (CR). That is, the *habit strength* of the learned S-R connection will be reduced, a process known as *extinction*.

Subjects respond with the learned response not only to the exact stimulus employed in the training but also to similar stimuli—e.g., tones of similar frequency, chambers of similar appearance—although the likelihood of the response is not quite so strong as with the original stimulus. This spread of stimulus effectiveness is known as *stimulus generalization*. Its value in the natural situation is apparent if one considers that no real life stimulus situation is ever exactly repeated, and that circumstances of similar appearance often do have similar significance for the organism. It is probably adaptive for an individual who has been painfully bitten by a large brown dog to have some degree of fear not only of that particular dog but of other dogs of similar size and color and even of other similar quadripeds. It would clearly be most often maladaptive to be equally fearful of all such creatures or of all objects, living and inanimate, of similar appearance in size or color. Generalization must therefore be balanced by *discrimination*. As the subject has further experiences, and reinforcement does not take place (all animals and even all dogs do not bite), those responses made to overgeneralized stimuli will, hopefully, be corrected by extinction, and the balance between generalization and discrimination necessary for satisfying interaction with the real world established.

Returning to consideration of the perceptual-cognitive or appraisal aspect of emotional behavior, we shall discuss further the proposition that classical conditioning may represent an essential, basic thread of the appraisal process. This process we view as the method by which the innate emotional reflexes of the individual are extended to include attitudes and expectancies which permit useful assessment of new and complex stimulus situations not "anticipated" in the evolution of the species. Consideration of the perceptual-cognitive (appraisal) aspects of emotional functioning in light of the model of classical conditioning (Figure 10.1) reveals some similarities and one important difference. The stimuli of innate emotional significance obviously correspond to the primary UCS of the classical conditioning paradigm. The emotional responses proper which they directly and reflexly evoke, correspond to the UCR, particularly if the visceral and metabolic responses associated with them are included. The initially neutral stimuli correspond to the CS, and a portion of their effect—once associations have been learned—follows the same automatic, reflexive route to the evocation of an inner motivational state. However, it is apparent, both intuitively and experimentally, that direct reflex-like processes from peripheral stimuli to motive state and motor discharge are not sufficient to conceptualize the appraisal process in higher forms and especially in man. There are intervening steps of great complexity, involving verbal responses (overt or silent) and related abstract thought, memory, foresight, and related cognitive activities. To take a simple example, it is not necessary to have actually experienced a dog bite to appraise dogs as dangerous. For most purposes, therefore, it is useful to describe the internal events involved in appraisal in more molar terms than that provided by the language of conditioning: thoughts, biases, memories, schemata, values, or "stimulus-outcome expectancies" (Mischel, 1973), to name a few examples.

Thus, whether in the form of a simple reflex or a complex internal network of mediating processes, we view appraisal of the meaning of the situation as the essential first step in the process of emotion in behavior.

Motivational-Effector or Drive-Discharge Aspects

So closely related are the concepts of "emotion" and "motivation" that some systems of psychological theory omit the former altogether while others treat emotion as one aspect, usually the subjective experience, of the larger topic of motivation (Young, 1973, p. 766).

Basic to the idea of affect as motivator is the concept of organisms phylogenetically programmed to survive by moving toward or maintaining closeness with stimuli experienced as beneficial, while moving away from or otherwise eliminating in effect those appraised to be dangerous. Thus the affects are most often initially classified as positive or negative, pleasant or unpleasant. In primitive biological forms we speak of tropisms, simple movements of the entire creature toward or away from particular stimuli. In higher forms, stereotyped metabolic, visceral, CNS-activated, and somatomotor patterns become elaborated around basic tropisms and are reflexly set into motion by appropriate stimulus conditions. These are the "instincts" or "fixed action patterns" of the ethologist. The development of animal forms, in which learning through individual experience has come to occupy a more prominent place in determining behavior, has reduced somewhat the fixed, stereotyped quality of these patterns. The somatomotor aspects, in particular, have become potentially much more flexible. However, for each motivational-emotional pattern there remains a core of basic behavioral direction (to fear is to avoid, to hunger for is to consume) and a closely related cluster of metabolic, visceral, and CNS responses necessary for the performance of that behavior. To be able to flee, for example, requires mobilization of energy resources, rechanneling of vascular supplies to the skeletal muscles, and a state of CNS arousal compatible with accurate sensory intake and rapid effector transmissions. This class of background of internal motor and CNS processes necessary for each emotional discharge we have termed the *enabling component.*

In its peripheral portions, study of the enabling component constitutes the field of psychophysiology. Psychophysiological and CNS aspects of the various emotional states will be discussed in Chapter 14. We shall return shortly in this chapter to some further comments about these enabling processes, but before doing so we must consider those motoric or discharge actions directed toward the sources of satisfaction or threat in the outer world. Within the limits set by the particular emotion-motivation involved, there is considerable flexibility in higher animals regarding the particular behavior selected to satisfy the need (motive). We say that the individual learns the most effective techniques by a process of trial-and-error learning—another term for instrumental conditioning.

Instrumental Conditioning

In an experiment typical of *instrumental* or *operant conditioning*, a hungry pigeon or cat is allowed free activity in a box constructed so that depressing a lever or turning a wheel releases into the box a measured amount of food. The subject, after a certain amount of random activity, makes the appropriate response, receives and eats the food. After a number of such experiences, the lever is pressed much more promptly and consistently when the subject is placed in the box (see Figure 10-2). We have just described instrumental learning of the *reward* type. In *escape* learning, the subject learns a response which is instrumental in getting it out of a painful or otherwise uncomfortable situation, for example, running to a marked corner of the box turns off the electrified floor. *Avoidance conditioning* is similar except that the discomfort may be avoided by responding to a warning signal with the proper response—the shock never occurs if the proper corner is selected when a warning buzzer sounds. Behaviors that are followed by a painful stimulus are, of course, avoided, or if already learned, suppressed by such punishment.

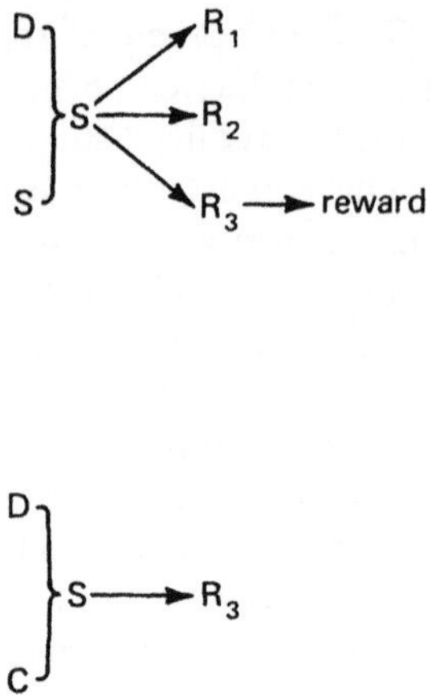

Fig. 10-2. Instrument conditioning. In a stimulus situation consisting of drives (D) and other stimuli or cues (C), the rewarded response will tend to be the one elicited by the same stimulus conditions on future trials (see text).

In instrumental conditioning, a new response becomes associated with a stimulus pattern, a response of which the subject is physically capable, of course, but one previously not high in the hierarchy of responses to that situation. Reinforcement in instrumental conditioning depends upon the performance of the "correct" response and consists of provision by the environment of some satisfying stimulation or the removal or avoidance of pain and discomfort. Reinforcement that promptly follows the "correct" response is more effective in strengthening the habit than delayed reinforcement. This principle, called the temporal *gradient of reinforcement*, has been invoked to explain, in part, the persistence of maladaptive behavior patterns in which the rewards are immediate (often in the form of relief of anxiety), while the "punishments" are frequently long-delayed and therefore ineffective in suppressing the behavior despite its net long-term negative consequences.

Another issue of some importance in instrumental conditioning is the *reinforcement schedule*, that is, the contingency relationship between the instrumental response and reinforcement. In a schedule of *continuous reinforcement*, every performance of the "correct" response is followed by reward (positive reinforcement) or the removal or avoidance of unpleasant stimuli (negative reinforcement).[2] Such a consistent schedule produces very rapid learning that is highly specific for the particular response. When the regularity of reinforce-

[2]Note that "negative reinforcement" is not the same as "punishment." Negative reinforcement produces new behaviors by the removal of unpleasant stimuli. Punishment reduces the emission of a particular behavior by introducing unpleasant stimuli. There is some disagreement about whether this reduction, which is not extinction but suppression of the punished response, is ever permanent or merely a temporary blocking. This issue, of course, has considerable importance for the use of punishment techniques in so-called aversion therapy (Rachman and Teasdale, 1969, p. 118ff) and, for that matter, in the socialization of children.

ment is varied, the schedule is one of *intermittent* or *partial reinforcement*. The important general fact to note is that habits based upon intermittent reinforcement are more stable, that is, more resistant to extinction when reinforcement is absent than those learned exclusively through continuous reinforcement.

Our model, in which the appraisal aspect of emotional behavior is extended by processes of which classical conditioning is the prototype and the motivational-effector aspect by learning basically instrumental in nature, corresponds to a theory of personality and psychopathology called the *two-factor learning theory* and is closely associated with the name of O.H. Mowrer (1947, 1950, pp. 275–317). This theoretical position, widely used in the planning and explanation of clinical techniques of *behavior therapy*, holds that classical conditioning is the essential process by which emotional-motivational meanings become attached to the many varied situations in which a complex organism finds itself, and the method by which problems are identified, and needs activated. Instrumental conditioning, the theory asserts, is a second factor—the one by which specific solutions to problems, methods for the reduction of drives, are acquired in the course of life experience.

It follows from such a theory that classical and instrumental conditioning typically occur together in any real situation. It is a mistake to try to characterize a situation as one of classical *or* instrumental conditioning. Even in the laboratory, in the instrumental conditioning situation there is inevitably an element of classical conditioning: the circumstances associated with reward or punishment themselves come to have emotional meaning, the box comes to be valued or feared. In the natural state (when the subject is not restricted by a harness), instrumental motor behavior accompanies classical conditioning: the animal searches for additional food, and his subsequent habits are affected by the outcome of that search.

In considering the learning of instrumental responses, it may appear as if any behavior physically within the subject's capability had an equal chance of being learned, given a particular situation of need and opportunity and the appropriate schedule of reinforcement. This has been the tacit assumption of many students of learning. It now appears from experimental evidence that there are phylogenetically determined innate limits upon what behaviors can be learned in response to particular motive states, or at least upon the relative ease or difficulty of that learning. For example, it is easy to train a pigeon to peck a lever to obtain the release of food pellets—pecking is part of the natural motor repertoire of food seeking and eating in the pigeon. It is very difficult to train a pigeon to peck in order to escape an unpleasant air blast, but quite easy to train it to fly to a shelf in the cage as the method of avoidance. Flying is clearly a part of the bird's natural repertoire for escaping danger. Seligman and Hager (1972a,b) speak of the "biological boundaries of learning" and of *preparedness*, a dimension along which behaviors may be measured with respect to their ease of learning as responses to particular motives. If behavior patterns can be ranked on such a dimension, and it appears that they can, the sharp dichotomy between instinctual and learned behaviors is seen to be a myth.

Seligman and others have also shown that the concept of preparedness applies to the classical conditioning situation as well. Some fears appear almost innate: it is possible to develop intense fears of other mammals and reptiles as a result of the briefest experience with only modest unconditioned reinforcement. Contrariwise, it is virtually impossible to condition fear to trees. The evolutionary value of such preparedness (and contrapreparedness) is obvious: a creature that fails to learn avoidance after one close brush with a predator may not get a second chance; a tree-dwelling primate who becomes phobic for trees after a single fall, on the other hand, has lost a basic facet of its adaptational capacity.

In some contrast to the almost total flexibility of learning potential assumed for the instrumental conditioning of somatomotor responses, it was for many years assumed that the autonomic and related internal behaviors (those we have described as the background enabling processes for somatomotor discharge) were fixed patterns quite impervious to instrumental conditioning. Once set in motion as part of the affective expression, they were thought to be beyond the influence of reward and punishment. The 1967 demonstration by Miller and DiCara (see Miller, 1975) of the possibility of modifying heart rate by instrumental techniques was followed by a series of studies with similar results with respect to blood pressure, skin resistance, EEG patterns, and other internal functions previously thought to be entirely automatic or "involuntary." This possibility of instrumental control, together with the development of techniques for sensitive, continuous monitoring of these parameters (biofeedback), while sometimes overblown and exaggerated, has added a major new dimension to the treatment of psychophysiologic (psychosomatic) and related disorders.

In the motivational-effector as in the appraisal aspect of emotional behavior, it must be emphasized that many complex mediating responses may be made internally before the actual motor act is performed. These symbolic processes may be considered vicarious performances of the behavior in which alternates and possible consequences are considered. Terms such as plans, strategies, cognitive maps, or "response-outcome expectancies" (Mischel, 1973) are often used to refer to these mental activities. Again we see that adoption of an instrumental learning model as a base concept for problem solving does not prevent the complementary use of more molar terms in the description of the process.

Interpersonal-Communicational or Transactional Aspects

The ultimate purpose of appraising one's situation for its affective significance and generating motives with their enabling and instrumental motor discharges is to permit interaction with the environment that is need-satisfying, safe, and reasonably "cost-effective." While some person-environment transactions involve the physical world and living organisms of other species, by far the most complex, troublesome, and therefore most interesting to the clinician are those involving other people. Patterns of interpersonal adaptation and maladaptation are so intimately tied up with personality and the neurotic disorders of personality that our entire Unit IV is devoted to their presentation, a presentation which will draw extensively upon the description of emotional-motivational behavior processes described in this section. We shall there offer a system for the classification of interpersonal behavior, and discuss the early life sources of interpersonal traits. For the present, we shall simply call attention to the existence of a transactional aspect of emotional behavior, noting as before that without such an aspect the intrapersonal (intrapsychic) aspects thus far emphasized become meaningless.

There is, however, one element in the communication of emotions that relates more directly to the present chapter than to later topics. The more reflexive, stereotyped kernels of somatomotor discharge related to the various emotions, the "fixed motor patterns," include elements that may well have survived in evolution more because of their communicational than because of their direct physical impact upon the environment. The mating displays and rituals of many birds and mammals are an obvious example. The threat conveyed by the posture and vocalizations of an angry cat may avert actual physical encounter by intimidating the adversary, and a similar effect may result from the reassuring effect of an animal assuming a submissive or retreating stance. In primate forms, and particularly man, the vehicle for these messages is shifted largely to the facial musculature (Izard 1971, 1977), but the messages have a similar capacity for near-universal understanding. The basic patterns of facial expression may be extensively modified by learned patterns deriving from family or cultural models, but the innate core is revealed in the widespread recognition accorded laughter, crying, and the facies of depression. Laughter and smiling, as well as crying, play an essential role in the communication between infant and mother, a relationship of critical importance for survival and healthy development.

Mood

Nowlis (1977) offers the following useful discussion of the definition of "mood" as contrasted with that of "emotion:"

> The most frequent distinction is that moods are longer and less intense than emotions. A related and less common distinction is that mood is background for emotion, both as predisposing antecedent and as lingering consequent of an emotional occurrence. A related difference in connotation is that mood more frequently implies that the antecedent or cause of the temporary disposition is unknown, vague, and remote. These characteristics of

> longer duration, low or moderate intensity, and vague cause are often implied when the term mood rather than emotion or emotional state is used .... Mood categories are more diverse than recognized in that special medical tradition which classifies all moods within one bipolar dimension: namely, elationdepression. They are, indeed, similar in range, diversity, and content to those of emotion. (pp. 263–264)

Clinical experience suggests one further aspect which may be useful in formulating the concept of mood, an aspect implied but not made explicit in definitions such as the one just quoted. Mood may usefully refer to that extension of emotion that is no longer maximally reactive to variations in incoming stimulation, a tendency to establish a new baseline or background or level of emotional "tonus" and to maintain it despite changes in the actual situation. As a result, of course, the level of individual emotional responses and of the entire behavior of the organism are affected. It is this tendency to become *autonomous* that, for certain mood dimensions such as depression, renders them singularly capable of disrupting and even overwhelming the total behavioral and biological functioning of the person, and therefore warrants the separate and extensive treatment of the subject in Chapter 13 and 14. To set the stage, we will first give some attention to the developmental aspects of the affect system and then to epidemiologic considerations regarding variations in a sense of "well-being" versus mental depression.

References

Engel, G.L. Anxiety and depression-withdrawal: The primary affects of unpleasure. International J. Psychoanalysis 43:89–97, March-June 1962.

Engel, G.L. Toward a classification of affects. In P.H. Knapp (Ed.) Expression of the Emotions in Man. New York, New York: International Universities Press, 1963, pp. 266–299.

Hamburg, D. Emotions in the perspective of human evolution. In P.H. Knapp (Ed.) Expression of the Emotions in Man. New York, New York: International Universities Press, 1963, pp. 300–317.

Izard, C.E. The Face of Emotion. New York, New York: Appleton-Century-Crofts, 1971.

Izard, C.E. Human Emotions. New York, New York: Plenum Press, 1977.

Miller, N.E. Application of learning and biofeedback to psychiatry and medicine. In A.M. Freedman, H.I. Kaplan, and B.J. Sadock (Eds.) Comprehensive Textbook of Psychiatry/II, 2nd ed., vol. 1. Baltimore, Maryland: Williams and Wilkins Co., 1975, pp. 349–365.

Miller, N.E. Clinical applications of biofeedback: Voluntary control of heart rate, rhythym, blood pressure. In H.I. Russek (Ed.) New horizons in cardiovascular practice. Baltimore, Maryland: University Park Press, 1975.

Mischel, W. Toward a cognitive social learning reconceptualization of personality. Psychological Review 80:252–283, July 1973.

Mowrer, O.H. On the dual nature of learning—a reinterpretation of "conditioning" and "problem solving." Harvard Educational Review 17:102–148, 1947. (Reprinted in Mowrer, 1950, pp. 222–274.)

Mowrer, O.H. Learning Theory and Personality Dynamics. New York, New York: Ronald Press, 1950.

Nowlis, V. Mood. In B.B. Wolman (Ed.) International Encyclopedia of Psychiatry, Psychology, Psychoanalysis, and Neurology, vol. 7. New York, New York: Aesculapius, 1977, pp. 262–265.

Rachman, S., and J. Teasdale. Aversion Therapy and Behavior Disorders: An Analysis. Coral Gables, Florida: University of Miami Press, 1969.

Seligman, M.E.P., and J.L. Hager (Eds.) Biological Boundaries of Learning. New York, New York: Appleton-Century-Crofts, 1972a.

Seligman, M.E.P., and J.L. Hager. Biological boundaries of learning: The sauce-bearnaise syndrome. Psychology Today 6:59, August 1972b.

Young, P.T. Feeling and Emotion. In B.B. Wolman (Ed.) Handbook of General Psychology. Englewood Cliffs, New Jersey: Prentice-Hall, 1973.

11

Attachment and Early Development of the Affective System

Consideration of the development of the affective system of the individual in its three aspects of appraisal, drive-discharge, and transaction requires an interactional approach to primarily maturational or learning perspectives. Affective development must be considered in relation to the situation or context. The context of major importance is the mother-infant relationship. Consequently, we will need to examine not only what is known about affective development within the individual but also what mother-infant relationship characteristics stimulate and foster this development. Likewise, the role of both the mother and infant in initiating and maintaining this relationship needs to be examined.

Initiation of affective development coincides with the initiation of the mother-infant relationship. One of the earliest manifestations of affect is in the process of attachment, which has been defined somewhat differently by various authors. The definition of Ainsworth (1973, p. 1) is representative:

> An attachment is an affectional tie that one person forms to another specific person, binding them together in space and enduring over time. Attachment is discriminating and specific.

Attachment is a two-way process. That is, the attachment of the infant to the mother and the attachment of the mother to the infant. Rosenthal (1973) contends that attachment is not a "thing" which results from the interaction of infant and mother, nor is it a trait or system or characteristic of the personality of either the infant or the mother. Rather, attachment is "a characteristic of the interaction itself" (p. 203). This view of attachment as an interaction process rather than a thing or result of mother-infant interaction enables the focus to be on understanding the process underlying attachment interactions and determining what characteristics of the participants, others, the situation, and previous interactions influence the interaction situationally and over time.

The classic nature-nurture controversy pervades consideration of the attachment process. The learning model of attachment emphasizes the influences of cultural, social, and experiential factors. This is in contrast to the ethological model, which emphasizes species specific behaviors having the biological function of survival advantage. Both models acknowledge given behaviors or capabilities which can then be "shaped" or "unfolded," and both acknowledge the necessary role of environmental stimulation in learning and maturation. A primary difference is that the learning model generally assumes a greater degree of environmental lability for human behavior systems than postulated in the ethological model.

Attachment of the Infant to the Mother

The infant's attachment to the mother does not occur suddenly. It gradually emerges during the first few months of life and continues to develop thereafter. Various sequential phases in the development of the infant's attachment to the mother have been noted. Ainsworth (1973) maintains that there are at least four major phases: (1) a phase during which social responsiveness is relatively undiscriminating; (2) a phase of discriminating social responsiveness; (3) a phase marked by emergence of active initiative in proximity-seeking, contact-seeking, and contact-maintaining behaviors; and (4) a phase identified by Bowlby (1969) as one of goal-corrected partnership. This goal-corrected partnership refers to the baby's altering of his/her behaviors on the basis of feedback received, so that it is in accordance with that of the mother. This last phase is seen as beginning during the previous phase, which Ainsworth (1973) maintains has a median age of attainment of about 7 months. Similarly, Yarrow (1961) maintains that the infant, during the period from 2 to 6 months of age, develops a stable and affectionate relationship to the mother. Thus, by approximately 6 months of age, there are indications of the existence of the attachment process in the infant-mother relationship.

Various behaviors of the infant have been recognized as precursors of attachment, in that they orientate an infant to his/her mother, signal to her, and actively promote contact with or proximity to her (Ainsworth, 1973). These precursor behaviors include rooting, sucking, postural adjustment, looking, listening, smiling, vocalizing, crying, and grasping. For attachment to occur, sufficient opportunity for interaction with mother is seen as necessary. These precursor behaviors serve to promote proximity which has the biological function of survival advantage. Developmentally, the ability to discriminate one person (mother) from another and the conception of object constancy are also necessary. It again needs to be emphasized that, while these precursors and cognitive and perceptual capacities necessary for attachment may represent species-characteristic behavioral systems, these do not develop wholly through maturation alone; they are strongly influenced by learning and environmental factors. One of the primary influences on these behaviors and capacities, as well as on cognitive and social development in general, is the nature of the mother-infant interaction or relationship.

The issue of time limits for the attachment of an infant to his/her mother stem from the ethological model of imprinting and critical periods. We have emphasized the evolving nature of the attachment process during the postnatal period, and the available evidence suggests that this is relatively established by about 6–8 months of age. Delineation of the upper time limit has presented major difficulties. Studies of institutionalized infants suggest that attachment is more likely to be optimal if the opportunity for interaction with one individual is provided during the first year to 18 months of life. This should not be taken as a definitive upper limit. We are aware not only of the adaptability of humans but also of the fact that we are capable of making attachments throughout our life span. It is not yet known what the upper limit is in terms of the establishment of the initial attachment and exactly how delays in the initial attachment affect capacity for subsequent attachments.

It was mentioned previously that one of the primary influences on the infant's cognitive and affective development and on the infant's developing attachment to mother was the nature of the mother-infant relationship. One of the main components of this relationship is the mother's attachment to the infant. The relationship is in turn influenced by maternal characteristics such as sensitivity, responsiveness, attitudes, and care practices, and infant characteristics such as sex, birth order, temperament, and state. We have already discussed many of these infant characteristics in Chapter 6. We will now consider mother's attachment to the infant, and then examine some of the maternal characteristics that influence the mother-infant relationship.

Attachment of the Mother to the Infant

Maternal attachment can be considered to be a particular variant of attachment, as exemplified by the definition of Robson and Moss (1970, p. 977): "The extent to which a mother feels that her infant occupies an essential position in her life." The components associated with this phenomenon include acceptance of imposition and obligations; a sense of possession, devotion, and responsibility for the infant's well-being; feelings of warmth, love, and protectiveness; positive anticipation of prolonged contact; need for and pleasure in continuing transactions; and a sense of loss with the infant's actual or imagined absence.

The original mother-infant bond has been considered of paramount importance.

> (It) is the wellspring for all the infant's subsequent attachments and is the formative relationship in the course of which the child develops a sense of himself. Throughout his lifetime, the strength and character of this attachment will influence the quality of all future bonds to other individuals. (Klaus and Kennell, 1976, pp. 1–2)

The primary issue in the ethological model perspective is that of the purported existence of a maternal sensitive period shortly after birth, during which time the initial mother-infant interaction must take place for attachment and later development to be optimal. According to this model, preprogrammed species-specific maternal behaviors are "released" should the mother have contact with the child during the critical period. Evidence for such a mechanism of attachment formation at the human level is mixed.

As contrasted with the ethological model, the learning model depicts attachment as a slowly developing process involving mutual learning and adjustment. Whatever the fate of the ethological model as it applies to humans, there is much evidence indicating that the mutual attachment of mother and infant is a gradually developing process.

Synchrony of the Relationship

An important characteristic of the mother-infant relationship is synchrony, that is, the extent of dovetailing of behaviors of the infant and mother. Synchrony is expected to facilitate the infant's development (Thoman, 1975), because it enables the infant's needs to be appropriately met, and feedback from the caretaker enhances signaling or communication skills. Each of the participants has a role to play in establishing synchrony. The infant must emit accurate cues as to needs or status, the mother must be sensitive and responsive to these cues, and, in turn, the infant must be responsive to the mother's interventions and ministrations.

There is much mutual learning which must go on for both infant and mother about the nuances of behavior patterns of each other and the rules of interaction which change constantly as a consequence of maturation and previous interactions. In early infancy, many authors (Bell, 1974; Brazelton, et al. 1974) make note of a homeostatic model of stimulation and arousal in that optimal levels of stimulation—neither too much nor too little—are sought. The early weeks are seen as an opportunity for mother to learn the rules about the infant's homeostatic needs in physiological matters as well as in attention. Brazelton et al. (1974) described the typical sequence of mother-infant interactional behaviors and noted the rhythmic, cyclical quality of attention and withdrawal: a buildup of excitement, then disengagement, and then reinitiation. The sequence of the infant's behavior involves initiation, orientation, state of attention, acceleration, peak of excitement, deceleration, and finally withdrawal or turning away. The development by mother of a sensitivity to her infant's capacity for attention and nonattention was seen as the most important rule for maintaining the interaction. With this sensitivity, she can adjust the rhythm of her behavior to that of her infant and thus maintain interaction. Lack of sensitivity results in maternal behaviors which prolong the infant's withdrawal of attention. Mother needs to learn which of her behaviors hold the attention of the infant and which activate and deactivate.

> Thus, the quality of each partner's display relative to the quality of the other's display is a measure of the match existing between their intentionality and affectivity. When synchronization is achieved, we feel we are observing a good interaction based on a mutuality of affect and intent. When it is not achieved, there is a dysrhythmia and lack of cyclic buildup of the behaviors into a smooth flow of phases (Brazelton, et al., 1975, p. 144).

Stern (1974) has shown that infants have relatively stable distribution of gaze-to-gaze intervals, but that these intervals can be differentially divided between gazes-at or gazes-away. He reports that infants initiated and terminated 94% of all mutual gazes, but that the maternal gaze and the accompanying constellation of vocal and facial behaviors exert a strong influence on eliciting and maintaining or holding the infant's gaze. Mother modulates her face and voice using the cues about the infant's state or arousal and quality of visual attention in order to elicit and hold the infant's gaze. Through this process, she helps the infant acquire schemata of human behavior and the precursors of interpersonal coping and defensive operations. Another rule for maintaining interactions that facilitate development is that mothers utilize periods of interaction to "model" more increasingly complex behaviors, with complexity being altered in relation to stage of infant development (Brazelton et al., 1974). Thus, constant readjustments are necessary to maintain the synchrony of interaction.

Moreover, the role of imitation as a nonverbal communication code that exists prior to verbal communication has been stressed (Pawbly, 1977). The capacity of the infant for imitation does not develop suddenly or simply as a function of maturation. It gradually emerges in the "context of the reciprocal pattern of social interplay between mother and child as a result of the mother's intention to communicate" (p. 219). The process begins with mother reflecting back or imitating aspects of the infant's behavior which she can endow with communicative significance. Mother's timing and placing of her reproductions are seen as important in fostering the infant's capacity for imitation.

There has been an emphasis upon the sensitivity of the mother and her capacity to adapt to the infant in such a way as to initiate, hold, and foster synchrony of interactions in accordance with homeostasis, in order to enhance development of more complex behaviors and skills. The point is beginning to be stressed that the postpartum period is a time for learning in which these sensitivities can develop. Initial difficulties are likely to be temporary and be resolved as learning proceeds.

Having considered the establishment of the infant's attachment to mother and mother's attachment to the infant and the characteristics and requirements of a synchronous mother-infant relationship, we have an appreciation of the context in which the individual's affective system develops. Now we will consider the development of the affective system.

Development of the Affective System

Again, considerations of affective development have reflected the nature-nurture polarity evident in all aspects of human development. Attention has been directed toward identifying which aspects of emotions are dependent on maturation and which are dependent upon learning. The maturational and learning perspectives have focused upon the changes in emotional expression and the changes in the efficacy of various internal and external situations in eliciting emotions which occur as the infant develops.

It used to be thought that as many as three emotions—fear, rage, and love—were present in infants at birth. However, it has gradually been recognized that infants do not exhibit a variety of emotional responses recognizable as such to adults. It appears that the only unlearned response of emotional significance occurring in infants is the startle pattern. It needs to be pointed out that recognition and identification of emotion even in other adults is poor unless the observer also has been able to observe the stimulus situation. Observing both the initiating situation and the individual's manifested response greatly increases the accuracy of the observer's identification of emotions as manifested in overt signs emitted by the "emoting" individual.

Bridges (1932), in a classic treatise, maintains that the only recognizable emotion at birth is undifferentiated excitement. All other emotions are seen as being derived from the undifferentiated excitement through the process of differentiation which results from maturation and learning. According to Bridges, the initial excitement is differentiated so that distress and delight are added to the infant's repertoire during the first two months of life. Further differentiation is depicted in Figure 11-1.

Not all child developmentalists concur with the number, sequence, and time periods of emotional development advocated by Bridges. The chief significance of her work is the indication that as the infant increases in age, an increasing number of emotions are able to be inferred reliably from the infant's increasingly differentiated behavioral responses to aspects of the environment.

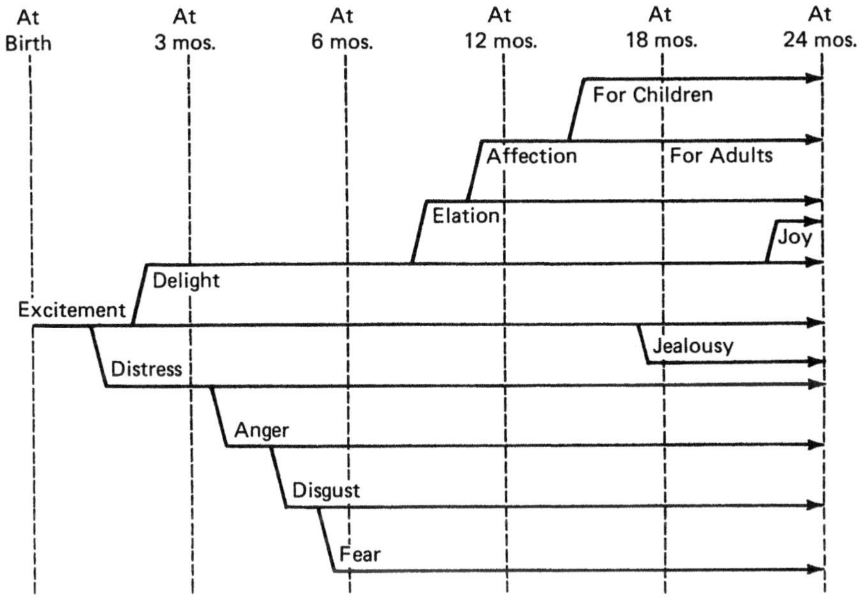

Fig. 11-1. Approximate ages of differentiation of emotions in early childhood.

Many aspects of the environment initially fail to elicit any recognizable emotional activity in the infant. As the infant increases in age, environmental objects and situations may increase or decrease in their effectiveness in eliciting emotional activity. This increased or decreased effectiveness reflects an interaction of maturational and learning processes in increasing the sensitivities and abilities of the infant. General sensorimotor and symbolic development underlies initial sensitivity to emotional situations. For example, the infant must learn the significance of snakes, or that one face is mother's and another is unfamiliar. Correspondingly, a decrease in emotional responses to environmental situations, such as the appearance of a stranger, may be attributed to the infant's increasing ability to adapt, to problem-solve, or to respond in an alternative manner.

In addition to changes in the variety of emotions displayed and in the effectiveness of environmental aspects in eliciting emotions, there are also changes in the frequency of some emotions with increasing age. There is some indication that anger increases in frequency until the second year of life and then decreases. With the increased capabilities for thought and action which accompanies increasing age, there is a tendency to remove the frustrating or bothersome situation and to display anger more subtly. With fear, it also appears that the number of observed instances decreases after the second year, but the frequency of anxiety increases. This probably reflects the child's increasing capacity to handle familiar situations and also to anticipate, on the basis of previous experience and learning, unpleasant or fear provoking situations.

The changes in the affective system are not simply a matter of increasing differentiation as a result of maturation. The role of learning in the acquisition of emotional respones to aspects of the environment has been well-demonstrated by work in the area of conditioned emotional responses. That is, through conditioning, aspects of the environment which previously did not elicit an emotional response can subsequently do so. The classic example is Watson and Raynor's experiment on conditioned fear reactions with "little Albert." It is of interest to present in part the authors' description of this conditioning process with little Albert and to realize that it appeared in the literature in 1920. Albert was described as a normal, healthy, relatively unemotional child. The authors describe their use of an unconditioned fear response to a loud noise to establish a conditioned fear response to a stimulus (white rat) which previously did not elicit a fear response. The following is a somewhat-edited version of the original Watson and Raynor article:

> At approximately nine months of age, we ran him through the emotional tests that have become a part of our regular routine in determining whether fear reactions can be called out by other stimuli than sharp noises and the sudden removal of support. In brief, the infant was confronted suddenly and for the first time successfully with a white rat, a rabbit, a dog, a monkey, with masks with and without hair, cotton wool, burning newspapers, etc. Manipulation was the most usual reaction called out. At no time did this infant ever show fear in any situation.
>
> The test to determine whether a fear reaction could be called out by a loud noise was made when he was 8 months, 26 days of age. The laboratory notes are as follows:
>
> One of the two experimenters caused the child to turn its head and fixate her moving hand; the other, stationed back of the child, struck the steel bar with a sharp blow. The child started violently, his breathing was checked and the arms were raised in a characteristic manner. On the second stimulation the same thing occurred, and in addition the lips began to pucker and tremble. On the third stimulation the child broke into a sudden crying fit. This is the first time an emotional situation in the laboratory has produced any fear or even crying in Albert.
>
> At first there was considerable hesitation on our part in making the attempt to set up fear reactions experimentally. A certain responsibility is attached to such a procedure. We finally decided to make the attempt, confronting ourselves with the reflection that such attachments would arise anyway as soon as the child left the sheltered environment of the nursery for the rough and tumble of the home. We did not begin this work until Albert was 11 months, 3 days of age. Before attempting to set up a conditioned response we, as before, put him through all the regular emotional tests. Not the slightest sign of fear response was obtained in any situation.
>
> The steps taken to condition emotional response are shown in our laboratory notes.

11 Months 3 Days

1. White rat suddenly taken from the basket and presented to Albert. He began to reach for the rat with the left hand. Just as his hand struck the animal, the bar was struck immediately behind his head. The infant jumped violently and fell forward, burying his face in the mattress. He did not cry, however.
2. Just as the right hand touched the rat, the bar was struck again. Again the infant jumped violently, fell forward, and began to whimper.

In order not to disturb the child too seriously no further tests were given for one week.

11 Months 10 Days

1. Rat presented suddenly without sound. There was steady fixation but no tendency at first to reach for it. The rat was then placed nearer, whereupon tentative reaching movements began with the right hand. When the rat nosed the infant's left hand, the hand was immediately withdrawn. He started to reach for the head of the animal with the forefinger of the left hand, but withdrew it suddenly before contact. It is thus seen that the two joint stimulations given the previous week were not without effect. He was tested with his blocks immediately afterwards to see if they shared in the process of conditioning. He began immediately to pick them up, dropping them, pounding them, etc. In the remainder of the tests, the blocks were given frequently to quiet him and to test his general emotional state. They were always removed from sight when the process of conditioning was under way.
2. Joint stimulation with rat and sound. Started, then fell over immediately to right side. No crying.
3. Joint stimulation. Fell to right side and rested upon hands, with head turned away from rat. No crying.
4. Joint stimulation. Same reaction.
5. Rat suddenly presented alone. Puckered face, whimpered, and withdrew body sharply to the left.
6. Joint stimulation. Fell over immediately to right side and began to whimper.
7. Joint stimulation. Started violently and cried, but did not fall over.
8. Rat alone. The instant the rat was shown the baby began to cry. Almost instantly he turned sharply to the left, fell over on left side, raised himself on all fours, and began to crawl so rapidly that he was caught with difficulty before reaching the edge of the table.

This was as convincing a case of a completely conditioned fear response as could have been theoretically pictured. In all, seven joint stimulations were given to bring about the complete reaction.

Conclusion

The main points of emphasis in this chapter on development of the affective system have been the gradual differentiation of behavior into more discrete and discernible responses; the importance of the context of a synchronous mother-infant relationship, which gradually evolves as does its component parts of infant's attachment to mother and mother's attachment to the infant; and the continual interaction of maturation and learning in the development of the attachment processes, of a synchronous mother-infant relationship, and of the individual's affective system. We have seen that the maternal characteristics of sensitivity and responsiveness influence these developments, and have previously (Chapter 6) considered the influence of infant constitutional characteristics such as sex, birth order, temperament, and state. As the infant progresses into childhood, the constitutional characteristics of temperament and state as they interact with maternal sensitivity, responsiveness, and environmental experiences will influence the continued differentiation of the individual's affective system. With regard to this continual interaction, it is important to keep in mind that it is not "the amount of stimulation per se, that influences developmental progress, but the appropriateness of the stimulation to the child's individual and developmental characteristics" (Yarrow, 1963, p. 106).

References

Ainsworth, M. The development of infant-mother attachment. In B. Caldwell and H. Ricciuti (Eds.) Review of Child Development Research, vol. 3. Chicago, Illinois: The University of Chicago Press, 1973.

Bell, R. Contributions of human infants to caregiving and social interaction. In M. Lewis and L. Rosenblum (Eds.) The Effects of the Infant on Its Caregiver. New York, New York: Wiley, 1974.

Bowlby, J. Attachment and Loss, vol. 1, Attachment. New York, New York: Basic Books, 1969.

Brazelton, T., B. Koslowski, and M. Main. The origins of reciprocity: The early mother-infant interaction. In M. Lewis and L. Rosenblum (Eds.) The Effects of the Infant on Its Caregiver. New York, New York: Wiley, 1974.

Brazelton, T., E. Tronick, L. Adamson, H. Als, and S. Wise. Early mother-infant reciprocity. In Ciba Symposium 33. Parent-Infant Interaction. Amsterdam: Associated Scientific Publishers, 1975.

Bridges, K. Emotional development in early infancy. Child Development 3:324–341, 1932.

Klaus, M., and J. Kennell. Maternal-Infant Bonding. Saint Louis, Missouri: C.V. Mosby Co., 1976.

Pawbly, S. Imitative interaction. In H.R. Schaffer (Ed.) Studies in Mother-Infant Interaction. New York, New York: Academic Press, 1977.

Robson, K., and H. Moss. Patterns and determinants of maternal attachment. J. Pediatrics 77:976–985, 1970.

Rosenthal, M.K. Attachment and mother-infant interaction: Some research impasse and a suggested change in orientation. J. Child Psychology and Psychiatry 14:201–207, 1973.
Stern, D. Mother and infant at play: The dyadic interaction involving facial, vocal, and gaze behaviors. In M. Lewis and L. Rosenblum (Eds.) The Effect of the Infant on Its Caregiver. New York, New York: Wiley, 1974.
Thoman, E. Sleep and wake behaviors in neonates: Consistencies and consequences. Merrill-Palmer Quarterly 21:295–314, 1975.
Watson, J.B., and R. Raynor. Conditioned emotional reactions. J. Experimental Psychology 3:1–14, 1920.
Yarrow, L. Maternal deprivation: Toward an empirical and conceptual reevaluation. Psychological Bulletin 58:459–490, 1961.
Yarrow, L. Research in dimensions of early maternal care. Merrill-Palmer Quarterly 9:101–114, 1963.

12

The Epidemiology of Well-Being

Epidemiology is a well established subdiscipline of medicine. An epidemiological perspective, which emphasizes the interaction of persons and environments and the multiple determinants of outcomes relevant to health and illness, complements the discussions of normal and disordered behavior in previous chapters. Epidemiology, like medicine, has tended to concentrate on pathology rather than health. Hence the title of this chapter might have been "The Epidemiology of Pathological Affect" or "The Epidemiology of Depression." The chosen title and the material presented intentionally make a point: Positive affect, satisfaction with living, and a general sense of well-being are the prevalent states documented by epidemiological research. We will first review that evidence which stresses nonpathology, and then discuss the distribution and prevalence of pathological affect. This sequence will help to make clear the complex and varied facets of human affect. We are also deliberately focusing on only one domain of affect—the sense of well-being.

Affect and the Epidemiologic Model

Human experience that underlies a sense of well-being or its absence is commonly an amalgam of positive and negative affect; on balance, the dominant experience is positive. While affect tends to reflect life circumstances in intuitively believable ways, a subjective sense of well-being is not, as will be indicated below, simply a response to objective indicators of material well-being. Substantial unhappiness and dissatisfaction are reported by at most 8% of the population in the United States. Pathological affect as expressed in clinical depression is observed in approximately 1% of the general population.

An epidemiological thoughtstyle calls attention to the distribution of health and illness of defined populations living in specified environments and to the explanation of the observed distributions of these conditions. Descriptive epidemiology is concerned with the rate at which pathological conditions appear in different populations at risk in different social and physical environments at different times. Consider, for example, the distribution of pathological depression as a manifestation of severe, sustained negative affect. An epidemiologist might inquire first about *incidence* of cases presented for treatment during a particular period of time and the *prevalence* of treated cases, which includes both new and continuing cases. Since research has repeatedly documented that treated cases of all kinds of pathology are frequently only a fraction of cases which can be identified in surveys of a population, epidemiological reports often refer to *true* incidence or prevalence in order to emphasize that treated cases are "the tip of an iceberg." When populations at risk are viewed as denominators and cases of the phenomenon of interest are viewed as numerators, the rates of the particular conditions observed in most populations are usually very low. For instance, less than 1% of the U.S. population is institutionalized at any point in time. This has been true for a number of decades. Moreover, best estimates of *treated* pathological depression indicate a prevalence of well below 1 in 100 persons in most populations. Furthermore, surveys of probability samples of populations indicate a prevalence of 6 to 8 persons per 100 for all *mental* disorders (Freedman et al., 1976, p. 190). Such information is a reminder that, in the absence of epidemics, even common forms of pathology are relatively rare events in populations, and treated cases of pathology are even rarer. Although these facts are useful for professionals who deal with pathology every day to keep in mind, it is also true that even statistically rare events accumulate in significant proportions of populous societies. Statistical rarity is not equivalent to lack of social or clinical importance.

An epidemiological thoughtstyle provides an illustration par excellence of a multivariate conceptualization and analysis of health and illness, as illustrated by the three types of interacting variables regularly considered by the discipline—agent, host, and environment (Table 12-1). Historically, the *agents* given primary attention were microorganisms; but over time, the list has been expanded considerably and will continue to expand. The concept *host* has stressed a wide range of intrinsic factors (genetic, maturation, ethnicity, behavior), and the concept *environment* has stressed a wide range of extrinsic factors (physical, biologic, social). It is axiomatic in epidemiology that observed patterns of health and illness in populations are best explained by taking all three types of variables into consideration simultaneously. Anyone who finds a good detective story appealing will be stimulated by classical multivariate studies in epidemiology that established the relationship between cigarette smoking and lung cancer, between vitamin deficiency and pellagra, and between fluoride and tooth decay (Lilienfeld, 1976, Chapters 1–3). A particularly appealing and instructive story from the annals of epidemiology is the discovery by John Snow, a physician in London, that the transmission of cholera in the epidemic of 1848–54 could be traced to the Southwark and Vauxhall Water Company. Snow traced the homes served by the water company and demonstrated that the incidence of cholera was nine times higher in these homes than in London generally. There is a public house in London built beside one of the ancient water pumps of the Southwark and Vauxhall Water Company, and epidemiologists from around the world still drop by to sign the pub register and lift a glass in honor of John Snow. Epidemiological studies have repeatedly demonstrated the correlation between noxious agents and deleterious outcomes. The fact that such correlations have always been imperfect has reinforced the importance of a multivariate analysis relating host, agent, and environment. Noxious agents are not equally distributed in environments. Hosts are not equally at risk even when they are in environments which expose them to noxious agents.

Table 12-1. A Classification of Agent, Host, and Environmental Factors Which Determine the Distribution of Diseases in Human Populations

I.	*Agents of Disease*—Necessary Etiologic Factors		
			Examples
	A.	Nutritive elements	
		Excesses	Cholesterol
		Deficiencies	Vitamins, proteins
	B.	Chemical agents	
		Poisons	Carbon monoxide, carbon tetrachloride, drugs
		Allergens	Ragweed, poison ivy, medications
	C.	Physical agents	Ionizing radiation, mechanical
	D.	Infectious agents	
		Metazoa	Hookworm, schistosomiasis, onchocerciasis
		Protozoa	Amoebae, malaria
		Bacteria	Rheumatic fever, lobar pneumonia, typhoid, tuberculosis, syphilis
		Fungi	Histoplasmosis, athletes foot
		Rickettsia	Rocky Mountain spotted fever, typhus
		Viruses	Measles, mumps, chickenpox, smallpox, poliomyelitis, rabies, yellow fever

(*Continued*)

II.	*Host Factors* (Intrinsic Factors)—Influences Exposure, Susceptibility, or Response to Agents	
		Examples
A.	Genetic	Sickle cell disease
B.	Age	
C.	Sex	
D.	Ethnic group	
E.	Physiologic state	Fatigue, pregnancy, puberty, stress, nutritional state
F.	Prior immunologic experience	Hypersensitivity, protection
	Active	Prior infection, immunization
	Passive	Maternal antibodies, gamma globulin prophylaxis
G.	Intercurrent or preexisting disease	
H.	Human behavior	Personal hygiene, food handling, diet, interpersonal contact, occupation recreation, utilization of health resources
III.	*Environmental Factors* (Extrinsic Factors)—Influences Existence of the Agent, Exposure, or Susceptibility to Agent	
		Examples
A.	Physical environment	Geology, climate
B.	Biologic environment	
	Human populations	Density
	Flora	Sources of food, influence on vertebrates and arthropods as a source of agents
	Fauna	Food sources, vertebrate hosts, anthropod vectors
C.	Socioeconomic environment	
	Occupation	Exposure to chemical agents
	Urbanization and Economic Development	Urban crowding, tensions and pressures, cooperative efforts in health and education
	Disruption	Wars, floods

From Lilienfeld, 1976.

Concerns about environmental pollution, which escalated in the 1960s, reinforced and broadened a long-standing concern of epidemiologists about the potentially noxious aspects of the physical environment. These epidemiologists also documented in detail how crowding, rapid culture change, lifestyles, and hostile interpersonal relationships had potentially deleterious consequences for health that are as real as the uncontrolled dumping of chemical waste into rivers and into the atmosphere (Cassel, 1976). Cassel's work on the social context of health and illness, and on the potential of medicine for devising helpful interventions that promote well-being as well as ameliorate illness, reflects the emergence of a distinctly new interest in social epidemiology. Cassel's emphasis on social factors in the determination of illness and on social interventions that may promote health provides a useful point of departure for discussing first the epidemiology of well-being and then the epidemiology of depressive illness.

Assessing Well-Being

Well-being has both subjective and objective components. The subjective components are reflected in the everyday awareness of happiness or sadness and of satisfaction or dissatisfaction as common experiences. In everyday speech, a person who is sad may be heard to label this affect as depression, but such negative affect in the typical situation is mild, temporary, alloyed with awareness of positive affect, and compatible with an overall evaluation of satisfaction with life. Social survey research in the United States has consistently found that most people, most of the time, tend to report a preponderance of positive affect and satisfaction with life.

Well-being also has objective components and, in assessing quality of life, many people tend to think first of these components—i.e., the tangible, material, measurable conditions such as health, life expectancy, income, and housing. By objective standards, the well-being of the population of the United States has steadily improved. Patterns of morbidity and mortality in the U.S., while not the best in the Western world, compare favorably. Since 1920, average life expectancy at birth has increased substantially, particularly for females, to the current 69 years for males and 76 for females. Approximately 75% of a birth cohort will survive to age 60, and 60% to age 70. Persons surviving to age 65 can expect, on the average, a substantial number of additional years (13 for males and 16 for females). In the past decade, poverty has become less common; and in the past two decades, the number of substandard households has decreased.

These positive, objective indicators of material well-being tell only part of the story. Do we find, as intuitively we might expect, that improving objective indicators of well-being are matched by improvement in subjective indicators? On the contrary, Americans appear to be doing better and report feeling worse. In recent decades, three large, reliable, social epidemiological surveys (Cantril, 1965; Bradburn, 1969; Campbell et al., 1976) have documented a slight but persistent decline in the report of positive affect (happiness) and a sense of well-being at the same time the objective indicators have been improving. Such findings strongly suggest that expectations play a prominent role in determining subjective judgments of well-being, and that

Table 12-2. Distribution of Responses to Feeling-State Items (%)

Feeling-State Item	Total Sample: Wave I	Total Sample: Wave III	National Sample[a]	Ten Metropolitan Areas Subsample of National Sample[b]
During the past few weeks did you ever feel:				
Positive feelings:				
1. Pleased about having accomplished something?	78	77	84	83
2. That things were going your way?	64	70	71	65
3. Proud because someone complimented you on something you had done?	67	66	71	63
4. Particularly excited or interested in something?	56	57	54	58
5. On top of the world?	29	33	33	38
Negative feelings:				
1. So restless that you couldn't sit long in a chair?	48	30	53	56
2. Bored?	38	33	34	34
3. Depressed or very unhappy?	33	30	30	30
4. Very lonely or remote from other people?	27	23	26	27
5. Upset because someone criticized you?	21	18	18	17
Number	2787	2163	1469	174

[a]National Area Probability Sample with Quotas (NAPSQ), June, 1965.
[b]Random subsample in ten largest metropolitan areas from NAPSQ, January, 1966.
[c]Actual N varies slightly from item to item because of differing number of "no" answers.
From Bradburn, 1969.

the discrepancy between expectations and outcomes is more important than the outcomes themselves in determining such evaluations.

The major theoretical and methodological arguments of Cantril and Bradburn regarding the measurement of subjective well-being are summarized by Campbell (1976) and Campbell, Converse, and Rodgers (1976). The findings regarding subjective well-being can be summarized briefly as follows:

1. Reliable, valid measures of affect and satisfaction indicate that Americans in the past decade report simultaneously a wide range of both positive and negative feelings (Table 12-2). These feeling states, on balance, tend to be

Table 12-3. Distribution and Relation of Affect Balance (Positive—Negative Affect) to Self-Ratings of Happiness

Affect Balance Scale	Difference	% Happy	% Not Happy	% Sample in Category
Positive—Negative	+4 to +1	96.3	3.7	49
Positive—Negative	+1 to −1	94.2	5.8	21
Positive—Negative	−1 to −4	69.9	30.1	30
N = 2726				

Adapted from Bradburn, 1969.

positive—that is, 8 out of 10 reporting at least a balance of positive and negative affect (Table 12-3). For 3 out of 10 the balance of affect is negative.

Similarly, Campbell and his associates (1976) report a large sample survey in which an Index of General Affect is derived from the average response on a seven-point scale to eight semantic differential items. In the semantic differential procedure used, individuals characterized their lives in terms of eight paired polar adjectives such as enjoyable/miserable, hopeful/discouraging, friendly/lonely, and worthwhile/useless. The mean response across items was positive 5.7. About 8% of respondents scored below the midpoint, indicating a predominantly negative characterization of affect (Table 12-4).

Interestingly, in Bradburn's research on affect balance, individual reports of negative and of positive affect are not highly correlated; and, in turn, each

Table 12-4. Distribution of an Index of General Affect

	Scale	%	
	1.00–1.94	0.6	
	1.95–2.94	1.6	7.8
Negative	2.95–3.94	5.6	
	3.95–4.44	6.8	
	4.45–4.94	8.6	
	4.95–5.24	6.1	
	5.25–5.44	6.2	
	5.45–5.74	7.3	
	5.75–5.94	8.7	
	6.25–6.44	9.7	
Positive	6.45–6.74	9.9	
	6.75–7.00	19.2	
Total		100.0	
Mean		5.675	
Standard Deviation		1.115	
N		2147	

From Campbell et al., 1976.

type of affect correlates with distinctly different sets of other variables. Positive affect was found to be associated with evidence of satisfying interpersonal contact, active social involvement, and numerous, varied personal interests. Negative affect, on the other hand, related to variables that are typically associated with poor mental health (e.g., poor adjustment at work, marital and family discord, anxiety, worry, and tension).

In sum, the prevalence of a positive balance of affect and a subjective sense of well-being appears to be high. Positive affect and a sense of well-being do not, however, preclude negative affect. The prevalence of a negative balance of affect is low—probably no more than 30 in 100 persons. It should be noted that this rate is many times higher than reported prevalence of treated pathological depression.

2. Most adults in the United States report overall satisfaction with their lives (Table 12-5). Survey research has also repeatedly demonstrated, however, that reports of affective states correlate only modestly (+.5) with reports of overall life satisfaction. A large number of individuals report that they are happy but not satisfied with life, or that they are unhappy but satisfied. This apparent contradiction has a plausible explanation. Clinicians who work with older persons frequently find that older persons, when asked "How are things going with you now?," respond "I am not happy but, overall, my life has been (or is) good." One would not be surprised, perhaps, to have a younger person respond to the same question with, "I am happy but dissatisfied with my life at present." Satisfaction appears to reflect a distinctly cognitive appraisal of the balance between personal aspirations and achievements, with perceived discrepancy predicting a report of dissatisfaction. Since we might expect actual discrepancy between aspirations and achievement to be

Table 12-5. Distribution of Overall Life Satisfaction

Level of Satisfaction/ Dissatisfaction	%
1. Completely dissatisfied	0.9
2.	2.1
3.	3.7
4. Neutral	3.7
5.	20.7
6.	39.6
7. Completely satisfied	21.7
Total	100.0
Mean	5.545
Standard Deviation	1.250
N	2134

From Campbell et al., 1976.

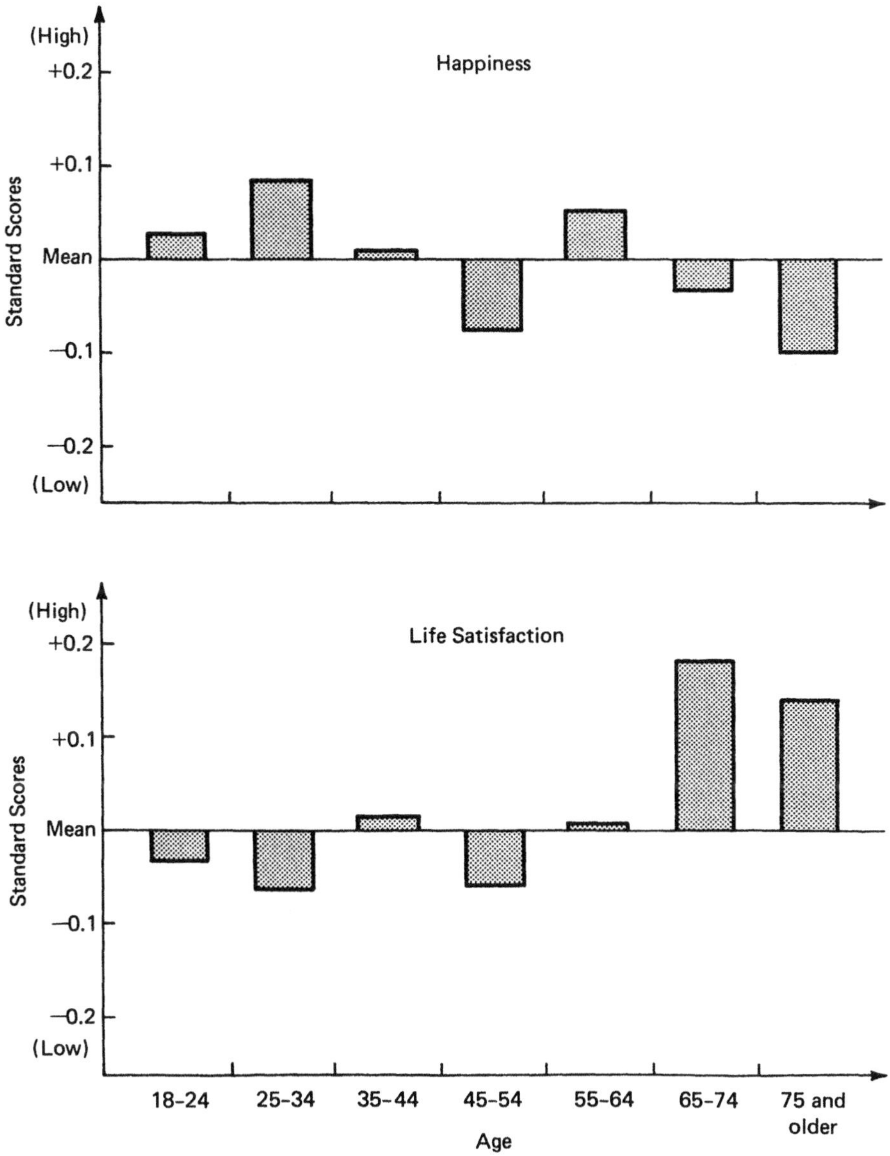

Fig. 12-1. Average levels of happiness and life satisfaction, by age (standardized scores) (From Campbell et al., 1976.)

inversely correlated with age, we are not surprised by the finding that younger persons tend to report happiness *and* dissatisfaction while older persons report unhappiness *and* satisfaction (Figure 12.1).

Overall, in probability samples of the U.S. population, most individuals report a positive balance of affect and above-average overall satisfaction with life; they also score above the midpoint of a composite Index of Well-being which combines general affect and overall life satisfaction (Table 12-6). The prevalence of well-being measured in various ways is over 70 per 100 respondents. Further, when this overall report of well-being is disaggregated into what Campbell and associates label as *domains* (e.g., marriage, family, health, neighborhood, and job), on average a positive assessment of each domain is observed. The prevalence of well-being is partly a function of socioeconomic status. As status increases, so does the prevalence of well-being. Contrary to a certain romantic mythology, there are some things that money and social position apparently can help secure, and a sense of well-being is one of them. Restated in negative terms, the prevalence of negative affect varies from the 30 per 100 persons who, report a negative balance of affect or that they have recently felt "depressed" and "very remote from people," to the 4 in 100 who are below the midpoint of the Index of Well-being.

Pathological Affect

While significant negative affect and the absence of a sense of well-being are not highly prevalent in a population, the evidence just reviewed indicates that rather substantial minorities report unhappiness, dissatisfaction with life, or both, If these estimates of prevalence of unhappiness and dissatisfac-

Table 12-6. Distribution of an Index of Well-Being

Scale	%
2.10–7.04	3.9
7.05–9.04	7.4
9.05–10.04	7.7
10.05–10.54	5.2
10.55–11.04	7.2
11.05–11.54	7.1
11.55–12.04	7.9
12.05–12.54	11.1
12.55–13.04	11.5
13.05–13.54	10.2
13.55–14.04	6.9
14.05–14.54	5.8
14.55–14.70	8.1
Total	100.0
Mean	11.768
Standard Deviation	2.207
N	2160

From Campbell et al., 1976.

tion are extrapolated to a population of over 200 million persons, there is clearly a great deal of negative affect and dissatisfaction with life endemic in society; and it is also apparent that a large number of distressed individuals never present themselves for treatment.

As noted earlier, the prevalence of treated depression is well below 1 in 100 persons. Actually, we do not know the true prevalence of pathological depression. As Gurland (1976) notes in a review of the epidemiology of depression, the prevalence of treated cases of depression almost certainly underestimates the true prevalence, but we do not know by how much. Pathological depression is difficult to establish in social surveys of noninstitutionalized individuals. Even the determination of the prevalence of treated cases is compromised by apparent differences in diagnostic style and conclusions of experienced clinicians. Comparative studies of the diagnosis of pathological depression in the United States and the United Kingdom indicate, for example, that clinicians in the United Kingdom tend more often to diagnose depression in criterion cases than do clinicians in the United States, quite possibly because they are less inclined than the latter to use certain alternative diagnoses, e.g., "schizophrenia." Gurland also argues that estimated true prevalence is affected by assumptions about the distribution of depression over the life cycle. There is a tendency to assume that children are not depressed and that the prevalence of depression is highest in middle age. Pathological depression in late life, Gurland believes, tends to be underestimated because it is assumed that observed negative affect is only a realistic appraisal of and response to the decrements of old age, and hence not pathological. Such an assumption is reinforced by the evidence noted above that reported unhappiness is a function of age. But, Gurland concludes, the prevalence of pathological depression, if properly diagnosed, appears to be very high in late life. He estimated the prevalence of mild depression at 3–4 per 100 persons 65 years of age and older, and the prevalence of severe depression at 2–3 per 100 persons. Since pathological depression is a treatable condition in late life and, as noted in a previous chapter, is inappropriately considered to be crucial evidence of organic brain impairment, a definitive clinical diagnosis of depression in the older patient is especially important.

We shall have more to say about pathological affect in later chapters.

Concluding Observations

The epidemiology study of subjective well-being reveals a very complex phenomenon. Well-being has cognitive and evaluative as well as affective components. A sense of well-being cannot simply be reduced to affect as indicated by the modest correlation between affect and life satisfaction. Even affect proves to be a complex amalgam of positive and negative feelings whose balance is not well-understood. Positive affect, satisfaction, and, hence, subjective well-being are, however, related to interpersonal relationships and integration into society.

Subjective well-being is the prevalent outcome of living for most individuals, most of the time. The prevalence of negative affect, dissatisfaction, and the lack of a sense of well-being is nonetheless high enough to call attention to the probability of a *true* prevalence rate for pathological depression which is much higher than the observed rate for treated pathological depression. The changing prevalence of subjective well-being and its components over the life cycle is apparent. So are the differences in prevalence by sex.

References

Bradburn, N. The Structure of Psychological Well-Being. Chicago, Illinois: Aldine, 1969.

Campbell, A., P. Converse, and W. Rodgers. The Quality of American Life. New York, New York: Russell Sage Foundation, 1976.

Campbell, A. Subjective measures of well-being. American Psychologist 13:117–124, February 1976.

Cantril, H. The Pattern of Human Concerns. New Brunswick, New Jersey: Rutgers University Press, 1965.

Cassel, J. The contribution of the social environment to host resistance. Am. J. Epidemiology 104:107–123, 1976.

Freedman, A., H.I. Kaplan, and B.J. Sadock. Modern Synopsis of Comprehensive Textbook of Psychiatry/II. Baltimore, Maryland: Williams and Wilkins, 1976, pp. 187–194.

Gurland, B.J. The comparative frequency of depression in various adult age groups. J. Gerontology 31:283–293, 1976.

Lilienfeld, A. Foundations of Epidemiology. New York, New York: Oxford University Press, 1976.

United States Department of Health, Education and Welfare. Suicide in the United States, 1950–1964. Vital and Health Statistics 20:5, August 1967.

13

Pathology of Affect: Psychological Aspects

Affects are profoundly involved in virtually all psychopathological conditions. For example, the acquisition of unrealistic fear as a learned response to objectively nonnoxious internal or external stimuli, and the subsequent development of operant behavior that serves to relieve or minimize these gratuitous fear responses, are central considerations in what historically has been called the neurotic process. Unit IV will address this matter in detail.

In certain pathological states, however, aberrant affective processes appear to be the basic core of the disorders in question. That is, they are not involved in a merely contributory and remotely causal way in the production of maladaptive behavior, but rather such behavior seems to be the more or less direct manifestation of a deranged affective system. Generally, these conditions, appropriately enough, are termed the affective disorders. They are most frequently observed in the form of psychic depressions of greater or lesser severity. The present chapter focuses on the psychology of depression.

The amount of human suffering caused by depressive affective moods or states, in both subclinical and clinical forms, in incalculable. Significant levels of depression can almost always be found in physically ill patients, and it is a very substantial component in most forms of psychiatric disorder—quite aside from those in which it is the essential feature. Some 25,000 to 60,000 (exact figures are difficult to unearth, for perhaps obvious reasons) Americans end their lives by suicide every year, the overwhelming majority of them doing so during and at least partly in consequence of, episodes of depressive mood. Only a fortunate few humans, it would appear, are able to live their lives in relative freedom from recurring bouts of "the blues"—intractable sadness and low spirits, explained more or less adequately by events surrounding them. Our task in this chapter will be to examine the principal phenomena of this mood state at the various levels of intensity in which it appears, and to pull together what is known and what may reasonably be conjectured concerning its causes—those that are antecedents and those that militate to maintain the state.

It is difficult, at first glance, to conceive of the depressive state as being in any way adaptive—either from an individual or a species preservation view. Its extreme manifestations include, for example, sleep disturbance, "paralysis of will," psychomotor retardation, loss of libido, loss of appetite, fatigability, indecisiveness, a penchant for suicide, and marked interpersonal passivity. Such characteristics seem ill-suited to survival even in a benign environment; in a primitive one, from an evolutionary view, they would seem—again at first glance—to be lethal. On reflection, of course, we know that many of the adaptive mechanisms of organisms miscarry (overshoot the mark, so to speak), often because they lag behind important changes in the conditions of living of the organism in question. Many of the so-called psychosomatic or psychophysiologic diseases of contemporary humankind (e.g., those based on a chronic mobilization of the organism for a "flight or fight" that would be gratuitous and inappropriate were it to be executed in the modern era) seem rooted in this type of biobehavioral anachronism. The common cold, whose defensive symptoms normally exceed by a large order of magnitude the actual threat posed by the invading organism, is another somewhat different case in point. Depressive moods, particularly in their more severe manifestations, may have a somewhat similar background, as conceptualized in the "conservation-withdrawal" hypothesis advanced by Engel (1962). By way of illustration, let us consider the following scenario.

Consider the situation of a prehistoric forest animal who suddenly falls into a pit having sides so steep and high as to be beyond its ability to escape. Since the creature cannot know initially of the hopelessness of its predicament, its first and most adaptive maneuver is a behavior pattern involving hyperarousal, mobilization of energy resources, and a vigorous, even desperate, attempt at escape. The emotional state involved is one that is usually called fear, with perhaps some mixture of rage. To continue in this frantic, hyperactive state indefinitely would be obviously and objectively maladaptive under the circumstances, lessening the organism's long-term chances of survival. The likelihood of self-inflicted injury would be heightened, energy resources would be depleted leading to bodily exhaustion, and the frantic activity would perhaps attract predators, all to no avail. An adaptive reaction, under the circumstances, would be for the animal to become inactive after a time, to detach itself from the immediacy of its peril, and to conserve energy resources—in short, in Engel's terms, to "withdraw." It is not unreasonable to believe that evolutionary pressures would militate in this direction, toward the substitution of a conservation-withdrawal behavior pattern should hyperarousal in the flight-fight (fear-rage) pattern of response to stress prove, over time, to be unproductive.

In order to be adaptive in some ultimate sense, such a conservation-withdrawal capacity would, of course, have to be time-limited in its manifestations, since indefinite prolongation of such a state would itself produce lethal effects for the affected organism and for its species. The response would have to be programmed in such a way as to provide for periods of its own interruption, making possible opportunities for reassessment of conditions to determine whether or not they continue to exceed the organism's range of control, or perhaps have changed so that energy mobilization and activity for flight, fight, or ordinary pursuits are once again appropriate. If our forest animal, trapped in the "hopeless" situation and following initial efforts to escape, rolls up in a ball and detaches itself from the situation for a time, and if it then arouses from this state at various intervals to permit reexamination of the current state of affairs, it may find that a tree was blown into the pit allowing for escape. Depressive affect, and indeed clinical depressive states in humans, seem in fact to exhibit this type of self-limiting quality. They tend to be episodic, quite likely on an innately determined basis. It is this quality, incidentally, that provides perhaps the soundest reason for intervening in the self-determination of depressed persons who are contemplating suicide.

Viewed in this light, depressive affect and its prolongation into a state of depressed mood constitute the typical second phase of a sequence of responses to unalleviated stress. The first phase consists of a fear (anxiety) response pattern that serves to mobilize the organism to avoid or to destroy the threatening intrusion. This phase, in which fear is probably basic but rage may dominate the overt behavior, persists so long as circumstances are perceived by the organism as potentially controllable. As the state of mobilized arousal continues but fails to be followed by a reduction or elimination of stress, the second, depressive phase tends to superimpose itself and eventually to dominate the organism's emotional state. The speed and completeness with which this second phase obtrudes in the sequence is determined by the interaction of many factors, only some of which are understood but which almost certainly include genetically determined variations in predisposition. However, acquired styles of perception, thought, and expectations favoring the appraisal of stressful situations as "hopeless" and oneself as "helpless" are probably the paramount determiners, as will be seen.

"Normal" Depression

The time-limited and perhaps ultimately adaptive character of depression is probably nowhere better illustrated than in the process of grieving, usually understood as the reaction to the death of a loved one but actually occurring in many other situations of important psychological loss (e.g., divorce, the "breaking up" of romantic relationships, retirement from a valued career, physical incapacitation by illness, etc.). The individual sustaining the loss will typically react in the fear (anxiety)-rage, followed by depression, sequence noted above. He will be observed to "withdraw" from substantial engagement with the vicissitudes of life for a greater or lesser period of time, seeming to husband emotional resources and to protect himself from the threat of additional psychic assault; psychologically, the individual "rolls up in a ball." Sullivan (1956), among others, has likened the grieving process to that of "erasing" (in the language of conditioning, "extinguishing") the pain of the loss by continuous re-creation, in fantasy, of pain-evoking images of the prior situation until they lose their emotional charge, enabling eventual reassessment of current conditions on a more objective basis. Meanwhile, the person renders himself in other respects emotionally anesthetic, being essentially unaffected by varied ambient events that would otherwise evoke a strong response. Eventually, the sadness abates, energy returns, zest is recaptured, and the person begins again to engage the world in an active manner—often stronger, in some ways at least, for having weathered the storm and reassessed his personal future. Such is the customary outcome of the adaptive process. But some few, of course, become "stuck" somewhere in the middle, to emerge again as fully functioning persons only after prolonged misery, if at all. As indicated above, adaptive processes sometimes go awry. It should be noted in this connection that intense, prolonged grief is associated with increased risk of mortality and physical disease, probably by virtue of the effects of such stresses on the neuroendocrine system—notably, a significant increase in adrenocorticoid activity (Klerman and Izen, 1977).

As has been suggested, and quite aside from instances of explicit loss and consequent grief, probably very few individuals in any population have never experienced periods in which they have felt dejected, sad, lacking in motivation, socially withdrawn, and so forth. The occasional experience of depression in its milder forms appears nearly universal in the species. We do not know, nor do we have precise criteria for deciding, when such experiences reach intensities that *require* professional attention. However, the similarities between "normal" and "pathological" depressions are so manifold, qualitatively speaking, that they strongly suggest an essentially *continuous* distribution on the severity dimension; there are no evident gaps, and instances of depression allocate themselves along the entire range from minimal to profound.

Blatt and colleagues (1976) have conducted a questionnarie survey of depressive experiences in normal young adults, using items that specifically excluded those manifestations believed to be indicative of the more severe, "pathological" levels of the condition—i.e., the generally agreed-upon "symptoms" of depressive psychiatric disorder. They combined various other measures in their battery of instruments, and factor-analyzed the resultant correlation matrix to determine the main organizational dimensions within this domain of self-report, separately for males and females. The factor structures were quite stable and similar for each sex. Three main factors emerged: (1) dependency (themes of self as weak, powerless, in need of nurturance and sustenance); (2) self-criticism, or the tendency to play down any positive qualities of the self and to indulge in self-abnegation; and (3) inefficacy, the sense that events in the world are impervious to one's own actions or efforts. As we shall see, these same themes are prominent in the expressive behavior of clinically depressed persons, including the tendency to display behaviors that invite—if they do not forcefully provoke—nurturant responses from the environment. These responses, more often than not, do not produce any discernible positive effect on the depressed person should they be offered, which they often are in at least the initial phases of depressive shutdown. As a general rule, however, depressive behavior is aversive to others, thus creating the conditions for a type of deviation-amplifying environmental feedback.

Pathological Depression

The distinction between normal and pathological is frequently blurred in psychiatry, certainly no less—and in many instances more—than in other areas of medicine. Such is the case with respect to depression, as we have seen. To a large extent, the *psychiatric diagnosis* of depression is a matter of establishing degrees of deviation from the norm along various *dimensions* of behavior. Fortunately, it is often the case that deviations across various pertinent dimensions are at least moderately correlated (that is, they tend to occur together in clusters), which suggests some underlying order to the phenomena even though the etiological significance of the clustering may remain obscure.

Beck (1967) has summarized the literature on the symptoms of psychiatric depression as follows:

A. Emotional manifestations
   1. Dejected mood
   2. Self-dislike
   3. Loss of gratification
   4. Loss of attachments
   5. Crying spells
   6. Loss of mirth response
B. Cognitive and motivational manifestations
   1. Low self-evaluation
   2. Negative expectations
   3. Self-blame and self-criticism
   4. Indecisiveness
   5. Distorted self-image
   6. Loss of motivation ("paralysis of will")
   7. Suicidal wishes
   8. Increased dependency

C. Vegetative and physical manifestations
   1. Loss of appetite
   2. Sleep disturbance
   3. Loss of libido
   4. Fatigability
D. Delusions
   1. Of worthlessness
   2. Of crime and punishment
   3. Nihilistic
   4. Of somatic alteration or deterioration
   5. Of poverty
E. Hallucinations (in 13%–25% of severely depressed patients)

In practice, clinicians make judgments as to the presence and severity of these various manifestations, the "diagnosis" being determined by a kind of weighted summing across the indications that are present. Beck concludes, on the basis of a variety of evidence, that there are few if any supportable arguments for establishing various types of depressive disorder based on symptoms alone. Differences among clinically depressed people (and between these and the "normally" depressed) are quantitative (more vs. less severe) rather than qualitative at the behavioral level, which is the level at which we are, for the present at least, largely constrained to operate in this matter. For example, in a random sample of 100 persons diagnosed clinically as "neurotically" or "psychotically" depressed (N = 50 each), the typical signs and symptoms of depression (aside from delusions and hallucinations, which are definitionally involved) were found in a large proportion of members of both groups (Beck, 1967). Similarly, Miller (1975), in an extensive review of psychological deficits in depression, concludes that there are strikingly few differences in such deficits among the various purported subtypes of depressive disorder; such differences are ones of *degree* rather than of kind.

Predisposing Variable

Descriptions of severe depressive disorder (and of the psychological opposite, mania) go back more than 2000 years, and yet it still remains in many ways a puzzling and paradoxical phenomenon. It is now virtually certain that a genetically determined diathesis is implicated as a predisposing factor in at least many instances of the disorder. The mechanism of transmission is as yet unknown, but it clearly does not follow any simple Mendelian pattern. The site or sites of biological vulnerability remain similarly obscure, although there is growing evidence that they may involve aberrations in the availability for use of neurotransmitter substances at pertinent synaptic sites (as detailed in Chapter 14). The frequent alleviation of the symptoms of the disorder by electroconvulsive therapy, and more commonly in recent years by pharmacological means, represents, of course, a strong case for an abnormal biological substrate in at least some cases.

A number of psychosocial variables have also been found to be associated with increased risk of depressive disorder. These include the following: (1) excessive dependence of self-esteem on external sources of evaluation (Becker, 1977); (2) excessive interpersonal dependency (although the research literature here is quite complex and occasionally contradictory) (Becker, 1977); and (3) the occurrence of bereavement in childhood due to loss of a parent—in Beck's (1967) series, 27% of these cases had experienced the death of at least one parent prior to age 16! Promising early investigations of a distinctive type of family background in predepressives have failed to be substantiated in later work, possibly because of pronounced cultural changes in the interim. Nevertheless, the basic idea of this early work—that the predepressive is subjected to simultaneous contradictory injunctions within his family of origin to succeed and not to succeed—is closely related to certain modern theories of the psychology of depression, as will be seen.

Precipitating Variables

It would appear that some disorders of affect occur without notable precipitating stress. These are so-called "endogenous" disorders of which the often dramatic bipolar manic-depressive syndrome is alleged to be an example. (In this disorder, the same patient experiences elated, hyperactive, often belligerent and dominating "manic" episodes along with depressive episodes in varied combinations, sometimes alternating in temporal contiguity.) In point of fact, estimates of the proportion of affective disorders in which precipitating circumstances are implicated vary from almost none (Winokur and Pitts, 1964) to almost all (Travis, 1933; Leff et al., 1970), but these estimates are clearly affected by the theoretical biases of investigators. In general, the broader the definition of "stress" (including, for example, some life changes that appear objectively positive—a promotion at work) and the more thorough the search of patients' immediately preceding histories, the greater the likelihood of discovering clear precipitants of the disorder. There is currently considerable doubt about the validity of a sharp distinction between "endogenous" depressions (those arising simply as a result of internal biological events) and "reactive" depressions (those caused entirely by life circumstances, past and present) (Leff et al., 1970; Thomson and Hendrie, 1972; Prange, 1973; Stainbrook, 1977; White et al., 1977). It seems true, however, that depressive affect, once evoked by whatever combination of internal and external factors, has the capacity to become a depressive mood and thus more *autonomous*, i.e., unresponsive to external psychological stimuli and to the appraisal (and reappraisal) processes as described in Chapter 10. Akiskal and McKinney (1975, p. 287) emphasize the clinical importance of recognizing this autonomous state because, when present, it requires additional, often somatic, treatment, since the patient may be too overwhelmed by depression and too unreachable to respond to human interactional (psychotherapeutic) techniques alone.

Paykel (1973) and colleagues have conducted a painstaking study of a representative sample of 185 depressed persons, comparing them with 185 matched controls from the general population of the same locale. Major differences were found between depressives and controls in both the number and quality of significant life events said to have occurred in the previous six months. For 8 of the 33 events on their schedule, differences between the groups were statistically significant, and a fair number of the remaining 25 probably would also have attained significance but for their generally low base rates of occurrence in the subjects' lives. Subject to possible biases created by retrospective distortion, the eight events occurring significantly more often in the immediately preceding experience of depressives were:

1. Increase in arguments with spouse ($p < .01$)
2. Marital separation ($p < .01$)
3. Start of a new type of work ($p < .01$)
4. Change in work conditions ($p < .05$)
5. Serious personal illness ($p < .05$)
6. Death of immediate family member ($p < .05$)
7. Serious illness of family member ($p < .05$)
8. Family member leaves home ($p < .05$)

Additional analyses of the data strongly supported the notion that undesirable, distressing prior events (as opposed to neutral or positive ones) were especially prominent in the lives of depressives. Moreover, it appears that actual or threatened *separations* from important others is a highly specific (although by no means exclusive) precipitant of depression, a fact amply documented throughout the symposium in which Paykel's referenced work appears (Scott and Senay, 1973). In only about 15% of the Paykel's series was there *no* identifiable precipitating stress.

Beck (1967), in his major and scholarly treatise on depression, lists the following as the most frequently encountered precipitating circumstances:

1. Situations that tend to lower self-esteem
2. Thwarting of important goals or the posing of an insoluble dilemma
3. Physical disease or abnormality that activates ideas of deterioration or death
4. Varied stressors occurring in a series
5. Single events of overwhelming magnitude, e.g. disasters
6. Highly insidious stressors unrecognized as such by the affected person

According to Beck, situations such as these will precipitate depression only in depression-prone individuals. The depression-prone person is one who harbors certain negative cognitive schemata (often latently) that become activated under stressful circumstances. These schemata are organized in terms of a "primary triad" consisting of negative views of self, negative views of experience in the world, and negative views of the future. In Beck's view, it is these negative cognitions that determine and color the depressive's dysphoric affect (rather than the other way around, as some would see it), although he allows for the possibility of circular feedback between negative cognitive schemata and affective structures. In any event, as depression deepens these negative schemata increasingly dominate the patient's interpretation of all life events, leading to characteristic disorders of thought. The latter include distortion and misinterpretation, perseveration, and loss of objectivity.

Psychological Theories of Depression

There is a well-established and well-known body of literature dealing with the "depressive" effects of early infantile deprivation and separation in both humans and animals. To summarize, and probably to oversimplify somewhat, this literature amply documents the devastating effects on psychological development of an absence of organism-environment interaction of a reciprocal and mutually contingent type. Some of these effects appear to be at least partially irreversible in terms of their refractoriness to a variety of compensatory measures introduced at later ages. Some people, in short, acquire a depressive stance toward themselves and the world very early in life, and this often remains essentially unchanged throughout their lives. These circumstances have prompted the development of various theories of depression that are basically elaborations of classical psychodynamic (chiefly Freudian) conceptions of the requirements of healthy development. We will forego detailed discussion of these views here, because the reader will doubtlessly encounter them in other contexts. Instead, we will concentrate on certain less-well-known but more contemporary and analytically precise (although as yet equally unproven) formulations of the depressive process that subsume and give some promise of extending the data base supporting these more classical views. In any event, it must be acknowledged that the occurrence of social deprivation and significant separations in early life, even if insufficiently severe to produce obvious childhood disorder, might well contribute (as some evidence suggests) to a predisposition to respond with depression to a variety of common stressors encountered in adult life.

Eastman (1976) has recently reviewed the major "behavioral" formulations of depression, all of them relatively new, and all of them focusing upon various aspects of behavior-consequence ("reinforcement") contingencies, albeit in very different ways in terms of details. The basic idea is that depression, as a set of *behaviors*, is a function of reinforcement contingencies. Insofar as a salient aspect of depression is an *absence* of behavior, particularly of an adaptive sort, the problem becomes one of accounting for the anomalies of reinforcement in the depressed individual's life that would explain this paucity of effective behavior. Several possibilities have presented themselves.

One type of behavioral formulation of depression is based on the idea of *inadequate reinforcement*, in terms of a reduced frequency of reinforcement, a poor quality of reinforcement, or an insufficient total quantity of reinforcement per unit time. Theoretically, any of these would indeed produce a paucity of operant (operating on the environment) responding. While this idea is attractive in possibly accounting for the *maintenance* of depression, it does not speak very effectively to the question of predisposing and precipitating *causes* of depressive episodes. It is true that much of the depressed person's behavior seems ill-adapted to the continuous *production* of positive reinforcement, particularly in the social realm, but how does it originate in the face of this very fact? Conceivably, such behavior is at first effective in generating succorance in the environment which then abates as the person's demands continue or increase, but this would still leave unaccounted for the initial emergence of extraordinary needs for succorance.

Another view emphasizes the notion of a loss of *reinforcable behavior* as a determinative aspect of depression. Such loss in the functional behavioral repertoire might occur as a consequence of: (1) behaviors that are aversively motivated (i.e., "defensive" behaviors), becoming so prepotent as to preempt most of the behavioral output; or (2) direct reduction of reinforcable behavior by various processes such as erratic or capricious occurrence of reinforcers, large and sudden environmental changes calling for new behavior, or generalized anger.

A third view of the vicissitudes of reinforcement as they relate to depression is that of a *loss of reinforcement effectiveness* by virtue or either underlying neurobiological events (such as any that might render the organism anhedonic) or the disruption of sequences of behavior on which reinforcement effectiveness is dependent—some reinforcements losing their hedonic charge unless they occur with other events in a sequence, as in certain aspects of sexual behavior.

A fourth view is basically similar to the first, but adds the notion that *aversive stimuli* (i.e., circumstances evoking unpleasant feelings leading to avoidance or escape behaviors) are the primary reasons for failure to obtain reinforcements that are in fact available.

The above views are not necessarily mutually incompatible, and each is supported by at least some evidence, however indirect. A more comprehensive theory to come out of behavioral science laboratories in recent years, one that in some ways subsumes much of the above, is the *learned helplessness* notion, advanced chiefly by Seligman (1975). Seligman's ideas originated in a simple but perhaps profound observation. If dogs are repeatedly subjected to painful, unpredictable, inescapable electric shocks, a majority of them will subsequently be unable to learn a very simple adaptive response enabling them to avoid or escape from additional shocks; these dogs simply stand and take the very painful stimulation, even though they could avoid it (as do unpretreated dogs) by making a modest motor response. It appears that these dogs just "give up," and thus the designation learned helplessness was coined to describe their state.

Utilizing data from a multitude of sources, although often somewhat loosely, Seligman has expanded this observation into a theory of depression as learned helplessness. Basically, according to this idea, the depressive is a person who has learned by an unfortunate type of characteristic experience that behaving "doesn't help," whether in the face of aversive or of positive incentives to do so. In other words, the depressed person has learned (believes) that hedonically relevant outcomes are *independent* of his/her own behavior. Thus, it is as possible for someone who has had it "all good" to become depressed as it is for someone who has had it "all bad," a suggestion that is not without some substance at a strictly observational level.

The condition of noncontingency between outcome and behavior may be schematized as follows:

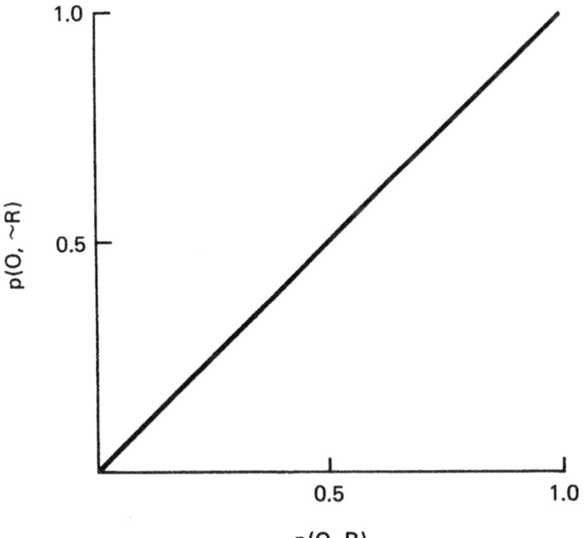

In this graph, where p (O,R) is the probability of the outcome when the organism responds, and p (O,~R) is the probability of the outcome when the organism does not perform the pertinent response, the diagonal function depicts the condition of noncontingency and represents the theoretical antecedent of "learned helplessness."

The basic work on learned helplessness was carried out on animals. It has subsequently been demonstrated that the condition is acquirable by normal human subjects, although it is by no means the only reaction such subjects have to noncontingency pretreatments. It is also clear that a large element of cognitive appraisal determines how humans will respond to such treatment. There is some evidence, as well as sound theory, suggesting that nonresponse-contingent *positive* reinforcement does indeed have debilitating effects on human subjects. However, the theory of learned helplessness as a basic aspect of depression has as yet not been adequately tested, and indeed it is not obvious how a direct test of this hypothesis could be performed.[1] It is, however, an attractive idea, and it does suggest a number of interesting connections with both the phenomena of depression (as indicated above) and other theories seeking to explain it, notably Engel's conservation-withdrawal hypothesis. The individual predisposed by earlier experiences in which he was truly helpless to influence sources of pleasure and pain will tend to appraise new situations as beyond his control and thus to move rapidly from the fear-rage positions to that of depressive affect, the position of "giving up."

Depression as a Psychophysiologic Disorder?

We have emphasized psychological factors in this chapter. Nevertheless, three facts about severe depression compel attention to aberrant biological involvement: (1) there appears to be a significant biologically based diathesis that is genetically transmitted in many instances of the disorder, (2) these disorders sometimes abate promptly with the administration of a variety of direct biological interventions, and (3) profound alterations in biological functions (e.g., sleep) often accompany the pertinent behavioral phenomena. On the other hand, there is certainly overwhelming evidence of a psychological causal element in most (if not all) cases of depression. The idea of an interaction between the two types of influences is certainly not new, but it is increasingly attractive as more is learned. Could it be, for example, that certain types of psychological stress (e.g., "helplessness"), when prolonged, might trigger transitory or persistent alteration in the chemical quality of synaptic clefts in particular brain pathways? It could be, and some evidence from varied sources suggests that it does. Akiskal and McKinney (1973, 1975) have developed a quite elaborate and sophisticated psychophysiologic model of depression that integrates in an effective way much of the information contained in this entire group of chapters on affect and mood. The succeeding chapter undertakes a detailed discussion of the neurobiological side of the coin.

[1]For a thorough discussion of the issues, see J. Abnorm. Psychol. 87(1), February 1978.

References

Akiskal, H.S., and W.T. McKinney. Overview of recent research in depression. Archiv. Gen. Psychiat. 32:285–305, 1975.

Akiskal, H.S., and W.T. McKinney. Depressive disorders: Toward a unified hypothesis. Science 182:20–29, 1973.

Beck, A.T. Depression: Causes and Treatment. Philadelphia, Pennsylvania: University of Pennsylvania Press, 1967.

Becker, J. Affective Disorders. Morristown, New Jersey: General Learning Press, 1977.

Blatt, S.J., J.P. D'Afflitti, and D.M. Quinlan. Experiences of depression in normal young adults. J. Abnorm. Psychol. 85:383–389, 1976.

Eastman, C. Behavioral formulations of depression. Psychological Review 83:277–291, 1976.

Engel, G.L. Psychological Development in Health and Disease. New York, New York: Saunders, 1962.

Klerman, G.L., and J.E. Izen. The effects of bereavement and grief on physical health and general well-being. In S. Kasl and F. Reichsman (Eds.) Advances in Psychosomatic Medicine. Basel, Switzerland: Karger 9:63–104, 1977.

Leff, M.J., J.F. Roatch, and W.E. Bunney, Jr. Environmental factors preceding the onset of severe depressions. Psychiatry 33:293–311, 1970.

Miller, W.R. Psychological deficit in depression. Psychological Bulletin 82:238–260, 1975.

Paykel, E.S. Life events and acute depression. In J.P. Scott and E. C. Senay (Eds.) Separation and Depression, Washington, D.C.: American Association for Advancement of Science, 1973, pp. 215–236.

Prange, A.J. Jr. The use of drugs in depression: Its practical and theoretical aspects. Psychiatric Annuals 3:56–75, February 1973.

Scott, J.P., and E.C. Senay. (Eds.). Separation and Depression. Washington, D.C.: American Association for Advancement of Science, 1973.

Seligman, M. E. P. Helplessness. San Francisco, California: Freeman, 1975.

Stainbrook, E.J. Depression: The psychological context. In G. Usdin (Ed.) Depression: Clinical, Biological and Psychological Perspectives. New York, New York: Brunner/Mazel, 1977, pp. 28–51.

Sullivan, H.S. Clinical Studies in Psychiatry. New York, New York: Norton, 1956.

Thomson, K.C., and H.C. Hendrie. Environmental stress in primary depressive illness. Archiv. Gen. Psychiat. 26:130–132, February 1972.

Travis, J.H. Precipitating factors in manic-depressive psychoses. Psychiatric Quarterly 7:411–418, 1933.

White, R.B., H.K. Davis, and W.A. Cantrell. Psychodynamics of depression: Implications for treatment. In G. Usdin (Ed.) Depression: Clinical, Biological and Psychological Perspectives. New York, New York: Brunner/Mazel, 1977, pp. 308–338.

Winokur, G., and F.N. Pitts. Affective disorder, I. Is reactive depression an entity? J. Nerv. Ment. Dis. 138:541–547, 1964.

References

[illegible]

14

Pathology of Affect: Neurobiological Aspects

In Chapter 9 the dopamine theory of schizophrenia was reviewed, along with experimental data showing that genetically and environmentally determined variations in enzyme biosynthesis can influence amine levels and, hence, behavior. We shall now turn our attention to the possible neurochemical bases for disorders of affect and mood, with specific attention being given to the "catecholamine hypothesis" of depression. In addition, we shall consider the CNS mechanisms involved in regulating certain other behaviors which are also disrupted in association with clinical levels of depression.

Theories of Emotion

There are nearly as many theories of emotion as there are psychiatrists and psychologists interested in the subject. An exhaustive survey of these theories is not necessary here. The interested reader may consult Young (1973) or Arnold (1960, pp. 91–165) for more extended discussion. We shall provide a brief overview sufficient to point out some lines of theoretical difference and some trends in theorizing about affect, as well as to relate a few of the better known theories to our earlier discussion.

An important nineteenth-century theory of emotion, that of William James, focused on explaining the subjective emotional experience. In this view, the experience of an emotion results from sensing the visceral and other bodily changes evoked (directly) by certain situations. Without such sensations, it is argued, there is no emotion. In this extreme version, the theory (often referred to as the James-Lange theory because of similar views of a contemporaneous Danish worker) has been attacked both logically and empirically. Surgical separation of the visceral afferent pathways to the CNS does not alter emotional expression and behavior. Visceral changes are too slow and too uniform to account for the variety of emotional experience.

The classical alternative to the James-Lange theory of emotion is that of Walter Cannon (Cannon-Bard theory). Cannon offered a reflex arc concept in which the thalamus plays the key role in assessing and determining the occurrence and nature of emotional response to incoming stimuli.[1] The hypothalamus is seen as the next portion of the arc, the highest point in the efferent system producing visceral responses and thereby enabling the production of skeletal behaviors. In this system, the cortex serves chiefly as an inhibitory modulator, damping thalamic activity which would otherwise result in excessive emotional response. Bard demonstrated that emotional expression is preserved, in somewhat exaggerated form, after decerebration, but lost when the transection is posterior to the caudal hypothalamus. Anatomically, the Cannon-Bard theory and most of those that have followed are more concerned with CNS function and are considered "central" theories of emotion, in contrast with the James-Lange view which focuses on the autonomic nervous system and is termed "peripheral."

The view of Papez extended the central theory of Cannon and Bard by implicating higher levels of the nervous system in the appraisal aspects of the emotional process. Diencephalic areas retain their position as links in the reflex arc, but the essential processes of discrimination and assessment of incoming stimuli for their emotional significance are now thought to be located in the limbic system, especially the hippocampus, amygdala, cingulate gyrus, fornix, and mamillary bodies. In MacLean's (1949, 1973) closely related concept of the triune brain, the limbic system is termed the "visceral brain" and is viewed as an early vertebrate evolutionary development layered upon the diencephalic and other brain stem areas, but itself later overlaid by the neocortex. The visceral brain, which includes the limbic structures already listed plus the septal area, provides (as in the Papez view) the initial emotional-motivational significance for incoming stimuli, but is regulated and subject to finer modulations in higher forms by the rapidly expanding neocortex which reaches its ultimate development in man. MacLean emphasizes the consequences to man of this evolutionary development, likening the neocortex to a rider in uneasy control of a spirited horse, the visceral brain. He sees these relationships as partial explanation of man's vulnerability to emotional turmoil and illness. This is essentially a horizontal or Jacksonian view of neural function, emphasizing evolutionary levels interacting with each other, the function of the higher levels being essentially that of control.

[1]The concept of "appraisal," to which we have given much attention, is the particular contribution of Magda Arnold (1960).

In some contrast to this Jacksonian model are more vertical concepts which identify neural systems extending over more than one anatomico-evolutionary level, each vertical system mediating some distinguishable behavior function such as appraisal of emotional significance, arousal and control of the level of consciousness, or activation of effectory pathways (Pribram, 1967). There also appears to be some support for the vertical position from recent neurochemical studies revealing multilevel CNS pathways, each with a characteristic neurotransmitter. At present, however, it would seem wise to view both vertical and horizontal conceptions of brain function, including the mediation of affect, as complementing positions needed to explain various experimental and clinical findings. The same may be said of central and peripheral views of emotion, or views which emphasize perceptual-cognitive (appraisal) aspects and those which emphasize emotion as motive or drive together with the visceral and somatomotor consequences of those drives. In each case, both aspects are required for a complete picture of the process.

The Catecholamine Hypothesis

In the mid 1960s, Schildkraut (1965), and Bunney and Davis (1965) advanced the hypothesis that depression results from a functional decrease in turnover of norepinephrine (NE) in the synaptic cleft of critical neurons in certain brain areas. On the other hand, mania might result from an excess of NE. They based this hypothesis on the observations that monoamine oxidase inhibitors and tricyclic antidepressants, both of which are effective in reducing symptoms of depression, all serve to increase the functional levels of NE in the synaptic cleft. Monoamine oxidase inhibitors slow the degradation of NE, while tricyclics prevent removal of NE from the synaptic cleft by blocking the reuptake mechanism. Additional support for the catecholamine hypothesis derived from the observation that reserpine, which depletes brain NE stores, evokes depression in about 25% of the patients treated for high blood pressure with this compound.

In an extensive series of studies, Bunney et al. (1971) attempted to document the effects on mood of specific alteration in brain levels of various biogenic amines. Their rationale for these studies is outlined in Figure 14-1, where it is seen that the neurotransmitters—NE, dopamine, and serotonin—do not cross the blood-brain barrier and hence do not affect brain amine stores when given peripherally. On the other hand, the precursors of these amines, L-dopa and L-tryptophan, do cross the blood-brain barrier, and it is possible to increase CNS levels of the monoamines by means of this "precursor loading" approach. The use of L-dopa to increase striatal dopamine levels to relieve symptoms of parkinsonism is based upon this approach. As is also shown in Figure 14-1, it is possible to decrease CNS catecholamine

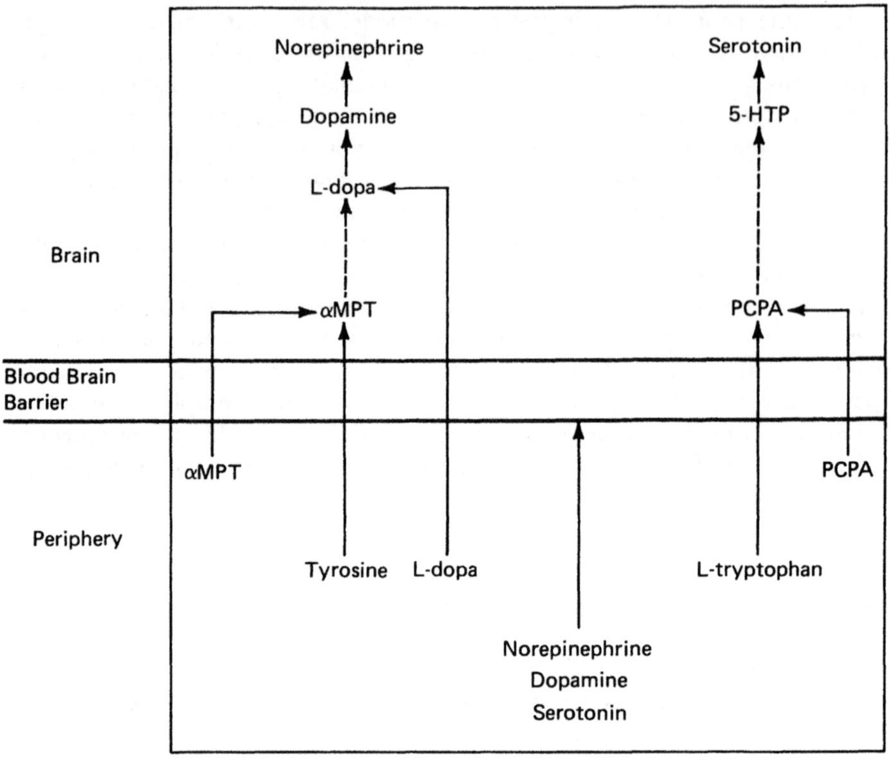

Fig. 14-1. Schematic representation of compounds affecting brain neurotransmitters.

levels by using alpha-methyl-para-tyrosine (AMPT) to block the conversion by tyrosine hydroxylase of tyrosine to L-dopa, and by using para-chlorophenylalanine (PCPA) to block the conversion by tryptophan hydroxylase of tryptophan to 5-hydroxytryptophan. Thus, pharmacologic means are available to both increase and decrease brain levels of such important neurotransmitters as NE, dopamine, and serotonin.

Since AMPT inhibits the synthesis of NE and dopamine, it would be predicted to decrease manic symptoms and increase depressive symptoms by decreasing the availability of these compounds in the brain. Five of seven manic patients treated with AMPT showed decreases in their manic symptoms; however, only two of these patients became worse again when placebo was substituted for AMPT. A particularly clear illustration of the apparent relation between AMPT administration and improvement of mania is shown in Figure 14-2. The day before starting AMPT, the patient was highly disturbed, as reflected in the nurses' daily mania ratings and in the observed behaviors of yelling, giving orders, and needing to be in seclusion. By the second day of AMPT administration, the patient was out of seclusion, well-groomed, and in very good control of her behavior. This improvement in behavioral status continued throughout the six days on AMPT until the

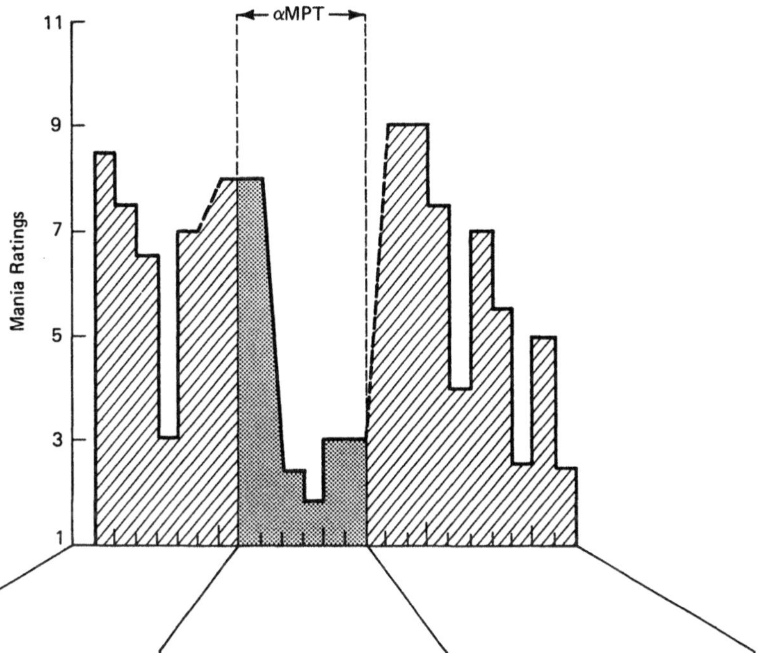

DAYS PRIOR TO αMPT ADMINISTRATION	DAYS ON αMPT	DAYS AFTER αMPT DISCONTINUED
DAY −3 Very talkative and seeking attention DAY −2 Talked nonstop from change of shift; intrusive behavior; placed in seclusion DAY −1 Remained in seclusion; yelling; demanding; giving orders	FIRST Demanding SECOND Out of seclusion in morning; neatly groomed; in very good control THIRD In very good control; busy baking bread in kitchen FOURTH Talking warmly about her brother's visit	DAY +1 Has been argumentative and resistive DAY +2 Flitting perpetually about the unit; constant chatter DAY +3 Loud and obtrusive behavior in hallway; in seclusion; loud and demanding DAY +4 Argumentative; extremely demanding; speech is pressured; grandiose

Fig. 14-2. Description of clinical improvement in mania with AMPT.

second and third days of placebo substitution, when her behavior deteriorated to the levels observed on day 1. It should be noted that the nurses making the observations and behavioral ratings on the NIMH research ward where this study was conducted were not aware of the shifts in medication from placebo to AMPT and back again to placebo.

Only 6 of 19 depressed patients treated with L-dopa showed a clinically significant improvement in their depressive symptoms in response to active drug administration. Of these, only four had relapses following placebo substitution. It is interesting to note that none of the responses to L-dopa occurred in patients with agitated (hand-wringing and pacing up and down) depressions, while six of seven patients with a history of bipolar affective illness (history of both manic and depressive episodes) showed an increase in manic behavior while on L-dopa.

With regard to increasing brain serotonin levels via administration of the precursor L-tryptophan, only one of eight patients so treated showed a significant clinical improvement on the drug and an increase in depression when placebo was substituted.

While providing some support for the hypothesis that treatment to decrease brain catecholamine levels is associated with a decrease in severity of symptoms among manic patients and that treatment to increase brain catecholamine levels is associated with symptomatic improvement among depressed patients, the findings of this study also indicate that both depression and mania are "biologically heterogeneous" conditions. A simple theory that levels of CNS monoamines are altered in one direction would not account for the observations made.

This point concerning heterogeneity can also be made in dispelling another misconception to which physicians, with their tendency to dichotomize and categorize, are prone. As noted in the preceding chapter, one hears of a contrast between depressions which are "endogenous" versus those which are "exogenous." The latter are felt to be in reaction to some stressful life event, such as a loss; while the former are felt to have their basis in biological (and hence genetically determined) characteristics of the individual, such as deficiency of brain tyrosine hydroxylase that could lead to decreased functional NE in the synaptic cleft. Just as was argued with regard to possible paths to increased dopamine levels in schizophrenia, it can also be argued that decreased brain NE levels can result from both genetic ("endogenous") and environmental ("exogenous") factors. If we assume that diminished levels of NE or serotonin form the basis whereby both genetic and environmental factors act to bring about a depressed mood, a graph similar to that in Figure 9-1 can be drawn to illustrate how genetic and environmental factors interact to bring about that change in affect and mood which we recognize clinically as depression.

To bring the argument concerning the catecholamine hypothesis of depression up to date, the latest evidence suggests that some patients with depression have as their primary defect a decrease in functional NE levels, as manifested by decreased urinary excretion of MHPG, a metabolite of NE which is felt to be derived mainly from central nervous system NE breakdown. These patients appear to respond better to a tricyclic antidepressant such as imipramine (Tofranil) which selectively blocks NE reuptake mechanisms. A second group of depressed patients appear to suffer from a deficit of brain serotonin, as manifested by normal to high urinary MHPG excretion and low cerebrospinal fluid levels of the serotonin metabolite 5-HIAA. These patients appear to respond better to the tricyclic amitriptyline (Elavil), a more specific blocker of serotonin reuptake.

On the basis of the above discussion, and despite the absence of final answers to the question of the role of the monoamines in determining affect and mood, the weight of the presently available evidence—both clinical and experimental—suggests the involvement of brain monoamine systems in the regulation of these mental states. When evaluating the patient who appears depressed, our confidence concerning the presence of a clinically significant depression is greatly enhanced when the patient also indicates to us the presence of certain changes in the "vegetative" functions of appetite, sleep, and sex. Our confidence in the monoamine hypothesis of depression might also be increased by the knowledge that brain monoamine systems are intimately involved in the regulation of these vegetative functions. While we cannot go into detail on these matters here, suffice to say that in fact such brain amine control of these functions has been amply documented in contemporary research. Thus we would expect that a patient with a depression resulting from decreased catecholamines in the CNS would also be likely to exhibit other signs of diminished catecholamine levels, such as decreased appetite and decreased sexual drive. Indeed, it is a measure of the brain's involvement in a depressive process that we are taking when we inquire after the patient's sleeping, eating, and sexual behaviors. When these are found to be disrupted in association with depressed mood, we have, in effect, performed a "bioassay" of the integrity of the brain monoamine system's functional status.

References

Arnold, M. Emotion and Personality. New York, New York: Columbia University Press, 1960.

Bunney, W.E., Jr., H.K.H. Brodie, D.L. Murphy, and F.K. Goodwin. Studies of alpha-methyl-para-tyrosine, L-DOPA and L-tryptophan in depression and mania. Am. J. Psychiat. 127:48, 1971.

Bunney, W.E., Jr., and J.M. Davis. Norepinephrine in depressive reactions: A review. Arch. Gen. Psychiat. 13:483–494, 1965.

MacLean, P.D. Psychosomatic disease and the "visceral brain:" Recent developments bearing on the Papez theory of emotion. Psychosomatic Medicine 11:338–353, November-December 1949.

MacLean, P.D. A triune concept of the brain and behaviour. In T.J. Boag and D. Campbell (Eds.) The Clarence M. Hincks Memorial Lectures, 1969. Toronto, Canada: University of Toronto Press, 1973, pp. 4–66.

Pribram, K.H. Emotion: Steps toward a neuropsychological theory. In D.C. Glass (Ed.) Neurophysiology and Emotion. New York, New York: Rockefeller University Press, 1967, pp. 3–40.

Schildkraut, J.J. The catecholamine hypothesis of affective disorders: A review of supporting evidence. Am. J. Psychiat. 122:509, 1965.

Young, P.T. Feeling and emotion. In B.B. Wolman (Ed.) Handbook of General Psychology. Englewood Cliffs, New Jersey: Prentice-Hall, 1973, pp. 749–771.

Unit IV

Personality and Interpersonal Functions

In Units I through III we have examined certain fundamental phenomena associated with organic brain dysfunction, biobehavioral dispositional influences on behavior, and variations in affect and mood as they may underlie and color the adaptation of individuals to the exigencies of life. In Unit IV we undertake to extend the analysis to a still more personal and individualistic level, to a consideration of those behavioral characteristics of a person that represent his or her unique way of having learned to deal with the world as he or she construes it—given constraints of a prior or concurrent nature emanating from organic limitations, constitutional predispositions, and prevailing affective proclivities and moods. In short, we shall be dealing here with behavioral phenomena normally falling within the rubric of "personality," with its origins, its functional characteristics, and the manner in which it may become dysfunctional for the individual and for those with whom he or she must interact in the course of everyday living.

15

The Nature of Personality

While there are many definitions of personality existing, little will be lost if, for the present, we limit ourselves to its most general and abstract meaning: Personality is an hypothetical construct referring to an organized system of reaction tendencies that mediates relations between the person and his/her environment, rendering the person's behavior distinctive and more or less uniquely identifying. The term derives from the Greek *persona*, or mask, the "face" the individual displays to the world, although in modern usage there is no suggestion of drama, or intent, or even necessarily of conscious awareness. The construct is a complex one in that it refers not only to "surface" behavior but also to its purported underlying causes, its "dynamics" so to speak, whether or not these may be accessible to the consciousness of the individual concerned.

The *scientific* necessity for the concept appears to rest on three common observations: (1) characteristic patterns of behavior vary from one person to another in ways that tend to be idiosyncratic and distinctively identifying; (2) each person's behavior exhibits a certain lawfulness or regularity, even if not surface consistency, across situations and over time; and (3) notwithstanding (2) above, a person's characteristic behavior undergoes modification in the face of changing circumstances and in ways not readily explained by any notion of rigid unfolding of an innately determined "program." It would seem, then, that a person's personality represents his or her largely acquired style of coping with the world, including certain underlying structural characteristics where, however, the system normally retains a degree of malleability on a continuing basis. Looked at in this way, early structuralizations might be of special significance, and indeed most theories of personality assume this to be the case.

Determinants of Personality

The origins of adult personality elude precise description. Given the multitude of influences that are undoubtedly implicated and the complexity with which they interact over time, there is little basis for believing that we will ever have an entirely satisfactory and complete account of how an individual comes to be the person he or she is. At the present time, in any event, we can at most point only to the major sources of influence, and then only on a very general level. Some of these have already been elucidated in previous chapters, and we begin here with a focused review of the pertinent earlier material.

Of the world's millions of people, only monozygotic twins share a common heredity; their common environment in some basic sense terminates with the splitting of the zygote, initiating what is in most respects an increasing environmental differentiation from that point. Every human neonate enters the world, therefore, with equipment that is at least in some aspects unique, and much of that equipment will profoundly affect the directions personality development will take.

External physical differences are an obvious part of these innate "givens." Anomalies of one sort or another, variations in size or physique, the appearance of the genitals (see Chapter 8), and the attractiveness of the child's features will all influence the behavior of others toward the newborn from its earliest moments of neonatal existence. These behaviors, constituting a special type of feedback experience, will in turn be registered and processed by the newborn within the limits of its processing capacity, and will be incorporated as part of its initial "sense" of what the self and the world is like. Such neonatal "prehensions" may determine to some extent the nature of the child's behavioral output, which in turn would further influence reactions in the social environment.

The child's behavior will also be determined in a more direct sense by innate, constitutional factors, as has been described at length in the foregoing Units of this work. He or she will have arrived in the world with predispositions to respond in particular ways to impinging stimuli, and some of these predispositions will vary from child to child. The child will also have certain prevailing characteristics of activity level, affect and mood, irritability, etc. that are to some degree distinctive and more or less independent of ambient events. Some of these characteristics, or their direct derivatives, may persist as background features in the individual's behavior over long periods, perhaps even a lifetime. Even if brief in duration, these temperamental qualities will often produce conformational reactions in others, thereby affecting the nature of the individual's social experience and in turn his or her cognitive understanding of self and the world.

In short, the underpinnings of personality are profoundly rooted in the biological organism. This fact notwithstanding, it is abundantly clear that much of what we regard as the behavioral manifestations of personality is acquired or learned. Or, to put it another way, personality is to an important degree formed out of life experience, albeit life experience that is determined to some extent by innate qualities in the individual. We merely wish to remind the reader once again that the product, adult personality, is a multidetermined phenomenon.

Personality and Behavior

In the final analysis, the concept of personality must be rooted in objectively observable phenomena, in behavior that can be tied more or less directly and explicitly to the concept(s) purporting to explain or account for it. While the basic notion of personality, as outlined above, has a certain intuitive appeal, it has been challenged very vigorously and effectively in recent years largely on the basis of persistent failures to demonstrate transsituational consistencies in the behavior of normal persons. That is, behavior as grossly defined tends to vary much more with normative situational constraints than it does with some presumed internal characteristics of the behaving person, all the more so if that behaving person is a random selection from the population of persons considered to be adaptive and well-adjusted, i.e., from the "normal" population. This observation suggests that consistency is itself a "trait" on which people vary, and indeed they do (Bem and Allen, 1974).

It is not wholly surprising that persons considered to be well-adjusted and normal should prove to behave in ways more or less dictated by situational constraints as conventionally conceived. Indeed, such an observation is almost necessarily tautological; abnormal behavior, practically by definition, is behavior that does *not* conform to a certain normative range of behaviors believed to be appropriate for any given situation. Much of abnormal behavior is not extraordinary or unusual per se, but is so only because it is enacted in contexts in which some other set of responses is believed called for. The person who frequently laughs and jokes is not especially remarkable; should he or she do so during the funeral proceedings for a deceased parent, there might be serious questions raised about that person's mental health. In other words, it is the case that much of the behavior of persons in general does indeed track fairly closely with situational requirements, whether deliberately or not. It would be a mistake, however, to conclude that any such phenomenon is universal. Moreover, such observations frequently ignore the more subtle aspects of a person's behavior, being addressed exclusively to the "what" of the behavioral content and neglecting important considerations of "how," of the stylistic features with which a behavioral act is carried out. A personal signature on a document is from one point of view merely a personal signature; from another point of view it is an expressive act—expressive of the signer's "personality." There may be a virtually infinite number of ways of signing a name, entering a room, lighting a cigarette, having sex with a partner, or writing a chapter on personality, although as far as we know none of these variations has been systematically studied. All of them would be missed in the typical research study purporting to deal with personality phenomena. The point is that different persons often do the same things in different ways, in ways that are manifestations of their differing personalities, although these differences may not be obvious in gross codings of behavioral acts.

If persons were wholly controlled by the external stimuli impinging on them and if there were no constancies, regularities, or redundancies in their behaviors, then there would be no point to the personality construct, *unless* it could be demonstrated that each person's behavior was *distinctively* and *differentially* controlled by these external stimuli. We have stated here the crux of a frequently misunderstood issue in the psychology of personality, one seemingly as often misunderstood by the purported leaders of the field as by lay persons. "Trait" theorists emphasize constancies in a person's behavior across situations; "situationist" theorists emphasize variance in behavior across situations. Both groups can marshal strong support for their positions, although to do so requires a certain selective inattention to contrary facts (Bowers, 1973; Wachtel, 1973; Carson, 1979). An exclusive preoccupation with personality traits, in the classical sense of transsituational consistency of behavioral acts, will inevitably lead to many errors of prediction, particularly in respect to normal or well-adjusted persons. Similarly, an exclusive preoccupation with situational control of behavioral acts will also lead to many errors of prediction, unless the situations considered are very constraining, behavior is coded quite grossly, and/or the persons to be considered are quite behaviorally adaptive. It may be noted in this connection that strongly trait-oriented theories of personality have almost always originated in clinical practice, e.g., psychoanalysis.

The the main outlines of the resolution of this problem are now quite clear. Modern situationists (e.g., Mischel, 1973) acknowledge that persons are differentially oriented in an internal sense such that, functionally speaking, the external stimuli they confront are in part products of what they are as persons. Similarly, trait theorists (e.g., Kelly, 1955) of the modern era seem to increasingly see the differences between persons as residing to an important degree in the perceptual and cognitive domains; different persons "construe" the same event in personally distinctive ways. For both groups, then, behavior is a product of the *interaction* of personal, internal variables and external, impinging events; to a large extent, personality becomes in this shared view a matter of idiosyncrasy of information-processing systems.

Major Theoretical Perspectives

As is so often the case in intellectual disciplines that have not yet attained maturity (perhaps especially so in those whose content intersects with strong positions of philosophy, values, religion, etc., as is the case here), "theory," if it may be so called, does not always bear an obvious or direct relationship to what may be established as empirical fact on an objective basis. Thus, the field of "personality theory" is an abundantly populated one, and one in which concepts are normally sufficiently removed from precise observation in empirically referenced variables and concepts that frank disconfirmation of theoretical constructs is rarely possible. Supposedly competing theories therefore proliferate, but they do not in fact compete in the normally accepted scientific sense. By and large, they compete (if at all) by their varying attractions to philosophically predisposed adherents, quite independent of the scientific quality of the evidence on which they are supposedly based. This is not to say that such theorizing is useless, or even that most theorists reject scientific objectivity as a base. A distinction must be made, however, between theory tentatively and flexibly utilized as an intellectual tool for ordering observations and theory as an approximation to some ultimate reality. A good case can be made that theoretical propositions in *any* science should be viewed more in the former than in the latter terms. In respect to personality at this time in our history, the case is virtually an ironclad one. We take the position, therefore, that one criterion of good personality theory is that it is explicitly tied to intersubjectively reliable observations, a requirement that would largely rule out many of the more frivolous contenders in the field, whatever their current popularity (which is often considerable).

There will be no attempt here to individually review all or even a substantial portion of the major extant theories of personality. That has been done in superb fashion by others, notably Hall and Lindzey (1970). However, certain dominant thematic elements characterize the field, and it may be useful to identify and describe these in broad terms so that the reader may become familiar with the differing approaches taken in accounting for individual personhood. The rubrics utilized are quite arbitrary and should not be taken with undue seriousness.

Personality as Adaptation to Primitive Drives and Mental Contents. A certain variety of classic personality theory, perhaps best exemplified in Freudian psychoanalysis, posits primordial inner drives and mental structures as being at the root of all personality formation. The foundation is thus connected with the biological history of the species; it is innate, primitive, and uncivilized, and in one form or another it remains active throughout the person's life. This, then, is the original "depth" psychology. Individual differences among persons are explained largely as a product of the peculiar adaptations and compromises essentially forced upon the individual by a social environment that is intolerant of his or her primitive and uncivilized proclivities. This clash of forces, moreover, largely occurs outside of the individual's awareness, because persons are not equipped to handle the intensities of affect that any such awareness would necessarily entail—thus the concept of an unconscious part of the mind wherein these psychic conflicts occur. Therefore, according to these views, an individual's personality at any point in time represents the form of balance or standoff he or she has been able to achieve in accommodating to these conflicting and dynamic forces that exist within. The term "dynamic personality theory," for perhaps obvious reasons, usually refers to this general class of viewpoints.

Personality as Learned Responses to Internal and External Environments. Theorists of a "behavioral" persuasion are often made uncomfortable by any proposition that assigns causal status to "mental" events or structures, or that posits constructs of a highly abstract kind far removed from observable events. The behavioral viewpoint on personality is perhaps best illustrated in the work of Dollard and Miller (1950), although it is of interest that this work was apparently intended to make Freudian psychoanalysis palatable to behaviorally oriented psychologists. In any event, the most radical forms of behavioral personality theory assert that the whole of adult personality is nothing more than a collection of "habits" or response tendencies acquired more or less automatically (although often accidentally) on the basis of the simple forms of learning known as conditioning. As was seen in Chapter 10, these simple forms of learning are of two general types: classical (Pavlovian, respondent) and instrumental (Skinnerian, operant) conditioning, although some would argue that this distinction is false and unwarranted. Classical conditioning is especially implicated in response modification of smooth muscle and glands, and thus in the control of emotion and affect, whereas instrumental conditioning is said to relate chiefly to overt behavior. Application of this behavioral viewpoint has been very successful in recent years in the treatment of variety of personality and behavior disorders that were heretofore somewhat refractory to other therapeutic approaches. It should be noted, however, that the success of a treatment technique does not necessarily in itself validate the general conceptions underlying its deployment. Interestingly, the most recent developments in "behavior therapy" have had a distinctly cognitive slant, which brings us to the next main approach to personality theory.

Personality as the Manifestation of Idiosyncratic Cognitive Structures. The dynamic and behavioral viewpoints outlined above have tended to underplay the significance of thought, cognition, or information-processing in personality formation or functioning. Indeed, in their more radical formulations they tend to assign a status to such phenomena that is frankly disparaging. Dynamic theorists often regard cognitions as being wholly determined by other, more "basic" processes, and some behaviorists consider them to be mere "mental waystations" of no significance whatever in the determination of "real" (i.e., observable) behavior. The origins of cognitive personality theory cannot be precisely located with respect to historical personages of note; the contributors are many. In recent times, Kelly (1955), Ellis (1962), and in certain respects Sullivan (1953) and Piaget (1954) deserve credit for extending and formalizing the basic notions. According to this general view, a person's characteristic behavior, including his or her affects and moods, is determined to a large extent by the manner in which he or she processes the information arriving at receptor apparatuses. Processing "style" (for want of a better term) involving features of memory organization, cue selection, enhancement or suppression, rules for assimilation or accommodation (encoding), preemptive constructs, etc., is in turn determined by the nature of one's past experience, especially past experience with significant other people such as parents. As we have seen, the cognitive viewpoint has essentially provided the means of satisfactorily resolving the trait-situation controversy in personality research.

Personality as Idiosyncratic Constraints on Awareness. This is a rather mixed category of dubious scientific significance; it is included here mostly for the sake of closure and completeness. We would place within this rubric various views on personality that are usually described as "phenomenological," "humanistic," or "existential." They tend to share the common scientific fault of failing to distinguish between mere values and genuine empirical and theoretical propositions, such that they become as often as not statements of what their originators believe should or ought to be the case in respect to human behavior rather than attempts to account objectively for what *is*. The general theme that ties these views together is the idea that persons would be happy, well-adjusted, fully functional, etc. if they could but see or "experience" important aspects of life or of themselves. The alleged critical missing data vary somewhat from one of these approaches to another, depending on the particular ax to be ground. They are often discoverable, however, in certain types of dramatic group experience involving "encounter" or even "basic encounter" which, if the search is successful, is often said to provide the person with "authenticity." A phenomenological approach to problems of personality, i.e., one that treats the momentary experiences of the person as important data, certainly has much to recommend it. However, serious and systematic efforts in this direction have not as yet produced much, and such efforts in any case have almost always occurred outside of the framework of the broad "theoretical" perspectives described.

It is not our intent in this chapter to make an informed choice among the various viewpoints presented, much less to attempt any comprehensive integration of the things they have to say about human personality. All of them have their uses in differing contexts, and probably all of them say at least some things worthy of serious consideration. We leave them behind for now, however, in order to examine the relationship between personality and social interaction. The astute reader will note many points of contact with the foregoing discussion as this material is developed.

The Structure of Interpersonal Behavior

Evidence from a variety of sources, reviewed in Carson (1969) and more recently in Kiesler et al., 1976), indicates that informal social behavior is organized according to a surprisingly simple arrangement of basic elements.

The basic elements constitute two orthogonal (i.e., independent) bipolar dimensions whose poles are usually described as dominance vs. submission and love vs. hate. They define a Cartesian space within which virtually any socially significant behavioral act may be located, a space that is usually conceived as circular in form and in its psychometric properties. This "interpersonal behavior circumplex" is illustrated in Figure 15-1. Conceptually, any interpersonal act may be coded with respect to its location on both principal dimensions, where the point of their intersection is considered "neutrality" on both of them. The location thus defined within the circumplex indicates both the "quality" of the act in question—defined as the segment of the circle occupied within its 360 degrees—and its "intensity," which would be proportional to the length of a vector running from origin (the point of intersection of the two dimensions) to the point defined by the particular behavioral act. The circle may be divided into as many appropriately labeled segments as would be justified by the qualitative discriminability of the actions to which they refer (see Leary, 1957, who proposes 16 such segments). For our immediate purposes we will deal only with the two dimensions themselves and with the four quadrants thereby generated.

The "normal" or well-adjusted person, is by definition, capable of enacting behaviors that would qualitatively encompass the full 360 degrees of the circle, depending upon circumstance; such behaviors would largely be confined to the moderate ranges of intensity. In other words, the normal person can be dominant or passive, hostile or loving, or any combination of these (in moderation) depending upon what is warranted or "called for" in a given

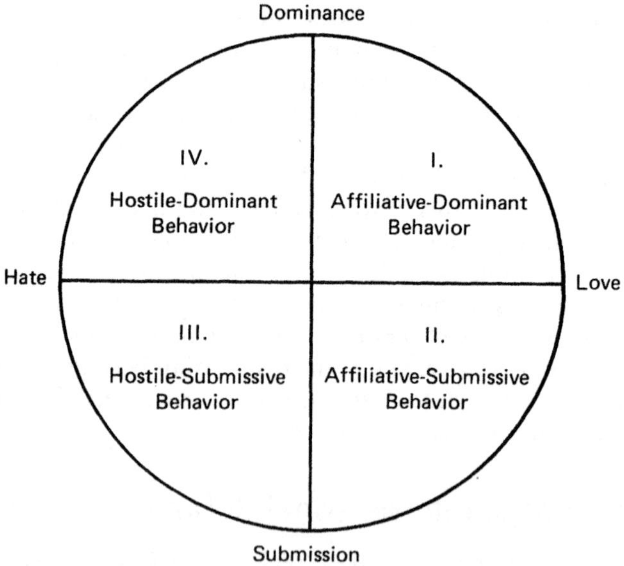

Fig. 15-1. The interpersonal behavior circumplex.

situation, including one in which his or her personal needs are a significant component. The "appropriateness" of a given behavior is determined partly by the impersonal social structure of the situation in which it is enacted, but also importantly by the behavior of other persons toward whom the behavior is directed. For example, "dominant" behavior cannot be very successfully carried off in the absence of someone who "submits." This point will be developed further in what follows.

While normal persons, in general, would be expected to be flexible in their behavioral output, adapting to the demands of the various social situations in which they engage, it is nevertheless true that most individuals exhibit distinct preferences for particular segments of the circle in terms of the relative frequency of the types of behavior they enact. To put it another way, a person expresses or manifests his or her personality in part by behaviorally claiming a particular portion of the circle as his or her own "thing." We use the term "claiming" here deliberately because, as will be seen, by behaving in the manner described the person places certain constraints upon the behavior of others with whom he or she interacts.

Social interchange is normally complementary in character, presumably because it facilitates transactions and eases awkwardness. The enactment of a given type of social behavior tends to "pull" responses of a given, complementary type from an interaction partner (Leary, 1957; Carson, 1969). Looked at in terms of the interpersonal behavior circle, these complementarities are readily specified: affiliative behavior tends to "pull" affiliative behavior, and hostile behavior "pulls" hostile behavior; submissive behavior tends to "pull" dominant behavior, and vice versa. In other words, interactions seem to go more smoothly and are less problematical for participants when they emit behaviors that are similar with respect to the affective (hate-love) dimension and reciprocal with respect to the "status" dimension. As we have seen, normal persons are capable of flexibility in the stances they take with respect to others, and by the same token normal relationships are dynamic and changing as the parties move from one form of interaction to another. However, in most relationships that are stable over time, there will be a discernibly prepotent pattern of interaction, reflecting at least in part the personal proclivities (personalities) of the interaction partners.

Personality, Motivation, and Inner Conflict

An important aspect of personality is certainly the motives that drive a person to behave as he or she does. Motives are of two general types: innate and learned. Innate motives (such as hunger, etc.) are inextricably linked to the biological functioning of the organism. Learned motives are those that are largely, although not necessarily exclusively, a product of the individual's experience. We say "not necessarily exclusively" because so-called learned motives often have, in the final analysis, some biological or "constitutional" foundation, even though their ultimate forms of expression are determined by life events. The motives of special pertinence to personality are those of the second type. Various lists and classifications of learned motives abound in the psychological literature, and it seems unlikely that a final consensus on their number and type will ever be approximated. A degree of arbitrariness will be required if we are to proceed with this matter. The main outlines of social behavior were presented above. In keeping with the principle that behavior reflects underlying motives, it will be consistent as well as convenient to limit discussion to four main "learned" motives. These four principal motives, then, would be *to love*, *to hate*, *to dominate*, and *to submit*. We might add *to be loved* and *to be hated* in recognition of the reciprocal character of much interpersonal exchange; for example, loving behavior might be the manifestation of a motive to love, but it might also reflect a need to *receive* love. There is also reason to posit a type of superordinate human motive, that of expression and confirmation of one's self-identity (Carson, 1969). A person might engage in much loving-dominant behavior not so much because he has strong needs to dominate and to love, but rather because he has strong needs to see himself and to be seen by others as lovingly dominant *or*, possibly even more importantly, to *avoid* the opposite attribution.

Whatever the precise motivational underpinnings, it is a fact that certain people routinely do avoid engaging in the behaviors pertinent to one or more of the principal motives identified above. It is as though their behavioral repertoires simply do not include greater or lesser portions of the behavior circle depicted in Figure 15-1. Such individuals usually also exhibit a concomitant *exaggeration* of behaviors that are in some sense opposite to those that are missing, as though the avoidance itself was driven by some powerful motive. We are essentially describing here the process of neurosis, and the driving motive is indeed a powerful one; it is called *fear*. The neurotic process will be described in greater detail in the following chapter.

References

Bem, D.J., and A. Allen. On predicting some of the people some of the time: The search for cross-situational consistencies in behavior. Psychological Review 81:506–520, 1974.

Bowers, K.S. Situationism in psychology: An analysis and critique. Psychological Review 80:307–336, 1973.

Carson, R.C. Interaction Concepts of Personality. Chicago, Illinois: Aldine, 1969.

Carson, R.C. Personality and exchange in developing relationships. In R.L. Burgess and T.L. Huston (Eds.). Social Exchange in Developing Relationships. New York, New York: Academic Press, 1979.

Dollard, J., and N.E. Miller. Personality and Psychotherapy. New York, New York: McGraw-Hill, 1950.

Ellis, A. Reason and Emotion in Psychotherapy. New York, New York: Lyle Stuart, 1962.
Hall, C.S., and G. Lindzey. Theories of Personality. New York, New York: Wiley, 1970.
Kelly, G.A. The Psychology of Personal Constructs. New York, New York: Norton, 1955.
Kiesler, D.J., A.J. Bernstein, and J.C. Anchin. Interpersonal Communication, Relationship, and the Behavior Therapies. Richmond, Virginia: Virginia Commonwealth University, 1976.
Leary, T. Interpersonal Diagnosis of Personality. New York, New York: Ronald Press, 1957.
Mischel, W. Toward a cognitive social learning reconceptualization of personality. Psychological Review 80:252–283, 1973.
Piaget, J. The Construction of Reality in the Child. New York, New York: Basic Books, 1954.
Sullivan, H.S. Interpersonal Theory of Psychiatry. New York, New York: Norton, 1953.
Wachtel, P.L. Psychodynamics, behavior therapy and the implacable experimenter: An inquiry into the consistency of personality. J. Abnorm. Psychol. 82:324–334, 1973.

16

The Process of Neurosis: A Distortion of Personality and Interpersonal Functioning

In the preceding chapter it was pointed out that personality appears to be largely a result of learning, i.e., of life experience. The concept of neurosis as fear-motivated inhibitions and exaggerations of the interpersonal behavior patterns of the personality was also introduced. The present chapter will carry that topic forward in greater detail.

As discussed in earlier sections of this book, personality functioning may be disrupted by behavior disorders at more basic levels, as in organic brain disease, schizophrenia, and the affective disorders. There is, however, a vast area of disordered behavior that is best understood as a primary distortion of personality itself and as the result of unfortunate experiences in the learning processes which determine personality. This great area of psychopathology may be called *neurosis* if the term is understood to mean behavior patterns resulting from *neurotic process* rather than its limited meaning of a list of disorders defined by specific symptoms such as hysterical paralysis, compulsive hand washing, or phobias for high places or insects. These specific symptom conditions, as we shall see, are merely special cases of the more general process.

A characteristic of neurotic process which distinguishes it from the more basic dimensions of psychopathology is the very personal quality of its behavioral effects. This reflects the essential role played by the personal meanings life experiences come to have for each individual, that is, by the way he or she construes various situations. Neurotic disorders of personality share with personality itself an element of uniqueness. Neurosis often coexists and interacts with disorders of other behavior functions, giving illnesses involving the other dimensions of disorder their particularly human quality. This characteristic, together with the fact that neurosis presents in every possible degree of severity from the "little bit of neurosis in everyone" to life-threatening illness, has caused some workers to deny its status as a true disease. They prefer to consider neurotic problems simply as "problems of living." There is an element of truth in this view. Neurotic disorders, with their essential component of personal meaning, are not impersonal diseases that have befallen the person. To see them as such would overlook the very aspect necessary for their treatment, but to omit the neurotic disorders from the realm of conditions worthy of the physician's understanding and help (in this sense, to deny them the title of "diseases") would greatly weaken the usefulness of medicine. There is neurosis in a great deal of human suffering, both behavioral and physical.

That the neurotic process is, in some measure, a universally shared experience can be of great diagnostic and therapeutic assistance to the physician. By drawing upon his or her own experience with unnecessary fears, the doctor can empathically understand those of the patient. Once the basic form of the process is grasped, there is nothing weird or bizarre about neurosis. One can literally feel oneself into the patient's world (the literal meaning of "empathy"), a world only quantitatively different from the fearful appraisals and fear-driven responses everyone has made in those situations to which our individual experience has attached the meaning of danger.

Before describing additional aspects of the neurotic process, let us turn briefly to some issues of terminology and formal classification.

Problems of Terminology: "Neurosis" in the Official Classification

The process of neurosis was first recognized in patients whose illnesses included distinct behavioral *symptoms*—behavior patterns such as nonorganic paralyses, compulsions, and phobias which were experienced by the subject as undesirable and alien, something to be rid of. From this beginning it became customary in clinical practice to list a group of diseases defined by these readily identifiable symptoms. In textbooks and official diagnostic manuals the term "neurosis" has usually been restricted to conditions with such symptoms. In the Diagnostic and Statistical Manual of Mental Disorders, 2nd edition (American Psychiatric Association, 1968), nine such symptom neuroses were listed: anxiety neurosis; hysterical neurosis; conversion type; hysterical neurosis, dissociative type; phobic neurosis; obsessive-compulsive neurosis; depressive neurosis, neurasthemic neurosis, depersonalization neurosis; and hypochondriacal neurosis. In that diagnostic system, two other areas of disordered behavior, personality disorders and psychophysiologic (psychosomatic) disorders, were presented as separate and distinct major classes of illness, different from the neuroses. Personality disorders were said to differ in that they manifested as long standing, deeply ingrained patterns of behavior. Psychophysiologic disorders were considered different in that physical symptoms in a particular organ system resulted from emotional factors.

In contrast to this traditional position in descriptive psychiatry, it has long been recognized by those especially concerned with the treatment of neurotic problems that processes identical with those producing neurotic symptoms played an important role in the formation of personality or "character," both normal and abnormal, irrespective of whether distinct symptoms formed a part of the pathology. Those personality formations that were abnormal were often termed "character neuroses," an apt term in this writer's opinion and one that might well have been more generally adopted. Similarly, psychosomatic problems in which neurotic process was usually involved were for a time called "organ neuroses." Despite the inelegance of this term, it too might have usefully been retained as a reminder of the more general importance of neurotic process.

The separation of the concept of personality disorders from that of neurosis was particularly unfortunate. As suggested earlier, neurotic processes exert their effects primarily on patterns of interpersonal functioning and thus on the personality of the individual. By 1908 Freud was aware that the processes he had begun to understand through the treatment of patients with neurotic symptoms also contributed to the development of traits of character. By 1933 Reich, at that time an important member of the Freudian group, could assert that, "the basis of a symptom is always a neurotic character" (1949, p. 42). And Fenichel (1945, p. 476), the encyclopedist of Freudian thought, at mid-century wrote: "All neuroses, except infantile ones, have their root in character." American neo-Freudian theorists have consistently emphasized character as the essential and primary manifestation of neurosis, viewing symptoms as merely "special cases of character trends" (Thompson, 1950, p. 64). (See also Horney, 1945, p. 220; Salzman, 1962, pp. 247–248.)

More recently, especially among writers within the classical (Freudian) psychoanalytic tradition, a distinction between "neurosis" and "character disorder" has been adopted and has further complicated terminology in this already complex area. The terms "character disorder" and "characterological" have come to mean deeper, more severe disturbances than those labeled "neurosis," the deeper disorders being thought to have their origins in infancy and very early childhood. They are often said to be more fixed (structural) in nature than the more malleable (dynamic) patterns of "true neurosis." We will shortly suggest that there are pathogenic processes that begin in the earliest developmental periods, and that these processes are usually more pervasive of the personality and less readily responsive to treatment than those stemming from later childhood periods. However, the similarities between these earlier, "deeper" processes and those universally called neuroses are more important than the differences. Thus we shall argue that neurosis should be retained as the common term for the entire area of psychopathology involving acquired personal meanings of excessive fears and their behavioral consequences. In any event, whatever important differences do exist between the so-called character disorders and true neuroses do not rest in the presence of disordered personality in the former and its absence in the latter. The personality is surely distorted in both, although this distortion may be in somewhat different directions. (To anticipate the latter discussion: the "deeper," earlier disorders are those we shall describe as resulting from trust-fear and submission-fear neurotic conflicts; the later and often less severe disorders will be viewed as the result of aggression-fear and independence-fear conflicts.) Behavior experienced as symptoms may or may not be present in either of these two varieties of disorder.

The recent revision of the official American psychiatrist nomenclature, known as DSM-III (American Psychiatric Association, 1980), contributes further to the complexities surrounding the term neurosis. The original intent of the task force preparing DSM-III was to omit the term altogether. Not even the traditional symptom neuroses were to be included as such. The reasoning behind this intent involved an effort to use a purely descriptive classification system for all areas of disorder in which etiology is not unmistakably clear, thereby leaving issues of etiology open to future research. Listing the neuroses together as a major class of disorders would have implied, it was felt, a bias in favor of a common etiology. Moreover, the presumed common etiology of the symptom neuroses is considered by many to underlie many descriptively diverse conditions not traditionally designated as neuroses (the view that has been taken earlier in this chapter). To attempt to classify them under a single heading on the basis of presumed common etiology would, the task force felt, significantly disrupt the entire proposed descriptive classification (Spitzer et al., 1977. p. 7).

However, when DSM-III came up for final approval by the American Psychiatric Association, there were vigorous objections to the proposed omission of the neuroses. A compromise was reached wherein the class of neurotic disorders is included at a level with the other major classes, but simply as a heading without any disorders included under it. The user is referred to various other major classes to which the traditional neuroses have (for descriptive considerations) been dispersed. At those places the traditional term is listed in parenthesis as a possible alternative. For example, under anxiety disorders is included "Phobic disorder (or Phobic neurosis)." Under somatoform disorders we find "Conversion disorder (or Hysterical neurosis, conversion type)" and "Hypochondriasis (or Hypochondriacal neurosis)."

The two areas of disorder, in addition to the symptom neuroses, that have been presented in this chapter as intimately associated with neurotic process are both given new prominence in DSM-III. Personality disorders are now a separate major "axis" in the system, with the consequence that consideration of a possible personality disorder is required in the diagnosis of every patient. Psychosomatic problems in the new system are now recorded in a more flexible and individualized manner by the use of a new class, psychological factors affecting physical condition, so that the behavioral contribution to any bodily dysfunctions may be indicated in the diagnosis. However, in accord with DSM-III philosophy of avoiding etiological bias, the concept of neurotic process is not specifically mentioned in relation to personality disorders or emotional factors in physical conditions. The DSM-III position is, therefore, in this respect distinctly different from the one adopted in this chapter and this book. We view neurosis as a major dimension of psychopathological process affecting personality primarily, and often including psychosomatic as well as distinct behavioral symptoms. We take the position that etiology is well enough understood to warrant classification on the basis of common pathogenic process.

The Importance of Neurosis

In the discussion of a multidimensional conception of psychopathology at the beginning of this book, note was taken of the widespread involvement of neurotic process in all areas of disordered behavior. The cases cited there each demonstrated such interactive involvement. In the discussions of schizophrenia and depression, the point was made that in most cases of these illnesses a factor of stress is necessary, in addition to whatever biological or other "constitutional" diathesis may be present. Such stresses are usually described in terms of external events (Holmes and Rahe, 1967; Holmes and Masuda, 1973; Paykel, 1973). However, it is obvious upon a moment's reflection that all individuals do not respond identically to the same external event. What is stressful to a particular person, and how severely the stress is experienced, depends to a major degree on what he or she has come to appraise as dangerous or threatening. This appraisal is often unrealistic, at least in the amount of threat perceived. It is thus a manifestation of learned habits of excessive, unrealistic fear response, the essential ingredient (as we shall see) of neurotic process.

Neurosis is a selector and an amplifier of stressful life events. Further, the stressful effect often outlasts by months or even years the external precipitating circumstance. The self-perpetuating, often escalating nature of neurotic process, once activated, is the most likely explanation for the prolonged impact of life events upon some apparently neurotically predisposed individuals. The "vicious circle, vicious spiral" nature of neurosis will be discussed in more detail shortly, following which the importance of neurotic process as extender as well as selector and amplifier of external stresses should become fully apparent.

Basic Theory of Freudian Psychoanalysis

We begin the more detailed discussion of neurotic process with a brief review of the theory of Freudian or classical psychoanalysis. Some understanding of Freud's contribution to theories of personality and neurotic illness is quite essential for the student of medicine. Many clinicians and theorists today work and write within the framework of classical psychoanalysis. Even those who do not, often consider Freud the reference point from which other approaches are to be viewed.

There are numerous textbook chapters (e.g., Meissner, 1980; Drellich, 1974; and entire volumes (Brenner, 1973; Waelder, 1960) devoted to an introductory presentation of Freud's theories. None is more useful, however, than the "Introductory Lectures on Psycho-analysis (1916–17)" that Freud himself delivered to medical and other students at the University of Vienna (Freud, 1963). These lectures reflect a middle period of his thinking and contain his most important and basic concepts. However, some of his later ideas are not included, so that one of the more recent sources listed above may be a useful supplement. In this single section of the present chapter, it is possible to select only the several Freudian concepts essential to our development of a theory of neurosis. These essential concepts are: (1) *psychic determinism* (and the related concept of *psychic reality*; (2) *the unconscious*; (3) *instinctual drives* (and the *id*); (4) the *ego*; (5) *intrapsychic conflict*; and (6) *anxiety*, the *defenses* (and *resistance*).

Psychic Determinism

Freud is usually described as a "hard determinist" with respect to psychological events, that is, in his view there are no accidental events in the mental life, and every such occurrence has a meaningful cause. Dreams and slips of the tongue (often called "Freudian slips") were his most clearcut examples, but he felt that neurotic symptoms and character traits as well could be explained in terms of the needs, wishes, fears, thoughts, and assumptions of the individual. This is another way of saying that mental activities have a causal power to determine subsequent behavioral events, that there is a *psychic* as well as a material *reality*. This concept of psychic reality is probably the important contribution. It is not necessary to take the extreme position that *all* behavioral events have antecedent causes in the mental sphere. Freud's extreme stand may have been a reaction against the prevalent view of his time that events without obvious, conscious psychological meaning were probably mere accidents or were understandable in purely physical terms (e.g., dreams as the result of an indigestible late dinner, and slips of the tongue the result of the distractions of a noisy room). What is important is that he called our attention to the possibility of *meanings* not immediately obvious and urged us to search for them as part of treatment efforts.

The Unconscious

Frequently, the meaning of neurotic and other behavior, as of dreams and slips of the tongue, is not apparent to the person involved. He or she may be quite unaware of connections between the behavior and certain thoughts and feelings, unaware that he or she has those particular thoughts or feelings. In psychoanalytic parlance, mental events out of awareness, particularly those not available to awareness without special effort and techniques, are said to be *unconscious*. (By contrast, more readily accessible material simply not in conscious focus at any moment is said to be *preconscious*.) It is a major tenet of psychoanalytic theory that the truly *un*conscious portion of the mental life is so because its recognition would be painful and therefore unacceptable to the person, *and* that these truly unconscious mental elements are of great importance in the development of neurotic illness and the personality in general. An active process, *repression*, is postulated whereby the person, without realizing that he or she is doing so, pushes unacceptable thoughts and feelings out of awareness. The Freudian unconscious is therefore a *dynamic* unconscious, maintained by the forces of repression but not without power to affect the mental life. The effects of the unconscious are thought to be reflected in dreams and Freudian slips, as we have seen, and may often be brought to awareness through special techniques such as hypnosis (Freud's earliest therapeutic tool) and *free association*. In this latter procedure, the mainstay of the psychoanalytic method of treatment, the patient attempts to avoid all "censorship" of his or her thoughts and to report freely whatever comes to mind.

Instinctual Drives

Freud attempted to relate his psychological concepts to physiology, although the neurobiology of his day permitted even fewer correlations than are possible today. One aspect of his theory that Freud considered most firmly rooted in biology, however, was that concerning the forces impelling the person into activity: the drives. Freud's term, *Triebe*, has unfortunately usually been translated into English as "instincts," a term which for most readers suggests behavioral sequences in which both motivation *and* predetermined patterns of complex motor activity are firmly linked in ways characteristic of each individual species of animal (e.g., nest building, courtship rituals, etc.). The human drives to which Freud had reference, while they do create tensions impelling the person in certain broad directions, do not determine exactly how this tension must be reduced. There is opportunity for much variation between people in drive reducing behaviors based upon differences in learning (instrumental conditioning) experience. By analogy with the concept of energy in physics, Freud conceived that there is a *psychic energy* associated with the drives.

Freud's thinking regarding the number and nature of the instinctual drives changed several times. In his final position he listed two: sex (libido) and aggression. This continues to be the view of present-day Freudian theorists, though many do not find it useful to think of the aggressive drive in terms of a "death instinct" as Freud did. Human behavior is seen as resulting from a mixture of these two drives, from "fusion" in varying proportions.

The sexual drive, defined as a mental stimulus toward pleasure deriving from various parts of the body (not the genitals exclusively), has been the more extensively discussed of the two drives. It is held that manifestations of this drive are apparent from early infancy on, and that there is an innate sequence of stages through which its development passes during infancy and childhood. During the first year and a half, roughly, the mouth and related structures are the focal point of the sexual interests, a conclusion originally derived from recollections of older children and adults during psychoanalytic treatment but also thought to be confirmed by direct observation of infants. This initial *oral stage* is followed, Freudian theory holds, by an *anal stage* covering the second year and a half of life, although there is considerable variation and overlapping in the timing of the several stages. The focus of bodily interest is now on the excretory functions and behaviors related to them and their products, behaviors such as retention and expulsion. There then follows, at about age 3, the *phallic stage*, during which the penis—or its analog, the clitoris—becomes the principal object of interest to the child. The phallic stage proper lasts some two to two and one-half years. It was long thought to be succeeded by a *latency period*, spanning roughly the grammar school years, during which the sexual drive is relatively inactive. However, many analysts now doubt that there is such a period of true quiescence. The final developmental stage of the libido begins at puberty and is called the *genital stage* (although this term is sometimes also incorrectly used for the earlier phallic period). This last stage is characterized in the normal individual by the pleasurable availability of adult sexual functions and other behaviors associated with mature human life.

Psychoanalytic theory postulates that biological variations between individuals (e.g., in the relative strengths of their drives) play some role in the differences of ease or difficulty experienced by children in traversing the various stages, but it is also held that the influence of family and other environmental forces are of major importance as well. Significant problems during any period may result in so-called *fixations* on the needs and gratifications of that period which then retain an undue importance for the individual—one part of the psychoanalytic explanation of later personality leanings and abnormalities as well as of neurotic symptoms. Thus, extremely dependent people may be viewed as "orally fixated," while those excessively concerned with cleanliness, order, and the accumulation and retention of possessions are said to suffer from "anal fixations." The libido may not only be fixated at early periods; having moved on to more mature stages, it may return or *regress* in its focus of interest to earlier modes and objects of gratification, especially if circumstances for its more mature satisfaction prove unfavorable. Neurosis is thus often conceived as a combination of regression to periods of partial fixation in the face of later life stresses.

The phallic stage is particularly important in classic psychoanalytic theory because the *Oedipus complex* occurs during that developmental period. For the child of about age 3, boy or girl, the mother continues to be the most important person and constitutes the strongest "object relation," to use the psychoanalytic phrase. This relationship now comes to include expectation on the child's part of participation by the mother in gratification of his or her maturing genital urges. The exact nature of this wished-for gratification is varied and often vague in the child's mind. Its realization, however, is viewed by the child as depending upon removal of rivals for mother's affection—especially father, who now becomes the focus of hostile, murderous wishes. These are followed by fears of reprisal, either as physical attack and damage or rejection and abandonment. The little boy may specifically fear castration as father's retaliation.

The male child, provided parents are reasonably tolerant and not overly threatening in response to oedipally motivated behaviors, eventually relinquishes his direct intense wishes to possess mother and takes his satisfaction from observing and vicariously experiencing his father, augmenting this experience by becoming as much like father as possible. Thus he establishes, through *identification* with father, much of his own (masculine) *identity*. Failure to accomplish this normal resolution of the Oedipus complex may occur if parental reactions are extreme or because of other unfortunate circumstances such as loss of a parent. Freudian theory also implicates constitutional predispositions toward abnormal resolutions such as excessive biological predisposition toward femininity. In any event, failure to adequately resolve the oedipal situation is, in Freudian thinking, given credit for a great deal of psychopathology—the various sexual dysfunctions, to be sure, but other symptoms and abnormal character traits as well. (At one point in Freudian thinking, virtually all acquired behavior disorder was attributed to unresolved oedipal conflicts, but the contribution of "preoedipal" [i.e., oral and anal] difficulties has now come to occupy a theoretically prominent place as well.)

Psychoanalytic theory presents the oedipal problems of the female child as more complicated than those of the male. The girl's renunciation of oedipal wishes for the mother is said to be based on shame, a sense of inferiority at her already castrated state ("penis envy") and rage at mother for allowing her to be born defective. As a result, she turns to father as the object of her love, and feels murderous rivalry toward mother. However, if development is normal, she eventually renounces expectation of direct gratification and resolves this childhood crisis by identification with mother, taking vicarious satisfaction from mother's relationship with father. (It should be noted that the original Freudian concept of the inevitability of shame and penis envy in the female has been vigorously challenged by many workers, including some within the Freudian psychoanalytic school.)

An additional consequence of normal resolution of the Oedipus complex through identification with the parent is said to be the beginning formation of the *superego*, the psychic system mediating moral precepts (conscience) and the ego ideals or personal aspirations. These are internalized as part of the process of resolution through identification with the parent.

The Ego

The superego, just mentioned, and the *id*, the system reflecting the instinctual drives, constitute two of the three components in Freud's description of the psychic apparatus or "structure." The third element is the *ego*, the system responsible for relating the individual (including his or her drives) to the demands of the superego and particularly to the demands of the outer world—often dubbed "reality" in Freudian writings. The ego, in basic Freudian theory, begins development in the first year of life, influenced by the maturing capacities of the individual and by interactions, both painful and satisfying, with the environment. Ego functions, in this view, include motor control, the acquisition of perceptual focus, and the accumulation of a store of memories and associations. The ability to modulate drives and to delay the discharge of the impulses they motivate also constitutes an important ego function. Related to the development of the ego and its beginning dynamic interactions with the id are the concepts of *primary process* and *secondary process*. This pair of terms is used in two distinct but related meanings. In the first usage, primary process refers to the tendency for drive tensions to be immediately discharged. Secondary process, on the other hand, refers to the ability to delay discharge in the form of behavioral efforts at gratification when this is necessary or desirable because of external circumstances. In Freudian theory, the organism is fundamentally motivated by a desire to achieve pleasure and avoid "displeasure." This is the so-called *pleasure principle*. With increasing ego capacity, the developing individual becomes able to delay gratification when necessary to avoid unpleasant consequences often imposed by reality upon unbridled demands for immediate and total satisfaction. The ego of the maturing child is thus said to increasingly employ the *reality principle*, utilizing secondary process to modify, but at the same time to serve, the more basic pleasure principle.

In their second meaning, the terms primary and secondary process refer to modes of thinking. Primary process thinking is characteristic of early life, of dreams and states of altered consciousness, and of the unconscious mental life in general. Secondary process thought, by contrast, is the ordinary thought we know in our waking lives: principally verbal rather than pictorial and following rules of syntax and logic. Primary process thinking is pathological if it predominates in the awake adult, but a state of balance between the two types of thought plays an important role in the mental life.

Intrapsychic Conflict

Psychoanalysts view the actual process by which life experience leads to pathology as involving conflict between instinctual (infantile sexual and aggressive) forces and antiinstinctual forces. The abnormal behavior is seen as a compromise between these forces. It may take the form of constricted, ineffectual personality traits (character neurosis) and may include specific neurotic symptoms such as those Freud studied in his early cases of hysterical conversion or obsessive-compulsive illness. By achieving this compromise through various defensive maneuvers (to be discussed shortly) the ego provides *primary gain*, a partial gratification of the instinctual demand and, at the same time, avoidance of the full force of overwhelming anxiety or guilt which would result from unmodified, undisguised expression of the instinctual impulse. The person protects him- or herself from full awareness of the instinctual desires. *Secondary gain*, on the other hand, refers to the subsequent exploitation of neurotic symptoms or character traits to obtain reward, tolerance, or special privilege from others. While not as central as primary gain to the development of a neurotic illness, secondary gain may at times become so powerful as to interfere with its treatment.

Anxiety and the Mechanisms of Defense

The concept of anxiety occupies a central position in the Freudian theory of the development of symptoms and other abnormal behavior from intrapsychic conflict. Freud's second *theory of anxiety*[1] suggests that at first anxiety is the result of the overwhelming of the ego in infancy or early childhood by stimuli from the environment or id impulses or both, but usually involving in some measure the instinctual drives of the id. Subsequent to such early "traumatic experiences," the ego learns to anticipate similar or associated

[1]A much earlier first theory asserted that anxiety was the result of transformation of dammed-up libido prevented from discharge by inner conflicts or external circumstances.

situations and to respond with *signal anxiety* as a warning to avoid the particular stimulus situation. Because anxiety is such a powerful and unpleasurable emotion, and because organisms are biologically adapted to give first priority to the pleasure principle, the ego adopts massive efforts to effect avoidance of the anxiety provoking stimuli, including the relevant id impulses. Any device by which the ego achieves that control of the instinctual drives necessary to prevent their emergence is known as defenses. These include a number of specific *mechanisms of defense*, some of which will now be described.

Repression is the process in which the ego actively bars from consciousness the unwanted id impulses and related memories or emotions. We often naively say that these memories have been forgotten. Repression is not a once-and-for-all process but one that must be continuously maintained, and the success of this maintenance varies under the changing pressures of maturation and environmental circumstances. Repression is often viewed by Freudians as the essential process in all defensive operations, the other mechanisms seen as devices to bolster repression.

Reaction formation is a defense mechanism whereby an unacceptable impulse is rendered and kept unconscious by overemphasis of its behavioral opposite. Hate is (apparently) replaced by love—or love by hate. It is important to recognize that reaction formation, like the other defense mechanisms, takes place unconsciously. It should be noted that in neo-Freudian theories of neurosis, purposive interpersonal behavior displaces intrapsychic self-deception as the central mechanism of defense. (This is also true of the integration of psychodynamic theories presented below.)

Isolation is a mechanism whereby emotions may be repressed from consciousness by disassociating them from thoughts and events, leaving the subject a relatively cold, unfeeling personality (at the surface). *Undoing* is a mechanism by which the individual attempts to reverse or disprove, as if by magic, the effects of unacceptable impulses (e.g., protesting "no offense intended" whenever making a hostile remark). *Denial* as a specific defense refers to denial of unpleasant or unacceptable aspects of external reality, often a denial of some portion of sensory experience itself (e.g., looking at the world through rose-colored glasses). *Projection* involves attributing one's own unacceptable wish or impulse to another person or to some impersonal outside force. *Turning against the self* is a process in which an instinctual impulse felt toward another, such as rage, is redirected toward oneself in fantasy or action. Regression, previously described as a more general process of falling back to the wishes and patterns of developmental periods that seem more secure, is also viewed as a specific mechanism of defense.

The reader's attention is called to the necessarily incomplete presentation of Freudian theory possible within this brief section. Consultation of at least one of the more extensive introductions previously cited is strongly recommended for those not already familiar with this topic. It is also very important to keep in mind the wide divergence of theoretical views that have developed within classical psychoanalysis itself, to say nothing of the many divergences and "defections" from psychoanalysis to which new names have been applied: individual psychology (Alfred Adler), analytic psychology (C.G. Jung), neo-Freudian or interpersonal psychoanalysis (Karen Horney and Harry Stack Sullivan), and adaptational psychodynamics (Sandor Rado), to mention only a few.

An Integrated Psychodynamic Theory of Neurosis

This final section is an abbreviated presentation of a theory of neurosis which is combined with valuable elements of classical psychoanalysis contributions from neo-Freudian psychoanalysis, adaptational psychodynamics, and learning or behavior theory (Hine, 1971; Hine et al., 1972, Chapters 5–8). The approach taken has been labeled "conflict-adaptational psychodynamics" to indicate its origins in the Freudian emphasis on intrapsychic conflict and the neo-Freudian and related theories which emphasize the interpersonal-adaptational aspects of behavior and its disorders. The purpose has been to distill from the literature of nearly 100 years a theory sufficiently brief to permit rapid assimilation by the student, but complete enough to provide real guidance in working with patients. It is intended that the theory be useful in itself, and also that its connections with the various "parent" disciplines and theories will serve the student as an introduction and basis for further study of the extensive literature on personality and its relation to neurotic illness.

Recognition of the Process of Neurosis

The presence of neurotic process in an individual may be inferred when three particular elements of behavior are observed. These elements are: (1) inhibition (avoidance) of one or more specific areas of useful, satisfying interpersonal behavior; (2) exaggeration of an area or areas opposite to those inhibited; and (3) the emotions of distress, namely fear (anxiety) and depressive affect, in a pattern of dynamic interaction with (1) and (2). For example, one may observe a person who consistently avoids expressing anger and other forms of aggression even in situations where those behaviors would prove useful and lead to satisfactions. In circumstances calling for aggression, the person displaying neurotic patterns of this type (which we shall later identify as reflecting aggression-fear conflict) typically becomes even less aggressive, tending instead to display exaggerated nonaggressive behavior. He may become overly nice and pleasant or exaggeratedly hurt and helpless, thus demonstrating to himself that he could not possibly have any angry feelings or aggressive impulses, and to others that he ought to be accepted as without aggression. If the exaggerated opposite (reaction formation) behavior is accepted by others, the person in our example will probably stabilize in a characteristic nonaggressive personality pattern. If, however, others continue to engage in one or another form of behavior calling for aggression (e.g., by continuing to frustrate, say, or to threaten), our subject will begin to experience and display the emotions of distress. He will become at first manifestly anxious and eventually somewhat depressed as well.

To be properly described as "inhibited," a behavior area must not only be significantly absent from overt, direct expression, but it is also necessary that indicators of its presence as a blocked impulse be evident in the form of disguised, indirect expression. Dreams, fantasies, slips of the tongue, out-of-character outbursts, unsolicited denials, and protesting too much have all come to be recognized as evidence that there are at some level of the psyche pressures toward the behavior that is absent from direct expression. A somewhat more subtle but even more regularly important such indicator is the impact on others of the reaction formation patterns we have seen as intended to disguise the inhibited behavior and confirm its absence. Imbedded in these exaggerated opposites is usually some of the very behavior they serve to deny. Consider the person who is so "nice" that others may seen unable to deny his "requests"—so that aggressive demands are served without revealing or recognizing one's aggression. As another example, can there be any doubt that those who spend time with a helpless and worried person, listening to his complaints and concerns, are being (aggressively) punished.

Upon finding his avoided behavior(s) called for, defensive reaction formations rebuffed, and his distress consequently increased, the person predisposed to neurotic reaction patterns, will attempt to reestablish emotional equilibrium by leaving the triggering situation and by instituting even more exaggerated defenses. He will resist any suggestions to recognize the avoided impulses or to engage in the avoided behavior. In fact, the term *resistance* is used in a technical sense to refer to the struggle against awareness and expression of one's inhibitions and defenses that are an inevitable part of the psychotherapy of neurosis.

Persons with active neurotic process of any severity tend to be relatively unhappy and miserable. Misery in life may, of course, be due to external circumstances over which the individual has no control, but when a person is persistently unhappy despite a life situation that could provide reasonable satisfactions, it is wise for the physician to suspect that the misery may be neurotically self-inflicted to significant degrees. The purpose of such recognition, of course, is not to justify ridicule or rejection of the sufferer, but rather to permit the doctor to offer help based upon a model of what is going on within the patient and in his interactions with the world.

A Classification of Neurotic Conflicts Based on Varieties of Interpersonal Behavior

In the foregoing description of the behavioral indicators of neurosis, reference has been made to inhibitions and contrasting exaggerations of *interpersonal* behavior. It is widely accepted that the tendency to neurosis is acquired as a result of childhood experiences with other people, especially one's parents. Some parents overdo, often unwittingly, their proper parental function of implanting sufficient fears of one's impulses to ensure the avoidance of real dangers, both physical and social. Excessive, unrealistic fears are taught and learned. It is thus not surprising that patterns acquired in an interpersonal setting might have their essential effects upon the interpersonal behavior of the subject. Nor is it surprising that the therapies considered most specific for neurotic disorder have a necessary interpersonal element at their bases. Some relationship with a therapist-teacher is required for modifying the earlier learned patterns. These considerations suggest the usefulness of a classification of varieties of neurosis based upon a classification of interpersonal behavior.

In Chapter 15, arguments were made for the usefulness of the Leary circumplex model of interpersonal behavior (Leary, 1957), a model based upon two axes and four major behavioral directions: dominance and submission on the vertical axis and hate (disaffiliation) and love (affiliation) on the horizontal. Learning excessive, inappropriate degrees of fear of one's natural impulses toward any one or more of these four behavioral modalities results in their inappropriate inhibition and thus in one or more of four varieties of neurotic conflict.

Consider Figure 16-1 (a modification of Figure 15-1) in which a second circle is added within the first. This figure depicts interpersonal behavior at the overt, direct level of expression, the level Leary calls level I. The inner circle now represents the various directions of behavior in its "healthy" form, motivated by the real (instinctual) needs of the person and flexibly responsive to the real possibilities for satisfaction inherent in various life situations. The outer ring of the circle represents exaggerated, inflexible, inappropriate behaviors motivated by excessive, unrealistic fears.

Figure 16-2 represents an idealized picture of normal (i.e., nonneurotic) interpersonal behavior at level I, the level of overt expression. Assuming observations have been made over a sufficient time span to provide a variety of opportunities in the real world, the normal individual will display the total range of interpersonal behaviors.

A second circle (without concentric rings, since we do not distinguish adaptive from maladaptive behavior at the level of disguised expression) is used to depict behavior expressed indirectly in symbolic or disguised forms (as in dreams, slips, imbedded defenses, etc.). Leary calls this level III. Using diagrams for level I and III (level II, the level of self-description, is not essential for our presentation), it is now possible to depict the four basic patterns of neurosis and to briefly describe each in its isolated, idealized form.

Aggression-Fear Conflicts (Figure 16-3). Healthy, appropriate expression of anger and other forms of aggression and disaffiliation are inhibited and largely unavailable to the individual, even when they would usefully add to

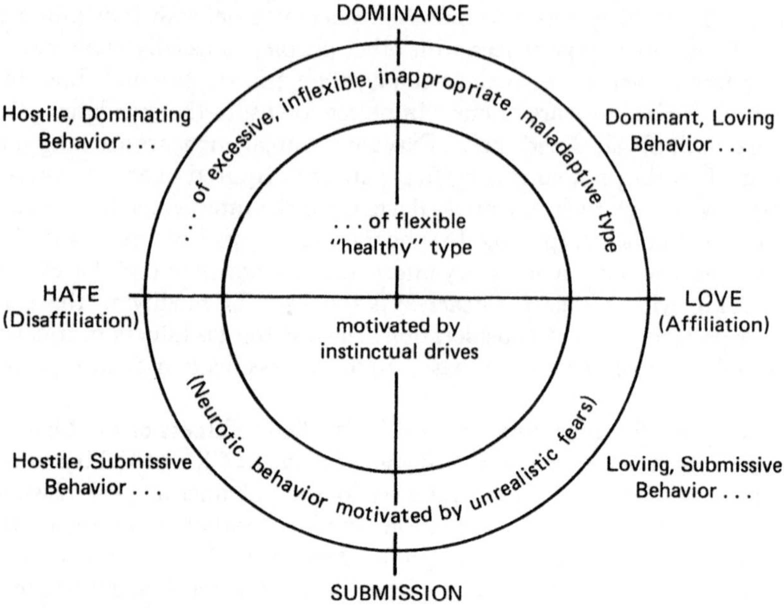

Fig. 16-1. The axes of interpersonal behavior and the interpersonal circle. In adapting the interpersonal circle to conflict-adaptational theory, the outer portion of the circle (at Level I) is regarded as depicting excessive, inflexible, and inappropriate (i.e., neurotic) interpersonal behavior in the various directions defined by the major axes. The inner ring of the circle (at Level I) represents the flexible (healthy) manifestations of the same behavioral directions. (From Hine, 1971.)

his satisfaction and safety. Affiliative, overly nice behavior is practiced in rigid, exaggerated fashion, particularly at those times when aggression is called for. In addition to level I behavior just described, evidence of the inhibited aggression is seen at level III in the form of aggressive dreams, perhaps occasional out-of-character hostile outbursts, and especially in the painful effects of exaggerated nonaggression on other people.

Independence-Fear Conflicts (Figure 16-4). Among the behaviors subsumed under the term "dominance" in Leary's schema, healthy independence or

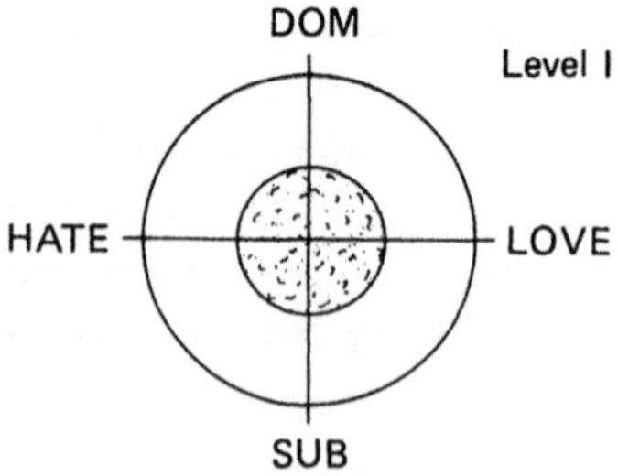

Fig. 16-2. Normal interpersonal behavior.

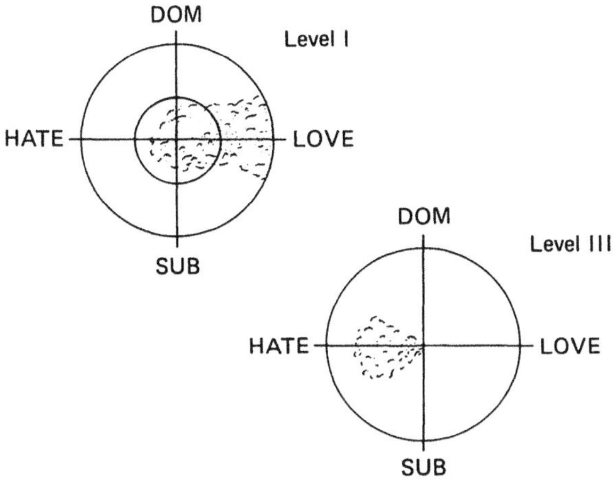

Fig. 16-3. Agression-fear conflict.

autonomy is the one frequently inhibited by neurotic fears. The person appears never to have adequately separated from parents in that he avoids adult, self-sufficient behavioral roles and thereby loses those satisfactions possible only by growing up. Helplessness and submission to others and the seeking out of strong people to lean on are both greatly exaggerated. The person becomes desperate at any suggestion of rejection by others and at the prospect of being alone. Autonomous, independent behavior is seen principally in dreams and daydreams.

Neurotic inhibitions of aggression and independence are frequently found combined in the same person (Mrs. R.L., Chapter 1, p. 100 , for example). There are variations in the degree to which each function is distorted, how-

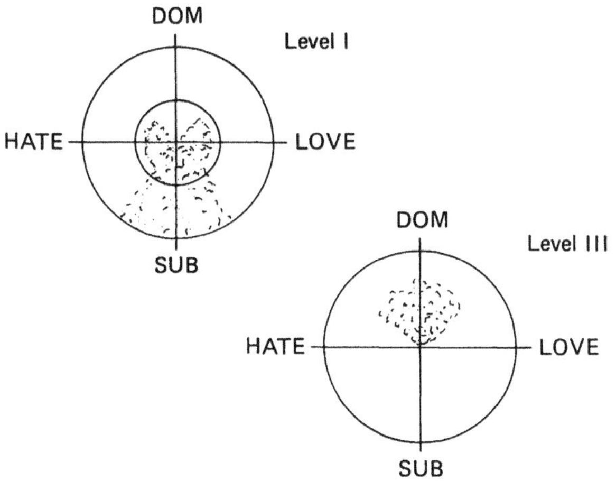

Fig. 16-4. Independence-fear conflict.

ever, and it is wise to consider them separately in formulating one's understanding of a patient.

Trust-Fear Conflicts (Figure 16-5). There is absence or relative absence (even in useful degree under safe circumstances) of free and direct expressions of love, intimacy, closeness, and trust. Instead one observes rigid, exaggerated, inappropriate expressions of suspicion, anger, defiance, bitterness, withdrawal, and social isolation. The level I behavior provokes and maintains the distance that the patient feels he must have to be safe. Fleeting glimpses of the underlying yearning for closeness may be apparent in the level III indicators (fantasies and half-hearted efforts to relate) if the patient will stay close long enough to reveal them and the observer can tolerate discomfort long enough to make the observations. (The case example of patient C.D. in Chapter 1 is an example of trust-fear conflictual processes.)

Submission-Fear Conflicts (Figure 16-6). There is inhibition of useful, healthy capacities to depend on others, and to allow oneself to be taken care of even when it may be necessary or would be satisfying and safe. The exaggerated patterns of self-defeating dominance and rigid self-sufficiency range from hostile, arrogant domination of others to excesses of benevolence and helpfulness.

Trust-fear and submission-fear conflicts frequently occur together, and submission fear is in part a less severe, more limited variant of the trust-fear pattern. Especially when the trust-fear element is large, the behavior resulting from this group of conflicts is excluded from the area of neurosis altogether by many theorists, being labeled instead with such terms as "characterological," "narcissistic," "borderline," "schizoid," or "paranoid"—all of which have come to have negative implications for prognosis

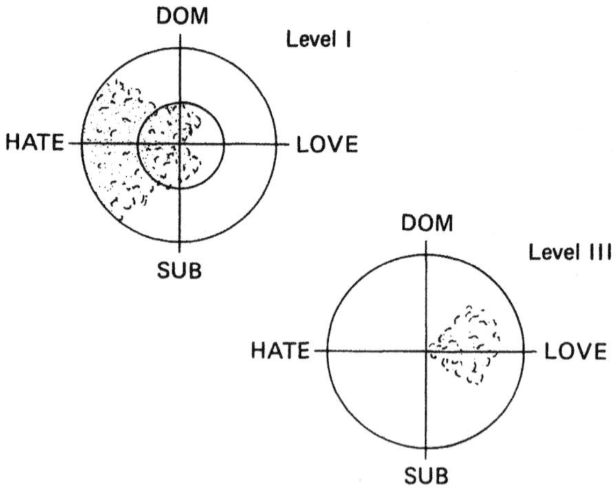

Fig. 16-5. Trust-fear conflict.

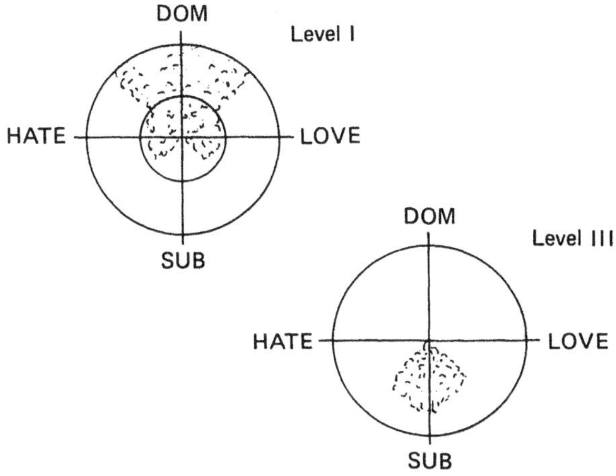

Fig. 16-6. Submission-fear conflict.

and therapy. As noted in an earlier section of this chapter, there are profound conflicts compared to those involving aggression and independence. They are often difficult to treat. We shall shortly suggest that they arise from very early periods of life. But they are learned, they do occur in varying degrees of severity, they are dynamic and involve active processes within the person and between the person and his environment, and they are often modifiable by the application of the basic principles of reeducative psychotherapy. For these reasons it is strongly urged that they be considered varieties of neurotic disorder rather than relegated to some different class of illness whereby the therapeutic guidelines provided by our knowledge of neurotic process may be lost.

The four types of conflict may occur in any and all combinations in any particular person. When they do occur in combination, they interact with one another to further aggravate the neurotic disorder. A frequently seen combination involves coexisting independence-fear and submission-fear conflicts (Figure 16-7). Neither healthy independence nor healthy, satisfying dependency is available to the person. He typically oscillates between the exaggerated extremes of attempting to dominate and control others and collapsing into helplessness. As each extreme is reached it triggers the corresponding neurotic fear: "My God, here I am all alone!" or "My God, here I am helpless and dependent on someone!" The person is then catapulted, as it were, by the pressure of fear to the opposite extreme of behavior.

Details of the development of personality, emphasizing the epigenetic schema of Erik Erikson, will be presented in Chapter 17. At this time, however, note must be taken of the probable sequence in which the several types of conflict are likely to be laid down in infancy and early childhood. For reasons that will be made clear shortly, the sequence is probably: trust-fear, submission-fear, aggression-fear, and independence-fear. Given this sequence

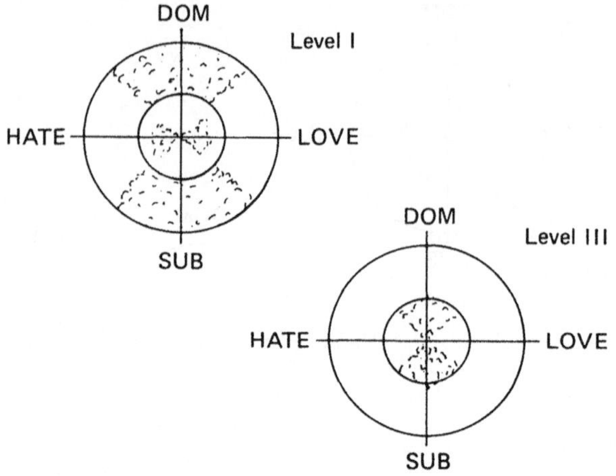

Fig. 16-7. Interlocking independence- and submission-fear conflicts.

and recognizing an important epigenetic principle which states that later developmental stages depend for their successful completion upon the successful completion of earlier stages, an important conclusion may be drawn concerning some probable combinations of neurotic conflicts. If the patient suffers from trust-fear conflictual problems, he will almost certainly have significant problems in the other areas as well. He will have come to the later stages already burdened with the interpersonal behavior constrictions resulting from excessive inability to trust. There is almost certain to be overreaction by parents and others to the extremes of defensive behavior this inability will generate. Excessive trust-fear–generated aggression will almost certainly lead to excessive punishment of aggression, for example, leading to excessive fears in that area as well. Thus we may say that in the presence of earlier conflicts those derived from later stages are almost always seen, but the reverse is not as consistently true.

It may seem surprising that sex has not been included in the list of neurotic conflicts. Certainly genital functions are frequently impaired to some degree in neurotically conflicted individuals. It is also true, however, that conflicts of major degree may exist without impairment of sexual function—but never without some impairment of some aspect of *relationship* with people. This finding leads to the conclusion that interpersonal patterns are more basic, essential loci of neurotic conflicts than sexuality per se. Sex is obviously an important, emotionally charged, vulnerable aspect of those same human relationships. Inhibitions of independence and the adult role may certainly interfere with one's ability to function comfortably in a behavior requiring a sense of freedom and adult competence. Inhibitions of intimacy and affiliation, and of submission, often interfere with sexual activity, for reasons that are immediately obvious.

The Process of Neurosis

The psychological process that gives rise to persisting unhappiness and misery in the absence of external disaster may be conceived as consisting of two opposite motive forces or emotions. One of these forces is a persistent drive toward some potentially satisfying interpersonal behavior. The other is learned, excessive, unrealistic fear of that drive and the associated behavior. Activation of the fear is triggered by the active presence of the drive. The distress produced by the resulting intrapsychic conflict gives rise in turn to intense, often desparate, efforts at behavioral resolution through avoidance of the drive-related behavior on the one hand and exaggeration of contrasting behavior on the other.

The behavior resulting from neurotic conflict, because it is preponderantly determined by unrealistic fear, is very likely to be inappropriate to the demands and opportunities of the real environmental situation, i.e., maladaptive. Such behavior tends to elicit from those in the environment responses which result chiefly in painful failure of need satisfaction and in direct painful punishment in the forms of rejection and retaliation. Although there may be initial short-term effects of reassurance and support from others, the long-term total effect is usually painful failure and reprisal. Of course some personality patterns, most notably the trust-fear driven pattern of overt hostility or withdrawal, typically elicit immediate retaliation and counterhostility from others. Thus, when hostility is neurotically exaggerated and pervasive, as in the trust-fear–conflicted person, it ensures that this person's worse fears will be confirmed. In the manner of a self-fulfilling prophecy, the world of other people will turn out to be a painful place. There is an element of self-fulfilling prophecy in much neurotic interaction: the exaggerately meek person invites caretaking, thereby confirming his fears that he is helpless; the dominant, hyperindependent person drives some people to fight for control or avoid, and therefore becomes more convinced himself that submission is likely to be painful. But even when the immediate, automatic interpersonal feedback is not painful and fear-confirming, the person who is not able to flexibly utilize all areas of behavior as required by changing circumstance is, over the long term, likely to have predominantly unsatisfying and painful interpersonal relationships.

Why does such a behavior pattern persist in the face of punishment? According to theories of instrumental conditioning, punishment should act as negative reinforcement and cause the behavior to be discontinued. The clinical fact is, however, that the conflictually predisposed individual, encountering rejection and other forms of punitive reaction from others, typically clings more fiercely than ever to his defensive, maladaptive patterns and even exaggerates them further. This fact has been termed the "neurotic paradox" by Mowrer (1950, pp. 486–487). Experimental demonstration that such a behavior paradox is possible is provided by the following:

> If a rat is put at one end of a straight alley about 4 feet long and if, after a period of ten seconds, the floor of the alley (consisting of a metal grill) is electrified, the rat will soon scamper to the opposite end of the alley and, if a small nonelectrified compartment is available, escape into it. After a few repetitions of this procedure, the subject, as might be expected, will run to the opposite end as soon as placed in the alley, without receiving the shock. What obviously happens is that the rat's fear becomes conditioned to the "danger situation" and, since the running response carries the rat out of that situation, with an attendant reduction in fear, this response is quickly fixated.
>
> Once this response is well established, it will persist for many trials; but the rat will tend to become more and more leisurely in making the run and will eventually delay beyond the ten-second period. If shock is not applied under these circumstances, the tendency on the part of the rat to flee from the end of the maze where it is introduced deteriorates still further; and ultimately the flight response will disappear completely.
>
> This behavior is, of course, in no way surprising, since it conforms perfectly to what is known concerning the extinction of avoidance reactions. What is surprising, however, is this: If, after a "conditioned" response of the kind just described is well established, the right half of the floor-grill, at the far end of the alley, is permanently electrified so that, in the process of getting from the starting point to the safety compartment, the rat must always receive at least a brief shock, the running response does not extinguish! Even though shock is never again experienced in the left alley, where the animal is introduced, flight from the area continues to occur indefinitely.
>
> [The rats] continue to cross the electrified segment of the floor-grill and get shocked, whereas if they merely "sat tight" in the first part of the alley, nothing would happen to them. Under these circumstances, the running response obviously gets "punished," and yet, instead of being inhibited by this punishment, it is apparently strengthened by it. (Mowrer, 1950, pp. 258–260)

A review by Melvin (1971) cites some 30 studies confirming the above findings. Similar results have been obtained in experiments using other species, using different punishment stimuli in the initial training and in the punishment-during-extinction phase, and using avoidance behavior other than running (e.g., bar pressing), thus demonstrating the generality of "vicious circle behavior." Furthermore, while the punishment-during-extinction procedure typically results in continued responding, it may result in an *increase* in performance (Melvin, 1971, pp. 101–102). This is a first step from vicious circle to vicious *spiral* behavior. Most important of all is the finding that behavior initially trained by any reinforcer other than pain (e.g., by positively rewarding the rat for running) cannot be converted into vicious circle behavior with any regularity. This finding attests to the essential place of pain-induced *fear* in the neurotic paradox.[2]

[2]Experimental psychologists are not in full agreement about the exact mechanism(s) by which painful, aversive stimuli exert their singular power in the learning of behavior. The interested reader may consult Seligman and Johnston (1973) and Levis and Boyd (1979) for two recent positions and reviews of earlier suggested explanations.

The vicious circle paradigm alone is not, however, a complete model of human neurosis. In the human situation, for one thing, there is no experimenter who replaces the subject in the feared start position. The person who is fearful of a particular external stimulus situation could probably arrange his life to avoid that situation—unless it included inevitably recurring, not-to-be completely-avoided inner needs, the instinctual drives of conflict theory. Conflict is an essential element of human neurosis; not only situations are feared but also one's own natural needs and impulses, from which there is no possibility of true avoidance or escape.

The vicious circle model also fails to describe the typically increasing severity of active human neurosis. In the animal experiment, only one maladaptive, "neurotic" solution is possible: needlessly running the electrified alley to avoid the now harmless start position. In human life, innumerable avoidance "solutions" are possible, so that as fear (and depressive affect) increases ever more desperate measures are employed: the dependent person moves toward total helplessness; the suspicious, distrustful individual becomes the hostile, accusing "paranoid" or the withdrawn, reclusive "schizoid." It is because of this tendency toward escalation in the human situation that we prefer "vicious spiral" to "vicious circle" for the characterization of human neurosis.

The irony of neurotic illness can be appreciated if one considers the following: In the severely conflict-prone individual, punishment, as we have seen, does not have the customary inhibitory effects on maladaptive behavior. It does, however, increase distress and the learned tendencies to fear one's natural drives. The person who acquires many strong patterns of unrealistic fear is likely to be caught in a vicious descending spiral of fear, followed by maladaptive behavior, followed by increased fear, followed by increased maladaptive behavior, and so on.

What then are the factors that determine whether the spiral will be activated in a predisposed individual, and whether, once activated, it will continue to turn or be interrupted and perhaps even reversed? Obviously these factors are numerous, complex, and interacting. They include both the intensities of the original learned fears and the circumstances of the individual's present life.

For some persons, the degree of predisposition and current life circumstances combine in unfortunate ways. As the spiral turns there is increasing narrowness of his range of behavioral possibilities. More and more desperate use is made of the remaining few. As one after another pattern is rejected by those around him, a stage may be reached at which the only apparent behavior consists of the physiological effects of the affects of distress; the patient is in a state of naked anxiety and/or depressive affect. In such states of panic and depression, massive and immediate supportive interruption of the spiral is often necessary for the preservation of life. Some measure of supportive therapy is necessary in the prevention of spiraling at any stage in the process of threatened or active neurosis.

In the absence of triggering circumstances and pressures, spiraling neurosis may not occur despite severe neurotic predisposition. The individual may find a person or group whose needs dovetail so completely with his neurotic behavior patterns that painful feedback does not occur and some satisfaction remains available. In that case, spiraling may be avoided or interrupted, and life continues at the level of limited happiness or tolerable misery. He remains, of course, vulnerable to changes in the circumstances with resumption of the active neurosis spiral.

There are times when the victim of neurosis may encounter a particularly fortunate combination of circumstances. Punitive retaliation for his inappropriate behavior is withheld or given in tolerable amounts, i.e., support is provided. But, at the same time, opportunities and encouragement are given for him to *challenge* the assumptions on which the unrealistic fears are based, and to try out, in graded steps, the behaviors he has so vigorously avoided. He is, in short, provided an opportunity for *reeducative psychotherapy*. Such therapeutic circumstances may occasionally be provided by family and friends, but the opportunity for their provision falls most often to members of the helping professions—an opportunity within which the physician may offer valuable service and derive much personal satisfaction.

References

American Psychiatric Association. Diagnostic and Statistical Manual of Mental Disorders, 2nd ed. Washington, D.C.: American Psychiatric Association, 1968.

American Psychiatric Association. Diagnostic and Statistical Manual of Mental Disorders, 3rd ed. Washington, D.C.: American Psychiatric Association, 1980.

Brenner, C. An Elementary Textbook of Psychoanalysis, revised ed. New York, New York: International Universities Press, 1973.

Drellich, M.G. Classical psychoanalytic school: The theory of neuroses. In S. Arieti (Ed.) American Handbook of Psychiatry, 2nd ed., vol. 1. New York, New York: Basic Books, 1974, pp. 737–764.

Fenichel, O. The Psychoanalytic Theory of Neurosis. New York, New York: Norton, 1945.

Freud, S. Introductory lectures on psycho-analysis (1916–17). In J. Strachey (Trans. and Ed.) The Standard Edition of the Complete Psychological Works of Sigmund Freud, vols. 15 and 16. London, Great Britain: Hogarth Press, 1963.

Hine, F.R. Introduction to Psychodynamics: A Conflict-Adaptational Approach. Durham, North Carolina: Duke University Press, 1971.

Hine, F.R., E. Pfeiffer, G.L. Maddox, P.L. Hein, and R.O. Friedel. Behavioral Science: A Selective View. Boston, Massachusetts: Little, Brown, 1972.

Holmes, T.H., and M. Masuda. Life changes and illness susceptibility. In J.P. Scott and E.C. Senay (Eds.) Separation and Depression: Clinical and Research Aspects. Washington, D.C.: American Association for the Advancement of Science, 1973, pp. 161–186.

Holmes, T.H., and R.H. Rahe. The social readjustment rating scale. J. Psychosomatic Research 11:213–218, August 1967.

Horney, K. Our Inner Conflicts: A Constructive Theory of Neurosis. New York, New York: Norton, 1945.
Leary, T. The Interpersonal Diagnosis of Personality. New York, New York: Ronald Press, 1957.
Levis, D.J., and T.L. Boyd. Symptom maintenance: An infrahuman analysis and extension of the conservation of anxiety principle. J. Abnormal Psychology 88:107–120, April 1979.
Meissner, W.W. Classical psychoanalysis. In H.I. Kaplan, A.M. Freedman, and B.J. Sadock (Eds.) Comprehensive Textbook of Psychiatry, 3rd ed., vol. 1. Baltimore, Maryland: Williams and Wilkins, 1980, pp. 631–728.
Melvin, K.B. Vicious circle behavior. In H.D. Kimmel (Ed.) Experimental Psychopathology: Recent Research and Theory. New York, New York: Academic Press, 1971, pp. 95–115.
Mowrer, O.H. Learning Theory and Personality Dynamics. New York, New York: Ronald Press, 1950.
Paykel, E.S. Life events and acute depression. In J.P. Scott and E.C. Senay (Eds.) Separation and Depression: Clinical and Research Aspects. Washington, D.C.: American Association for the Advancement of Science, 1973, pp. 215–236.
Reich, W. Character Analysis (1933), 3rd ed. New York, New York: Orgone Institute Press, 1949.
Salzman, L. Developments in Psychoanalysis. New York, New York: Grune and Stratton, 1962.
Seligman, M.E.P., and J.C. Johnston. A cognitive theory of avoidance learning. In F.J. McGuigan and D.B. Lumsden (Eds.) RSP Contemporary Approaches to Conditioning and Learning. New York, New York: Wiley, 1973, pp. 69–110.
Spitzer, R.L., M. Sheehy, and J. Endicott. DSM-III: guiding principles. In V.M. Rakoff, H.C. Staner, and H.B. Kedsward (Eds.) Psychiatric Diagnosis. New York, New York: Brunner/Mazel, 1977, pp. 1–24.
Thompson, C. Psychoanalysis, Evolution and Development. New York, New York: Hermitage House, 1950.
Waelder, R. Basic Theory of Psychoanalysis. New York, New York: International Universities Press, 1960.

17

Personality: Developmental Aspects

We have defined personality as a hypothetical construct referring to an organized system of reaction tendencies that mediates relations between the person and his or her environment, and rendering the person's behavior distinctive and more or less uniquely identifying. In this chapter we are going to consider this uniquely "identifying signature"—personality—from a developmental perspective. It is beyond the scope of our present endeavors to consider the developmental postulates of the major theories of personality; the interested reader is directed to the classic work of Hall and Lindzey (1957). Furthermore, it is not the goal of this chapter to present the one "best" theory. The goal is to facilitate understanding of the process of personality development.

Theories of personality differ in basic assumptions about the nature of human development in terms of the locus of change and the nature of the change process. The locus of the developmental dynamic refers to whether developmental change is viewed as occurring as a consequence of changes within the organism or because of changes external to the organism (Looft, 1973). Theories that assume that man is active and changes as a result of his own initiations are referred to as *organismic*, of which Piagetian theory is an example. Theories that assume that man changes primarily in response to environmental changes are referred to as *mechanistic*, of which Skinnerian theory is an example.

Theories based on either an organismic or mechanistic assumption about human development tend to differ from each other on several other dimensions. Organismic theories, locating the developmental dynamic internally, see changes as qualitative and discontinuous resulting in universal developmental stages. The whole is viewed as more than the sum of its parts. Mechanistic theories, locating the developmental dynamic externally, see changes as quantitative and continuous. Relativism rather than developmental universals are posited, and the whole is viewed as predictable from its parts or elements.

It has been maintained that the organismic and mechanistic theories have outlived their usefulness and that a new relational model of development is needed "that perceives human social and mental development as the confluence of many interrelated and changing subsystems, including the biological, social, cultural and historical" (Looft, 1973, p. 51).

Another basic assumption about human development that differentiates theories of personality is the nature of the process of change and its determinants. One view, the biogenetic, stresses the universality of development related to maturation, while the other view, the sociocultural, sees development as relative to individual experience.

Biogenetic theories see personality development—as all development—as directed by genetically determined physiological factors that are immutable, inevitable, universal, and relatively unaffected by environmental factors. Three representative examples are the theories of Hall, Freud, and Gessell.

One of the main tenants of Hall's theory is the law of recapitulation. The experiential history of the human species is considered part of the genetic structure of each individual. Individuals develop through predetermined stages from primitiveness to civilized behavior, i.e., a recreation of the development of the human race. The individual and species stages are:

Individual	Species
Infancy	Animal stages
Childhood	Hunting and fishing stage
Youth	"Humdrum life of savagery"
Adolescence	Transition and turmoil, i.e., "storm and stress" of the development of civilization

The implications of Hall's view would be that since socially unacceptable types of behavior were necessary in social development, they must be tolerated.

The traditional Freudian view, with its emphasis on innate drives and universal psychosexual stages, is also a biogenetic view. Excessive frustration of these instinctual drives may lead to neurosis. Thus the implication would be for acceptance, love, and leniency in childrearing practices.

Gessell's view, although it makes some allowance for individual variation and external influence, is also basically an evolutionary conception of development with predetermined maturational phases unfolding in orderly sequence. Biology determines the order of appearance of behavior traits and developmental trends.

Sociocultural views arose from the influences of behaviorism, learning theory, and cultural anthropology during the first decades of this century. The biogenetic view was challenged. Although biogenetic factors were acknowledged to contribute broad developmental dispositions, experience was seen as the most important determinant of man's nature. Cultural relativism replaced postulates of universality. Cultural relativism emphasizes the importance of social institutions and cultural factors in human development. These factors are seen as able to channel and alter the influence of the biological factors. Social and cultural factors, for example, are seen as determining whether different roles for children and adults are experienced as continuous or discontinuous. It has been pointed out that stages can be culturally induced by discontinuities in childrearing methods and educational practices. The implications of the sociocultural view are that personality and behavior can be significantly modified by environmental factors. Empirical cross-cultural research provides support for sensorimotor, preoperational, and concrete operational forms of thought as universal, but formal operational thought seems to be relative and dependent upon forms of education (Looft, 1973). However, similarities in development across cultures are not viewed by the sociocultural theorists as evidence of universality because the similarities could be dissolved by the application of a unique set of environmental contingencies to each person.

The discerning reader knows that, as we have done in previous chapters, we will advocate an interaction view of nature-nurture. The question is not what is given, acquired, or what is due to the interaction, "it is rather the infinitely more complex question of what specific biological or environmental events or combination thereof, in what degree, and under what circumstances, operate to influence a specific pattern of personality development or behavior" (Weiner, 1970, p. 12).

Throughout this book we have been espousing a transactional point of view about human behavior that leads us to consider personality as being formed out of life experiences that are determined to some extent by innate qualities of the individual that are rooted in the biological organism. Previously, we have considered the innate or constitutional factors and characteristics that the neonate brings into the world. We have discussed the various dimensions of individual differences, including physical, state, and temperament characteristics, and their effect on and interaction with the environment. We have presented the context of immediate and lasting importance as that of the mother-infant relationship. The importance of maternal sensitivity and responsiveness in establishing and maintaining a synchronous relationship and the importance of such a relationship to attachment and affective development has been stressed. Thus the view of personality and its development that we are presenting is one that is transactional, views man as both active and reactive, and views development as reflecting the confluence of maturation and learning.

Social Learning Theory

How personality development proceeds in this transactional view can be accounted for by a social learning theory perspective. Social learning theory represents the extension of learning theory principles to account for development and modification of human social behavior (Bandura and Walters, 1963). Personality development is seen as a consequence of organism-environment interactions resulting in unique learning histories and unique patterns of learned attributes, competencies, and traits or characteristics. Individual idiosyncratic behavior patterns are viewed as a consequence of idiosyncratic social learning histories. Each person experiences the environment in a unique way because the meaning and impact of stimuli are acted upon and modified by cognitive transformation, that is, the processing of environmental stimuli and construing of reality by the individual.

Social learning theory does expand traditional stimulus-response learning theory in several important ways (Bandura and Walters, 1963). In addition to classical (Pavlovian) and operant (Skinnerian) conditioning, a third type of learning is emphasized: observational learning. Much social behavior is not learned through the process of reinforcement of successive approximations but through observation and imitation. This led to the recognition of the value of vicarious reinforcement and also to the inclusion of cognitive variables as legitimate behaviors to study as well as motor responses. Thus behavior is broadly defined to include observable and potentially observable events including thoughts, feelings, and motor responses. The focus is on identifying the physical, emotional, cognitive, and social stimuli that elicit and maintain specific behaviors.

Both prosocial and deviant patterns of response can be accounted for by the same social learning principles. Traits or personality dimensions are considered in terms of habit hierarchies. The individual learns a variety of response patterns to the same social cues, and if some response patterns result in more reinforcement than others, these can become dominant (e.g., dependency behaviors). The strength of a particular response pattern to other response patterns determines whether they are exhibited in a wide or narrow range of situations according to the principles of discrimination and generalization.

The same social learning principles are considered to apply throughout the life span. Social learning theory does stem from a mechanistic, sociocultural view of human development. Thus development is viewed as continuous and relative, so that no universal hierarchical progression through developmental stages is postulated. Chronological age is considered a rough index of environmental experience, and correlations of behavior with age are not considered to be of fundamental importance.

Developmental Tasks

This view of personality development as reflecting transactions between biologically based dispositions and psychosocial context proceeding according to social learning theory principles is particularly suited for a life-span perspective; that is, a perspective that considers personality changes and development throughout the entire life span and not just limited to childhood and adolescence.

The biologically based drive toward growth exhibited by the individual combined with the demands, constraints, and opportunities provided by the social environment gives rise to the concept of developmental or psychosocial tasks that need to be accomplished during the course of the life span. Two principal sources of developmental tasks can be postulated: (1) the biological changes which present the individual with new opportunities, needs, and problems of adjustment; and (2) the expectations of the society and of the person regarding social roles that change with age (Havighurst, 1973).

The concept of psychosocial task is an integral part of Erikson's theory of personality development. Erikson (1963) reorganized psychoanalytic theory in the light of anthropological findings and emphasized the social conditions with which the individual must contend during development. Consideration of Erikson's theory will provide an example of a theory that, while basically organismic, bridges biogenetic and sociocultural views.

The essential features of Erikson's concept of epigenesis are: (1) the innate *ground plan* which determines the sequence and times of emergence of the various biobehavioral potentialities; (2) the dependency of each biologically based behavior area on the quality of *psychosocial interaction* which it obtains at the time of its emergence and developmental crisis; and (3) the *interaction of stages* whereby recognition is given to the fact that the interactions and outcomes of each stage depend not only on the environment at that time but also on whatever the individual brings with him from the resolution of earlier crises.

Erikson's theory postulates eight psychosocial tasks or issues each of which are prominent at a certain stage of development from birth to adulthood. Healthy movement to a subsequent stage requires successful resolution of the preceding stage. The tasks are presented in terms of resolution of a conflict with two possible outcomes: one negative and one positive. Erikson's stages are depicted in Figure 17-1. It is useful to think of these conflicts as represent-

VIII. Maturity								Ego Integrity vs. Despair
VII. Adulthood							Generativity vs. Stagnation	
VI. Young Adulthood						Intimacy vs. Isolation		
V. Puberty and Adolescence					Identity vs. Role Confusion			
IV. Latency				Industry vs. Inferiority				
III. Locomotor-Genital			Initiative vs. Guilt					
II. Muscular-Anal		Autonomy vs. Shame, Doubt						
I. Oral Sensory	Basic Trust vs. Mistrust							
	1	2	3	4	5	6	7	8

Fig. 17-1. Erikson's eight ages of man. (From Erikson, 1963.)

ing an essential developmental task at each stage or age. Thus, the task to be accomplished during the first year of life is basic trust. During ages 1–6, establishing autonomy is the task. The major developmental task of adolescence is the establishment of identity.

One of the utilities of a theory based on developmental tasks that arise out of biological changes and personal and societal expectations is that it can accommodate advances in our understanding of and changes in both biological and psychosocial issues. For example, Hine (1971) has suggested a downward extension of Erikson's psychosocial stages of development to reflect development and developmental issues during approximately the first six months of life. This extension is depicted in Figure 17-2. We have previously considered the areas encompassed in this extension in Unit I (on basic mental functions) and Unit II (on dimensions of biobehavioral dispositions).

Another utility of a theory based on developmental tasks is that it is applicable to a life-span approach to personality development. There are a number of developmental tasks or experiences that are typically confronted during the adult years. These include marriage, parenthood, occupation, postparenthood, retirement, grandparenthood, and widowhood (Ahammer, 1973).

In addition to changes occurring in our understanding of biological and sociocultural factors that influence development, another source of change can be actual historical development in our society. Looft (1973) has pointed out that historical developments "have changed the very nature of psychological development within individuals" (p. 50). At one time in our history Freud's focus upon achieving a stable sexual orientation may have been the essential developmental achievement in youth. At a later time, this goal could be subordinate to establishing a stable identity, as Erikson postulated. This in turn could become subordinate to the establishment of some other goal more in tune with current issues, such as "commitment" as suggested by Mead (Looft, 1973).

Conclusion

> Situations are as much a function of the person as the person's behavior is a function of the situation. (Bowers, 1973)

Thus, with that statement, we may have come full circle in the consideration of personality from a developmental perspective. Frequently the science of human behavior proceeds in pendulum fashion, with each successive theory or position exerting an initially corrective and balancing influence on the prevailing view but in turn proceeding too far only to be in need of correction by the subsequent swing of the pendulum. It is hoped that we have gained in our understanding of the process of personality development as we rode the pendulum swings of nature-nurture, maturation-learning, biogenetic-sociocultural, organismic-mechanistic, universal-relative, structure-

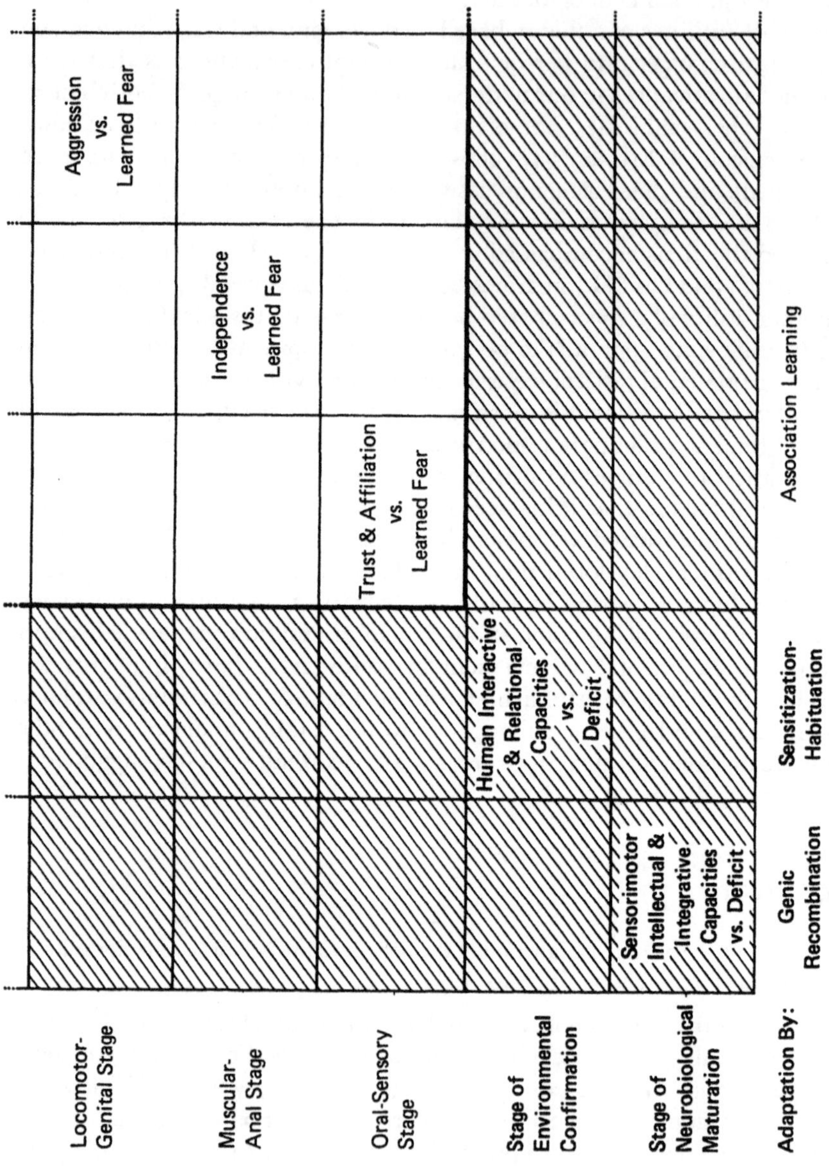

Fig. 17-2. Proposed extension of Erikson's epigenetic schema by the addition of two earlier stages. (From Hine, 1971.)

task, and trait-situation. We have learned that there are no main effects, that everything is an interaction, and that views that proceed on a main effects model are not sufficient for the complexity of the multiply determined and manifested dimensions of human behavior. Specifying the interaction effects is the task. Person variables, situation variables, and moderator variables all are necessary for our continuing search for understanding of the most idiosyncratic aspect of human behavior.

References

Ahammer, I.M. Social-learning theory as a framework of the study of adult personality development. In P.B. Baltes, and K.W. Schaie (Eds.) Life-Span Developmental Psychology: Personality and Socialization. New York, New York: Academic Press, 1973.

Bandura, A., and R.H. Walters. Social Learning and Personality Development. New York, New York: Holt, Rinehart and Winston, 1963.

Bowers, K.S. Situationism in psychology: An analysis and a critique. Psychological Review 80:307–336, 1973.

Erikson, E.H. Childhood and Society. New York, New York: Norton, 1963.

Hall, C.S., and G. Lindzey. Theories of Personality. New York, New York: Wiley, 1957.

Havighurst, R.J. History of developmental psychology: Socialization and personality development through the life span. In P.B. Baltes and K.W. Schaie (Eds.) Life Span Developmental Psychology: Personality and Socialization. New York, New York: Academic Press, 1973.

Hine, F.R. Introduction to Psychodynamics: A Conflict-Adaptational Approach. Durham, North Carolina: Duke University Press, 1971.

Looft, W. Socialization and personality throughout the life-span: An examination of contemporary psychological approaches. In P.B. Baltes and K.W. Schaie (Eds.) Life-Span Developmental Psychology: Personality and Socialization. New York, New York: Academic Press, 1973.

Weiner, I.B. Psychological Disturbance in Adolescence. New York, New York: Wiley, 1970.

18

Role Theory and the Social Self

Systematic observation of organisms in their natural environments has always been important in science. Observed regularities in patterns of behavior in animals, including the human ones, are frequently the outcomes which scientists want to describe precisely, classify, understand, explain, and predict. While explanation and prediction are the ultimate goals of science, the penultimate goals of description, classification, and understanding are necessary precursors which prove to be quite challenging in themselves. The ethnographic tradition in anthropology and sociology has produced documentation of similarities and differences in behavior between and within groups which gave rise to the concepts of *culture*, *role*, *status*, and *norms*. Such constructs do not explain observed patterns of human behavior, but they do provide essential and useful tools for describing the social contexts in which human beings interact. In emphasizing the social context of behavior, this chapter complements the other chapters in this Unit which focus primarily on intraindividual aspects of behavior.

The two constructs noted in the title of this chapter, *role theory* and *social self*, are commonly encountered in the literature of the social sciences and social psychology. Discussions of role theory and the social self draw heavily, and rather obviously, on the commonsense association between social behavior and dramaturgy. Life indeed appears to be a stage on which individuals (persona) appear to play parts (roles). Culture provides a script which locates the actors, feeds them stage directions and lines, and designs the scenery. Social groups provide the audiences who react with approval or disapproval. Players are coached and directed. They play well or badly. They are sometimes out of character. They are different offstage and onstage.

One has no difficulty in recognizing the applicability of dramaturgical metaphors to the ways commonly used to describe everyday experience.

Role performance in social groups is not left to chance. The coaching of the young by adults observed in families and other social groups tends to produce predictably recognizable performances. Most individuals most of the time appear to want to behave in ways they are expected to behave. Erving Goffman popularized this observation in his widely read book, *The Presentation of Self in Everyday Life* (1959). Individuals are asked implicitly and explicitly, "Who are you?" They also ask themselves, "Who am I?" The answers to both questions tend to be congruent and, to a substantial degree, tend to reflect recognizable, shared social roles related to gender, age, occupation, marital status, and so on. The *self* Goffman had in mind is phenomenological, relatively conscious, and decidedly social. The social self therefore cannot be equated with the more comprehensive and complex concept of personality or even of ego. However, social self is reasonably close to Erikson's construct of *identity*, which he defined as a satisfying sense of sameness which is acceptable to significant others (1959).

Role theory, in summary, provides a useful perspective for understanding the successful and unsuccessful presentations of self in everyday life. In the sections which follow, some basic insights from research on role theory and the social self will be reviewed briefly and illustrated. Those who wish to pursue the issues in depth are referred to the excellent article by Sarbin and Allen (1968) which focuses on the relevance of role enactment, role expectations, and individual characteristics for understanding stability and change in self-perception and behavior.

Role Enactment

Children at play are observed to try a variety of roles. They play or, more accurately, they *play at* roles like doctor, nurse, patient, mother, father, policeman, robber, cowboy, indian, or soldier. In play they costume themselves with the stereotypic cultural symbols associated with the roles, and experiment with related tones of voice, demeanors, postures, and gestures. If one observes the process of role entry, role play, and role exit in children, differential emotional involvement is apparent at different stages in the process. The child appears to move affectively into the role, to be momentarily absorbed in the role, and then to move affectively out again. This differential degree of absorption has been designated variously as *organismic involvement* or *role distance*. This child's play has its counterpart as adults work at role enactment. Adults typically have to enact a number of roles during a day, and the transition between roles provides an opportunity to observe the taking leave of one role and the taking on of another. Consider, for example, a physician who leaves home in the morning in ordinary clothing. At the office or in a hospital, distinctive clothing (a white coat) and tools (a stethoscope) are added prior to beginning work. When leave is taken from the workplace, the distinctive role symbols are relinquished. In a very literal sense, one steps out of the role. There is a certain amusement in imagining a physician who would insist on staying in the occupational role while interacting with guests at a party or with spouse or children. A physician suiting up for surgery and unsuiting after surgery also provides a recognizable illustration of role transition. Similarly, clergymen suit up for and disrobe following ceremonial occasions. But clergymen in some religious organizations illustrate a relatively rare but recognizable characteristic of some social roles: they preempt or pervade other roles. In churches with high liturgical traditions, clergymen are required to remain in uniform and in role in public. Until recently, persons in military service faced the same kind of requirements. Currently, persons in military service can remove the symbols of military service when they are properly on leave and off the military base.

The number of roles which a person plays and the degree of involvement in each role varies (Figure 18-1), but extensive involvement for sustained periods of time in a single role is not expected, encouraged, or usually permitted. Sustained total absorption of a person in a role is suggestive of pathological behavior. This is so, in part, because the unrelieved enactment of a single role regardless of audience or situational appropriateness is incongruous, deviant, and maladaptive. Also, there are many indications that being onstage and in character is emotionally very demanding for many roles. William James, for example, observed that the role of a teacher was very exacting insofar as it required the teacher to remain intellectually engaged and in step with students. Professional actors performing before audiences and therapists relating to patients experience similar demands and seek the relief of being offstage and out of such demanding roles periodically.

The fact that role enactment is usually for the benefit of audiences calls attention to the interpersonal dimensions of behavior. Roles are almost always observed to be in sets. *Physician* makes us think of *patient*, *teacher* of *student*, *priest* of *parishioner*, *husband* of *wife*, *parent* of *child*, and so on. The sets can in fact be very extensive and complex, as indicated by the vast array of interlocking statuses and roles of health professionals observed in a teaching hospital designed to provide care for patients. Such role sets provide an immediate audience to which the performance of particular roles in the set are directed.

Role enactments tend to be set and situation-specific. A physician who generalizes the role appropriate to patients at bedside, in the examining room, or in surgery to sets or situations that include, for example, family members or academic colleagues who are not physicians, does so at considerable risk of assessment, ridicule, or outright rejection. With the social situation properly specified, a physician may inquire about intimate details of personal life and touch a nude or partially draped patient without regard to

Zero. Noninvolvement

I. Casual role enactment

II. Ritual acting

III. Engrossed acting

IV. Classical hypnotic role taking

V. Histrionic neurosis

VI. Ecstasy

VII. Object of sorcery and witchcraft (sometimes irreversible)

Role and self differentiated	Role and self undifferentiated
Zero involvement	Maximal involvement
Few organic systems	Entire organism
No effort	Much effort

Fig. 18-1. Scale representing dimensions of organismic involvement. (From Sarbin and Allen, 1968.)

gender. Moments later, outside the consulting room, exactly the same questions or touching would be considered improper, offensive, and unacceptable. The fact that change in audiences may require changes in roles is one basis for the observation that personal behavior does not generalize in a simple way across situations. Whatever relatively stable personal trait may characterize an individual's preferred enactment of roles appears to be titrated by the perceived expectations and demands of the relevant audiences in various situations. Hence, personality theorists have found it necessary and useful to distinguish situational behavioral *states* from relatively persistent behavioral traits.

Since different situations may provide different audiences, individuals can and do seek out particular audiences in order to enact preferred roles. One meaning of *primary group* in sociology is that the membership of such groupings share a sense of belonging together and a community of fate; a primary group of friends or kin typically constitutes a preferred and receptive audience that tolerates a considerable degree of offstage and idiosyncratic behavior. One cannot choose one's audience, however, nor does the presence of an audience ensure that the actor will play to it in a simple way. Persons of high status may ignore or treat with contempt audiences whose members have a lower status. In some situations, an individual may ignore another individual who is physically present, treating him or her as a nonperson or as "not present" as in the case of a preoccupied walker on a crowded street or a partially nude student behaving offstage in a dormitory, oblivious to janitors or maids. However, in most public situations one expects individuals to acknowledge the presence of audiences, and it is disconcerting for individuals to persist in acting as though they are offstage and "not present" in group situations.

Imagination does provide some freedom from ordinary and usual audiences. This freedom is implied in the playacting behavior of children and in the fantasy of the mythical figure in our literature, Walter Mitty, who projects himself with ease into a wide range of heroic roles to the enthusiastic approval of equally mythical audiences. Since the number of roles which may be played is always larger than the number realistically available at any given time, adults, like children, tend to anticipate playing the roles they expect to play or want to play before some preferred audience. A first-year medical student provides an obvious illustration of anticipatory role enactment. The beginning student has a general knowledge of the script for enacting the role of physician vis-à-vis nurse, technician, administrator, and patient. The student understands in a general sense the props (the white coat, the stethoscope, the name tag ending in M.D., and the physical settings for doctor-patient interaction) and the etiquette for interaction long before the props and the etiquette can be displayed with aplomb (Merton et al., 1957; Becker et al., 1961).

Role Expectations

Culture provides the script for role enactment, and audiences provide the behavioral reinforcement. Learning theory and the process of socialization ensure an outcome in which most people, most of the time, enact a variety of roles in an orderly, recognizable fashion. This does not at all require us to believe that persons are automatons without individuality. While social groups do tend to develop consensus about expectable behavior in a wide range of situations, there is considerable latitude for individual variation. First, as already noted, individuals usually have an opportunity for some choice in the audience before which they perform regularly. Second, audiences permit individuals to go offstage into relatively private worlds, as though the need for emotional relief is understood. Some social groups even institutionalize opportunities for offstage behavior to be brought onstage for limited periods, as in the case of Mardi Gras in the French tradition or, more commonly, the cultural permission of unusual behavior observed at professional and business meetings called "conventions." Third, consensus about the requirements for role enactment is not usually either total or exact. Social groups may permit considerable latitude in the acceptable enactment of roles. This is necessary in part because multiple, complex roles must be negotiated. A mother may be without a spouse and also be a worker. A physician may also be a religious missionary and an organizational administrator. Role enactment, furthermore, may be minimal or involve considerable personal embellishment. In the sociological literature, role *making* as well as role *taking* is recognized. Different boundaries of tolerable performance are clearly demonstrable from group to group and from society to society. These boundaries may change over time, as illustrated by the changing definitions of gender roles in contemporary society. Legal sanctions may define the essentials of certain role enactments, as in the case of a physician's responsibility for patients or of a parent for offspring. An officer of an organization may have the basics of role enactment defined by a constitution and by-laws. Yet, an equally palpable indication of the existence of expectations about role performance is found in the everyday experience of embarrrassment, shame, and guilt.

In simpliest terms, embarrassment reflects discomfort stemming from being onstage but out of character. This discomfort implies that one should be but is not (or does not know how to go about) meeting a role expectation, as in the case of a performer who forgets or muffs lines or is generally out of character. Of even greater interest is the experience of being embarrassed for someone else, which is the vicarious experience of another's failure to perform adequately. Shame is a more intense affect than embarrassment. A social group may publicly shame an individual for improper role enactments; the shaming may be expressed spontaneously in booing, hissing or cries of outrage, or ritualistically in ceremonies of disparagement and banishment (e.g., defrocking and excommunication). Guilt is both a legal concept and a powerful affect. A jury of one's peers can declare one guilty of unacceptable behavior and assign appropriate punishment. The individual so charged may or may not *feel* guilty. On the other hand, an individual may *feel* guilty for some real or imagined social transgression in the absence of literal trial by jury. The self-imputation of guilt and related self-disparagement are noted here as social facts commonly reported by individuals, indicating the internalization and acceptance of social expectations about role performances. The internal dynamics of personal feelings of guilt is the domain of psychology and psychiatry; however, the origins of the phenomenon are distinctly social.

While many aspects of role expectation are embodied in law, regulations, or explicitly common knowledge, some aspects are implicit and inferential. A particularly interesting illustration of implicit expectations which guide role performance is found in the etiquette of touching persons. Edward Hall (1966), an anthropologist, has reported that definitions of personal and private space may vary widely across cultures. In the United States, individuals, particularly if they are strangers, avoid touching one another except in formal, ritualistic fashion such as hand shaking. Hall notes that it is usually possible to interpose a 12-inch ruler between individuals in conversation. The body is personal space which is rarely touched except by intimates, and even then the touching is very restricted in amount and location. Touching, it appears, is guided by implicit but effective rules.

A strict application of restrictive rules of touch would make a physical examination in medicine impossible. How is this restriction negotiated? Special rules are applied for the doctor-patient role set, and the situational redefinition is signaled by a number of ritualistic and formal requirements such as draping the body, having a third person present, and restricting the unusual touching to a limited number of publicly defined places. Even with these redefinitions, individuals who are learning to touch others in ways that are usually culturally prohibited experience some apprehension until the initial affect is neutralized by repetition.

Skill in Role Enactment

Dramaturgical role performances are not of equal quality. Some performers appear to audiences to be more in character than others and to convey that fact exceptionally well through demeanor, posture, gesture, and inflection. Excellent performances certainly reflect coaching and direction. The real-life counterpart of differences in role enactment onstage is a socialization process in which parents and adults generally coach and direct children regarding role enactments. Medical students, for example, are explicitly taught how to do a physical examination and how to interview a patient; they also have innumerable opportunities to observe role models not only doing these tasks but also displaying the finer points of role enactment such as demeanor, gesture, and intonation and the display of the paraphernalia which signal *physicians* to others.

One does not have to be a physician to be able to act like one, as professional actors in a number of successful television series on medicine have demonstrated. Of equal interest is the occasional appearance of a charlatan who appropriates illegitimately, but nonetheless enacts successfully, a physician's role in interaction with patients and other health personnel. Clearly, certain highly visible social roles have easily recognizable stereotypic components which can be taught and learned.

The most obvious handicap in developing adequate role enactments for some individuals is the absence of competent tutors, coaches, and directors. This handicap is illustrated by immigrants to a new society, by migrants from an isolated rural area to a city, and by individuals who have been reared in families flawed by a missing or socially incompetent parent.

Actors are to some extent born and not simply made by adequate coaching and directing. Research has not, however, identified a profile of personal characteristics which ensures exceptional role enactment (Sarbin and Allen, 1968) across a variety of situations. The most consistent positive correlates of exceptional role enactment are general intelligence and empathy, although the evidence is clearer on the former than on the latter. Empathy refers to the ability to put oneself in another's place (i.e., to take the role of the other) and to imagine correctly the other's private feelings and probable responses in particular situations. In general, a positive relationship has been found between role enactment and age, intelligence, social maturity, and perceptual ability. However, intelligence accounts for more of the differences in role enactment aptitude than any other variable.

Self-Role Congruence

In dramaturgy, roles are enacted by a character, a *persona*. Historically, the persona had a stage identity revealed not only by the roles to be enacted but also by costume and, in ancient theater, by a mask. The actor was not the persona. In the same sense, one's *social identity* cannot be simply equated with the cognitive organization of personal qualities which is designated as *self*. We would, however, expect the two constructs to be consonant in the typical case. As noted earlier in this chapter, individuals appear to want to become and be what they are expected by significant others to want to become and be. We do not know the epidemiology of incongruence between self and social identity or the precise incidence and prevalence of flawed social identities which are associated with self-rejection and disparagement. We do know that all societies generate some potential for role conflict and for incongruity between role expectations and preferred conceptions of self. Highly differential societies have a particularly high potential for these stressful outcomes.

A highly differential society such as our own may appear to offer a wide variety of role opportunities but, at the same time, proscribe role taking for individuals in a particular ascribed status. *Ascribed* status is often associated with organismic and hence personally uncontrolled characteristics such as age and sex. Drinking and driving are legally proscribed for the young. Mandatory retirement may be prescribed for older persons. Historically, women and black persons have been severely restricted in the types of occupations open to them. Kardiner and Ovesey (1951) have illustrated the importance of distinguishing between the social identity of blacks and their conceptions of self. A black person, while conforming exactly to stereotypic social role performance of the dominant society, may reject this identity as unacceptable and demeaning. If alternative social identities are repeatedly denied, rage, however internalized and controlled, is the likely outcome. Kardiner and Ovesey hypothesized from their clinical experience that the more outwardly conforming middle-class black males were to the social identity required by the dominant society, the more internalized rage would be revealed in psychological analysis.

Individuals who perceive their social identity to be flawed by an ascribed characteristic or by an impairment may go to great lengths to conceal or correct the flaw. Individuals whose personal and social gender identity are mismatched may seek to change gender. Prior to the black movement of the 1960s which began to assert that "black is beautiful," many blacks indicated a preference for relatively light-skinned marital partners and attempted to lighten their own skin and straighten their hair. Plastic surgery is sought by some individuals who wish their appearance to match their perception of some cultural norm of attractiveness. Dieting and programs which offer the prospect of weight reduction, and hence conformity to cultural preferences for slimness, attract hundreds of thousands of individuals. The management of the impressions an individual wants to make on others, a common activity in social groups, becomes an imperative and a preoccupation for those who perceive themselves as socially flawed and stigmatized. A common response of those who consider their identity seriously flawed or stigmatized is withdrawal from social groups or withdrawal to social groups of similarly flawed individuals (Goffman, 1961). Such withdrawal controls the audience to whom the social self is presented and may permit the development of new techniques of impression management for presentation to general audiences. Goffman argues that socially flawed individuals tend to develop "careers" in which deviant behavior becomes a stable lifestyle reinforced by audiences composed of other deviants.

A phenomenological account of how roles are learned reinforces the conclusion that social identity and the social self are substantially a product of role enactment; individuals learn that some roles are socially rewarded *and* personally satisfying. This, in fact, is essentially the argument of Erik Erikson who refers to *identity* as a satisfying sense of sameness *and* an awareness that personal preferences for interpersonal behavior are socially approved. This is also the dominant argument in the sociological literature. *Identity* and *self* are social products. Such an argument does not require the conclusion that identity and self are totally passive products of social interaction. This is certainly not the case. We have already noted above that persons may be active agents who seek out situations in which roles they perceive to be attractive may be enacted, rewarded, and hence reinforced. However, the opportunities for personal choice of performance sites and the inherited or learned aptitudes for role performance are limited. The result is inevitably flawed identity, self-disparagement, and deviance for some and compensatory fantasy for many.

Role enactment, even if not preferred or chosen, can and does have an impact on social identity, and the perception of this fact is powerfully illustrated by Zimbardo's prison experiment. In order to illustrate the impact of enforced role enactment on interpersonal behavior and self-evaluation, Zimbardo and his associates at Stanford advertised an opportunity for male collegians to earn some money by participation in an experiment, otherwise not described to potential participants. Applicants were screened by conventional psychological tests to ensure the selection of conventionally normal, middle-class young adults who were then randomly assigned to be either guards or prisoners in an experiment which simulated a prison environment. Prisoners were systematically depersonalized by having their heads covered with stockings, by the removal of all personal effects, by the use of numbers rather than names when referring to prisoners, and by having guards subject prisoners to demeaning and punishing behavior and arbitrary rules. Guards were costumed to fit stereotyped images of police authority. The experiment was to continue for 14 days.

The hypothesized transformations of behavior worked too well and much quicker than expected. In a matter of a few days some of the prisoners began to behave passively and submissively in the face of unexpected brutality on the part of the guards. When an increasing number of prisoners began to display pathological responses, the experiment was terminated. In a debriefing session, both prisoners and guards reported that, in the contrived situation, they increasingly came to think of themselves and to behave as prisoners or guards. The role enactment had temporarily transformed social identities and perceptions of the self. In retrospect, Zimbardo had misgivings about the ethics of such experimentations precisely because he had been able to demonstrate the transformation of identity with such ease. Situational factors appear to be relatively powerful determinants of social behavior, identity, and self-perception.

References

Becker, H.S., et al. Boys in White: Student Culture in Medical School. Chicago, Illinois: University of Chicago Press, 1961. Erikson, Erik. Identity and the life cycle. Psychological Issues 1:1:, 1959.

Goffman, E. The Presentation of Self in Everyday Life. Garden City, New Jersey: Doubleday, 1959.

Goffman, E. Asylums. Chicago, Illinois: Aldine, 1961.

Hall, Edward. The Hidden Dimension. Garden City, New Jersey: Doubleday, 1966.

Kardiner, A., and L. Ovesey. The Mark of Oppression. New York, New York: Norton, 1951.

Merton, R.K., G.C. Reader, and P.L. Kendall (Eds.). The Student-Physician: Introductory Studies in the Sociology of Medical Education. Cambridge, Massachusetts: Harvard University Press, 1957.

Sarbin, T.R., and V.L. Allen. Role theory. In G. Lindzey and E. Aronson (Eds.) The Handbook of Social Psychology, 2nd ed., vol. 1. Reading, Massachusetts: Addison-Wesley, 1968.

Unit V

Socialization and Social Integration: Aggression and Its Control

In this unit, we discuss the fifth and final behavior function area in our schema, namely, social integration. More specifically, we deal with that subarea of social behavior most frequently of concern to the physician because it is the one most often disordered. Such behavior is usually termed aggressive, impulsive, or antisocial.

19

Pressures Toward Socially Disintegrated Behavior: The Sources of Aggression

The approach taken in this book assumes that successful socialization is socially integrative. In the typical case, the developing individual acquires information about society's expectations and develops associated emotional patterns required to give that information motivational significance. Individuals know how to order their behavior so as to derive the benefits provided by the society and avoid the punitive sanctions imposed by that society for major deviations from its norms. Socialized individuals typically want to do what they are expected to do. They also want to perform the behaviors that are socially approved and will fear, to a degree appropriate to the real consequences, to engage in major transgressions of law, custom, and role expectations. These statements are not intended to rule out the possibility that the individual may want and attempt to change the society, even at the risk of failure and retaliation. But, in the socially integrated person, activities aimed at protest and reform will, not be undertaken blindly and impulsively but rather from a position of cognitive and emotional appreciation of the society, a position that increases the probability of success while reducing where possible the likelihood of personal cost and distress. Moreover, the events of everyday life are not free of conflict since the objectives of individuals and social groups are sometimes contradictory. Social groups may, in fact, ritualize conflict in the form of contests in which aggressive behavior is condoned and applauded. Violent collective behavior in the form of war may have a socially integrative effect for combatants and produces heroes distinguished by the success of their violence. Nevertheless, the survival of individuals and social groups depends on keeping expressions of aggression within tolerable bounds. Uncontrolled aggression is a threat to orderly development of individuals and to the functioning of social groups.

Failure to acquire the knowledge and motivation for the control and inhibition necessary for social integration produces the behavioral pattern that has come to be known as psychopathic, sociopathic, or antisocial personality disorder. Lack of adequate impulse control is the defining characteristic of the dimension of psychopathology we have termed impulse disorder, an abbreviated form of "impulse control disorder." By viewing this condition of inadequate control as a dimension, we recognize that it may be mild or severe—so severe in some cases that even though the drives or impulses themselves are quite normal in intensity, the person regularly engages in socially unacceptable behavior in a personality pattern that appears unmodifiable by societal disapprovals and punishments. Such persons approximate the picture of "true" or "pure" psychopathic personality described by Cleckley (1976), in which lack of impulse control is, for all practical purposes, the sole source of the disordered behavior.

Much more frequent than cases of clinical psychopathy, however, are those in which the impulse disorder element is not the whole story and excessive pressure *for* socially unacceptable behavior also plays a part. This chapter deals with this second element in failure of social integration, the sources of abnormally strong motivational pressures toward uncontrolled aggression. While excesses in any interpersonal behavior may disrupt necessary social integration, extremes of aggression usually have the most immediate and most intense impact upon others, and some form of aggression is therefore usually implicated in the behavior of persons identified as sociopathic. The discussion in this chapter will therefore focus on aggression, its behavioral variations and motivational (affective) sources. We shall consider:

1. A definition of aggression and its subclassification, and a comment on the epidemiology of aggression
2. A review of some major theories on the nature of aggression, including the question of whether mankind is innately aggressive in the sense that aggressive behavior is a biological imperative
3. Additional aspects of the relationship of fear and anger (avoidance and aggression), particularly some ways in which this relationship may result in socially unacceptable behavior

Definition and Classification of Aggression

A useful definition is provided by Moyer (1976, p. 2): Aggression is "overt behavior involving intent to inflict noxious stimulation or to behave destructively," usually directly toward another organism but at times toward inanimate objects. The inclusion of the goal-directed intent in the definition, while it may be difficult to assess and thus often creates problems in application to particular instances, is necessary if the meaning of the term is to have significance for understanding behavior. Thus, accidental injury or destruction of an animal or person who darts in front of one's car is not usually considered an aggressive act by the driver, but an attempt to discharge a gun at someone is certainly aggressive even if the gun misfires and no harm results. Aggression may involve focused, direct physical attack on other persons but may also be indirect, as when one sets harmful or destructive forces in motion without direct involvement or when valued property or status is damaged rather than the body of the victim. Aggression may be verbal or symbolic, as in the sarcastic "put down" or public slander, or it may be ritualized in sports involving physical contact. Although Moyer considers hostility and aggression equivalent terms, it seems to us that hostility usefully connotes the presence of anger (rage, hatred) as an underlying motivational force.

In his definition of aggression, Moyer does not include assertiveness, behavior intended solely to advance the interests of the subject without any purpose of inflicting harm or destruction on another. This is in some contrast to our broader use of the term in discussing neurotic conflicts of an aggression-fear type (Chapter 16). The two areas of behavior and motivation are both so regularly inhibited in neurosis that their combination in a single conflict type seems justified. For the purpose of this chapter, however, Moyer's distinction will be adopted.

While all aggression is destructive in its intent under Moyer's definition, all aggression is not motivated by the emergency emotion of anger. This fact is the basis for an important classification of aggression into the subvarieties, *predatory aggression* and *affective aggression*. The destructive behavior inflicted by the predator upon its prey or, for that matter, by the browsing animal upon the foliage, is certainly destructive both in intent and result. However this behavior is very different from the aggression of an animal defending itself or its offspring, competing with others for scarce resources, and reacting to pain or crowding. The same organs (teeth, claws, hooves) may be employed, but similarities between predation and other forms of aggression are very limited. Consider the following passage from Konrad Lorenz (1966):

> The fight between predator and prey is not a fight in the real sense of the word: the stroke of the paw with which the lion kills his prey may resemble the movement that he makes when he strikes his rival, just as a shotgun and a rifle resemble each other outwardly; but the inner motives of the hunter are basically different from those of the fighter. The buffalo which the lion fells provokes his aggression as little as the appetizing turkey which I have just seen hanging in the larder provokes mine. The differences in these inner drives can clearly be seen in the expression movement of the animal: a dog about to catch a hunted rabbit has the same happy expression as he has when he greets his master or awaits some longed-for treat. From many excellent photographs it can be seen that the lion, in the dramatic moment

> before he springs, is in no way angry. Growling, laying back the ears, and other well-known expression movements of fighting behavior are seen in predatory animals only when they are afraid of a wildly resisting prey. (pp. 25–26)

Lorenz, it will be noted from the foregoing, considers predatory behavior so distinct from "fighting behavior" that he chooses to eliminate it altogether from his definition of aggression. Moyer (1971) includes predation with the concept of aggression, but supports the point made by Lorenz:

> The topography of behavior (i.e., the motor patterns) in predatory attack by the cat is quite different from a type of aggression which has been called "affective." The former involves relatively little emotional display. The cat does not hiss or growl, but slinks close to the floor and makes a silent, deadly attack on the rat. In "affective" aggression, however, there is evidence of pronounced sympathetic arousal. The back arches, the tail fluffs out, the animal hisses and growls, and may attack in a flurry of scratching and biting. (p. 224)

J.P. Scott (1971) makes the point again and adds an evolutionary perspective:

> While the possibility exists that a predator might, so to speak, get its wires crossed and deliver the kind of behavior toward a species mate which it normally uses in killing its prey, such behavior seldom occurs. Prey-killing and social fighting are subject to different sorts of selection pressures and consequently have evolved in different directions. (p. 17)

Reis (1974) provides a tabulation of behavior differences between affective and predatory aggression (Table 19-1). Further evidence of the validity of this distinction will be provided in Chapter 20 with the citation of studies pointing to quite distinct anatomical and neurochemical pathways mediating these two major subtypes of aggression.

Distinguishing predatory from affective aggression is not intended to suggest that the former is without affective-motivational sources. No doubt hunger or appetite and related emotions of pleasant anticipation (see quotation from Lorenz above) are involved in predation. However the term *affective* in this classification schema is clearly intended to refer to that group of emotions most closely associated with the kind of aggressive behavior that can exceed its adaptational, socially integrative purposes—occasionally in nonhuman forms, but very frequently in man. These are the affects of anger, rage, hatred, and the like.

If the distinction between predatory and affective aggression is not made, erroneous conclusions about the sources of human aggression are easily drawn. There has, in fact, been a line of thought suggesting that man, being at least partially carnivorous and having a long prehistory of hunting for food as well as gathering, must therefore be constituted with a spontaneously recurring, inexorable internal pressure to periodically go out and kill or

Table 19-1. Some Characteristics of Affective and Predatory Agression

Affective Agression	Predatory Agression
Intensive, patterned automatic activation, especially sympathoadrenal	Little autonomic activation
Threatening and defensive postures	Stalking postures
Menacing vocalization	Little vocalization
Attack is with claws, frenzied, mutilating	Attacks by biting, lethally directed to back of neck
Initiated by somatic (especially nociceptive) as well as exteroceptive stimuli	Initiated by exteroceptive stimuli, usually visual
Generally lowered threshold for agression (irritability), not always goal-directed	No irritability
Intra- as well as interspecific	Interspecific
May be used only for display	Always aims at success
Not usually related to feeding	Related to feeding
Probably quite hormonally responsive	Probably less hormonally responsive

From Reis, 1974.

injure someone or some thing. Fromm (1973, pp. 124–181) has extensively reviewed these explanations of human aggression as an appetitive function based upon the view of "man the hunter." He cites in particular the theories of S.L. Washburn (Washburn and Aris, 1958; Washburn and Lancaster, 1968) and D. Freeman (1964). Fromm, and other writers are critical of this predatory view of human aggression for a number of reasons. Man and his primate relatives do not have the muscular and dental equipment characteristic of animals adapted primarily for predation (Scott, 1973, p. 711). The employment of hunting as a major source of food was a secondary development in human evolution, necessarily dependent upon the creation of tools (weapons) (Scott, 1973, p. 712). Animal species that are among the most effective predators (wolves, cats) are often least aggressive in other contexts, while certain totally herbivorous forms (rhinoceroses, elephants, African buffalos) are among the most easily aroused to rage and destructiveness (Scott, 1971, p. 17; Moyer, 1976, p. 135). However, the most compelling argument of all against a predatory explanation of human aggression is the one already cited: predatory aggression and affective aggression are two very distinct patterns in terms of behavior, psychophysiology, and central nervous system mediation.

How frequently is aggression behavior that is clinically significant or societally intolerable observed? A definitive answer is not possible, and no reliable estimates of the incidence and prevalence of significant aggression exist. Societies tolerate certain types of dramatic outcomes of violent behavior such as homicide or suicide, and from these tolerations we know that such events are relatively rare. We know that our society has, over several decades, incarcerated slightly less than 2% of the population, presumably to control intolerable behavior of one sort or another but not necessarily for the kinds of aggressive behavior that are of interest in this chapter. Furthermore, observations confirm that violent behavior (e.g., suicide and homicide) varies by gender and age, with homicide being more common with males and decreasing with age, and with suicide also being more common among males but increasing with age. There are no definitive studies of the incidence and prevalence of sociopathy. The absence of an epidemiology of aggression probably reflects a problem of case identification. Identifying in a population where aggressive behavior clearly reflects a *predisposition* toward pathological, antisocial behavior as distinct from sporadic, situational violence is difficult to do.

Review of Major Theories

Is Mankind Innately Aggressive?

Even if we accept the mounting evidence that predation is a behavior pattern basically different from the other major forms of aggression, it is still possible that there has evolved in the vertebrate line an innate, spontaneously recurrent pressure to attack with intent to harm or destroy. There could be an independent *appetite* for aggression, a type of instinctual drive like those for food, water, and sex such that in the absence of the specific satisfaction there is a buildup of pressure to levels eventually experienced as painful. Such an appetitive need presumably depends upon some internal signaling mechanism (e.g., central nervous system centers sensitive to low levels of blood sugar) and does not require external stimuli, though its activity may at times be triggered or augmented by outside circumstances. There is, of course, obvious adaptational value to appetitive systems that "spontaneously" set the organism into activity to correct states of low blood sugar and dehydration. Survival of the species may depend upon internal pressures to seek out and mate with a sexual partner, even in the absence of external triggering stimuli. Are there, possibly, survival advantages in a similar appetitive system for nonpredatory aggression?

Konrad Lorenz, the world-famous ethologist, contends that aggression has survival value and that human aggression, while not related to predatory behavior (see quotation above), is indeed an instinctual function. Lorenz's position is that aggression developed in vertebrate forms because of selection pressures for mechanisms to ensure spacing of members of a species over the available habitat, to establish a hierarchial social order ("pecking order") within animal societies, and to ensure that the genes of the more robust males would be transmitted to future generations. He also argues, though less persuasively, that without aggressive urges there could be no impulses toward love or attachment and therefore no social order, art, or science—that hate somehow necessarily precedes love and cooperation between members of a species. These conclusions are based chiefly on systematic observations made by Lorenz on certain species of birds and especially certain fish in which the males instantaneously attack other males coming within the sensory field and in which the mating patterns of male and female include much aggressive behavior. To these observations he adds informal descriptions of human behavior in which the person may be said to be just "looking for a fight" without known provocation.

Lorenz also suggests that in nonhuman forms there are innate patterns for interrupting fighting within species before it leads to major injury or death. Intraspecific aggression is often ritualized in ways that make serious damage unlikely (i.e., confined to attacks on the least vulnerable body parts) and includes stereotyped "submission" movements by one participant that "turn off" aggression by the other. He believes these control patterns evolved as needed, depending upon the potential lethality of the species. That is, strong innate inhibitory patterns developed in carnivores equipped with deadly claws and fangs and in other physically powerful animals; weaker innate inhibitions were sufficient in less lethal species such as the relatively harmless primates. Mankind's problem—the problem of being the only species that regularly destroys by fighting large numbers of its own members—is explained by Lorenz as being a result of the sudden (on an evolutionary time scale) development of conceptual thought and verbal speech and the resulting capacity to produce tools that are easily turned into lethal weapons. Mankind thus finds itself a group of creatures with spontaneously recurring, appetitive urges to attack, without strong innate inhibitory controls and in possession of weapons of incredible deadliness!

The implications of an appetitive view of human aggression are that there really is no way to reduce the innate pressures. Any solution to individual and mass destructiveness must lie not only in accepting the inevitability of the instinctual pressures but also in concentrating on ways to reinforce activities that are less destructive and perhaps even socially beneficial. Lorenz has steadfastly maintained that his theory does not imply pessimism or resignation to the inevitability of violent crime and war. His principal suggestion is for the draining off ("catharsis" is a term often used by other writers) of aggressive pressures by redirecting them (into sports, for example, or even into the breaking of cheap pottery). He also believes, as noted above, that intense involvement in art or science or other cultural activities may serve a similar redirecting function.

Since Lorenz began to put forward this view, and particularly since the first German edition of his *On Aggression* in 1963 (Lorenz, 1966), there have been a great many vigorous critiques and rebuttals (Lehrman, 1953; Fromm, 1973; Bandura, 1973; Montagu, 1973), most concentrating upon his view of aggression as an appetite. Even Niko Tinbergen (see Hall, 1974), Lorenz's fellow ethologist and friend, chides him on this point:

> I think it is unfortunate to phrase it so that one says man has an innate urge to fight. Konrad always links innate and urge in one breath. But while man's knee reflex is innate, there is certainly no urge to jerk the knee. By not separating these two questions, I think Konrad has created a lot of misunderstanding. (p. 78)

Very important objections to the appetite view of aggression are also raised by the behavioral zoologist J.P. Scott who concludes that the behavior patterns of nonpredatory aggression, including those involving members of the same species, are almost certainly derived from the *defensive* patterns of each animal form. These activities are primarily designed for avoidance and escape, but in all species with anatomical potential for inflicting damage (amphibians being a possible exception) they include the possibility of a shift to defensive attack under certain conditions (Scott, 1970, 1971, 1973, 1975). Scott (1973, pp. 708–709) views the functions of space regulation and the facilitation of reproduction as secondary developments taken on in some species by what is primarily a defensive behavior system. Both Moyer (1976, pp. 276–277) and Scott observe an absence of the signs of appetitive buildup relievable *only* by the expression of aggression in animals "deprived" of opportunity for aggressive behavior. Scott (1970, p. 573) writes: "An animal or human being can live satisfactorily for long periods without ever showing overt fighting or feeling unpleasant emotions or hostility, provided external stimulation for fighting is kept to a minimum." Anger, like fear, is primarily a *reaction* to stressful circumstances, including those perceived as stressful—not a spontaneous appetite.

Even the subvariety of affective aggression, known as "irritable aggression" (Moyer, 1975, 1976), that probably most clearly approximates descriptively the animal "out looking for a fight" is dependent upon at least one of a number of antecedent factors: pain, frustration, deprivation (as of food or sleep), social isolation, crowding, and various physiological dysfunctions (Moyer, 1976, p. 188). Physiological dysfunctions include tumors of the temporal lobe and limbic system, temporal lobe epilepsy, the epileptoid conditions of episodic dyscontrol (Mark and Ervin, 1970; Monroe, 1970), hypoglycemia, premenstrual tension, Lesch-Nyhan syndromes, and the sequelae of encephalitis [the list is from Moyer (1976, p. 202) and Fromm (1973, pp. 103–109)]. Only these pathophysiological states among the sources of irritable aggression fail to qualify as situational stimuli, and they are clear instances of disordered brain function, hardly qualifying as examples of normal, phylogenetically evolved, adaptive patterns of appetitive aggression.

A further argument in rebuttal of the concept of aggression as an appetite raises the question of whether a spontaneous urge to destroy, unrelated to circumstances, and an internal pressure to attack in the absence of danger or frustration and without concern for possible retaliation or other undesirable consequences could possibly confer selective advantage upon an animal species. Again J.P. Scott (1968) makes the telling point:

> In short, the physiological evidence is against Lorenz's notion of the spontaneity of aggression, and indeed, it is difficult to see how such a mechanism for spontaneity could have evolved. Fighting is an emergency reaction, and it is hard to imagine how natural selection would lead to the development of a mechanism of continual internal accumulation of energy which would unnecessarily put an animal into danger. (p. 138)

Scott (1973) summarizes his own view of aggression as follows:

> Thus it is possible to set up a relatively simple theory of the dynamics of hostility and aggression. The basic mechanism is that of driving away another individual who has produced, or appears to have produced, painful external stimulation or an internal emotion of a noxious or unpleasant nature. Since a wide variety of social stimuli and social conditions can produce unpleasant sensations, this mechanism will account for the wide variety of causes that may be associated with aggressive behavior and hostile feelings. Whatever behavioral and emotional responses are elicited, they will be organized by the processes of learning in accordance with the principles of either classical or operant conditioning. (p. 718)

Is mankind innately aggressive? If the question means is there an innate capacity to respond to certain stimuli with aggression, the answer is clearly *yes*. We know there are differences between species and between strains within species in the tendency to aggress (Scott, 1975). Human beings are probably somewhere toward the high end (low threshold for aggression) of that distribution and thus, in a second sense, innately aggressive. Furthermore, Lorenz may be correct in that portion of his theory that suggests that man must pay an evolutionary price for the development of conceptual thought, symbol use, foresight, and an enormous capacity for association learning. We would shift Lorenz's emphasis somewhat to suggest that these human capacities may lead to excessive generalization and anticipation in the perception of danger, and thus to overuse. This may be further aggravated, as noted by Hamburg (1972), in that man's heritage of aggressive tendencies may no longer have the survival advantages in the modern urban-industrial environment our species has so rapidly constructed for itself that it did in those epochs in which it evolved. In these meanings too, man may be said to carry some burden of any innate tendencies toward aggression.

However, there is a profound difference between viewing these innate patterns as designed to meet circumstances *when and if* those circumstances occur and viewing the aggressive patterns as reflections of inevitable appetitive expressions of some vital need. Many circumstances known to stimulate aggression can be modified and, by relearning, so can our perceptions of them as well as our behaviors in response to those perceptions. If this view of the modifiability of aggression behavior is correct, the conclusion that mankind is not appetitively innately aggressive is an important one.

The Frustration-Aggression Hypothesis

The most widely known theory of aggression using the concepts of experimental psychology (learning theory) and clinical psychology is the *frustration-aggression hypothesis* (Dollard et al., 1939). This theory stresses that, to an important degree, aggression is affected by situational variables and by learning. These authors state: "The proposition is that the occurrence of aggression always presupposes the existence of frustration and, contrariwise, the existence of frustration always leads to some form of aggression" (p. 1). *Frustration* is defined as any interruption of goal-directed behavior in which the organism is engaged. Dollard and associates (1939, pp. 21–22) make it clear that the inspiration for their theory came largely from Freud's work. They cite a number of passages from his early clinical reports that include examples of frustration leading to aggressive wishes and behavior. However, they are also careful to make clear that Freud's later theoretical writings, particularly his postulation of a "death instinct" to account for much aggressive affect and behavior, pursue a different line of thought from theirs. Freud's theoretical position on aggression, developed in his later work, is today most often linked with that of Lorenz rather than Dollard (see Fromm, 1973, pp. 14–20).

The generality of the frustration-aggression hypothesis, as originally stated, has been challenged. Is frustration always the cause or even the only significant cause of aggression? Does frustration, when present, always lead to aggression? As early as 1941 Neal Miller, one of the original authors, found it necessary to "weaken" the second proposition: Frustration does not always lead only to aggression but also instigates other behaviors. Other investigators found that other stimuli (e.g., pain, attack, threat, insult) lead to anger and aggression even more consistently than does frustration. Again, from another perspective, we see that aggression cannot be understood fully without the inclusion of perceived danger and the related concepts of fear and defense. The threatened-thwarted individual in effect teeters between fear and anger, flight and attack. Berkowitz (1962), while proposing one of many modifications offered for the frustration-aggression hypothesis over the years, attempts to deal with this fear-anger oscillation and its resolution:

> The major feature of this analysis, then, is its emphasis upon the degree of harm the individual actually suffers or anticipates. However. . . , whether fear becomes the dominant emotion, at least in some situations, may not depend entirely on the absolute amount of hurt the person experiences. Rather, *the extent to which this emotion is stronger than anger may be a function of the*

> *individual's perceived power to control or hurt his frustrator relative to the frustrator's power to control or harm him.* [Italics in the original.] He is more strongly afraid than angry when he believes he can receive serious harm from the frustrating agent, but is relatively unable to hurt him in return. (p. 45)

The frustration-aggression hypothesis has stimulated a great many useful observations, experiments, and theoretical discussions (see Buss, 1961; Berkowitz, 1962, 1969; Feshbach, 1970). Most revisions of the hypothesis have been intended to reflect increasing recognition of the complexity of the topic. Thus, in addition to the issues already mentioned, it has been recognized that attribution of intent is often of critical importance in determining whether anger and aggression will follow pain or frustration. Perception of a painful blow to the shoulder as deliberate and hostile is far more likely to elicit aggression than viewing it as an accidental jostle. This example also reflects a major trend toward the inclusion of cognitions and other mediating variables (thoughts, memories, plans, expectancies, etc.—see Chapter 10) in conceptions of the psychology of aggression. Thus the original hypothesis is now somewhat overlaid with the newer formulations that were stimulated, but its essential position on the nature of the instigation of aggression makes it of continuing importance. It is a theory that emphasizes the reactive nature of aggression as a drive and as behavior. Because it includes a place for anger as a drive, does not, as Bandura seems to suggest, make it an instinct theory in the tradition of Freud and Lorenz. It is true that Dollard and associates believed that aggressive drive could be rechanneled (Freud's "displacement") and drained off ("catharsis"), but they saw the drive state as one continuously responsive to the situation. If frustration diminished, so did the pressures for aggression—without having to be discharged as aggressive behavior (Dollard et al., 1939, pp. 53–54). This emphasis on reaction, both initial and continuing, is different from the emphasis of instinct theory, a difference which gives the frustration-aggression hypothesis a central place in the development of the psychology of aggression.

Social Learning Theory

The frustration-aggression hypothesis places major focus on the stimuli for aggression and the motivational or drive state that they instigate. These aspects of the sequence of emotional behavior are roughly equivalent to those we termed in Chapter 10 the perceptual-cognitive (appraisal) and the motivational portion of the motivational-effector. To complete the behavior sequence, more attention to the specifics of the motor output and feedback on consequence (instrumental conditioning) aspects was required. This has been supplied chiefly by the development of social learning theory. Within this newer frameword Albert Bandura has most particularly contributed to the understanding of aggression.

The essentials of Bandura's (1973) position are twofold. First, he holds that there is no drive or motivational state specific for aggressive behavior or any other particular behavior but simply an undifferentiated state of arousal triggered by aversive stimulation and influenced by anticipated consequences based on previous stimulation and influenced by anticipated consequences based on previous reinforcement experience. Second, he suggests that aggressive behavior is one of a number of instrumental behaviors possible in response to arousal and will be emitted to the degree that it has been reinforced relative to the alternate possibilities.

With the increased emphasis upon the social consequences of behavior as reflected in complex patterns of instrumental reinforcement, it can no longer be assumed that aggressive behavior will result from the activation of aggressive drives, even if one disagrees with Bandura and assumes there are such specific drives. One cannot make this assumption even if the aggressive drive is prepotent over others currently active. Aggressive behavior as a response may have been so extinguished by nonreinforcement together with the reinforcement of alternatives in the learning history of the individual that the probability of its occurrence is very low. Aggressive behavior may also have been inhibited by punishment, although, as we have previously noted (Chapters 10 and 16), the consequences here are more ambiguous since punishment (pain) is itself a stimulus for aggression but punishment also induces fear with its potential for maintaining behavior even in the face of that punishment (vicious circle).

Social learning theory also places major emphasis upon the importance of mediating processes as a necessary expansion of the traditional conditioning models, particularly when these are applied to human beings. People can learn and thus begin to change their behavior patterns by thinking and talking (often to themselves) and by remembering and anticipating. The social learning theory emphasis on these processes has been a stimulus for the development of a form of therapy, usually called "cognitive," that is in some respects intermediate between but also combining important aspects of traditional psychotherapy and the early forms of behavior modification. Techniques that are based on learning theory include an active challenging of patients' cognitive assumptions about themselves and the world and teaching them to "dialogue with themselves" to modify misconceptions (e.g., Beck, 1976; Ellis, 1974; Mahoney, 1974).

Also closely related to social learning theory and its emphasis upon mediating processes is the concept of *modeling*. The concept, briefly stated, is that individuals can learn behaviors by observing others engaging in them without actually performing the observed behaviors themselves. Attention is of course essential, together with some "coding" of the behavior into verbal and/or pictorial memory traces. Other conditions such as the prestige of the model(s) and relation to the learner also influence the success of the learning. There may be very extended lapses of time between the observation and the first performance of the behavior by the subject. This phenomenon, popularly known as imitation, is familiar to parents and to casual students of behavior. However, social learning theorists have defined the conditions for its occurrence more precisely and related it to other aspects of learning, socialization, and therapy. The social significance of modeling has been much discussed in such areas as the effect of television violence on the behavior of children and adults. Experiments have consistently shown increased aggressive behavior in groups of subjects following observation of aggressive behavior by live actors or in filmed sequences. This behavior is compared with the pretesting of the same subjects as their own controls, or with the behavior of matched control groups viewing scenes without violence but similar in other respects (Bandura, 1973, pp. 68–89). Thus, modeling is another variable that must be considered in understanding the determinants of aggression and expected outcome of programs employed to reduce violence. Parents who aggressively punish a child for aggressive behavior are not only inhibiting the aggression and inducing pain and fear with their potentially complex consequences, but also may be modeling aggressive behavior for the child.

One further aspect of Bandura's theory remains to be considered: his notion of an undifferentiated arousal state as motivation for behaviors. It is almost certainly true that the varied words we have to denote emotions do not each represent a behaviorally specific, physiologically distinguishable motivational state. Fear and anger, as we have noted many times, are very similar; some workers would say they are identical psychophysiologically. But to suggest that the riddance emotions—fear-anger, the conservation-withdrawal emotion of depressive affect, and the approach-and-maintain emotions of joy and contentment—are three identical states of arousal at the peripheral or CNS levels not only strains credibility but contradicts evidence from psychophysiology, neurophysiology, neurochemistry, and neuropharmacology. Many of these findings are reviewed in the neurobiology chapters of this book. The famous experiment of Schacter and Singer (1962) in which subjects who were injected with adrenalin (on some unrelated pretext) interpreted the sensations of arousal produced entirely on the basis of social cues: those interacting with angry stooges reported bodily feelings of anger; those with happy stooges, feelings of joy. This experiment is often cited as evidence for the nondifferentiation of emotional states. Such an interpretation is unwarranted. What the experiment does show is that feedback from the periphery alone is probably not sufficient to permit subjective differentiation of various emotional states, certainly not when those peripheral stimuli are artificially induced. The findings certainly do not rule out different CNS components for different emotions, nor do they rule out the possibility of psychophysiological differences between the major emotions when those emotions occur as part of a natural reaction of the organism, as Schacter and Singer themselves noted.

Among other things, the preceding paragraph points out the importance of a theoretical model of aggression (and other emotion-behavior patterns), which includes a place for conceptualizing the biological level of the process and for including the data from that level of inquiry.

A Psychobiological Model of Aggression

Two major, current theoretical models of aggression attempt to integrate the psychological levels of the process with biological factors. Several aspects of the theoretical system of J.P. Scott (1975) have already been presented by way of contrast with the view of Lorenz. The second important model is that recently proposed by K.E. Moyer (1975, 1976). Moyer's definition of aggression was cited at the beginning of this chapter. We shall now consider his theory further because it provides a useful overview of the sources of aggression and an excellent framework for integration with the more detailed neurobiological material to be presented in the chapter that follows.

The pivotal concept in Moyer's theory is the *neural system*, a complex of neurons involving several brain levels. Such a system tends to function as a unit in that its neurons tend to fire together to mediate some particular activity. There are, in Moyer's view, neural systems for a variety of brain-behavior functions, including aggression. Rather than a single or double system for aggression, as suggested by those workers who subdivide aggression into predatory and affective varieties, Moyer proposes seven types of aggressive behavior with a separate neural system for all but the last.

The types of aggression suggested by Moyer are: (1) predatory, (2) intermale, (3) fear-induced, (4) maternal, (5) irritable, (6) sex-related, and (7) instrumental. Definitions of each variety are based upon two principal factors: (1) the specific stimuli which characteristically elicit the particular aggression; and (2) the distinctive pattern of motor activity which characterizes each. Moyer terms this second factor the "topography of the response."

Predatory aggression is a pattern of attack stimulated by the presence of, and directed against, the natural prey of a given species. The motor pattern is relatively fixed for a given species and, as described above in the quotations from Lorenz and from an earlier paper of Moyer himself, involves relatively little preliminary activity or affective display. Moyer views predation as a type of aggression quite distinct from all others.

Intermale aggression is evoked in the sexually mature males of many species by the stimulus of a strange male conspecific, i.e., a male of the same species to whom the subject has not become habituated by frequent prior contact. Immature males do not usually fight but often engage in play that simulates adult intermale aggression. The motor activity (topography) for intermale fighting is the most rigidly ritualized of all types of aggression. It conforms most closely to the ethological concept of an instinctual, innate "fixed action pattern." Serious injury to either participant is rare; the rituals take the form of attack on less vulnerable anatomical areas, while the more deadly "weapons" of the species are often not a part of the pattern. Flight by one of the combatants usually ends the pattern; the "victor" does not typically pursue. In some species, assumption of a ritually prescribed submissive posture by one combatant usually ends the fight. Often the result of intermale aggressive encounters is the establishment of a more or less lasting dominance-submission role relationship between the two animals.

In *fear-induced aggression*, the stimulus for the activity is the presence of some threatening agent. Because Moyer restricts use of the term fear-induced aggression to those aggressive actions preceded by an attempt to escape, it follows that confinement or some barrier to escape is also a necessary stimulus condition. The barrier may be physical or it may be some strong attachment to some element of the situation in which threat occurs. Moyer's example of such an attachment is that of the mother to her offspring, an indication that the distinction between this and the next variety of aggression may be less than sharp.

Maternal aggression is elicited by the proximity of some threatening agent to the young of a female. The topography usually includes, as in fear-induced aggression, an initial effort to move the offspring away from the intruder. In some species the actual attack, if avoidance is impossible, is believed to be more direct and without prelude than is usual in other forms of nonpredatory aggression.

Irritable aggression is characterized by the relative absence of specific triggering stimuli; the subject will attack almost anything. Topographically there is absence of the initial effort to escape, but there does not appear to be any important feature distinguishing the attack pattern in irritable aggression from other affective types. What is characteristic of this type is the array of background or antecedent conditions that appear to predispose the animal to it—to lower the threshold of the neural system or, using Moyer's alternate phrasing, to raise the neural sensitivity. In an earlier section of this chapter we have listed some of the antecedent conditions for irritable aggression; a major portion of that list is taken from Moyer. He includes: frustration; deprivation of food, water, sleep, substances to which the organism has become addicted, and social contact; pain; and the various conditions of CNS pathophysiology detailed in the earlier section. Surprisingly, crowding, a widely recognized precondition for aggression, is not included in Moyer's list.

Sex-related aggression is defined as aggression elicited by the same stimuli which elicit sexual behavior. It occurs mainly, but not exclusively, in the male. It is often an important component of the courtship and mating behavior; and its motor patterns are varied, sometimes involving much affective display, but in other species resembling the predatory pattern.

Instrumental aggression, when it occurs in pure form, is considered by Moyer to be no different from any other instrumentally learned behavior. Because pure instrumental aggression is without a specific motivation source, he does not postulate a separate neural system more specific than that which mediates operant conditioning in general. As a human example of instrumental aggression he cites the working behavior of the bombardier in combat or the syndicate "hit" man. In discussing social learning theory we have already noted that there is an instrumental element to be considered in most aggressive behavior patterns, however they may be initially motivated.

It is not clear at this time whether these seven types of aggression will provide the most useful classification for this area of behavior. The present writer would favor combining fear-induced, maternal, and irritable under the heading "affective" or, if the organic conditions were omitted, "fear-induced." But Moyer's classification is valuable as a survey of the phenomenology of aggression. Moreover, his theoretical system does not stand or fall on the question of whether seven is the right number for types of aggression. Its essential concept, as we have said, is the neural system for the mediation of a behavior pattern—in this case some form of aggression. We now return to further consideration of this concept.

The collection of neurons tending to function as a unit, that Moyer calls a neural system, is designed to provide constant interaction between stimulus pattern and organism such that cessation of stimulus turns aggression off. The system is also capable of various levels of sensitivity: from those at which the threshold is so high that no stimulus, however intense or appropriate, will provoke activity, to that of sensitivity so high that almost any strength and all degrees of appropriateness of stimulus will trigger activation. Ongoing activity in the system increases its sensitivity to new stimuli. In his monograph, Moyer (1976) lists and discusses in great detail three additional major influences on the sensitivity of the neural systems for aggression: blood chemistry, heredity, and learning.

By blood chemistry, Moyer refers particularly to the concentrations of sex hormones: male hormones and those controlling the female reproductive cycle. Low levels of blood sugar are also cited as a less frequent example of this type of influence. Influences may be long-term in their effects; he calls these "chronic behavior tendencies." The influence of hereditary factors would certainly be predominantly of the long-term type. Influences may also be considered in terms of their effect on system sensitivity at a particular moment. Moyer calls the state of momentary sensitivity produced by the sum of influences the "neurological set." Blood chemistry effects may be both long- and short-term. The relatively permanent effects of high androgen levels in utero or shortly after birth on the aggressive tendencies of biological females would be an example of the former; irritability produced by a sudden drop in blood sugar illustrates the latter.

Under the heading of learning influences, Moyer again includes both long- and short-term influences. Learned patterns that might increase the sensitivity of a neural aggression system would be the acquisition of threat or frustration significance by previously neutral stimuli such as classical conditioning in its simple or cognitively mediated versions. Patterns of instrumental reinforcement of aggressive behavior are, as we have discussed, also important in this same context. Both of these learned influences would usually be long-term. Beyond learning itself, Moyer appears to include experiential effects perhaps better described as continuing, reverberating activation of a neural aggression system, activation which would make the system more sensitive to new stimuli. These would be the more typical short-term influences deriving from life experience. Moyer's (1976, p. 20) example is that of a schoolgirl embarrassed earlier in the day by a sarcastic teacher. The girl, stumbling over her pet dog in the evening, gives the animal a vigorous kick. Learning patterns are not necessarily absent from this short-term example, however. One wonders what habits of unrealistic fear and shame may have been previously set up in this girl in her relations with authority persons to cause restimulation of her neural system for irritable aggression to be maintained for hours after the incident at school.

Aggression and Fear: Neurosis as a Source of Aggression

Throughout this chapter and in earlier parts of this book, the relationship between fear and anger and between fear and aggressive behavior has been described as complex. In this final section we shall try to summarize this topic and to refer again to a clinical phenomenon of considerable importance: socially unacceptable aggressive behavior in which neurotic process plays a major role.

We have repeatedly suggested that fear and anger together are the elements of an early stage of an organism's reaction to stress and to stimulus situations perceived as having or likely to have painful or other disruptive impact upon the subject. Of these two emotions, fear is perhaps in some primordial sense the more basic. As Scott (1973, p. 708) points out, escape and avoidance are characteristic of animal behavior in the most primitive phyla, whereas aggression has evolved only among arthropods and vertebrates. Thus it may be justifiable to say that, in the basic stress-induced response pattern, fear drives the anger expressed as fear-induced aggression (Moyer) or defensive aggression (Scott). Whether avoidance or aggression dominates behaviorally at a given moment is determined by the interaction of situational and a number of organismic variables.

If, as a result of unfortunate learning experiences, the fears are unrealistic and inappropriate for the current setting, and if that setting cannot be avoided, a vicious circle of recurrent fear and needless avoidance is likely. Some increased proclivity for aggression is undoubtedly a part of that pattern. If, however, the subject's aggressive impulses and behavior have themselves been previously punished and become themselves stimuli eliciting unrealistic fear, aggressive behavior will be inhibited and nonaggressive behavior of an exaggerated degree substituted to allay the fear. This is the well-known neurotic pattern we have described as aggression-fear conflict (Chapter 16). In this condition, overt, undisguised expressions of aggression typically occur only as occasional outbursts, under conditions of intense pressure and failure of the exaggerated defenses to elicit outside support.

Of more direct importance to our study of social integration of the individual and its failures are those cases in which punishment (not always intended as such, of course) has been regularly directed against loving, trusting, affiliative, intimacy-seeking behaviors and against tenderness, interpersonal warmth and openness, comfortable submission, and dependence on others. Under these conditions, trust-fear (affiliation-fear) and submission-fear conflicts develop in which *aggression itself seems the only means of escape from danger*! Descriptions and discussion of the "antisocial" behavior generated as defense in such cases have been presented earlier in this volume (see the case of C.D. in Chapter 1) and are also found in the psychiatric literature under a variety of diagnostic labels [see Hine et al. (1972, p. 114 and footnote) and the more recent paper of Vaillant (1975)]. Our purpose here is to reiterate, against the background of discussions of affect, the concepts of conflict and aggression, the point initially made in Chapter l in the discussion of the patient, C.D. At times socially unacceptable behavior may be entirely the result of failure to acquire the necessary social inhibitions. Much more commonly, however, such lack of inhibition combines with recurring patterns of fear-driven anger and aggression to produce the so-called sociopathic personality traits. That is to say, there is a neurotic element in most impulse disorders.

References

Bandura, A. Aggression: A Social Learning Analysis. Englewood Cliffs, New Jersey: Prentice-Hall, 1973.

Beck, A.T. Cognitive Therapy and the Emotional Disorders. New York, New York: International Universities Press, 1976.

Berkowitz, L. Aggression: A Social-Psychological Analysis. New York, New York: McGraw-Hill, 1962.

Berkowitz, L. (Ed.). Roots of Aggression: A Re-examination of the Frustration-Aggression Hypothesis. New York, New York: Atherton, 1969.

Buss, A.H. The Psychology of Aggression. New York, New York: Wiley, 1961.

Cleckley, H. The Mask of Sanity, 5th ed. St. Louis, Missouri: Mosby, 1976.

Dollard, J., L.W. Doob, N.E. Miller, O.H. Mowrer, and R.R. Sears. Frustration and Aggression. New Haven, Connecticut: Yale University Press, 1939.

Ellis, A. Humanistic Psychotherapy: The Rational Emotive Approach. New York, New York: Julian Press, 1974.

Feshbach, S. Aggression. In P.H. Mussen (Ed.) Carmichael's Manual of Child Psychology, 3rd ed., vol. 2, New York, New York: Wiley, 1970, pp. 159–259.

Freeman, D. Human aggression in anthropological perspective. In J.D. Carthy and F.J. Ebling (Eds.) The Natural History of Aggression. New York, New York: Academic Press, 1964, pp. 109–127.

Fromm, E. The Anatomy of Human Destructiveness. New York, New York: Holt, Rinehart and Winston, 1973.

Hall, E. A conversation with Nobel Prize winner Niko Tinbergen. Psychology Today 7:65–80, March 1974.

Hamburg, D.A. An evolutionary perspective on human aggression. In D. Offer and D.X. Freedman (Eds.) Modern Psychiatry and Clinical Research. New York, New York: Basic Books, 1972, pp. 30–43.

Hine, F.R., E. Pfeiffer, G.L. Maddox, P.L. Hein, and R.O. Friedel. Behavioral Science: A Selective View. Boston, Massachusetts: Little, Brown, 1972.

Lehrman, D.S. Problems raised by instinct theory: A critique of Konrad Lorenz's theory of instinctive behavior. Quarterly Review of Biology 28:337–364, 1953.

Lorenz, K. On Aggression. New York, New York: Harcourt, Brace and World, 1966.

Mahoney, M.J. Cognition and Behavior Modification. Cambridge, Massachusetts: Ballinger, 1974.

Mark, V.H., and F.R. Ervin. Violence and the Brain. New York, New York: Harper and Row, 1970.

Miller, N. . The frustration-aggression hypothesis. Psychological Review 48:337–342, 1941.

Monroe, R.R. Episodic Behavioral Disorders: A Psychodynamic and Neurophysiologic Analysis. Cambridge, Massassachusetts: Harvard University Press, 1970.

Montagu, A. (Ed.). Man and Aggression, 2nd ed. New York, New York: Oxford University Press, 1973.

Moyer, K.E. A preliminary physiological model of aggressive behavior. In B.E. Eleftheriou and J.P. Scott (Eds.) The Physiology of Aggression and Defeat. New York, New York: Plenum, 1971, pp. 223–263.

Moyer, K.E. A physiological model of aggression: Does it have different implications? In W.S. Fields and W.H. Sweet (Eds.) Neural Basis of Violence and Aggression. St. Louis, Missouri: Warren H. Green, 1975, pp. 161–195.

Moyer, K.E. The Psychobiology of Aggression. New York, New York: Harper and Row, 1976.

Reis, D.J. Central neurotransmitters in aggression. In S.H. Frazier (Ed.) Aggression. (Research Publications, Association for Research in Nervous and Mental Disease, vol. 52.) Baltimore, Maryland: Williams and Wilkins, 1974, pp. 119–148.

Schacter,S., and J. . Singer. Cognitive, social, and physiological determinants of emotional state. Psychological Review 69:379–399, 1962.

Scott, J.P. That old-time aggression. In A. Montagu (Ed.) Man and Aggression, 2nd ed. New York, New York: Oxford University Press, 1968, pp. 136–143.

Scott, J.P. Biology and human aggression. Amer. J. Orthopsychiat. 40:568–576, July 1970.

Scott, J.P. Theoretical issues concerning the origin and causes of fighting. In B.E. Eleftheriou and J.P. Scott (Eds.) The Physiology of Aggression and Defeat. New York, New York: Plenum, 1971, pp. 11–41.

Scott, J.P. Hostility and aggression. In B.D. Wolman (Ed.) Handbook of General Psychology. Englewood Cliffs, New Jersey: Prentice-Hall, 1973, pp. 707–719.

Scott, J.P. Aggression, 2nd ed. Chicago, Illinois: University of Chicago Press, 1975.
Vaillant, G.E. Sociopathy as a human process: A viewpoint. Arch. Gen. Psychiat. 32:178–183, February 1975.
Washburn, S.L., and V. Avis. Evolution of human behavior. In A. Roe and G.G. Simpson (Eds.) Behavior and Evolution. New Haven, Connecticut: Yale University Press, 1958, pp. 421–436.
Washburn, S.L., and C.S. Lancaster. The evolution of hunting. In R.B. Lee and I. DeVore (Eds.) Man the Hunter. Chicago, Illinois: Aldine, 1968, p. 293.

20

The Neurobiology of Aggression

As noted in the previous chapter, it is convenient to subdivide aggressive behavior into two general types, affective and predatory. In addition to the differing behavioral characteristics of these two types of aggressive behavior, there is considerable evidence that they also have different neurobiological substrates. In this chapter we shall review this evidence, concluding with a consideration of the implications of the experimental studies, conducted almost exclusively in animal models, for aggressive behavior in humans.

Neuroanatomical Pathways and Neurobiological Factors

The neuroanatomical pathway involved in mediation of affective aggression extends from the prefrontal cortex, to the amygdala, to the lateral hypothalamic area, to the periaqueductal gray matter, and into the caudal brain stem. Stimulation at any point in these areas can elicit the complete picture of affective aggressive behavior in the cat or rat. Only in the caudal brain stem do various components of the complete rage reaction begin to drop out. On the other hand, ablation at various points of these brain areas can result in a marked reduction in aggressive behavior. For example, the lynx is an extremely aggressive animal, not permitting a human to even approach it without eliciting a rage response. Following bilateral lesions of the amygdala, this animal becomes quite gentle, allowing itself to be petted like an ordinary friendly housecat!

In contrast to such knowledge of the neuroanatomical pathways involved in mediation of affective aggression, relatively little is known concerning brain sites involved in mediation of predatory aggression. The most that can be said is that projections from hypothalamic sites to the ventral midbrain tegmentum appear to be important. One further bit of evidence is that bilateral ablation of the olfactory bulb in rats results in an increase of one form of predatory aggression, mouse killing, in this species.

To characterize further the neurobiology of aggressive behavior, it has been necessary to advance beyond the classical approach of stimulating or lesioning various brain areas and inferring the function of those areas from observed changes in the animal's behavior. As with other aspects of the neurobiology of behavior described in earlier chapters, an approach based on a consideration of brain neurotransmitter systems has been extremely fruitful in attempts to understand brain mediation of aggressive behavior. We shall now review the role of various neurotransmitters in mediating aggressive behavior. In these studies, affective aggression has been investigated using the model of irritable aggression. Two animals, usually rats, are placed in an enclosure from which they cannot escape and subjected to painful stimuli—usually electric shocks delivered through a metal grid floor. The number of shocks resulting in species-specific attack behavior are counted, and the degree of aggressive behavior is expressed as the percentage of shocks delivered to the animals which result in clear-cut attack behavior. For predatory aggression, the model which has been most frequently employed is that of mouse killing by the rat. A rat is placed in a small enclosure with a mouse. Usually within less than 1 min, the rat, if it is a mouse killer, will kill the mouse employing a behavioral pattern exactly like that described for predatory aggression in Table 20-1.

The involvement of biochemical factors in the facilitation or inhibition of predatory and affective aggression has been illustrated in a variety of animal studies. The catecholamines, norepinephrine and dopamine, have opposite effects on the two classes of aggressive behavior. In contrast, acetylcholine facilitates both classes of aggression, and serotonin inhibits both classes.

Norepinephrine

Eichelman and Thoa (1973), in extensive series of studies, employed various means of manipulating the functional activity of norepinephrine (NE) at receptors in the brain and observed the effects upon *irritable* aggression. Administration of L-dopa, amphetamine, or tricyclic antidepressants, each of which increases functional NE levels, was found to result in an increase in attack percentage in the shock-induced fighting paradigm of the rat. Intracisternal injection of 6-hydroxydopamine (6-OHDA), a neurotoxin specific for catecholamine neurons, resulted in an increase in irritable aggression. At first, this might appear to contradict the findings of increased aggressive behavior after drugs known to increase functional NE levels, since after destruction of catecholamine neurons there would probably be less NE available to stimulate receptor sites. The increased fighting after 6-OHDA does not develop immediately but appears gradually over the course of several days. This suggests that the effect of 6-OHDA to increase fighting behavior may be a result of increased stimulation of NE receptors secondary to denervation supersensitivity. Support for this interpretation was provided by the observation that chronic administration of either L-dopa or amphetamine (which by virtue of increased stimulation of NE receptors by newly synthesized neurotransmitters would be expected to reduce any denervation supersensitivity) blocked the facilitation of irritable aggression by 6-OHDA.

In contrast to the use of pharmacologic means to increase stimulation levels of NE receptors, rats subjected to chronic immobilization stress exhibit a two- to threefold increase in shock-induced fighting. This increase in aggressive behavior appears to be the result of increased NE synthesis in the hypothalamus, as indexed by an increase in hypothalamic levels of both NE and the rate limiting enzyme in its biosynthesis, tyrosine hydroxylase.

Thus, chronic stress, administration of L-dopa, and denervation supersensitivity after 6-OHDA would all be expected to increase the functional stimulation level of brain NE receptors. All of these treatments are associated with an increase in irritable aggression in the rat. In contrast, chronic administration of L-dopa to animals with denervation supersensitivity after 6-OHDA would be expected to reduce the denervation supersensitivity, and this treatment is found to reduce irritable aggression in 6-OHDA–treated animals.

Another means of altering functional NE levels in the brain is by chronic administration of the element lithium. By virtue of effects to facilitate reuptake of NE by presynaptic membranes and by effects upon intracellular metabolism of NE, lithium is felt to decrease functional NE levels. Eichelman and Thoa (1973) found that chronic administration of lithium resulted in decreased numbers of attacks in the shock-induced fighting paradigm.

The most parsimonious interpretation of the above findings is that stimulation of NE receptors in the brain is involved in the mediation of affective aggressive behavior. The available data are insufficient to specify with confidence the site of the relevant NE receptors. However, the finding of Lamprecht et al. (1972, see Chapter 8) that NE synthesis after immobilization stress was increased only in the hypothalamus would strongly implicate that structure as the site of the relevant NE neurons.

With regard to *predatory* aggression, it appears safe to conclude that NE receptors are inhibitory of this form of aggressive behavior. In contrast to the increased shock-induced fighting in the rat after administration of drugs known to increase functional NE levels, the use of these agents is found to block mouse killing behavior by the rat. Mouse-killing behavior in the rat is an interesting phenomenon. Even within a single rat strain there is considerable variation from rat to rat with regard to mouse killing. However, within a given rat this characteristic is quite stable; that is, if a given rat is found to be a mouse killer on one occasion, it will always be a mouse killer. On the other hand, a rat that is not a mouse killer on the first occasion of testing will never be a mouse killer no matter how many times it is subsequently tested. Thus the finding that administration of drugs that increase functional NE levels is uniformly associated with a block of mouse killing in rats that are known mouse killers permits us to conclude that NE receptors are involved in inhibition of predatory aggressive behavior.

Dopamine

Although the evidence is not so extensive or detailed, as in the case of NE, activation of dopamine receptors appears to facilitate irritable aggression and possibly to inhibit predatory aggression. Thus its actions with regard to aggressive behavior appear to parallel those of NE. It is impossible to say, given the present state of knowledge, whether this is merely a reflection of the fact that dopamine is the immediate precursor of NE and thus would be expected to correlate highly with NE effects, or whether there are more specific effects of dopamine receptor stimulation upon aggressive behavior.

Acetylcholine

Stimulation of acetylcholine (ACh) receptors by intracerebral injection of ACh itself or of such agonists as carbachol is associated with a weak (compared to increased NE stimulation) facilitation of *affective* aggression. In contrast, the administration of ACh or carbachol has been found to facilitate *predatory* aggressive behavior. Administration of ACh greatly enhances frog killing by the rat, and this facilitation is blocked by the ACh antagonist atropine. Injection of carbachol into the lateral ventricle of the rat converts non-mouse-killers into mouse killers.

Thus, the major involvement of ACh in the regulation of aggressive behavior appears to be in the facilitation of predatory aggression.

Serotonin

To complete our survey of the role of brain neurotransmitter systems in the regulation of aggressive behavior, we need only note that administration of PCPA, which decreases brain serotonin levels, is associated with an increase in both affective and predatory aggressive behavior. Furthermore, administration of 5-hydroxytryptophan to bypass the PCPA block of serotonin synthesis returns serotonin levels to normal and also returns levels of predatory aggressive behavior to those obtained prior to PCPA treatment.

Table 20-1. Different Actions of Some Central Neurotransmitters on Two Classes of Aggression

Neurotransmitter	Class of aggression	
	Affective	Predatory
Norepinephrine	↑↑	↓
Dopamine	↑?	↓?
Acetylcholine	↑	↑↑
Serotonin	↓	↓

Adapted from Reis, D.J. Neurotransmitters in aggression. In S.H. Frazier (Ed.) Aggression. (Res. Publ. Assoc. Res. Nerv. Meut. Dis., vol. 52) Baltimore, Maryland: Williams and Wilkins, 1974.

To recapitulate, the findings which have been summarized above are illustrated in Table 20-1. The catecholamines NE and dopamine have opposite effects on the two classes of aggressive behavior: facilitatory for affective aggression and inhibitory for predatory aggression. ACh, on the other hand, facilitates both classes of aggression, but appears to have its major effect in the facilitation of predatory aggression. Finally, serotonin appears to be inhibitory of both forms of aggression.

Implications for Human Aggression

First, there may be parallels between the two classes of aggressive behavior and the two general types of arousal. Clearly, affective aggression would appear analogous to the defense response system with its increased motoric activity, emotional display and cardiovascular activation pattern appropriate for flight or fight.

Whereas affective aggression appears to activate the brain's defense system, predatory aggression could well serve as one means of activating the sensory intake arousal system. There is much correspondence between the predatory animal's observable behavior and a state of vigilance, as mediated by the sensory intake arousal system. It would certainly be advantageous for the animal stalking its prey to activate a sensory intake system. The key contradiction between the two schemata involves the assertion that there is "little autonomic activation" in association with predatory aggression. This statement is probably in error. The stalking carnivore is clearly in an "activated" state; one need only observe the cat stalking a mouse or bird. Furthermore, there is clear evidence of autonomic arousal; one need only look at the pupillary dilatation of the cat's eyes, a sure sign of sympathetic arousal. An additional explanation for the erroneous assumption of little autonomic arousal involves the cardiac deceleration that is characteristic of the sensory intake system. It would be easy to interpret the lack of a heart rate increase during stalking as evidence that there is no sympathetic nervous activation. However, a more detailed assessment of the status of the skeletal muscle vasculature would reveal—and has revealed in animal studies—an active, sympathetically mediated vasoconstriction during sensory intake behaviors.

A second problem in understanding the complex involvement of neurotransmitters in the activation of aggressive behavior concerns the observation that NE receptors are inhibitory of predatory aggression, while hypothalamic NE receptor stimulation appears essential for the muscle vasoconstriction during sensory intake behavior. Again, we must consider that there are many NE pathways in the brain, and that at different sites NE stimulation can have different, even opposite effects. For example, stimulation of posterior hypothalamic NE receptors is associated with an *increased* sympathetic vasoconstrictor outflow; in contrast, stimulation of NE receptors in the nucleus tractus solitarius is associated with a *decreased* sympathetic vasoconstrictor outflow. As with the possible activation of the defense system not only by NE-facilitated affective aggression but also by exercise and mental work, the NE-facilitated sensory intake system could be activated by NE-inhibited predatory aggression. However, it could also be activated, to use an illustration among humans beings, by such non-NE-related behaviors as listening to another person giving instructions or searching for onions in the grocery store.

An additional implication of the animal studies reviewed earlier in this chapter involves the possible neurobiological basis for the frequently observed increased incidence of overtly aggressive behavior among socioeconomically deprived groups. Could it be that socioeconomic "immobilization" experienced by those trapped in an inner city ghetto has effects upon hypothalamic NE similar to the effects of chronic physical restraint upon hypothalamic NE in the rat? If so, could this knowledge contribute to our understanding of the mechanism whereby the disadvantaged in our society are driven to increased aggressive acts? These questions could perhaps be answered by measuring hypothalamic NE levels in persons killed during the commission of aggressive acts (e.g., a mugging or a robbery) and comparing them to NE levels in persons with no history of aggressive behavior who had been killed in automobile accidents. In addition to possible implications for understanding the increased levels of aggressive activity among certain socioeconomic groups, the experimental studies which were reviewed could also help identify pharmacologic strategies appropriate for the reduction of aggressive behavior. Before considering these, however, we should remind ourselves that understanding the neurobiological basis of aggressive behavior in human beings and therefore the possible means for its control in no way frees us from being concerned about the mediating effects of environmental conditions. Environmental conditions may act via the putative neurobiological mechanisms to induce aggressive behavior. It may be more important to correct the conditions that subject a portion of our society to socioeconomic immobilization than it is to know that by preventing hypothalamic NE levels from rising among those so immobilized we can curb their aggressive behavior.

Pharmacological Agents and the Control of Aggression

All commonly used antipsychotic agents have been reported to reduce aggressive behavior among hospitalized psychiatric patients in whom aggressive outbursts were a prominent feature of the clinical picture. These agents are known (see Chapter 9) to block dopamine receptors, and this blocking effect could be important in their capacity to reduce aggressive behavior of disturbed patients.

As noted earlier, lithium has effects which decrease the functional NE levels at receptor sites and has been found to decrease aggression in animals. In addition, lithium has other effects which could enhance even further its capacity to inhibit aggressive behavior. It has been shown to decrease ACh turnover and synthesis (Vizi et al., 1972). It has also been found to increase serotonin production in the brain (Sheard and Agahjanian, 1970). Thus lithium has effects upon all known neurotransmitters which have been implicated in the mediation of aggressive behavior, and in each case that effect is to decrease the expected aggressive behavior. It is not surprising, therefore, that there are several reports of decreased aggressive behavior in various human populations in response to lithium therapy (Sheard, 1975; Tupin and Smith, 1977).

Other Considerations

The possible association between EEG abnormalities, particularly those indicative of temporal lobe dysfunction, and episodic aggressive behavior should be noted. There are clearly isolated cases where a temporal lobe seizure focus can be correlated with problems of aggressive behavior and where the institution of anticonvulsant therapy with diphenylhydantoin resulted in a significant reduction in aggressive behavior. It is unlikely, however, that such a mechanism is involved in any but a tiny proportion of individuals with aggressive behavioral problems. For example, a review of the charts of 700 patients with temporal lobe or psychomotor epilepsy found that only 4.8% had any history of destructive or assaultive behavior. Moreover, a detailed analysis of the data available found other variables such as age and sex to be better predictors of assaultive behavior than the abnormal EEG.

Most of us would conclude intuitively that the male of the species is more aggressive than the female. There is some evidence that testosterone levels are elevated in young criminals with a history of aggressive, antisocial behavior. However, the administration of testosterone to experimental animals is not associated with an increase in aggressive behavior, nor is the administration of antiandrogen agents reliably associated with a decrease in aggressive behavior.

This chapter necessarily ends with a note of caution. It should be clear that the neurobiological control of aggressive behavior is not a simple one-to-one relationship between a single structure or neurotransmitter and the output of aggressive behavior. Obviously, the past history of the individual and the present environment are woven into the neurobiological substrate in complex ways. Nevertheless, it is possible to discern some reliable interrelationships among the involved systems. Hopefully, progress in the various fields concerned with the study of aggression, from sociology to neurobiology, will keep pace, and our ability to curb the destructive effects of this behavior will improve.

References

Eichelman, B.S., and N.B. Thoa. The aggressive amines. Biol. Psychiat. 6:143, 1973.

Sheard, M.H. Lithium in the treatment of aggression. J. Neur. Ment. Dis. 160:108, 1975.

Sheard, M.H., and G. Agahjanian. Neuronally activated metabolism of serotonin—effect lithium. Life Sci. 9:285, 1970.

Tupin, J.P., and D.B. Smith. The long-term use of lithium in aggressive prisoners. Psychopharmacol. 9:48, 1977.

21

Impulse Disorders Associated with Cerebral Dysfunction: A Developmental Perspective

This Unit concludes with a consideration of the association of impulse disorders with cerebral dysfunction. Two specific disorders, hyperactivity or minimal brain dysfunction (MBD) and Gilles de la Tourette's syndrome, will be presented as useful examples. The state of knowledge about these disorders is by no means complete, and we stress the complexity and uncertainty of interactions of nature-nurture and organic-psychological factors in understanding aggressive behavior. Our intention is to develop an awareness of the influence of cerebral factors in manifestations of impulse disorders. We will consider briefly what is known about etiology and manifestation of impulse disorders and the implications for management.

Hyperactivity

The diagnostic terms *hyperactivity* and *minimal brain dysfunction* are controversial and lacking in consensual definition among both clinicians and research investigators. Increasingly it has been recognized that some children demonstrate behavior which resembles sequelae of brain damage, such as hyperactivity, impulsivity, antisocial behavior, disturbances in motility, emotional lability, perceptual disorders, and developmental lag, but in whom no conclusive evidence of brain damage could be found. The inference that brain damage and brain dysfunction necessarily underlie impulse disorders is therefore debatable and debated.

The classification of *minimal brain dysfunction* is now known to encompass a number of heterogeneous groups which need to be delineated into more specific and homogeneous subgroups. Some progress has been made, but even today the interchangeable and synonymous use of the terms *hyperactive child syndrome, minimal brain dysfunction syndrome (MBD)*, and *learning disabilities* is still common. This is particularly true of *MBD* and *hyperactivity*, although hyperactivity is generally recognized as one subgroup of the broad spectrum of behaviors linked together under the category of MBD.

The term *hyperactive child* refers to a child "who consistently exhibits a high level of activity in situations in which it is clearly inappropriate, is unable to inhibit his activity on command, often appears capable of only one speed of response, and is often characterized by other physiological, learning, and behavioral symptoms and problems" (Ross and Ross, 1976, p. 12). Some of these behavioral symptoms are often concomitant with hyperactivity (e.g., impulsivity), while others may be a response to the patient's own feelings of inadequacy, such as lack of self-esteem. The primary behavior essential for inclusion in this classification is hyperactivity. Thus the hyperactive child syndrome is itself not homogeneous but heterogeneous. However, the use of a core symptom to define a type of impulse disorder is an improvement on the umbrella term *minimal brain dysfunction*.

The developmental disabilities cube, initially presented in Chapter 4, is a useful vehicle for considering etiology and manifestations involving the cognitive-intellectual, neuromotor, physical, affective-personality, and learning dimensions of functioning as these dimensions relate to an understanding of impulse disorders. We will now consider each of these dimensions.

Cognitive-Intellectual. In terms of level of intellectual functioning, research suggests not only consistently lower levels of functioning but also greater variability in performance of hyperactive children compared to controls. Moreover, interaction effects among several personal and situational variables have been found to lead to downward spirals in functioning. In addition to manifestations of intellectual deficit, a number of other cognitive deficits have been noted in hyperactive children (Wender, 1971). These included shortness of attention span, poor concentration, and difficulty organizing hierarchically, so that as much attention is directed toward the irrelevant and peripheral as to the relevant and essential aspects of an idea or event.

Some differences in the hyperactive child's cognitive style have also been noted. As contrasted with same aged, equally intelligent controls, the hyperactive child's cognitive style is viewed as more impulsive, field dependent, and constricted in control of attention and slower in response to repetitive tasks (Ross and Ross, 1976).

Neuromotor. Motor hyperactivity is a cardinal manifestation of the hyperactivity syndrome. Often it is noticed in the first days of life with parents reporting restless, colicky babies with sleeping problems (Wender, 1971). Impaired coordination is another frequent finding. The driven nature and forced responsiveness of the hyperactive child are the essential aspects. That is, the activity level of children differs qualitatively rather than quantitatively from normal activity. There is also evidence that these qualitative differences are not apparent in free play situations but are evidenced in structured situations.

Physical. Physical manifestations of MBD and hyperactive children found on clinical examination are the so-called "soft" neurological signs. These soft signs are slight, inconsistently present findings not clearly associated with localized neuroanatomical lesions (Wender, 1971). Soft signs include a number of fine and gross motor deficits such as fine choreiform movements, jerky eye tracking, and associative movements as well as sensory impairments such as finger agnosia and difficulty with graphesthesia and stereognosis (Touwen and Prechtl, 1970). The value of soft signs has been questioned because they are transient, often not reproducible, not well standardized and common under the age of 7. Schmitt (1975) maintains that at best soft signs are evidence of neurologic immaturity. Wender (1971) reports the prevalence of soft signs in approximately 50% of MBD children referred for psychiatric consultation. However, he also points out that the diagnostic usefulness of soft signs is limited because they occur in a moderate number of persons who are apparently normal. The evidence of abnormal electroencephalograms in MBD children is also inconsistent. Although an excessive amount of slow-wave activity is a frequently reported result, Cantwell (1975) remarks:

> There are no EEG abnormalities specific to the syndrome. There is even some question as to whether hyperactive children have a greater number of EEG abnormalities than carefully matched equal normal and non-hyperactive emotionally disturbed children. (p. 44)

Affective-Personality. Wender (1971) maintains that: "The emotionality of MBD children shows four major types of dysfunction: increased lability, altered reactivity, increased aggressiveness, and dysphoria" (p. 21). Frustration tolerance is notably poor, with poor impulse control resulting in recklessness, poor judgment, and acting-out behavior. The typical MBD child is portrayed as resisting social demands and controls by adults but as controlling with playmates who tend to be younger.

Because of the increased frustrations, negative feedback, and lack of academic and social success, the MBD and hyperactive child must be considered at risk for developing emotional, personality, and behavioral difficulties throughout the various stages of development. Cantwell (1975), reporting on follow-up studies, maintains:

> These data strongly suggest not only that the hyperactive child syndrome is a precursor to significant psychiatric and social pathology in adulthood but also that alcoholism, sociopathology and hysteria are the likely psychiatric outcomes in adulthood. (p. 59)

Learning. Academic performance is a function of many factors including motivation, adequacy of teaching, as well as emotional status and integrity of the central and peripheral nervous systems. It is not difficult to see that many children who exhibit a sufficient number of the above mentioned symptoms to be considered MBD or hyperactive would have difficulties with learning in school. Some have estimated that one-half to two-thirds of MBD children manifest such difficulties. The type of learning problems displayed is not specific to hyperactivity or MBD and can range broadly from general academic delays to difficulties in reading and sloppy writing to specific learning disabilities such as dyslexia (reading difficulties), dysgraphia (writing difficulties), and dyscalcula (arithmetic difficulties).

Keogh (1971) has proposed three hypothetical mechanisms to explain the learning problems of hyperactive children. One is that both the behavioral and cognitive manifestations are caused by some type of neurologic impairment. The second considers the motor activity of the hyperactive child as interfering with attention and thus disrupting acquisition. A third view attributes the learning problems to too-rapid decision making, so that hyperactive children respond before they have enough information to respond accurately.

More research is needed in this area, especially in terms of identifying procedures for educational remediation which are effective with specific, homogeneous subgroups of MBD children. It is likely that the three mechanisms proposed by Keogh (1971) are all operative, that is, that each is operative with a particular subgroup. What is clear is that functioning in school is impaired very early in the school careers of hyperactive children, and this impairment interacts with other factors such as failure and motivation problems throughout the child's school years to produce a downward spiral in school performance

Changes in Manifestation Over Time

Not only are there changes in the manifestations of MBD and hyperactivity over time, but over time the view about these changes has changed. Recent findings have challenged the previously held view that hyperactivity was primarily a problem of middle childhood which generally was favorably resolved by adolescence. It is now recognized that hyperactivity may span the developmental stages from the last trimester of pregnancy well into adulthood.

Cantwell (1975) reviewed a number of follow-up studies of hyperactive children and paints the following picture of the hyperactive child in adolescence:

> Hyperactivity *per se* seems to diminish with age, but the children are still more restless, excitable, impulsive and distractible than their peers. Attentional and concentration difficulties remain major problems. Chronic, severe underachievement in almost all academic areas is a characteristic finding. Low self-esteem, poor self-image, depression and a sense of failure are common. Antisocial behavior occurs in up to one-quarter and a significant number have had police contact and court referral. (p. 58)

Another recent advance has been the early identification of manifestations in infancy and even prenatal and neonatal factors which would place a child at risk for the subsequent manifestations of MBD and hyperactivity later in childhood. The work in the area of temperament, which we discussed in Chapter 6, has helped in focusing attention on precursors in infancy of hyperactivity in childhood. The infant characterized by high activity level, irregularity, nonadaptability, high intensity, and negative mood is considered to be at particular risk for behavioral and learning problems later. Well-controlled longitudinal follow-up studies are needed to elucidate these and other manifestations in infancy and early childhood and their relationship to functioning in middle childhood, adolescence, and adulthood. Once the precursors are identified, early intervention can be developed to reduce the need for primary and secondary clinical management of problems which have become associated with the behavior patterns.

Etiology

Organic Factors

Although there is considerable diversity in the symptoms that comprise the MBD or hyperactive syndrome, these basically suggest behavioral disorders with neurological implications. One inference is "that cerebral abnormality is the primary basis for the presenting behavioral disturbance" (Benton, 1973, p. 29). The inference of cerebral abnormality is suggested by cases in which exclusion of other known causes for similar behavior, such as environmental deprivation or primarily emotional disturbances or peripheral nervous system damage or even frank central nervous system damage, is indicated. Such evidence, however, remains inferential.

The adoption of the adjective *minimal* in discussions of brain dysfunction adds nothing to the clarity of the concept and does not counter the fact that observed behavior is a translation of behavioral abnormalities (which are relatively minor as compared to mental deficiency or cerebral palsy) into a hypothetical malfunction of the brain. Furthermore, many studies have shown that cerebral lesions in children must be extensive or have specific disorganizing effects in order to result in significant behavioral abnormalities (Benton, 1973). Consequently, the behavioral disorders constituting MBD and hyperactivity can hardly be considered to have resulted demonstrably from "minimal" cerebral dysfunction. Benton's (1973) remarks are worth considering in full:

> These considerations lead to the conclusion that, if MBD is to be retained as a diagnostic category, it is reasonable to adopt the working hypothesis that it is caused by major (not minimal) cerebral abnormality. Presumably this conclusion is as true for a relatively discrete deficit such as developmental dyslexia as it is for a more pervasive disturbance such as hyperkinesis. It is also reasonable to assume that the cerebral abnormalities underlying such contrasting behavioral deviation differ in nature and that no single type of neural dysfunction is likely to be identified as responsible for diverse manifestations of MBD. (p. 31)

The fact that MBD children are a heterogeneous group in terms of behavior characteristics also suggests that the causes of the behavior are heterogeneous. Syndrome analysis is needed to define more homogeneous subgroups of MBD childen in terms of behavioral characteristics which can then be related to more specific etiological factors.

Wender (1973, p. 21) has speculated about a possible biochemical deficit as the basis for MBD, and postulates some primary psychological deficits that might account for the observed behavioral abnormalities seen in some MBD children. Heightened arousal, he believes, may contribute to reduced concentration, attention, and inhibition of responses to the irrelevant. The resulting psychological deficit is seen, in turn, as accounting for social noncompliance and academic difficulties. Another postulated psychological deficit is diminished capacity for positive and negative affect which results in diminished sensitivity to positive and negative reinforcement. This deficit may account for both the MBD child's greater difficulty in being socialized and for the child's tendency to be bored quickly. These two primary psychological deficits are considered secondary to disorders of monoamine metabolism which may occur on a genetic basis.

Wender believes that the dramatic quieting effect and improvement of selected drugs on complex psychological function, such as cognitive, social, and interpersonal behavior, suggests something about the etiology of behavior disorders. Stimulant and antidepressant drugs act in various ways to increase the functional activity of areas in the central nervous system in which serotonin, dopamine, and norepinephrine are neurotransmitters. It is known that serotonin acts to decrease motoric activity, while dopamine and especially norepinephrine increase activity and decrease sedation.

Wender points out that a subgroup of MBD children are apparently not hypoactive but hypoaroused, as evidenced by studies of heart rate, GSR, and EEG data. Stimulants such as amphetamines are seen as useful with this group in that these drugs inhibit dopamine reuptake and diminish attentional and affective abnormalities. The improvement in these psychological deficits in turn produces improvement in behavior.

Theoretical formulations similar to these of Wender, in conjunction with empirical investigations of syndrome analysis, are needed to identify homogeneous subgroups of MBD children with specific and different etiologies. These behaviorally and etiologically homogeneous subgroups could then be related to specific management approaches.

Environmental Factors

As we have maintained previously, an individual's functioning always represents an interaction among organic and environmental factors. A number of environmental factors have been postulated as having an etiological role in hyperactivity. Some (e.g., traumatic events such as severe illness, injury, prenatal and perinatal problems) are environmental events which may produce cerebral damage and related manifestations of MBD or hyperactive behavior. Other damage-producing environmental agents postulated as having an etiological role in MBD and hyperactivity include food additives, lead poisoning, and radiation. The effects of these agents are in the preliminary stage of scientific investigation, and the interested reader is referred to the consideration of the current evidence by Ross and Ross (1976).

Additional environmental factors postulated as having etiological significance are psychogenic factors such as learning and childrearing practices. One view postulates that the irritable, negative, nonadaptable child is a product of inadequate parenting. The recent work on mother-child interactions, especially the recognition of the reciprocity of these interactions, along with the work on infant temperament patterns and the effects these have on the caregiver have provided fertile grounds for investigation of the interaction of a number of etiological factors. The methodologies now exist to engage in increasingly definitive longitudinal investigations of these factors, as well as risk factors on the basis of organic damage or dysfunction, as they relate to subsequent behavior and learning disorders and of the effectiveness of early intervention efforts. Psychogenic factors, while not believed to have a significant etiological role in hyperactivity and MBD generally, may be the causative factor in some subgroups. Thompson and Schindler (1976) have postulated that some children viewed as hyperactive may in effect be exhibiting embryonic mania. The role of depression in the hyperactivity syndrome has also been considered (Zrull et al., 1970).

Management

Consideration of management of impulse disorders referred to as MBD or hyperactivity stems from the current understanding of the multiple behavioral manifestations and etiologies. Most frequently, multiple treatment strategies with three major modes are advocated: pharmacological, psychotherapeutic, and educational. We will consider each of these modes separately, with recognition that an integrated treatment program is a necessity.

Pharmacological Treatment. The "paradoxical response" of MBD children to the amphetamines has been repeatedly noted. The dramatic effectiveness of this medication in improving behavior has been a consistent finding with heterogeneous groups of children. In fact, Wender (1971) maintains:

> It was the common responsiveness to amphetamines which constituted one of the reasons for grouping this seemingly heterogeneous group of children together under the cognomen "minimal brain dysfunction." (p. 88)

The dramatic effectiveness of stimulant medication is reflected in a general quieting, increased attentiveness and persistence, decreased distractibility, decreased daydreaming, increased sensitivity to reward and punishment and then to social and self controls, increased introversion, and better academic performance (Wender, 1971).

Before considering in more detail the response to stimulant drugs, we must consider how amphetamine acts to produce such changes. Snyder and Meyerhoff (1973) present a concise description. Amphetamine is chemically similar to the catecholamines, dopamine and norepinephrine. Both methylphenidate (Ritalin) and the tricyclic antidepressants seem to act in a way similar to amphetamine. Amphetamine increases the amount of norepinephrine or dopamine available at synapses for receptor stimulation. It can mimic catecholamines at their receptor sites, and it inhibits monoamine oxidase, an enzyme that degrades the catecholamines. It impairs the reuptake inactivation of the catecholamines and can release them directly into the synaptic cleft. It has been found that *d*-amphetamine is considerably more potent than *l*-amphetamine in inhibition of reuptake inactivation and in synaptic release affecting norepinephrine neurons, but similar in affecting dopamine neurons. This difference in potency is useful in determining which behaviors are mediated by which neurotransmitter. If *d*-amphetamine is more effective than *l*-amphetamine in eliciting a behavioral effect, norepinephrine may be responsible. If *d*-amphetamine and *l*-amphetamine have similar effects, dopamine would be the implicated neurotransmitter. Snyder and Meyerhoff (1973) point out that some results indicate that brain dopamine is involved in the mediating effects of amphetamine upon symptoms of MBD. However, there is also evidence which suggests norepinephrine pathways as mediating the alerting effects of amphetamine.

It has been pointed out that the paradoxical effect in the response of MBD children to stimulant medication may only be apparent. The erroneous impression of paradox results from confusing behavioral and pharmacological effects. Furthermore, Satterfield (1975) hypothesizes that there is a subgroup of hyperactive children who have low CNS arousal and insufficient

CNS inhibition. It is the insufficient inhibitory control over motor functions which is seen as resulting in excessive and inappropriate motor activity. Poor inhibitory control over sensory functions could result in distractibility and response to the irrelevant as well as the relevant stimuli. Stimulant medication is hypothesized to increase arousal and inhibitory levels which in turn enable the child to attend and inhibit motor and sensory overresponsiveness.

Having considered how stimulants work on the central nervous system and some possible mechanisms of effect, we can return to a consideration of the effects of stimulant medication upon the behavior of hyperactive and MBD children. Although Eisenberg and Conners (1971) acknowledge that the findings of a majority of the drug investigators are difficult to accept with any confidence because of the inadequacy of most study designs, they do accept the previously reported dramatic effects:

> Effects on activity level and motor performance are generally in the direction of more controlled, skilled performances, particularly where goal directed striving is an important component of the task. Various perceptual, intellectual and performance tasks have been enhanced by the stimulants in children with a variety of behavioral disturbances, most notably in those with poor impulse control and impulsivity. These changes are most likely a function of enhanced attention to the tasks or control over response, or both. Effects on mood and personality are less well understood, though often the drugs appear to produce sense of well being and a vigorous, zestful approach to the environment. (pp. 416–417)

Ross and Ross (1976) have explanations of the reported improvements in specific behaviors attributed to medication. The effect of stimulant medication on activity level is seen as situation-specific. That is, there is no pervasive general reduction of activity but a decrease in extraneous activity and task-irrelevant behavior in demand situations. The improvement of an array of fine motor tasks is seen as resulting from the acquisition of more selective control of motor behavior. Studies of the effects of drugs on classroom behavior of MBD children have not focused upon factors such as problem solving or academic achievement but instead have considered more repetitious routine tasks which require sustained attention and effort. Gains in performance on standardized intelligence tests have been a consistent finding, but again attention and motivation improvements rather than any significant change in "intelligence" are produced.

A number of other medications that have been used with varying success in hyperactive and MBD children will be mentioned but not discussed. These include caffeine, Cylert, tricyclic antidepressants, Benadryl, and the phenothiazines Thorazine and Mellaril. The interested reader is directed toward the reviews by Millichap (1973) and Eisenberg and Conners (1971).

Behavioral Management. Behavioral management refers to a variety of procedures such as psychotherapy and behavior therapy. Although the usefulness of and necessity for psychotherapeutic intervention with MBD and hyperactive children has been questioned (Wender, 1971), the extremely negative social and personal consequences of impulse disorders argues for consideration of any potential therapeutic benefit. Drug therapy may enable greater motor control and attention, but improving a child's self concept or his stimulus value to parents, teachers, and peers will not automatically occur. Behavioral management may contribute to beneficial changes in at least three ways. The first is to assist the child and his family to understand MBD or hyperactivity and to appreciate the child with impulse disorder as having unique strengths as well as weaknesses; with appropriate therapy, improvement can be reasonably expected. The second is to assist the child and family in dealing with any secondary or reactive emotional or behavioral problems that might exist. The third is to use behavioral management approaches to reduce and alter disruptive behavior, such as hyperactivity, poor frustration tolerance, and temper outbursts, and to increase appropriate behaviors such as impulse control and attention.

Frequently, by the time a child is brought to a clinic for evaluation there has been a history of dissatisfaction and conflict within the home and school. There tends to be a focusing upon the problem behaviors and areas of dissatisfaction. A thorough interdisciplinary diagnostic evaluation is necessary to reach a formulation which will present a holistic view of the child's strengths and weaknesses, assets and problems. A common problem for a family, but especially for a child, is overgeneralization of weakness and inadequacy. These children understand that they are different, have less success at many things, and get more negative feedback than other children; they tend to overgeneralize these problems to produce a pervasive feeling of inadequacy. A major role for behavioral management is to accurately identify different competencies and provide appropriate remediation plans and expectancies that build on these competencies.

A particular area of concern in behavioral management involves drug therapy. The reason for prescribing a certain drug, the anticipated effects (including possible side effects), and the necessary monitoring all need to be explained in detail to the child and his family. This is necessary to ensure accurate administration and reporting of behavioral change as well as compliance. The need for matching specific treatment approaches to specific problems has been recognized, and efforts are being made to determine what type of treatment is effective with particular problems in specific situations. Research in this area should enable better matching of problem, therapist, and technique and should increase the effectiveness of psychotherapeutic interventions over that which is customarily reported (Levitt, 1971).

Behavior therapy techniques, primarily operant conditioning and modeling, have been demonstrated to be effective in altering the inappropriate and disruptive behavior of hyperactive or MBD children (Patterson et al., 1965). The process of behavior therapy is based on learning principles and begins with a functional analysis of the problems. A functional analysis includes not only a consideration of the problem behaviors but also the physical, emotional, cognitive, and social stimuli which elicit and maintain these behaviors. Behaviors can be conceptualized as falling into three categories: behavioral excesses (e.g., hyperactivity), behavioral deficits (e.g., short attention span), and behavior under inappropriate stimulus control (e.g., out of seat in classroom). Behavior is viewed as being maintained by its consequences, and procedures such as extinction, shaping, differential reinforcement of other behaviors, and modeling are utilized to eliminate undesirable behavior and foster more appropriate behavior.

Behavior therapy other than operant conditioning and simple modeling has also been utilized. Meichenbaum and Goodman (1971) have developed a treatment program to help the child acquire voluntary control over behavior through internalization of self-controlled verbal commands initially modeled by an adult. Behavior therapy in the form of biofeedback is also beginning to be utilized (Braud et al., 1975).

Educational Management. There is little argument that children exhibiting MBD or hyperactivity present special educational needs and problems. There is a growing awareness that an overemphasis on the medical basis of hyperactivity and MBD can interfere with effective education of these children. Classification as MBD or hyperactive can provide sophisticated and respectable excuses for nonteaching and poor teaching (Bateman, 1973). Frequently, such children are perceived as "a patient and not as a learner who is ready to learn and profit from classroom instruction at least at some level" (Forness, 1975, p. 159). Some clinicians consider the etiology of MBD to be irrelevant to remedial education, while others see little educational utility in this diagnosis because of the heterogeneity of symptoms and behaviors included.

Presently, there is no one definite school program for the hyperactive child any more than there is one kind of hyperactive child. However, some frequently occurring problems have been recognized. For example, Forness (1975) identifies three problems that need to be met with a hyperactive child. First, there are attentional problems. Reducing distractions or reducing interfering motor behavior through medication has sometimes been useful. A second problem is motivation. It is necessary to decrease disruptive behavior and provide success experiences so that good behavior and performance can be reinforced. The third problem is impulse control. It is frequently necessary to teach hyperactive children how to learn before trying to teach them content. For example, many hyperactive children have to learn to inhibit responding until they have sufficient information to answer a question or solve a problem. Educationally what is needed is to meet children at their particular level, determine and behaviorally specify what a child needs to learn, analyze these objectives into teachable units, and then present concepts and skills along with opportunities for response and practice and subsequent reinforcement or correction (Bateman, 1973).

Concluding Remarks

Consideration of impulse disorders associated with cerebral dysfunction suggests the need for integrated, multifaceted diagnostic approaches to the complex problems presented by these children. Typically, diagnostic assessment must be interdisciplinary or multidisciplinary, and management must include drug therapy, educational intervention, and behavioral intervention in varying combinations. Careful matching of specific intervention techniques with particular problems in order to improve the clinical management of these children is required. Future research on MBD must focus on homogeneous subgroups of these impaired children so that well-controlled drug intervention studies can be done and specific behavioral and educational remediations developed. Although the estimates of incidence vary with the diagnostic criteria used, the reporting, personnel and the method of investigation, the conservative estimates of from 4% to 10% MBD children in the U.S. (Ross and Ross, 1976) indicate a compelling need for improved diagnostic and management procedures.

Gilles de la Tourette's Syndrome

Another impulse disorder associated with cerebral dysfunction is Gilles de la Tourette's syndrome. This disorder has prompted considerable interest because of its rarity and the opportunity it provides to clarify the interaction of neurological and/or psychological etiological factors associated with tic-like motor movements and vocal utterances. Although accurate estimates are difficult to obtain because of the suspected large number of undiagnosed cases, a prevalence rate of 4 per 100,000 with a male to female ratio of 3:1 has been reported. Much of the information about this disorder has been provided by Shapiro and his co-workers and the interested reader is directed to their recent book (Shapiro et al., 1978) and to a recent review (Thompson, et al., 1979).

The differential diagnosis of Tourette's syndrome from other movement disorders including chorea, dystonia, and tics of childhood is based on the characteristic course of symptoms starting between the ages of 2 and 13 with simple involuntary tic-like movements or noises. Fifty percent present initially with a single or simple tic. This most frequently involves the eyes, head, or face but sometimes includes sniffling, hacking, throat clearing, tongue protrusion, snorting, barking, or other noises. Some patients present initially with two to eight such symptoms. Eventually, all develop involuntary movements and noises. Coprolalia (vulgar language) develops in approximately 60% of cases. The symptoms wax and wane in intensity, the symptom pattern changes with movements progressing from simple to multiple tics, and new symptoms replace previous ones. The general progression of symptoms is cephalocaudal, and the symptoms become worse at times of high stress, fatigue, excitation, and anger but improve with relaxation and sleep.

As mentioned previously, there has been considerable controversy regarding the organic as opposed to the psychological etiology of Tourette's syndrome. Previously, the psychological view dominated, with patients exhibiting Tourette's syndrome being described as obsessive-compulsive personality types. The associated characteristics of obedience, perfectionism, and difficulty with overt expression of anger were frequently noted. The tic behavior was then perceived as a symbolic expression of hostile impulses. The traditional Freudian defense mechanisms of displacement and dissociation were seen as operating so that hostile impulses could be directed to more generalized expressions of hostility through vulgar language and gestures.

Gradually, the dominance of a psychological view of Tourette's syndrome as a manifestation of obsessive compulsive neurosis has weakened as evidence of organic abnormality has accumulated. Shapiro and his co-workers initially reviewed the literature as well as their own patients with respect to psychopathology, birth history, family histories, and demographic information. They found no relationship between Tourette's syndrome and a variety of factors such as mother's age at birth, history of abortion, birth history or birth order, social class, family history of mental illness, and tics. However, about half of their sample (14 out of 27) had abnormal developmental histories including hyperactivity and perceptual difficulties, which indicates the need for further investigation. Intellectual functioning of patients with Tourette's syndrome was not found to be different from that of the general population. Common psychopathological factors and dynamic conflicts, including obsessive-compulsive symptoms and inhibition of hostility, were not characteristic of patients with Tourette's syndrome, were unrelated to diagnostic and etiological considerations, and were thought to be irrelevant to treatment. The etiology of Tourette's syndrome was postulated to be of undetermined organic impairment of the nervous system. Evidence for the organic basis of the syndrome is accumulating from neurological, neuropsychological, biochemical, and familial studies. Shapiro et al. report that 76% of their sample of 30 patients evidenced signs of mild or moderate organicity on psychological tests, 58% on neurological evaluations, and 50% on both psychiatric evaluations and electroencephalographic results. The findings were mixed in that some of the data suggested a right hemispheric involvement while other data suggested left hemispheric involvement, and it is generally believed that the basal ganglia are involved. Neuropsychological test results (Thompson et al., 1979) have also provided mixed results. Thus, for the most part, results of neurological, EEG, and neuropsychological assessment have suggested the importance of chronic diffuse organicity rather than definitive localizations of impairment.

Additional support for an organic etiology has been provided by the marked effectiveness of the drug haloperidol. Snyder and associates (1970, 1972) have suggested that dopamine is the neurotransmitter responsible for stereotypic movements following amphetamine administration. They have made the argument for dopamine as a neurochemical mediator of stereotypic behavior. It has also been shown that dopamine is the neurotransmitter most selectively blocked by haloperidol. Snyder et al. (1970) have postulated dopaminergic hyperactivity in the corpus striatum as the pharmacological mechanism for Tourette's syndrome, but this has not yet been substantiated.

The previous focus on psychological etiology followed by the present emphasis on organic etiology has tended to obscure interaction effects. The importance of the interaction of neuropsychologic substrates and intrapsychic and family influences is being recognized. This has led to an increasing appreciation of the possible multiple components involved. The primary example is with regard to differentiation of the voluntary and involuntary aspects of the disorder. It is clear that while patients report a strong press to make a certain movement, utterance, or behavior, they are able to monitor the time and form of the presentation. For example, a less socially obvious tic can be substituted for a more obvious variety in an effort to avoid the negative social consequences of detection.

The differentiation of voluntary and involuntary factors in Tourette's syndrome has been aided by the contributions from learning theory. Tics can be viewed as a conditioned avoidance response which was evoked initially by stress and reinforced by subsequent reduction in anxiety. Subsequently, a variety of behavioral approaches including mass practice and operant methods have been utilized successfully with Tourette's syndrome (Doleys and Kurtz, 1974; Rosen and Wesner, 1973). It has been recognized that the syndrome can serve the individual as an instrumental response and can be manipulated by varying contingencies and reinforcements.

In summary, the consideration of Tourette's syndrome has progressed from an either/or approach, to etiology, to a consideration of multiple components and interactions. Neurological, neuropsychological, and psychopharmacological results suggest organic dysfunction as the basis for Tourette's syndrome which interacts with psychological stress factors such as tension, fatigue, and anxiety to result in multiple and changing manifestations with both voluntary and involuntary components. Pharmacological (primarily haloperidol) and learning-based therapies have been effective and may be differentially effective with various components of the syndrome. Multiple methods of management are necessary, given that unwanted side effects may lead to discontinuation of medication.

Consideration of impulse disorders associated with cerebral dysfunction suggests the necessity for a holistic, multifaceted, and multimodal approach to understanding and management. Some impulsive behavior can have its basis in the neuropsychological substrate, but manifestation is always the resultant of the interaction with environmental factors. Delineation of the heterogeneous categories into more homogeneous subgroups is a necessity for increasing our understanding of the multiple organic and environmental components involved and development of effective intervention and management strategies.

References

Bateman, B.D. Educational implications of minimal brain dysfunction. Ann. NY Acad. Sci. 205:245–250, 1973.

Benton, A. Minimal brain dysfunction from a neuropsychological point of view. Ann. NY Acad. Sci. 205:29–37, 1973.

Braud,L.W., M.N. Lupin, and W.G. Braud. The use of electromyographic biofeedback in the control of hyperactivity. J. Learning Disabilities, 8:420–245. 1975.

Cantwell, D.P. (Ed.). The Hyperactive Child: Diagnosis, Management, Current Research. New York, New York: Spectrum Publications, 1975.

Doleys, D.M., and P.S. Kurtz. A behavioral treatment program for the Gilles de la Tourette's syndrome. Psychological Reports 35:43–48, 1974.

Eisenberg, L., and C.K. Conners. Psychopharmacology in childhood. In N.B. Talbot, J. Kagan, and L. Eisenberg (Eds.) Behavioral Science in Pediatric Medicine. Philadelphia, Pennsylvania: Saunders, 1971.

Forness, S. Educational approaches with hyperactive children. In D.P. Cantwell (Ed.) The Hyperactive Child: Diagnosis, Management, Current Research. New York, New York: Spectrum Publications, 1975.

Keogh, B. Hyperactivity and learning disorders: Review and speculation. Exceptional Children 38:101–109, 1971.

Levitt, E.E. Research on psychotherapy with children. In A.E. Berger and S.L. Garfield (Eds.) Handbook of Psychotherapy and Behavior Change: An Empirical Analysis. New York, New York: pp. 474–494. 1971.

Meichenbaum, D.H., and J. Goodman. Training impulsive children to talk to themselves: A means of developing self control. J. Abnormal Psychol. 77:115–126, 1971.

Millichap, J.G. Drugs in management of minimal brain dysfunction. Ann. NY Acad. Sci. 205:321–334, 1973.

Patterson, G.R., R. Jones, J. Whittier, and M.A. Wright. A behavior modification technique for the hyperactive child. Behavior Research and Therapy 2:217–226, 1965.

Rosen, M., and C. Wesner. A behavioral approach to Tourette's syndrome. J. Consult. Clin. Psychol. 41:308–312. 1973.

Ross, D.M., and S.A. Ross. Hyperactivity: Research, Theory, and Action. New York, New York: Wiley, 1976.

Satterfield, J.H. Neurophysiologic studies with hyperactive children. In D.P. Cantwell (Ed.) The Hyperactive Child: Diagnosis, Management, Current Research. New York, New York: Spectrum Publications, 1975.

Schmitt, B.D. The minimal brain dysfunction myth. Amer. J. Dis. Child. 129:1313–1318, 1975.

Shapiro, A.K., E.S. Shapiro, R.D. Bruun, and R.D. Sweet. Guilles de la Tourette's Syndrome. New York, New York: Raven Press, 1978.

Snyder, S.H. Catecholamines in the brain as mediators of amphetamine psychosis. Arch. Gen. Psychiat. 27:169–179, 1972.

Snyder, S.H., and Meyerhoff, J.L. How amphetamine acts in minimal brain dysfunction. Ann. NY Acad. Sci. 205:310–320, 1973.

Snyder, S.H., K.M. Taylor, J.T. Coyle, and J.L. Meyerhoff. The role of brain dopamine in behavioral regulation and the action of psychotropic drugs. Amer. J. Psychiat. 127:199–207, 1970.

Thompson, R.J., Jr., and F.H. Schindler. Embryonic mania. Child Psychiatry and Human Development 6:149–154, 1976.

Thompson, R.J., Jr., A.N. O'Quinn, and P.E. Logue. Gilles de la Tourette's syndrome: A review and neuropsychological aspects of four cases. J. Pediatr. Psychol. 4:371–387, 1979.

Touwen, B.C. and H.F.R. Prechtl. The neurological examinations of the child with minor nervous dysfunction. Clinics in Developmental Medicine No. 38. London: Spastic Society with Heinemann Medical. Philadelphia, Pennsylvania: Lippencott, 1970.

Wender, P. Minimal Brain Dysfunction in Children. New York, New York: Wiley, 1971.

Wender, P. Minimal brain dysfunction: Some recent advances. Pediatric Annals 2:42–54, 1973.

Zrull, J., J. McDermott, and E. Pozanski. Hyperkinetic syndrome: The role of depression. Child Psychiatry and Human Development 1:33–40, 1970.

Unit VI

Behavioral Medicine: Implications of Behavioral Science for Medicine

Behavioral medicine is defined as the *interdisciplinary* field concerned with the development and *integration* of behavioral and biomedical science knowledge and techniques relevant to health and illness, and the application of this knowledge and these techniques to prevention, diagnosis, treatment, and rehabilitation. Most medical students will not be choosing psychiatry as a clinical specialty. In all areas of medicine, however, it is important to have a working knowledge of both basic behavioral science principles and their clinical implications for mental health and illness. Therefore, in the preceding chapters of this text we have focused primarily upon basic behavioral science and its relationship to problems of mental and behavioral functioning—the concerns of psychiatry as a clinical discipline in medicine. It is becoming increasingly important to note that recent developments indicate the importance of behavioral science for problems of physical health and illness—the domain of the emerging field of behavioral medicine as defined above. Since most of the audience for whom this volume is intended will be entering the various nonpsychiatric specialties, we have included this Unit on behavioral medicine to introduce the reader to those aspects of behavioral science with direct relevance for issues of etiology and pathogenesis of physical disorders, for issues of disease outcomes, and for issues of prevention, treatment, and rehabilitation of physical disorders.

22

Introduction to Behavioral Medicine

Before going into a detailed consideration of the issues with which this unit deals, it is in order to introduce the reader to the historical and theoretical contexts out of which behavioral medicine has emerged. To understand what is new about behavioral medicine it is necessary first to consider how it differs from that field which has traditionally concerned itself with the links between emotions and illness: "psychosomatic medicine." Historically, psychosomatic medicine focused its main attention on the role of specific personality traits and the neurotic conflicts growing out of those traits in the etiology and pathogenesis of disease. While the focus initially was on seven disorders—duodenal ulcer, asthma, Grave's disease, essential hypertension, ulcerative colitis, neurodermatitis, and rheumatoid arthritis—in recent years the scope has enlarged to include all illness. Yet the historical concern with such intrapsychic phenomena as personality and neurotic conflict determined to a large extent that interventions in psychosomatic medicine would be directed toward correcting or reducing conflicts or changing personality. Thus therapy focused on the spontaneous verbal productions of the patient with the goal of achieving insights that would hopefully ameliorate the disease process.

A major impetus for the emergence of behavioral medicine as a distinct field has been the realization on the part of many that the application of "talking therapies" has not had any observable impact on the physical disease processes for which they have been employed. This realization has led many leaders in psychosomatic medicine to conclude that psychosomatic medicine has had essentially little lasting impact on medicine in general over the past three decades.

In contrast to this primary focus in psychosomatic medicine upon personality factors and neurotic conflicts and their role in the etiology and pathogenesis of disease, behavioral medicine focuses primarily on the overt behavior of the patient and upon modifying behavior as a means of preventing or treating disease. Based on the research in learning and conditioning of I.P. Pavlov and B.F. Skinner (see Chapter 10) and the extension of this research into the clinical area by Joseph Wolpe and A.A. Lazarus, behavioral medicine does not focus upon the patient's verbal reports and free associations but rather upon the direct observation and quantification of the patient's overt behavior in real-life situations, followed by the application of the principles of learning theory and behavior modification, with the goal of directly changing the behaviors or pathophysiology that appear important in the initiation and/or maintenance of the disease process. The similarity of this goal of direct modification of pathophysiologic processes to the traditional pharmacologic approaches taught to physicians may account for the apparent ready acceptance of behavioral medicine in the medical community.

Thus a second stimulus for interest in behavioral medicine among nonpsychiatric physicians has been the demonstration in a growing body of clinical research that such behavioral treatment approaches as biofeedback and relaxation techniques are effective in the actual direct treatment of such physical disorders as headache, chronic pain, and insomnia—all disorders that had heretofore proven unusually resistant to the traditional pharmacologic approaches that students learn in medical school. In contrast to the talking therapies employed in traditional psychosomatic medicine approaches, these behavioral treatment approaches have not only found a ready acceptance in many facets of the medical community, but their use has also become increasingly widespread in a variety of biomedical treatment settings ranging from primary care, to neurology group practices, to oncology services in tertiary medical centers.

Finally, a third factor in the recent emergence of behavioral medicine has been the discovery in large-scale epidemiological studies that certain behaviors or lifestyles are "risk factors" for such major medical disorders as cancer and coronary heart disease. The relative failure of public education in achieving the anticipated dramatic changes in such risk factor behaviors as cigarette smoking and nonadherence to antihypertensive regimens has convinced some leaders in clinical medicine that behavior modification approaches that have proved effective in changing behaviors associated with mental disorders might also prove useful in attempts to modify behaviors that increase risk of major physical illness. In addition, a behavioral medicine concept, the "type A" *behavior* (*not* personality) pattern, has recently achieved the status of major independent risk factor for coronary heart disease—a status that was never achieved for any disease by any concept associated with psychosomatic medicine.

With the foregoing introduction in mind, we shall review in Chapter 23 the evidence that behavioral factors play a demonstrable role in the etiology and course of major illness, using coronary heart disease as an example. In Chapter 24 we shall focus on the use of behavioral approaches in the prevention and treatment of physical disorders.

23

Behavioral Factors in Coronary Heart Disease

Such large-scale prospective epidemiological studies as the Framingham Heart Study have identified certain characteristics or lifestyles which predict the subsequent occurrence of clinical manifestations of coronary heart disease (CHD). High levels of serum cholesterol and blood pressure and the habit of cigarette smoking have been termed "risk factors" for CHD. However, the best combination of these risk factors do not allow for the identification of which specific individual will develop CHD, and appear to account for no more than 50% of the variance in CHD rates in any population studied thus far. Thus it has become evident that additional risk factors must exist, and the search for these has led naturally to a consideration of the role of behavioral factors as potential risk factors for CHD. There is extensive evidence that stressful life events may be playing a role in the precipitation of acute clinical events related to CHD, and the role of the social milieu—particularly the availability of social support—also appears of key importance in modulating the impact of stressful life events. Most impressive of all has been the recent emergence of a specific behavior pattern, termed the type A (coronary-prone) behavior pattern, as an established risk factor for CHD of equal magnitude to the traditional physical risk factors (cholesterol, high blood pressure, and cigarette smoking).

In this chapter we shall review the findings that implicate social factors in the causation of CHD, as well as the evidence leading to the now general acceptance of type A behavior as a CHD risk factor, along with the findings of recent research indicating that one particular aspect of the global type A pattern, hostility, is especially important in CHD pathogenesis. We shall also review evidence indicating the importance of psychosocial factors in determining the response of the major symptom of CHD, angina pectoris, to medical treatment approaches aimed at relief of this debilitating clinical symptom.

Behavioral Factors in the Etiology of CHD

Stressful Life Events and Social Support

With respect to stressful life events, there is now extensive evidence that a wide variety of changes in one's social milieu increases the risk of CHD. Such effects have been reported for major changes in place of residence and occupation, and in association with discrepancies between the culture of upbringing and one's current sociocultural situation (status incongruity). These findings suggest that increased mobility may be a factor in the precipitation of acute CHD events. Another theme in the life-change literature relates to the deleterious impact of various kinds of losses. A number of studies have found increased CHD morbidity and mortality rates among widows and widowers in the year following the death of their spouses when compared to men and women of similar age whose spouses had not died. In addition to loss of significant persons, the loss of one's role also appears to predispose to the appearance of clinical CHD. A significant increase in CHD mortality has been observed among persons recently retired in comparison to age-matched controls who continued to work.

In addition to findings as those described above which suggest the involvement of stressful life events in more chronic processes leading up to the expression of CHD, there is also an extensive literature made up of anecdotal reports of sudden cardiac death occurring in settings of intense emotional excitement, such as the sudden and unexpected news of the death of a loved one, a personal attack upon one's honesty from a group previously thought to be friendly, or being threatened with bodily harm, during a robbery. Besides such obviously negative situations, positive life events have also been reported to occur just before sudden death—e.g., the occasion of suddenly seeing a long lost relative. In most cases autopsy studies have shown that the persons suffering sudden death in these situations had preexisting coronary atherosclerosis, though there are some reports of no underlying disease. In these latter situations the presumed mode of demise was the precipitation of cardiac arrhythmias.

While the type of anecdotal evidence cited above is suggestive, it is impossible to subject the hypothesized role of stress to prospective testing since not all people exposed to such life events die as a result, and it is virtually impossible to foresee when such events will occur and to whom. A more systematic evaluation of the role of one's social milieu in the etiology of CHD emerges from a growing body of research aimed at determining the role of *social support* as a factor in subsequent health status. Social support has been defined as information available to the individual leading to the following beliefs: (1) that one is loved and cared for, (2) that one is esteemed and valued by other individuals or groups, and (3) that one belongs to a network of communication and mutual obligation (e.g., at one's place of work).

There is now much evidence that persons with higher levels of social support are able to adapt more effectively to a wide variety of illnesses. For example, pregnant women on an army base whose husbands were shipped overseas on maneuvers during their last trimester experienced significantly more complications during delivery than women whose husbands had not been transferred. High levels of social support appear to protect against CHD events, while low levels appear to confer higher risk. For example, in a nine-year follow-up study of over 6000 persons living in a California county, those who reported fewer contacts with others and fewer friends experienced a higher mortality rate due to CHD than persons with more friends and contacts. This relationship between social support and CHD mortality was found to be independent of health status at baseline as well as such other risk factors as obesity, cigarette smoking, and sedentary lifestyle.

Indirectly implicating high levels of social support as providing protection against CHD is a recent study of Japanese immigrants to the United States. There were no differences between those developing CHD and those free of CHD in terms of diet, age, serum cholesterol, blood pressure, or cigarette smoking. What did distinguish the CHD and non-CHD groups, however, was the degree to which each group adhered to traditional Japanese cultural patterns. Those free of CHD were far more likely to read and write Japanese, to have visited Japan recently, and to have a physician or dentist of Japanese descent. The researchers conducting this study hypothesized that the closer and more intimate ties with family and friends characteristic of traditional Japanese culture may have resulted in higher levels of social support available to those immigrants who adhered to Japanese cultural patterns, with the result being that they were insulated against forms of societal stress that may lead to CHD.

Thus there is ample evidence that one's relationships with those in the social environment play an important role in the etiology and pathogenesis of CHD. More specifically, it appears that lack of contact or of satisfying contact with others predisposes to increased CHD risk. Turning from the influence of factors in one's social environment, we shall now consider characteristics of the individual which predispose to increased CHD risk.

Type A Behavior Pattern

A number of years ago, two cardiologists in San Francisco, Meyer Friedman and Ray Rosenman, noted that virtually all of their patients with CHD displayed a rather characteristic behavior pattern consisting of high levels of competitive achievement-striving, speed and impatience and hostility. To test whether this behavior pattern is prospectively associated with increased CHD risk, they devised a standard interview for assessment of this behavior pattern which they termed the *type A behavior pattern*. They then began a study which eventually enrolled 3000 middle-aged men in the San Francisco area, half of whom were type A and half of whom showed an absence of type A characteristics (these were termed type B). Each subject in this study (widely known as the Western Collaborative Group Study) was also characterized with respect to levels of the known risk factors as well as detailed histories regarding diet and exercise habits and clinical signs of CHD. Among those free of CHD at intake, the type A men experienced over twice as many CHD events as did the type B men over an $8\frac{1}{2}$-year follow-up period. Moreover, this increased CHD risk among the type A men was not mediated by any influence of the traditional CHD risk factors. As a result of these findings, as well as the demonstration of increased risk among those characterized as type A by a questionnaire used in the Framingham Study, type A behavior pattern is now generally accepted as a risk factor for CHD that is of equal magnitude as and independent of the traditional risk factors (cholesterol, blood pressure, and cigarette smoking).

What remains unknown are the mechanisms whereby the increased risk is mediated. On the one hand, type A behavior could predispose to acute events among those who already have extensive coronary atherosclerosis. On the other hand, it is also possible that type A behavior plays a role in atherogenesis itself, as well as in the precipitation of acute events. It is important to determine which of these influences is operative, for if type A behavior is involved in atherogenesis, then efforts to prevent its deleterious effects on health should begin early in life, since it is now generally accepted that the processes involved in atherogenesis also begin as early as adolescence.

Ultimately, the answer to this question must await prospective studies in which type A behavior is assessed early in life and the individuals followed over an extended period—up to 25–30 years—to see if type A persons have increased risk. Preliminary evidence is available, however, which suggests that type A behavior pattern is associated with increased levels of coronary atherosclerosis (CAD). Several studies have been carried out among patients referred for coronary arteriography to evaluate suspected CAD, with the goal of determining whether type A patients have increased CAD levels. Three studies have found a positive association between type A behavior pattern and increased CAD levels, while there are two studies (both from the same group) which fail to find an association. In addition to these studies in highly selected clinical populations, there is another study which has been carried out in relatively young, healthy Air Force personnel who have undergone coronary arteriography to determine coronary status after having shown electrocardiographic changes suggestive of CAD. Type A behavior pattern was found to correlate with increased CAD in this study. Thus, while the final story remains to be told, the weight of current evidence supports the conclusion that type A behavior pattern is associated with increased levels of CAD as well as with increased rates of CHD events.

In our research program at Duke University Medical Center, we have recently been trying to identify psychological characteristics in addition to type A behavior which might be related to CHD and CAD. Among patients referred for coronary arteriography, we find that those with high scores on a scale from the Minnesota Multiphasic Personality Inventory (MMPI, a standard psychological assessment instrument) that measures hostility (Ho) are more likely to have clinically significant lesions on their coronary arteriograms than are patients with low Ho scores. As shown in Figure 23-1, both Ho scores and type A behavior pattern are related to CAD levels independently of each other and of gender. There is a striking progression in the proportion with significant CAD, ranging from only 12.5% among non-type A women with low Ho scores, to 46% among type A women with high Ho scores, to 82% among type A men with high Ho scores. (The interested reader might want to refer to Chapter 7 to see how hostility and type A behavior might be learned.)

Again, the interpretation of findings such as these in a highly selected clinical population is clouded by the possibility that any relationship of psychosocial factors to CAD in such a sample may not be operative among normal, healthy individuals. Since the Ho scale is derived from the MMPI, an instrument which has been in wide use over several decades, it has been possible to go back to samples of individuals who completed the MMPI over 25 years ago and who have been followed for CHD over the ensuing interval. Thus far we have evaluated the prospective relationship of Ho scores to CHD morbidity and mortality in two independent samples: one of employees in a single plant and one of medical students, both of whom completed the MMPI 25 years ago. In both samples, high Ho scores were found to be significantly correlated with increased risk of developing clinical manifestations of CHD as well as of dying from CHD. These findings greatly strengthen the case for a causal role of high hostility levels in the pathogenesis of CHD, particularly among the medical student sample, since it is likely that most of the persons evaluated 25 years ago (average age of 25) did not have advanced atherosclerosis at that time.

Since the basic processes involved in atherogenesis have yet to be fully defined, any attempt to specify the mechanisms whereby type A behavior or hostility contribute to the pathogenesis of CHD must remain speculative. The most widely accepted current theory of atherogenesis holds that *injury* to the endothelial lining of arteries is involved in both the initiation and the progression of the atherosclerotic plaque. Research currently in progress in a number of centers is attempting to identify cardiovascular and neuroendocrine responses among type A persons which could be logically inferred to increase their rate of endothelial injury.

While final answers are obviously not now available, the results of these studies have been remarkably consistent in at least one regard: whenever

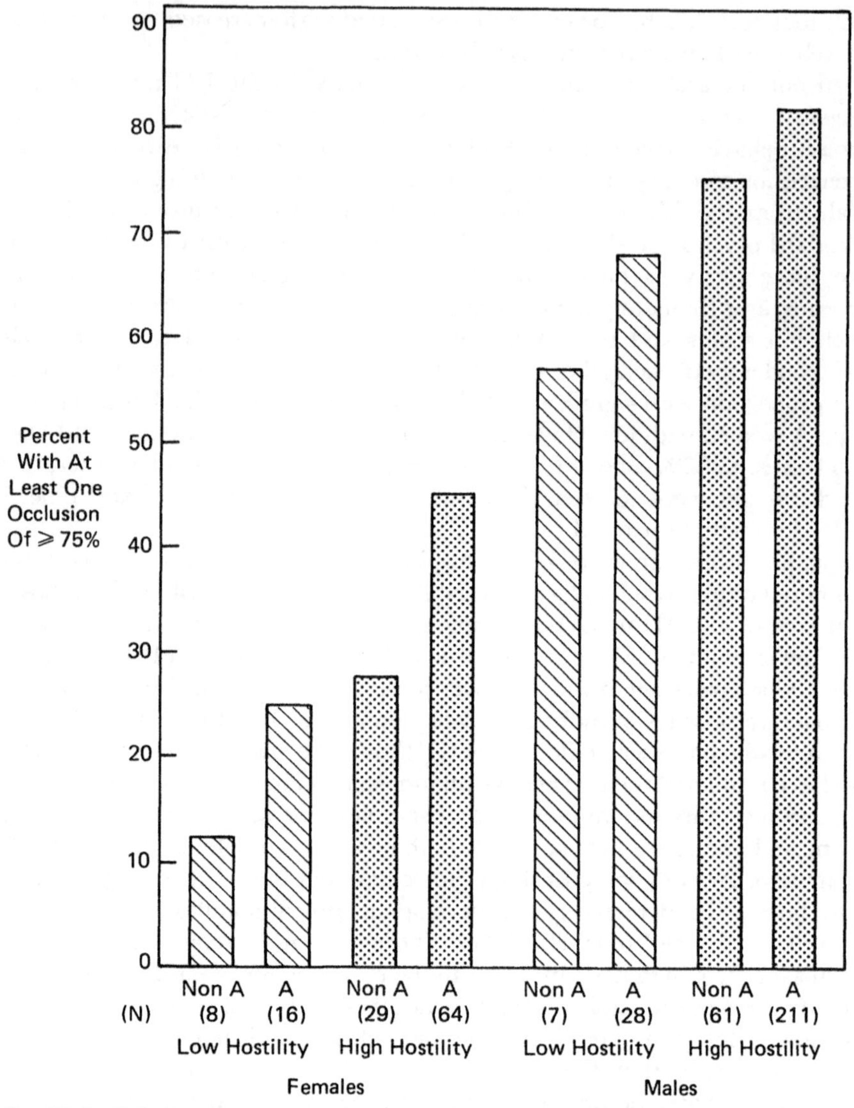

Fig. 23-1. Relationship of Type A behavior pattern and hostility to presence of significant coronary occlusion (at least one artery with luminal narrowing of 75% or greater) shown separately for men and women. (From Williams et al., 1980.)

differences are found between the cardiovascular or neuroendocrine responses of type A and type B subjects to any experimental stressor, it has always been the type A subjects who are hyperresponsive. A number of studies have found type A subjects to show greater heart rate and/or blood pressure responses to a wide variety of stressors, including the structured interview to determine type A behavior, a competitive puzzle-solving task, reaction time tasks, and competitive TV "pong" games. Additionally, there are several studies in which plasma catecholamines are found to increase more among type A subjects during similar stressors. Most recently, there is emerging evidence that type A subjects show hyperresponsivity of other hormones as well. During performance of mental arithmetic, type A men have been found to increase plasma cortisol levels three times as much as type B men, while the plasma testosterone response of type A men during a reaction time task is twice as large as that of type B men. Both cortisol and testosterone have been found in experimental studies to increase levels of atherosclerosis in animal models of atherogenesis. Further suggesting a role for cortisol in atherogenesis is the finding in the Air Force sample mentioned earlier that higher cortisol levels are related to increased severity of CAD on coronary arteriography.

In summary, it is possible to advance a rather plausible argument that type A persons are at greater risk of developing CHD, and that this increased risk is related to higher levels of hostility among type A persons as well as excessive cardiovascular and neuroendocrine responses to stress. As these psychological and physiologic characteristics which may be responsible for increased CHD risk are defined with greater and greater specificity and precision in both preliminary "retrospective-prospective" studies and in experimental laboratory studies, it will eventually be possible to undertake definitive prospective longitudinal studies of healthy young persons with the goal of confirming hypotheses regarding pathogenetic mechanisms relating behavior and CHD. Of course, with such information in hand, the ultimate goal of primary prevention of CHD will be much closer than is now the case.

Behavioral Factors and Response to Treatment in CHD

In addition to a role in the pathogenesis of CHD, as outlined in the preceding section, there is also emerging convincing evidence that psychosocial factors are important determinants of response to treatment once CHD is clinically manifest. In addition to prolongation of life, a major goal of medical treatment in patients with clinically evident CHD is to provide relief from the debilitating symptoms of angina pectoris. For only a minority of the surgically treated patients—those with lesions of the left main artery and, possibly, three-vessel disease—is it clear that survival is better with surgical treatment. In over half the patients treated with coronary bypass surgery in this country annually, the only documented benefit is better relief of anginal pain than could be achieved with medical (i.e., nitroglycerine, propranolol, etc.) treatment. Thus failure to obtain adequate relief of angina with medical treatment is the most common indication for coronary bypass surgery.

If it were possible to identify prior to a trial of medical treatment those patients unlikely to respond with adequate pain relief, then extra or more intensive medical or behavioral treatment attention in this group could result in a better clinical response. Since over half of the $2 billion annual cost of coronary bypass surgery in the United States is expended to obtain pain relief for patients who failed to respond to medical treatment, the potential savings in treatment costs are great.

Since indices of coronary anatomy and left ventricular function that are potent predictors of survival among CHD patients have not been found to predict pain relief, we have been assessing over the past several years a variety of psychosocial factors among patients referred for coronary arteriography to Duke University Medical Center. Recent analyses of these data in a sample of over 500 medically treated patients have identified two psychosocial characteristics which predict pain relief after six months of medical management, independent of cardiac status. Patients with high scores on the MMPI hypochondriasis (Hs) scale and who are not working at the time of the initial coronary arteriography are far less likely to achieve pain relief than patients who are working and who have low Hs scores. Both of these characteristics were also found to predict pain relief in a sample of patients evaluated subsequently to the original sample in whom the basic analyses were performed. Thus it appears that high Hs scores and being unemployed are valid indicators of a low likelihood that patients will obtain relief of angina with medical management.

Both of these characteristics are highly plausible predictors of failure to obtain pain relief. At the start of our clinical study over five years ago, we predicted that high Hs scores would predict failure to obtain pain relief. This is because persons with high Hs scores are typically more sensitive to all bodily sensations, including pain, than persons scoring low on the Hs scale. In addition, in studies of patients treated with surgery for low back pain, patients scoring high on the Hs scale were relatively less likely to obtain relief of their low back pain. With respect to work status, it should be recalled that one form of social support is information that one is part of a network of communication and mutual obligation—a type of information that would be more likely provided to those who are actively employed than to those who no longer work. Thus higher levels of social support, with their effect to improve patients' ability to cope with illness, may be responsible for the better pain relief obtained by patients who are working.

Summary and Conclusions

In this chapter we have reviewed evidence that behavioral and psychosocial factors are involved in the pathogenesis of CHD as well as in the response to treatment of patients with CHD. We chose CHD to illustrate the application of behavioral science to the problem of etiology and pathogenesis of physical disease because this is the area where the most research has been done and the most convincing findings have been found. A similiar if less extensive review could have been devoted to the role of behavioral factors in the pathogenesis of cancer. For example, in both of the cited prospective studies of the relationship of MMPI hostility scores to CHD morbidity and mortality, it was found that high Ho scores also predicted increased mortality due to cancer. In addition, there are numerous experimental studies using animal models which show that various forms of stress result in attenuation of immune function, assessed in terms of both antibody formation to a specific antigen and killer-cell activity. Since impaired immune surveillance has been implicated in tumorogenesis, it is possible that stress and personality effects on immune function could be playing a role in the pathogenesis of cancer.

We hope that assimilation of the material presented in this chapter will lead the medical student to a greater appreciation of the importance of behavioral factors in the etiology and pathogenesis as well as in the determination of response to treatment of major medical disorders. In addition to its importance for understanding disorders of mental and emotional life, we believe that this relevance of behavioral science for physical disease provides compelling reason for the inclusion of basic behavioral science in the preclinical curriculum. As we shall see in the next chapter, the case is strengthened even further by a consideration of the relevance of behavioral science for issues of prevention and treatment.

Bibliography

Surwit, R.S., R.B. Williams, and D. Shapiro. Behavioral Approaches to Cardiovascular Disease. New York, New York: Academic Press, 1982.

Weiss, S.M., J.A. Herd, and B.H. Fox. Perspectives on Behavioral Medicine. New York, New York: Academic Press, 1981.

24

Behavioral Approaches to Prevention and Treatment of Physical Disease: Practical Applications

The recent upsurge of interest in behavioral medicine is due in part to the hope that application of behavior modification techniques will prove effective in modifying risk factor behaviors and lifestyles, thus improving our ability to prevent such major diseases as cancer and coronary heart disease. Additional impetus has come from the demonstration in the mid-1960s that application of instrumental conditioning techniques, or biofeedback, could be successful in directly modifying physiological functions previously thought to be beyond voluntary control. While there continues to be controversy in academic psychology regarding the precise mechanisms whereby control is achieved in humans, that early work has spawned a new clinical specialty of behavioral medicine whereby biofeedback and other behavior therapy techniques have come to be used on an ever-increasing scale in the direct treatment of a wide range of physical disorders that had previously proven resistant to traditional clinical medicine's treatment approaches. In this chapter we shall review this burgeoning area which might be termed "applied" behavioral medicine.

General Clinical Principles

The first step in treatment must be diagnosis. With respect to behavioral approaches to treatment of medical disorders, this means that in addition to the routine medical diagnostic procedures necessary to arrive at the correct diagnosis, it is also necessary to carry out a *behavioral assessment* of the patient's problem. This involves taking a careful history regarding the situations in which the symptom is worsened, the things the patient has learned to do which reduce the symptom, and the specific parameters of the symptom. This almost always involves *record keeping* by the patient over a period of one to three weeks of the level of the symptom (e.g., headaches) over the course of each day. This serves several functions. First, it enables both the patient and the physician to determine whether there are any characteristic patterns in worsening or improvement of the symptom. If, for example, the headache increases in intensity toward the end of each working day and is generally absent on the weekends, it is likely that work-related stresses are causing increased muscle tension which leads to the headache, and that interventions to either reduce those stresses or to prevent them from causing increased muscle tension will prove effective in treating the headache. It is important to note that patients will often be unaware of such temporal patterns in their problem. Thus the clinical history alone is often insufficient to discover such patterns; only by having the patient maintain a daily log of symptoms which is filled out four times a day (on arising, at lunch, dinner, and bedtime) can an accurate picture of the symptom topography be obtained. In addition to aiding in the diagnosis of the possible precipitating factors, record keeping serves other useful functions as well. Not only does the physician come to note possible causal factors, but the patient, by focusing on the symptom and keeping careful track of its occurrence, also comes to recognize situations that are likely to cause increased symptoms. This increasing awareness will often help the patient to take steps on his or her own which reduce the exposure to the stress and lead to clinical improvement. Perhaps this is why clinical experience has shown that those patients who do not maintain accurate records of their symptoms generally do not show a good response to behavioral treatment. Another reason may relate to the requirement in behavioral medicine that the patient become an active collaborator in the treatment process. Those patients who are unwilling to make the effort to keep records of their symptoms may be the same ones who are either uncommited or unable to participate in their own treatment.

A very frequent second step in behavioral treatment of various physical disorders, particularly those involving pain related to excess muscle tension, is the use of some form of *relaxation* technique. Frequently this will involve biofeedback approaches. For example, EMG electrodes are attached to frontalis and trapezius muscles of the patient with muscle tension headache, and the EMG levels are displayed (i.e., "fedback") to the patient using either visual or auditory signals so that the patient can gain a more accurate sense than his or her own sensory apparatus permits of whether the muscles in question are increasing or decreasing in activity. This feedback helps the patient to obtain better control over muscles in the same way as seeing where the golf ball goes after it is hit by the putter.

Biofeedback is often used in conjunction with other noninstrumented techniques. One such technique which has proved very effective is Edmund Jacobsen's *progressive muscle relaxation* exercises. These involve having the patient begin with the muscles in the lower body and gradually move up the body ending with the head in a process that includes first tensing each muscle group, then allowing it to relax passively while focusing attention on the sensations of relaxation. Other techniques which have been used to achieve general relaxation effects include autogenic training (slowly repeating self-directive phrases to oneself—e.g., "my hands are heavy and warm" for patients with Raynaud's disease) and meditation.

Not only have these techniques been evaluated in controlled clinical outcome studies for a variety of disorders and found to be more effective than no treatment or attention placebo approaches, they have also been found to have physiologic effects—decreased blood levels of catecholamines and cortisol—which support the conclusion that they are genuinely effective means of modifying potentially pathophysiological processes in the body. Unlike pharmacologic approaches (a benzodiazepine muscle relaxant, it might be recalled, is the most frequently prescribed medication in this country and the world), these behavioral relaxation techniques do not have problems with addiction and psychological dependency, clouding of consciousness, and various physical side effects. In addition, they represent something of a "paradigm shift" with respect to the roles of the doctor and the patient. Whereas the patient is traditionally the passive recipient of the doctor's treatment activities, in behavioral medicine the patient is an active participant in the treatment process. Indeed, without the patient's active involvement in record keeping, regular relaxation exercises, etc., behavioral treatment is not possible. With the growth of the "holistic" health movement and increased consumerism among purchasers of medical care, the behavioral approach to treatment has become much more acceptable to patients than in previous times when "doctor's orders" were considered (though not necessarily acted upon) as absolute.

Another general type of behavioral technique is the use of various behavior modification techniques to achieve better self-management or habit control among patients.

Thus it is evident to us that the physician of tomorrow will need to have knowledge of behavioral approaches to medical treatment, not only because such approaches are more effective than currently available treatments, but also because his or her patients will demand that these approaches be employed. With the foregoing in mind, we shall in the remainder of this chapter provide an introduction first to behavioral approaches to prevention of disease and conclude with a brief review of those medical conditions which have been found to respond to behavioral treatment approaches. As the reader will observe, the general principles outlined in this section will be employed in various combinations to achieve prevention and treatment goals.

Behavioral Approaches to Prevention of Disease

There is probably no better evidence for the need to devise better means of helping people to change risk-conferring behaviors than the fact that more than 50 million Americans continue to smoke, despite the indisputable evidence that cigarette smoking increases the risk of both cancer and coronary heart disease, and despite the massive public education efforts mounted to bring this information to the public's attention. Of particular concern is the observation of increased smoking rates among women, especially female teenagers. This is apparently responsible for the increasing rates of coronary disease and lung cancer among women. Whereas lung cancer was a very rare cancer in women 20–30 years ago, it is projected to become the leading cause of death among women within the next decade.

Cigarette smoking is indisputably a behavior. Since public education efforts have not been as successful as had been hoped in changing this behavior, the question is asked: Can behavior modification techniques be of help to persons wishing to stop smoking? The answer to this question is probably yes. However, the real problem is that most persons who are currently smoking cigarettes are profoundly addicted to nicotine, such that the process of withdrawal is so immediately aversive and the potential benefits so far in the future that most current smokers do not present themselves to smoking cessation clinics employing behavioral approaches (e.g., aversive techniques like the rapid smoking technique, which induce mild nicotine poisoning to make cigarette smoking so unpleasant that the client is able to stop). Based on such observations, behavioral scientists studying the cigarette-smoking problem have concluded that rather than focusing more attention on current smokers, a more effective use of resources would attempt to influence preaddictive smokers—beginning in the sixth and seventh grades—to curtail the incidence of smoking before they become addicted or nicotine-dependent.

Richard Evans, a social psychologist at the University of Houston, has pointed out the ineffectiveness of approaches depending only on educational efforts and fear arousal (e.g., showing seventh graders slides of tumorous lung sections). He has proposed that teenagers and preteens must be taught social skills that will enable them to cope with the many pressures to smoke to which they are subjected by the media, peers, family, and such role models as teachers and public figures (don't forget John Wayne, who licked the "big C"). Whether this approach, based on principles of applied social psychology, will achieve the goal of preventing teenagers from taking up the cigarette habit, only time and extensive evaluation research will tell. Preliminary studies suggest that it can be effective. If successful, the reduction in suffering, death, medical care costs, and lost productivity directly attributable to cigarette smoking would provide the strongest evidence of the benefits of applying behavioral science knowledge and techniques to medical problems.

It is possible to sketch a similar scenario with respect to the contribution of type A behavior to CHD risk. Studies now in progress have used record keeping (of episodes of anger and hostility), relaxation techniques, and group therapy (to help hostile type A men learn to accept help and care from their peers) in an integrated program designed to reduce the risk of a second myocardial infarction among type A men who have recently suffered their first infarct. Again, preliminary results are encouraging in that the treatment group appears to show a significant reduction in recurrence rate compared to control groups who are receiving routine medical care.

Behavioral Treatment of Disease

The initial demonstration provided by basic psychophysiological research that so-called autonomic functions can be brought under voluntary control through the use of biofeedback techniques has led to the widespread use of biofeedback and other behavioral techniques in the direct treatment of a wide variety of medical disorders. It is important to note that the term "direct treatment" refers to the fact that the goal is direct reduction of pathophysiological processes, rather than indirect modification by reduction of "underlying psychopathology" which is hypothesized to cause the pathophysiology. For purposes of illustration, we shall briefly review the evidence for the effectiveness of behavioral approaches in the treatment of neuromuscular disorders, muscle tension headache, and insomnia.

Neuromuscular Disorders

Electromyographic (EMG) feedback has now been found in numerous studies to be superior to standard physical therapy approaches to neuromuscular reeducation following a stroke. Since in this situation lower motor neurons remain intact, it appears that feedback from either spastic or paretic muscle groups enables the patient to utilize other descending pathways to achieve improved control over the involved muscle groups. Spasmodic torticollis, or wry neck, is another debilitating movement disorder which has proven unusually resistant to both pharmacologic and surgical treatment efforts. EMG biofeedback has been found in several studies to provide significant relief for this distressing symptom.

Muscle Tension Headaches

Muscle tension headache is a very common problem, afflicting over half the adult population at one time or another. For some patients the occasional use of mild analgesics becomes ineffective in dealing with the symptoms, and this disorder can assume quite serious proportions resulting in major disability and even narcotic addiction. Numerous controlled outcome studies have shown that a combination of EMG biofeedback and muscle relaxation techniques are effective in achieving significant reduction in headache frequency and severity in over 70% of patients who require more than the occasional use of mild analgesics. Long-term follow-up studies have shown that treatment of muscle tension headache represents a very gratifying area for the behavioral medicine clinician, since even patients with a long history of debilitating headaches resistant to even the most vigorous pharmacologic interventions can be brought to a relatively headache-free state within two to three weeks of treatment employing any of the muscle relaxation techniques commonly in current use, and the benefits are maintained over long follow-up periods.

Insomnia

Sleep onset insomnia is a very common complaint in general medical practice. It probably accounts for a substantial proportion of the very high level of prescriptions for minor tranquilizers and soporifics, not to mention the record sales of over-the-counter sleep aids. Paradoxically, the chronic use of sleep medications is probably the most common cause of sleep-onset insomnia, since by coming to be dependent upon a sleeping pill the patient learns that he or she cannot fall asleep without taking the pill. Those who specialize in the evaluation and treatment of sleep disorders have concluded that sleep-inducing medications have no place in the long-term management of the patient who has difficulty in falling asleep.

When careful evaluation establishes the diagnosis of idiopathic sleep-onset insomnia (complaints of difficulty falling asleep, 6 or less hours of sleep per night, and daytime drowsiness in the absence of any identifiable biologic cause), a combination of relaxation-training and stimulus-control procedures has been found to be a highly effective treatment for this common and distressing symptom. It has been found that many patients with insomnia have acquired "bad habits" in association with bedtime practices. For example, many patients will read or watch TV on retiring, many will have a snack, and others will rehash the day's events over and over in their minds or plan the next day's activities. All of these actions are incompatible with falling asleep, and by their frequent association with the act of going to bed the patient gradually "learns" to associate going to bed with sleep-incompatible behaviors—leading to the problem of sleep-onset insomnia.

Clinical researchers have evolved a "behavioral prescription" for sleep onset insomnia which can be summarized as follows:

1. Go to bed only when you feel sleepy.
2. Set your alarm for the same time and get up at that time every morning regardless of how much sleep you obtained the night before.

3. Avoid daytime naps.
4. Use the bed and the bedroom only for sleeping. Do not engage in sleep-incompatible activities (e.g., reading, snacking, TV watching, etc.) in your bed or bedroom.
5. When you go to bed, practice one of the relaxation techniques (e.g., progressive muscle relaxation or meditation—"counting sheep" is a form of meditation), and if you do not fall asleep within 10 min, leave the bedroom immediately and return to bed only when you feel sleepy again.
6. Repeat step 5 as often as necessary during the night until rapid (i.e., within 10 min) sleep onset occurs.

Other Conditions

This brief review has been selective, rather than exhaustive. Active research, currently in progress, is aimed at evaluating the effectiveness of behavioral approaches in the treatment of essential hypertension, diabetes mellitus, anticipatory nausea and vomiting associated with cancer chemotherapy, and a number of other clinical problems.

Summary and Conclusions

In view of the high prevalence of sleep-onset insomnia and the vast amounts of money spent on sleep aids, it is surprising that these highly effective behavioral treatment approaches are not more widely employed. Similar arguments can be advanced with respect to the other conditions and public health problems addressed in this and the preceding chapter. We suspect the absence of instruction regarding behavioral medicine principles and techniques in medical school curricula is responsible for this state of affairs. We urge the medical student readers of this text to pursue knowledge of behavioral medicine approaches, as outlined in greater detail in the selected bibliography at the end of this chapter. Just as demand for better care on the part of your patients will eventually convince you of the need to acquire clinical expertise in this important emerging area of medicine, so will your pressure on medical school faculties lead to the time when behavioral medicine assumes its appropriate place in the medical school curriculum alongside other time-proven disciplines.

Bibliography

Evans, R.I. Smoking in children: Developing a social-psychological strategy of deterrence. J. Prev. Med. 5:122–127, 1976.

Pomerleau, O.F., and J.P. Brady (Eds.) Behavioral Medicine: Theory and Practice. Baltimore, Maryland: Williams and Wilkins, 1979.

Williams, R.B., and W.D. Gentry (Eds.) Behavioral Approaches to Medical Treatment. Cambridge, Great Britain: Ballinger, 1977.

Author Index

A page number in *italics* indicates the page on which the full reference is given.

Subject Index

The letter *f* after a page number denotes "figure," and the letter *t* denotes "table."

Batch number: 10844669

Printed by Printforce, the Netherlands